PRAISE FOR *BLACK WOMEN'S RIGHTS*

"An authoritative and compelling articulation of historical, political, legal, social, creative, and ubuntu-responsive conceptions and navigations of power, leadership, and empowerment by women of African descent. Distinguishing and celebrating past and current symbols and markers of transformative leadership in the face of unrelenting prejudice and injustice, Carole Boyce Davies forecasts the twenty-first century as the era of inclusive, equitable, and ubuntu-responsive leaderships and worlds. This rare global picturing in a single publication responds to challenges of and offers a model for studying corresponding and consonant yet dispersed experiences and enterprises of women of African descent."

—Besi Brillian Muhonja, James Madison University

"Pioneering feminist scholar Carole Boyce Davies' book is a groundbreaking, cogent, meticulously researched, penetrating analysis of Black women's political leadership around the globe, including their feminist writings and activism, in a variety of cultural contexts—Africa, the United States, Brazil, and the Caribbean. Boyce Davies challenges readers to reimagine the complexities of our engagements and entanglements with racist and patriarchal paradigms in various historical periods. Included are provocative interviews and rare portraits of powerful Black women—if maligned or neglected—including 'alternative president' Winnie Mandela (South Africa), Madame President Ellen Johnson Sirleaf (Liberia), and Congresswoman Shirley Chisholm (U.S. presidential candidate)."

—Beverly Guy-Sheftall, Women's Research &
Resource Center, Spelman College

"Carole Boyce Davies is an exceptional international and interdisciplinary scholar who has written an extraordinary book on Black women and political leadership in the pan-African world. Erudite, engaging, and conceptually rich, she brilliantly critiques and celebrates women's struggles, achievements, and aspirations in the constructions and circularities of power. It is a compelling read and represents a major contribution to studies of leadership that tend to be Eurocentric and malecentric."

—Paul Tiyambe Zeleza, Case Western Reserve
University; formerly Vice Chancellor (President), United
States International University–Africa, Kenya

"To godmother a literary work is to bear the privilege of first seeing the pulse of its verse. / To comment on a literary work is to bear the privilege of first seeing the pulse of its words. / In the narrative of a Black woman intellectual, we behold the emergence of voices, the reconstruction and recreation of space-times, the *axé* of change.

"What fascinates me about this work is the care, the reverence in the exercise, the respect for the histories reflected in the crucible of time. I accompanied Carole Boyce Davies to Ile Axé Omi Ohu Aro in Miguel Couto, Nova Iguaçu, a sacred territory led by Iyá Mãe Beata De Iemanjá, a beloved practitioner of the system of Afro-Brazilian spiritual/cultural Candomblé worship, who is remembered here. Among those referenced in contemporary advancements and recognitions for the specificity of Black women's struggles in Brazil: Benedita da Silva, who emerged from a movement in the favelas; Jurema Batista, Cida Bento–CEERT, Sueli Carneiro, *Geledes* in São Paulo, having produced knowledge on Black women; and Marielle Franco the Afro-Brazilian political activist assassinated on March 14, 2018, clearly for her political positions advanced as one of the most visible contemporary representations and articulations of Black Left Feminist leadership. Such projects by hopeful Black voices like this make clear the range of versions of our history. The frame contains tense elements, but also sensitive ones. It proposes circularity, self-realization, empowerment. I thank Carole Boyce Davies for wanting to share it in such a beautiful way, opening with integrity the true path of dreams and resistance by the women here portrayed as sources of inexhaustible lived experiences, rescuing the feminine soul as instrument for human transformation."

—Lia Viera, poet, ASPECAB Negras, Rio de Janeiro, Brazil

"The uniqueness of Carole Boyce Davies; approach—as expressed in her trailblazing *Black Women's Rights: Leadership and the Circularities of Power*—is always how she makes complex ideas easy to understand. This book gives the reader an understanding of Black women's political leadership in the context of our assumption that political leaders should be male. In its elegant analysis, this book questions the fundamentals of male leadership which in actuality are given to males by females. From Shirley Chisholm to Ellen Johnson Sirleaf to Mia Mottley in the Caribbean, Black women have now taken the mantle of leadership around the world and one can easily predict that Black women's political leadership will continue to grow and bring related issues to the fore. This book inspires and is strongly endorsed as it sets out the blueprint of Black women's political leadership. It is a book that all women, but especially Black women, aspiring female leaders around the world, should see as fundamental to their lives and aspirations."

—Siga Fatima Jagne, Commissioner Gender and
Social Affairs, ECOWAS Commission

Black Women's Rights

Leadership and the Circularities of Power

Carole Boyce Davies

LEXINGTON BOOKS
Lanham • Boulder • New York • London

Published by Lexington Books
An imprint of The Rowman & Littlefield Publishing Group, Inc.
4501 Forbes Boulevard, Suite 200, Lanham, Maryland 20706
www.rowman.com

86-90 Paul Street, London EC2A 4NE

British Library Cataloguing in Publication Information Available

Library of Congress Cataloging-in-Publication Data Available

ISBN 9781793612380 (hardcover) | 9781793612397 (epub) | ISBN 9781793612403 (paperback)

To My Teachers and Students:

Dr. Mary Fair Burks, co-founder of the Women's Political Council in 1946, in Montgomery Alabama, which led to the Montgomery Bus Boycott who was my memorable undergraduate literature professor. I was pleased to learn about her activism years later.

Léon-Gontran Damas, one of the founders of the Négritude Movement, my professor and later thesis advisor at the African Studies and Research Center at Howard University, was always caring and hospitable in his engagement with students, often inviting us to dinner in his home in South West Washington, D.C. Above all, he provided the kind of tangible gesture as I left for graduate studies in Nigeria that will never be forgotten though he passed before I was able to reconnect upon my return.

The many students I have had the pleasure of teaching, learning from and sharing knowledge with over the years in diverse global locations: Trinidad and Tobago; Binghamton and Ithaca, New York; Miami, Florida; Oxford and London, England; Cachoeira and Salvador da Bahia and Brasilia, Brazil; Durban, South Africa; Athens, Greece; Beijing, China; Havana, Cuba.

Giving my students always "the space to be brilliant" has provided me in return with some of the most creative, joyful, intellectually stimulating and enriching moments in my life.

Contents

Acknowledgments

A work of this breadth could not be done without the collaboration of several people in different locations who provided sources and references, read chapters, suggested names, and otherwise ensured that there was good coverage of the subject from their particular vantage points. My practice includes inviting scholars, writers, knowledgeable people from areas to read the relevant chapters and offer comments on the content of the material emanating from their own communities. My interest in this topic started years ago when I created a project to study Black Women in Brazil titled "Women, Creativity and Power" and which interviewed political leaders, writers, and *mães do santos,* culminating in the essay, "Re-/Presenting Black Female Identity in Brazil: Filhas de Oxum in Bahia Carnival" (1998), and an interview which saw the conjunction between spirituality and creativity in "Afro Brazilian Women, Culture and Literature. An Introduction and Conversation with Miriam Alves" (1998). My Afro-Brazilian activist and writer friend, Lia Viera, from Niteroi, hosted me in her beautiful city and one day took me to meet and interview Jurema Batista, then a *vereadora* (Rio councilwoman) and on another day her *mãe do santo.* Thus I offer here sincere appreciation to my Brazillian *gente* which includes Conceição Evaristo, Miriam Alves, Lia Viera, Milson Manuel dos Santos, the no-longer-with-us-in-person Lino d'Almeida, Angela Figueiredo, Vanicléia Silva Santos, Vanda Vaz, Eudes Lopes and several other colleagues/friends. I am pleased that all the readers from Brazil concurred on the content of the chapter which dealt with Brazil. I have felt always Brazil to be a second home from the start so though I hesitated at first to include the chapter on Brazil during the pandemic, on the basis of my not being able to physically conclude the project by doing final work myself on the ground in Brazil, it came together with a great deal of support and encouragement from Brazilian friends who were adamant Brazil should not be left out. In this context, Maíra dos Palmares Souza Santana who served as a research assistant for the Brazilian portion of this project was amazing in scouring archives to find the range of Afro-Brazilian women in politics available and in the end provided much more material than I could use in that important closing chapter of this work. Maíra was meticulous and detailed, both energized by and simultaneously humble in her approach to this project and for this I am grateful. My colleague, historian Vanicléia Silva Santos, has been a superb sister-friend along the way, ensuring that no critical names were left out, providing some of her own knowledge in the process. Eudes Lopes, then an anthropology Ph.D. student at Cornell, became a great supporter and friend as well, with great ideas always and confident interest on the need for the Caribbean and Brazil and indeed Latin America in general to be seen in their geo-spatial and historical "New World" conjunctions. Keisha-Khan Perry provided timely essays on Lélia Gonzalez which helped shape the nature of the chapter on Brazil. The wonderful conference organized by Christen Smith at University of Texas provided a renewed meeting with *Geledes* founder Sueli Carneiro who I met over 20 years ago during my first visit to Brazil as a member of a large NEH group, organized precisely to develop continuing interest by scholars already involved in research or wanting to begin projects on Brazil. But it was great hearing her continued work and then having a chance to read her paper which confirmed my thinking about the centrality of Lélia Gonzalez. Ângela Figueiredo was a timely meeting at CEAO (Centro de Estudos Afro-Orientais) in Dois de Julho, Salvador da Bahia, three years ago which led to her inviting me to teach in the international summer school — *Escola Internacional Feminista Negra Decolonial* in Cachoeira during the summer of 2019. Thank you, Eudes Lopes for often on-the-spot translation help and affirmation as I brought this work to a close.

Sincere gratitude to Desiree Lewis for feedback on the chapter on Winnie Mandela and for suggesting the work of Sisonke Msimang and to sister-scholar-friend, Amina Mama for camaraderie. Leo Wilton, my former teaching assistant, now Professor of Psychology and Race at Binghamton University, years ago gave me a copy of Winnie Mandela's, *491 Days* which he acquired during a sabbatical period in Johannesburg. This book ended up being absolutely critical to this work. It was important to the fleshing out of a chapter on Winnie Mandela which actually began to be written in Senegal in 2019 but technically had a start years ago when I wrote "Collaboration, and the Ordering Imperative in Life Story Production," based only on on the first Winnie Mandela autobiography and which was published *in De/colonizing the Subject. The Politics of Gender in Women's Autobiography* (1992).

For the chapter on Africa as well, sincere thanks to Aminata Dramane Traoré who graciously gave me an interview in her complex in Bamako, Mali. Mme. Ndaiye Ramatoulaye Diallo, former Minister of Culture of Mali provided instinctive friendship, she said reciprocally because she had a former classmate from Trinidad and Tobago who helped her adjust to university life in the United States when she was a young student. I am grateful for the follow-up interviews she provided with amazing photographs I am unable to share in this manuscript. In Mali as well, I was pleased to meet for the first time Samiah Nkrumah, the daughter of Osagyefo Kwame Nkrumah of Ghana, whose interview is included in this study. All of the amazing and beautiful women in Dakar must be recognized: the then staff of the Museum of Black Civilizations (MCN): Oumy Diaw, Fatoumata Sy, Fatoumata Lo, secretary of the director, and especially Halima Diallo who had just completed her thesis on "Women Leaders in Senegal" and shared her findings. Super thanks to Babacar Mbow for providing translations when necessary, for mounting that exhibition in the MCN and using my words in the wall text of the exhibition on Black Women and the Production of Knowledge. Stylist extraordinaire Oumou Sy, always so generous and beautifully talented, provides best examples of African woman's aesthetics of power, is my sister-friend and head wrap fashion guru during my visits to Dakar. My former student Siga Fatima Jagne Jallow, Commissioner for Gender and Social Affairs of ECOWAS (The Economic Community of West African States) during this period of study has been a major staple, in this process, providing documentation and intellectual affirmation, speaking remotely to my Black Women and Political Leadership class during the height of the COVID-19 virtual teaching. Thank you, Hilary Jones, then a history professor at FIU, for an early reading of this chapter.

My dear friend Abena P.A. Busia, now Ambassador of Ghana to Brazil and former Rutgers University professor, has been an amazing constant in my academic life since we met years ago as we both navigated our first African Studies Association meeting at the start of both of our academic careers. Thank you to another dear friend and colleague, Anne Adams, Professor Emerita in Africana Studies at Cornell University, and her daughter Zora. Stopping by my office to share with me a pizza on Halloween Night when I was working on the bibliography actually helped me bring that aspect of the project to conclusion on that very night rather than delaying it to the next day which was my inclination to avoid another late Ithaca night. My dear student and later research and teaching assistant who is now a special assistant to the World Trade Organization's Director-General, Ngozi Okonjo-Iweala, was the lovely Nicole Naa Adoley Mensa who the class loved. I expect some day will be one of those African women leaders we discussed. This acknowledges all your work Nicole and above all your grace and diligence.

For the Caribbean aspects of this study, major thanks are due to Yvonne Bobb-Smith for reading and offering feedback but above all providing on-the-ground information necessary to complete that chapter during pandemic closures which foreclosed possibilities of travel. Opal Palmer Adisa, then Director of IGDS (Institute for Gender and Development Studies), University of the West Indies, based in Jamaica graciously shared her children's book which developed from her research on Portia Simpson Miller, titled *Portia Dreams* (2022) but also provided contacts with the assistants to Hon. Portia Simpson Miller. Rhoda Reddock always provides intellectual camaraderie and intense historical and sociological knowledge from which I grow always. Eudine Barriteau, thank you for your examples in articulating Caribbean feminism and your prior work on this subject of women and political leadership. Linda Carty, my erstwhile upstate New York Caribbean sister so happy to change her praxis location to the Caribbean, is the kind of friend who always brings sanity and realness often to our sometimes crazy academic encounters with, and resistance to, academic patriarchy. Thank you, former colleague and T& T homie Dwight Nimblett and his assistant both of Florida International University for a critical favor. Howard Dodson, former Chief of the Schomburg provided a timely connection for my conversation with former President of Liberia, Ellen Johnson Sirleaf. In Mali, artist Abdoulaye Konate did the same for my conversation with Aminata Dramane Traoré as did Modibo Souare for a meeting and subsequent conversation with then Minister of Culture Ramatoulaye Diallo.

Always the anchor for realness, my family in Trinidad, especially Walda Waithe, Ilori Waithe, Margaret Boyce George, Wendell George, Mennen Walker Briggs, Joyce Walker Thompson, provide that grounding that one needs outside the academy, as do friends like Neila Todd and Eintou Pearl Springer. Daughters Jonelle Demby and Dalia Davies Flanagan, son-in-law Brian and granddaughters, Ila Rose Flanagan, Nomi Michelle Flanagan, and grandsons, Lev Bryson and Brian Demby, bring love always. Babacar M'bow partner in struggle as in life.

Working on the African American experience of women is a constantly unfolding process. Thank you, Dorothy Jenkins Fields, for sharing information on Gwen Cherry. My friends Phyllis Baker, Linda Spears-Bunton, Loretta McNeir, Valerie Lyle Patterson remain consistently supportive, space-giving while understanding. Berthe Petit is my sister-friend who makes sure I represent always. Rosemari Mealy, Cheryl Roberts, Elizabeth Ross, thank you for being so dear. Colleagues and friends in Ithaca and Cornell especially Mukoma wa Ngugi, Edward and Dee Baptist, Ishion Hutchinson, Russell Rickford, N'dri Assie Lumumba, Lyrae van Clief Stefanon, Derrick Spires, Anne Adams, Mary Anne Grady Flores, Helena Viramontes, Zillah Eisenstein, Satya and Chandra Mohanty provide continued supportive community. The John Henrik Clarke, Africana Librarian, Kofi Acree and night manager Saah Nue Quigee came through all the time with essays and other research items I could not find on my own and above all support and care. My many energetic students in courses on Black Women and Political Leadership have been amazingly inspirational . . . with statements like this one from a spirited presentation on Winnie Mandela describing Nelson in a reversed domestic ascription: "He was the husband of Winnie Mandela and that's all we will say about Nelson Mandela in this presentation."

Finally, one of the political contexts for doing this study resides in the fact that I joined the faculty of the Africana Studies and Research Center at Cornell University which in its more than 50-year history, founded in 1968, has maintained a distinctively male-dominated leadership paradigm. Studying and writing about this phenomenon as in "The Persistence of Institutional Sexism in Africana Studies" *AAIHS on line journal*, September 17, 2018,. https://www.aaihs.org/the-persistence-of-institutional-sexism-in -africana-studies, allowed me to think through how such a progressive intent could end up with a sexist legacy and thereby to reach beyond the specifics of the structural frameworks of the department to understand how male supremacy works nationally and internationally.

Much of this discussion of rights was aided by my completing an LLM in international human rights law in 2001 which has helped me to put many of these claims into a larger context and led to an essay "Black Voting Rights, Kwame Toure, Barack Obama and the Im/Possibility of a Black President" *Pluriel Magazine* (June-July, 2008): 42–43 which looked at institutional power and race in the US context. Thank you, Jeremy Levitt for encouraging my first published essay on this subject which definitely led to this larger work: "Writing Black Women into Political Leadership: Reflections, Trends and Contradictions." *Black Women and International Law: Deliberate Interactions, Movements and Actions*. Ed. Jeremy Levitt. Cambridge UK: Cambridge University Press, 2015: 23–34.

Readers and editors of this manuscript have contributed substantially to the present organization of this work and have helped me to clarify my ideas along the way, particularly the title of this work. The editors at Lexington Books who initially sought this work and those like Sydney Wedbush who actually realized it are offered sincere gratitude. Still as always, I assume, as my own, any limitations in expression, content and full coverage even as I aspire to fully represent. Such is the nature of writing.

COVER ART ACKNOWLEDGMENT

When I studied the intent and presentation of Wangechi Mutu's "The Seated Ones," exhibited in the MET Façade (September 2019 to June 2020), I saw these powerful sculptures immediately as in conversation with this work, confirmed by her statement that: "The poised, stately figures I have created for The MET facade derive inspiration from my interest in ancient and modern practices that reflect on the relationship between women and power across various traditions . . ." (https://www.metmuseum.org/press/exhibitions /2019/wangechi-mutu-artist-statement).

Amazing timing has produced a fortuitous result for the cover which features Wangechi Mutu's The Seated IV. A visit from artist Peter Wayne Lewis and his wife Catherine Schneider Lewis to our house in Miami produced one evening a conversation in my backyard about the need for an amazing cover for this work, after discussions I had with art historian Frieda High about finding a work that captures the power of women as leaders, creative individuals in their own right. When I told Peter that Wangechi's work spoke to me for this purpose, he indicated right away that she was a friend and called her there and then saying all the time. "It's done!" Wangechi answered from Kenya in a time frame of about 2:00 a.m. Nairobi time and after we chatted briefly about what I wanted, she asked me to send a text and an email request the next day. Everything else fell into place within a week. My daughter Dalia Davies Flanagan that same evening did mock-ups of what the cover could look like. A sincere debt of acknowledgment and appreciation are due to Peter Wayne Lewis who I have met, visited, hung out and traveled with in Dakar Senegal, Beijing, China, Miami, Florida, Boston, Massachusetts when he invited me to give the MASSArt Lecture and New York City after his exhibition at the Skoto Gallery. Here then is another example of synchronicity, friendship and deep love for art as for the scholarly-creative experience.

Thank you Wangechi Mutu for use of a detail from "The Seated IV" 2019 Bronze Edition of 3 Courtesy of the Artist and Gladstone Gallery, New York and Brussels, The Metropolitan Museum of Art, Photo by Joseph Coscia, Jr.

Introduction

"I Am a Woman's Rights":
Power and Parity Politics

"Talking about rights," as voiced by Sojourner Truth (Isabella Baumfree, c. 1797–1883) in her legendary 1851 speech at the Women's Rights Convention in Akron, Ohio, provides an early and relevant example of the ongoing articulation of the quest for Black women's rights as embodied politics.[1] Indeed, the conjunction Sojourner created between Black people and women in general is precisely where Black women, both denied rights and articulating the right to these, reside as a kind of absence which scholarship and writing by generations of Black women have consistently made present. While there has been some distortion in the way the speech has come down into history, Margaret Washington in *Sojourner Truth's America*[2] indicates that "the *Bugle* reported that Sojourner began with 'I am a woman's rights'" (229). Indeed, we have several reports of Sojourner using the language of rights as in another statement: "that women shall have their rights, not rights from you" but what actually belongs to them.[3] And in 1866, she is indicated as saying, "I am about the only colored woman that goes about to speak for the rights of the colored woman."[4] Thus, we have some of the earliest assertions of a claim for Black women's rights and thereby Black women's assumption of a rights discourse as a key and basic political position. Sojourner would combine, both in her body and discourse, the principle of that Black woman's rights discourse. She would consistently campaign for Black Civil Rights as well for land and for the 15th amendment to the US constitution which ostensibly gave Black people the right to vote[5] but because it focused on race without gender, actually gave Black men the right to vote even when racism thwarted its full realization. Additionally, in a claim that would be called reparative justice today, she saw the acquisition of land as "her people's entitlement and the key to their economic independence, industry and mobility" (356). In the United States women would get the right to vote in 1919 but generally that "women" meant white women, again given the stipulations and barriers placed by anti-Black racism to full democratic enfranchisement up to the present. Still, it would

1

take that entire 20th century for women everywhere in the world to get even basic rights to vote.[6]

Given that each of these freedom movements has taken sometimes a century to be realized, this work asserts from the outset that the 21st century, despite its racial and gender setbacks, will advance the full participation of women in creating a transformed and equitable world. Just as W.E.B. DuBois called the 20th century, the century of the color line,[7] we can similarly assert the 21st century as the century for claiming Black women's right to leadership. The lessons and positions already advanced by a range of women in leadership throughout the 20th century provide guidance for subsequent generations of women who will no longer be kept away from the sources of power that can effect change and provide simultaneously a more equitable world.

A half a century ago, South African writer Bessie Head who titled her novel *A Question of Power* (1974), opened the space for a literary work to engage what the absence of power can mean in a Black woman's life trajectory as she navigates the state, the combinations of white and male supremacy and her own struggles for a pathway through their various blockages. Bessie Head, we note, was also involved in political organizations and campaigns against *apartheid* which would have also impacted her particular angle of literary creativity as did her deliberations on questions of power at institutional and personal levels.[8] It is necessary therefore to engage these unfulfilled assertions from political actors as from literary activists, from Sojourner to Bessie Head and beyond, via this work, *Black Women's Rights: Leadership and the Circularities of Power.* The literary articulators often imagine new worlds; the political actors work to execute these imaginaries. My claim in this work follows Claudia Jones (1915–1964) in asserting that women, representing "half the world" demographically, are therefore due half of the world's resources and an equal share of its power.

"HALF THE WORLD"

The history and trajectory of "half the world"[9] discourses indicate that these were central to Black women's emancipatory politics in the early 20th century. Frances Watkins Harper (1825–1911), African-American poet, short story writer and abolitionist activist is one of the first to publicly assert: "I know that no nation can gain its full measure of enlightenment and happiness if *one-half of it is free, and the other half fettered.*"[10] The implications of this "half the world" framing is significant as it referred to both racial and gender subordination simultaneously. In that framing, the assumption was that the enslavement or absence from participation of "half a nation" meant the absence of fulfillment of the founding democratic premises of any nation. In this case Watkins Harper was talking about the enslavement and continued racialized and gendered oppression of Black people in the United States which she described as "wrongs" instead of "rights." But the implications for women who at that time were also mounting a movement for equitable belonging in the United States make it applicable specifically to Black Women as a community to which she belonged. The question of rights then has dominated the discourse of Black women in many different locations.[11]

The "half the world" formulation was created and justified by Claudia Jones, a Black left activist-intellectual who explained her argument in various texts and in multiple frames using the statistical data of her day to make her arguments. As Secretary of the Women's Commission of the Communist Party, USA, she used this byline as the title for her column, "Half the World,"[12] where she was explicit in describing a gendered position that advanced issues that pertained to the status of women all over the world. Published in the early 1950's in the *Daily Worker*'s Woman Today Section, the "Half the World" column was targeted first at reaching and organizing an audience of women and second, at raising what the party called the "woman question"[13](77) for a general audience. Further, in her 1948 essay "For New Approaches to Our Work Among Women," Claudia Jones had argued similarly that: "To begin with, women represent over half the nation."[14]

The world demographic share in which women are consistently identified between 49.6 and 51% of the world by United Nations and other population assessments, serves as the legitimate basis for equality and above all access to at least half of the word's resources and representational structures. In Claudia Jones's framing:

> *To begin with, women represent over half the nation.* Moreover, there are nearly sixteen million women wage-earners, one fifth of whom are heads of families. Thirty-seven million are housewives in cities or farms. Eight percent of these are working mothers. There are forty-seven million women eligible to vote in the United States, over a million and a half more than men. (738–739)[15]

While for Claudia Jones, the logic of "half the world" carried the essential materialist-feminist assertion that "women make up half the world's population and as such need to be similarly represented in terms of resources, access and identification" (738), this ends up being a practical issue of apportionment and therefore of the need, minimally, for parity. In other words, the "half the world" formulation remind us that we are still negotiating the rights of "half the world" to be full participants in the world in which we live.

Thus, by the time we get to the United Nations Decade for Women, (1975–1985), the discourse and logic of "Half the World" would become entrenched in the formation of the Convention for the Elimination of All

Forms of Discrimination Against Women (CEDAW) which passed in 1979 after being declared in 1967. It is significant that The Declaration of Mexico on the Equality of Women and their Contribution to Development and Peace, a resolution adopted by the UN at the end of the International Women's Year World Conference in 1975 begins with a "half the world" framing as follows:

> *Aware* that the problems of women, who constitute *half of the world's* population, are the problems of society as a whole, and that changes in the present economic, political and social situation of women must become an integral part of efforts to transform the structures and attitudes that hinder the genuine satisfaction of their needs.[16]

Relatedly, Ghanaian writer Ama Ata Aidoo would use a similar proportional representation frame as she observed similar limitations to women's full emancipation caused by the ways that marriage has disadvantaged "half of humanity." In her words: [. . .] marriage has proved singularly effective as an instrument of suppression. It has put half (or often more than half) of humanity through mutations that are thoroughly humiliating and at best ridiculous (263).[17]

Black Women's Rights: Leadership and the Circularities of Power is stimulated titularly, in part, by a conversation I was fortunate to have with former Liberian president Ellen Johnson Sirleaf in 2018 in which when I asked her about women and leadership she responded: "Yes, we want the Power and if we can get it the leadership."[18] She felt that women should not refuse ever if they are offered a leadership option as men rarely refuse these opportunities whether they are credentialed or prepared or not. Embedded in that statement though is a subtle distinction between leadership and power. But there is also Eudine Barriteau's edited collection *Love and Power: Caribbean Discourses on Gender* (2012) which engages the issue of power also in its title articulating at the same time a concept of power mitigated by love.

This work examines the articulations of "Half the World" discourses in legal, political, and social and creative texts in a variety of selected African and African diaspora locations, guided by the locations which have visibly advanced women in leadership positions and comparable women's rights organizations. It was important to be affirmative and to pursue these understandings of what happens when women are empowered, as opposed to attempting to justifying minor or tokenized inclusions of one or two women in leadership positions, in representations in organizations, boards, supreme courts and other positions which impact but often do not provide the advancement of a variety of social processes. As these pertain to Black women's rights, the aim was to examine the nature of these implementations of policies advanced by international organizations in several locations. A timely and relevant work is Stanlie James's *Practical Audacity. Black Women and International Human Rights* (2021) which interviewed fourteen 20th century activist women inspired by the work of luminous figures in the United States such as Mary McLeod Bethune (1875–1955). She defines these women as "Black female human rights practitioners" whose work she credits with informing "the development of international human rights" (9). She therefore asserts that "Black women have an illustrious, often unsung history (in international human rights) that incudes participation in and leadership of a wide range of organizations and social movements" (10).[19]

THE PARITY FOR "HALF THE WORLD" CLAIM

In June, 2010, the Senegalese parliament approved a "parity law" asserting that women who represent 52% of that country's population still hovered around 20% of representation in the various elective bodies and therefore required all political parties to introduce absolute gender parity in electoral lists for all elected representation, national or local. While the actual acquisition of parity remains to be fulfilled, in the Senegalese case, as in others, the ability to indicate it as a legal principle provides the destination of those rights which will have to be fulfilled over time. Credit for the assertion of the Senegal Parity Law is given to the leadership of Aminata Diaw (1959–2017) as a sociologist and women's rights activist who saw this policy through to completion.[20] Significantly, Senegal has already had a short-lived, principled woman prime minister (2013–2014) in Aminata Touré who was also before that the Minister of Justice, conscious of women's rights, and who left the office rather than be compromised with presidential decisions that she did not support. An earlier prime minister, Mame Madior Boye (2001–2002) during the presidency of Abdoulaye Wade also had a short-lived prime ministership. The extent to which competent and prepared women end up not being able to function under corrupt male leadership adds another theme to be pursued in discussion of the nature of 20th century post-colonial independence and male-dominated, nation-state politics.

In other words, my assertion is that the extent to which parity becomes a legitimate articulation of equality for women globally, is contingent on this right to leadership becoming common place, advanced in popular global assertions and actualized in political representation and without demands to compromise. To do less, in Watkins Harper's words, and in Claudia Jones formulation, is to automatically accept that *half of the world,* in this case women, have no rights to determine how the resources of the world are distributed and what the actual progression of humankind should be like.

We recall Thomas Sankara's (Burkina Faso progressive leader 1983–1987) valiant but also short-lived effort to redress the imbalance which relegated half of his nation's population (women) to erasure and lack of representation, expressed in his classic question: "Did we realize we are talking about the living conditions of 52% of the Burkinabe population, away from towns, in the rural areas?"[21] In many ways, his position is attuned to that of Black left activists like Claudia Jones who made the same arguments and with African women's rights proponents who work steadily towards equal representation. However, according to ONU Femmes (UN Women), *"Femmes en Politique"*: 2019, Burkina Faso still has only 14.3 representation of women in parliamentary positions.

This work on *Black Women's Rights: Leadership and the Circularities of Power* is guided by several research questions which were posed to women in political leadership positions, responses to which informed some of our discussions and conclusions. A selection of these responses accompany this study of women in political leadership in a variety of world locations. These questions continue to guide analyses of the praxis of Black women in political office and the actuality of the gradual rise of Black women to political office.[22]

While some countries have used the language of providing quotas to account for women's absence, the language and philosophy behind quotas, on their own, carry a complicated political trajectory. They have had, nonetheless, a certain impact as used by several countries at party, legislative and national levels to ensure some participation of women. Relatedly, as we see in the case of Brazil, racial quotas have had a significant impact on the advancing of Afro-Brazilians through the educational process and therefore into more contemporary professional and political roles. According to Mona Lena Krook, author of "Reforming Representation: The Diffusion of Candidate Gender Quotas Worldwide," who has studied their history and application and uses four models (international imposition, transnational imposition, international tipping, and international blockage), there is always a degree of cross-national diffusion (310) particularly since most states like to follow international norms and regional practices and strategies end up having impact on individual states.[23]

Above all, the role of women's self-organizing and modes of resistance have also created conditions by which representation was struggled for and attained. A good example is the case of Sudan in 2019 where parity became a more descriptive formulation for activism on behalf of women's access to leadership. In that case, parity was applied as well towards equality in educational attainment as in political representation, though it has since been challenged by masculinist male military proclivities. Thus, the question of the absence or presence of women and political leadership remains a global phenomenon in a variety of intersecting areas which highlight the circularities of power to which we refer.

Still, it is clear that the idea of *half the world* remains aspirational as generally political representation for women in 2021 hovered around 23% worldwide. Even so, representation remains uneven. Rwanda notwithstanding with 61% women is sometimes indicated as presence without power. At present, a number of African countries have a parity law which means that, as surprising as it seems, African countries will be in the lead of having women elected or appointed to the highest levels of leadership. This possibility becomes glaringly visible as the major world power, which the United States is, has never ratified the Equal Rights Amendment nor CEDAW. This means that women's advancement is based on individual assertion in keeping with US late capitalist politics, the legendary and masculinist "throwing one's hat in the ring" or the "putting oneself out there" of Shirley Chisholm in 1972, Hilary Clinton in 2016, Amy Klobuchar, Elizabeth Warren, Kamala Harris in 2019. South Africa for example has a parity policy which indicates that: "In the elections for local councils in South Africa, parties must seek to ensure that 50% of the candidates on the party list are women."[24] In 2006, the ANC (African National Congress) adopted a 50% gender quota in local elections. The quota was extended to national elections as well in 2009. By September 2021, women represented 46% of the National Assembly.[25]

Still, the case of Senegal remains a striking example of one way in which the acceptance of parity increased its representation of women by over 20% in one election cycle, following the introduction of a parity law which says that for each election the slate should have 50% representation of women or it would not be approved, the representation of women in parliament in 2019 is indicated at 41%, though this is not geographically even across the country. Interestingly then President Abdoulaye Wade (2000–2012) had proposed, as well, a 50% representation of women in the African Union in 2002. So, it was not surprising that he also proposed it for Senegal which adopted Law No. 2010–11 of May 28, 2010, allowing 43.03% of women representation in the National Assembly. Signed in 2010 by President Abdoulaye Wade,[26] the law obliged all political parties to place women and men in an alternating manner on candidate lists, aiming at a male-female ratio of 50%. In cases of non-compliance, the electoral commission (CENA) had the authority to reject lists, and thus exclude parties from competing in elections. The direct result was that the 2012 national election saw an increase of women representatives from 22.7% to 42.7% in the National Assembly, and from 16% to 47% in local legislatures in the 2014 local election. According to Marianne Toraasen "Gender parity in Senegal—A Continuing struggle" (2017), it remains still a struggle, particularly as it pertains to Muslim strongholds like the Muslim holy city of Touba which rejected putting women on any legislative lists (7).[27]

For Halima Diallo, who wrote an M.A. thesis on the subject, it is a policy still "flouted by men" for "while the law favored the massive entry of women parliamentarians (43%) into the National assembly, men continue to debate their legitimacy."[28]

The Charter of Political parties in Angola encourages the promotion of equal opportunities and equity between men and women as well as gender representation and recommends no less than 30% representation in their governing bodies (Article 20 of Law 22/10 on Political Parties). There is a direct equivalence of 30% of women political parties. In 2012 (Section 151 (3) in Cameroun, "a new electoral code" was adopted whereby gender became a legal prerequisite in the compilation of all candidates for elections. By the end of 2019, women were 31% of the parliament.

All of these above-identified cases of the legal advances of representation reveal that there is a direct equivalence with women's accession to political leadership once institutional barriers are removed. For Torasen, using Ali Tripp's analysis, based obviously on the Rwanda and Liberia cases, "in the aftermath of a destructive civil war, an institutional vacuum appears. In this political space, new constitutions and electoral laws are implemented. Women's movements often use this opportunity to claim their rightful place in the new society and create women-friendly laws and institutions like gender quotas."[29]

However, the case of Senegal where the creation of a women's rights organizations has consistently pushed for women's advancement is more instructive. The creation of COSEF (Conseil Sénégalais des Femmes) founded in 1994 was preceded by textual analyses and assertions such as those by African feminist Awa Thiam's *Black Sisters. Speak Out: Feminism and Oppression in Black Africa* (1986), one of the first books to assert an African feminism. AAWORD (Association of African Women for Research and Development) a Pan-African organization of women was founded in 1977 in Dakar and advanced a variety of projects for economic, social and political rights, led by a variety of assertive Senegalese and other African women academics and activists. Aminata Diaw (1959–2017) sociologist and intellectual activist who advanced women's rights positions in West Africa from the 1970's onward was posthumously identified at the CODESRIA 2018 general assembly as one of the leading energies and campaigners behind the passage of the Parity Law in Senegal. And we cannot forget the work of novelist and women's rights activist Mariama Ba (1929–1981) whose *So Long a Letter* (1982) laid out descriptively the issues facing women in contemporary polygamous marriages and the lack of protection of their rights at their husbands' demise.

SWAPO, the South West African People's Organization founded in Namibia in 1960 was in its origin an African Liberation Organization, as were several others on the continent with male and female fighters, which when it came to leadership ended up male-dominated. It is only in 2013 that it introduced an amendment allowing equal representation of men and women 50–50 in the party's organs and structures. This policy has given women an opportunity to participate on an equal footing with their male counterparts in the country's legislative elections. According to UN Women, Angola has 46% representation in parliament. Similarly, for Burundi in which Article 108 of the 2014 Electoral Code stipulates that at least 30% of the members of the National Assembly must be women and Article 127(4) also indicates that lists muse be gender balanced so that at least one in four candidates must be a woman. We note that in the Rwanda case which today has 61% of representations the stipulation of a minimum of 33% of women is indicated in all decision-making bodies.[30]

While there are studies in the field of political science on quotas and even an international database which updates the use of quotas in parties, at legislative and national levels, all over the world, the Senegalese example of the language of parity as opposed to quotas has more utility for a few reasons: For one thing, the logic of quotas suggests that those in power give over a minor portion of those tools of power, incrementally, to a subordinate group. Parity which carries the language and logic of bringing one thing in par or at the same level as another, then has to do with a redistribution of resources so that there is more evenness in the sharing of those benefits. Thus, in the Senegalese case while depending on one's point of view, *parité* has been seen by patriarchal power as a negative word, meaning, "I no longer accept my husband's authority," according to Senegalese cultural workers, instead, the national language of *parité* has made it also into Wolof and has also provided the language for some redefined domestic cultural practices for women who claim equality or sharing of household responsibilities.[31]

The point is that these personal and political rights and processes consistently have to be negotiated and re-advanced in the context of male or white supremacist frameworks. The most recent case is that of the women of Sudan who were publicly active and instrumental in the movement to remove the dictator Omar al-Bashir in April, 2019, and then have to struggle again for full participation in the transitional government, only to be thwarted by a military coup on October 25, 2021. This resistance to sharing leadership with women, we know, is a consistent pattern which has been documented by women who were active in various liberation struggles across Africa in the lead up to independence. Sudanese women nevertheless have asked for parity: "the representation of women in all government institutions, executive bodies, legislative and the judiciary including at decision making with a percentage of not less than 50% as a temporary measure while giving due consideration to female youth" (MNSM Declaration).[32] Still, this produced only four (4) out of the fourteen (14) ministers nominated by the prime minister with portfolios in Foreign Affairs, Labor and Social Development, Youth and Sports and Higher Education, but definitely, *not* parity.[33]

So, in advancing a study of Black women and political leadership, the history and trajectory of "half the world" discourses must be advanced in a few directions. First of all, such a paradigm assumes equality as a given. This study also allows us to launch an examination of the articulations of "Half the World" in legal, political, and social and creative documents in a variety of selected African and African diaspora locations, with an open question: Why it is so difficult to have equal representation? Such a framework nonetheless keeps alive an overarching question about whether the goal is a "parity of power" with men or are we working towards a world of circulating power as opposed to hierarchical power relationships?

What happens after women attain leadership is still material for ongoing discussion. Often the idealized qualities asserted tend to challenge the ways that women continue to be represented. Thus, we maintain a series of open questions to women leaders:

1. What is leadership in your thinking?
2. What is your leadership story (your pathway to leadership)?
3. Are there issues you are able to address better as a woman? Do you use a gender lens when solving problems?
4. How do you balance your personal life and professional? And what is your advice to young girls and women today trying to figure out how they can balance their lives?
5. Is there a difference between women's leadership and men's use of political power?
6. How would you describe your leadership style?
7. Do you see yourself carrying forward any traditional (African, African-American, Caribbean, or other) leadership methods in your various projects?
8. Do you think anything changes, or will change, when more women get to political power?
9. Do you feel that women in positions of power are scrutinized more heavily on issues such as competence?
10. What about physical appearance, clothing, family? Have you had any experience with negative responses to you as a Black woman that you are willing to describe or give examples of this?

The process of developing this work includes examining the lifestories of Black women who have attained political leadership as well as the surrounding issues that rendered them visible. These included Shirley Chisholm's two political autobiographies, *Unbought and Unbossed* (1970) and The *Good*

Fight (1973). While the former *"Unbought and Unbossed"* became her sig-
nature statement and is therefore more well known, the second *"The Good
Fight"* in which she goes into her political campaign provides additional
details about the intricate nature of her own process, thinking, achievements
and includes texts of her speeches. The Chisholm example as this study pro-
gressed was clearly pivotal in the campaigns of women in wider geographical locations than the United States impacting the Caribbean and Europe
as well as evidenced by Diane Abbott in the United Kingdom. Her *Diane
Abbott. The Authorised Biography*[34] describes coming to the United States as
a guest of the Congressional Black Caucus and being consistently energized
by what transpired as far as the taking of office by Black elected officials in
the United States was concerned and absolutely being inspired by Shirley
Chisholm's daring.

Yet, there are still relatively few accounts either by themselves or by
others of Black women in political office. In Brazil, *Benedita da Silva: An
Afro-Brazilian Woman's Story of Politics and Love*[35] is still perhaps the only
text of its kind in the field of study of Afro-Brazilian women's political history though there are a few forthcoming books on Léila Gonzalez in process.

The model of documenting one's political process as a Black woman politician is an important step in beginning a campaign for that politician but is also
necessary at the conclusion of serving one's office. This project reveals that
this final rear-view mirror approach is just as significant in having an assessment, by self and by others, in the aftermath of one's leadership trajectory
as was demonstrated by the work of Eudine Barriteau on Eugenia Charles in
the Caribbean. Such studies will advance us beyond the few available ones
of Black women politicians available. With the rise of Kamala Harris to the
Vice Presidency of the United States and her own book, *The Truths We Hold*
(2019), we expect that there will be numerous continuous and follow-up
self-assessments (magazine and journal articles, edited collections and mono-
graphs) which will generate and enhance continuing studies in the fields of
Political Science and Black and Women's Studies and in African American
History. Stacey Abrams's two political autobiographies, *Lead from the
Outside. How to Build Your Future and Make Real Change* (2019*)* and *Our
Time is Now. Power, Purpose and the Fight for a Fair America* (2020), are
only the beginning in my view for someone who is already a prolific writer.
In this way then, the literary and the political come together in the writing of
their lifestories and experiences as is the intent of this work.

While this study has focused on Black women and political leadership,
there are a variety of adjacent fields through which one can also study Black
women's leadership trajectories. Black women and leadership profiles are
available in religion, entertainment, especially film and music industries,

academic institutions, and definitely activism at the community grassroots or local and national levels. Each of these deserve and will eventually have their own studies with time. A number of autobiographies of Black women in entertainment such as Grace Jones, *I'll Never Write My Memoirs* (2016) or the subsequent Cecily Tyson, *Just As I Am: A Memoir* (2021) are also deserving of further study.

My own personal experience as a Black woman working through some of these same questions of inequality in the academy has in some ways prompted this study. This was documented in my article on "The Persistence of Sexism in Africana Studies"[36] which in many ways included the fact that the larger institutional contexts, with their racialized gendered structures and expectations, indeed facilitated or continue to support these male-dominated processes, even sometimes with women at the head of these academic institutions. In response to ongoing issues and charges of sexism in Africana Studies at Cornell, I offered my own challenge after witnessing the relaying of leadership from man to man in that department in a fifty plus year loop which continues still.[37] Black women on the faculty of various universities who raise issues of misogyny or misogynoir are often seen as not being collegial and therefore the problem as opposed to the recalcitrant and sometimes incompetent male leadership. My position is that in the same way that white people benefit from white supremacy even when they are not directly practicing but have ancestors who benefitted and passed it down, Black men acquire leadership and the benefits of male supremacy in similar ways. Black men in Africa and the African Diaspora are therefore culpable if not actively, as in their charges against racism, resisting and challenging these forms of gender oppression. Misogyny and sexism or in Moya Bailey's term *misogynoir*,[38] are built into these institutions in which we work and are sometimes heightened or practiced, more or less, in various ways in academic departments, governments, businesses, industries, depending on institutional histories.

In some ways then, this text was written to try to understand this experiential phenomenon even as I also lived it, to respond to Claudia Jones's ongoing question: "*Why are they so frightened about the political views of* one *[Black] woman?* Or, why is it so hard to hear and respond to the assertions of Black women?" In this regard, teaching a class on this subject and seeing students develop this topic in their various projects which identified Black women leaders around the world advanced and multiplied the possibilities as we studied how women get to political leadership and how they navigate and exercise power once they have attained same. Students energetically pursued research on political figures and created podcasts as they were able to get access to local and state politicians in their various communities.

This project therefore does not offer major conclusions. It is not a political science study; it was interested in the manifestation of leadership as expressed, narrativized, and represented by women of African descent in a selected number of African diaspora and regional contexts. Instead of offering conclusions, it witnesses, opens up space for specific locations as well as global/relational discussion as we collectively pursue developments in the field and await advancements, promises, understandings and conclusions. This then is only the opening salvo, an early and preliminary contribution to what will be an evolving field of study. The Museum of Black Civilizations in Dakar, for example mounted an exhibition on Black Women and the Production of Knowledge to which I contributed conceptually and which has become a popular site for women just to sit and contemplate the various women in world leadership.[39] This prompted a follow-up exhibition on African Women and Political Leadership sponsored by United Nations Women (Africa) after a tour of that exhibition. A corresponding conference on the subject was the last public event I attended in March 2020 in Dakar, Senegal, before the pandemic-generated closures.

"WOMEN OF THE WORLD UNITE"[40]

Black Women's Rights: Leadership and the Circularities of Power is organized into seven chapters focused largely on Africa and the Americas, already assumed incomplete since the African Diaspora exists in the entire world and since we are in a consistently evolving scenario of access sometimes happening in unexpected ways as in the presidency of Samia Suluhu Hassan in Tanzania who became president in March 19, 2021 following the unexpected death of her male predecessor.[41] The confirmation of Judge Ketanji Brown Jackson to the United States Supreme Court finally passed the Senate on April 7, 2022, declared publicly by another Black woman, the sitting Vice President of the United States, while this work was in press. Still, I imagine, and therefore forecast, many more gains, based on my guiding principle that this is the century for the realization of Black women's leadership. While we accept that a particular limitation of a work such as this one is that we must admit that we are still striving towards full representation, surprising political, social and environmental conjunctures create amazing qualitative leaps in sometimes unexpected ways. A materialist reading reveals that the historical issues that produced contemporary social conditions in Africa and the Americas, places with the largest populations of Black people of African origins, the products of forced transatlantic migration of Africans, means that the demographic realities suggest enduring possibilities for the revelation of Black people's desire for and access to power to decide their present and futures. Thus, the unfolding scenario is that with each passing year, more and more women are being recognized or are entering representational politics which makes all works of this nature open to continuous revelations and, thereby, new insights and understandings of how access to political representation and its related power networks operate. As such, this study only marks a particular time period, largely the first two decades of a new millennium and ten years before the target realization of UN Sustainable Goal 5 of gender equality.[42]

The concept of the circularities of power used in this work is in part informed by Foucault's notion that power circulates and does not lie only within the purview of the dominant or oppressive force, but also is situated in those who respond to it and/or claim its creative possibilities. Sara Mills cites as salient Foucault's assertion that "power is conceptualized as a chain or as a net, that is a system of relations spread throughout the society, rather than simply as a set of relations between the oppressed and the oppressor. And, second, individuals should not be seen simply as the recipients of power, but as the 'place' where power is enacted and the place where it is resisted. Thus, his theorizing of power forces us to reconceptualize not only power itself but also the role that individuals play in power relations—whether they are simply subjected to oppression or whether they actively play a role in the form of their relations with others and institutions" (35). Foucault's suggestion that "we need a new economy of power relations"[43] or that we take "the forms of resistance against different forms of power as a starting point" (780) allows us to position women wanting to access the power/knowledge complex in order to create more circulations of power is critical to this study's orientation. And clearly these are "transversal" struggles as we see the movements of women across Africa and the African Diaspora geographies.

"Circularities of Power" as a concept thus takes into consideration the various ways that power circulates in a variety of locations. When Stokely Carmichael as representative of the Black youth activists of his 1960's generation claimed "We need Black Power!"[44] he was asserting simultaneously a resistance to the state white supremacist dominating assumption that it alone had power while calling Black communities into claiming their own power. Yet, for many Black women, that power remained male-centered, transient, and limited. We see this in Elaine Brown's titling *A Taste of Power* (1993) which identifies what it meant when women also access power to just get a "taste" in Black male dominated institutional contexts. A more recent work titled *Power Hungry. Women of the Black Panther Party and Freedom Summer and Their Fight to Feed A Movement* (2022) also engages the question of accessing power but reveals Black women activists' projects to ameliorate the food insecurity which plagued Black communities, especially the children.[45] Yet, in several contexts when Black people, often men, come to power as in becoming mayors of major US cities, or leaders of countries they often operate at the behest of entrenched state practices which have historically disadvantaged people of color. So how does one assess the circularities of power when practiced by Black conservative women like the Lieutenant Governor of the Commonwealth of Virginia in the United States, Winsome Sears in 2021[46] who is explicit in her identification with white male state power? The famous "Trust Black Women" mantra used to document the predominant population of Black women and their savvy political stances and voting power in national elections, still has to be contextualized in terms of the way that power circulates and the ideological contexts and class positions and politics of its actors.

This is therefore the kind of ongoing project which will be elaborated on consistently with closer and further study of specific locations. Reports and studies such as *Discussing Women's Empowerment: Theory and Practice* (2001) pursue some of these issues by studying as international agencies do the various processes in place to have women access power, looking at examples from South Africa, Mexico, and selected Muslim Societies. Work in the United States continues to be advanced by new developments and the successes and shortcomings of the election of Kamala Harris, a Black woman of South Asian and Caribbean ethnic descent to the Vice Presidency. *Sisters in the Statehouse: Black Women and Legislative Decision Making* by Nadia Brown (2014)[47] is one such work approaching the study of Black women in US politics from the field of political science.

Black Women's Rights: Leadership and the Circularities of Power first of all poses Black women as alternative and possible transformative leaders at the highest levels and suggests that in several instances Black women could have already occupied these positions except for social and political gender and race-based barriers. This work also operates from the perspective that not all women elected to office live or deliver transformative practices or actually assume or apply power to enhance the lives of those they represent. Indeed, they can also be conduits (if wittingly or unwittingly used) for repressive patriarchal state power. Still, the study of issues of creativity and power is linked, in the initial formation of this project as in the ongoing and deliberate need to study Black women's use of power once they access political leadership.

Chapter 1: "Assuming the Right to Leadership: Black Women and Political Power." As an opening chapter we begin with the assumption of political leadership and move through the various conceptual definitions, intents, and meanings as these pertain to leadership in general and the differences in presentation of these issues by women and feminist scholars. Transformative feminist leadership then occupies the distinct pole of the attainable model as advanced by scholars who prefer not just leadership as a given model in the masculinist terms that it has been presented but a new world model which advances the rights of women to full participation in their societies.

Chapter 2: "Feminist Literary Leadership in African Women's Writing" argues that African women writers had consistently put forward critiques of women's place in society and thereby had provided the critique of dominant paradigms in their societies which would be subsequently addressed in political fields and enshrined in the Protocol of the Rights of African Women (2006). The point here is that writers through their use of the imaginative projection of possible worlds were already able to advance some of the issues that would end up being realized. We assume here as well that some writers like Toni Morrison provide the kind of creative-theoretical framings as for example her challenge to "invisibility" in the US African-American context.

The central argument of *Black Women's Rights: Leadership and the Circularities of Power* comes to full visibility in chapter 3: "Alternative President: Nomzamo Madikizela-Mandela's Challenge" which displays the different political trajectories of Nelson Mandela and Nomzamo Winnie Madikizela-Mandela. Though she never attained full elected political leadership to this position, it is my contention that she nevertheless functioned as an "alternative president" of South Africa and not as a first lady, in the absence and incarceration of her husband until his release when he became President of South Africa. This is a bold argument which actually sees Nelson Mandela's leadership struggle as not only against the apartheid state but also to ensure the subordination of his wife's leadership paradigm.

The actualizing of political leadership in the Presidency of Ellen Johnson Sirleaf and the grassroots international leadership of Wangari Maathai are the concerns of chapter 4: "'Yes. We Want the Power!' Writing African Women's Political Leadership with Ellen Johnson Sirleaf and Wangari Maathai." Here we study what happens when women actually attain political leadership, inside or outside of institutional structures; what is achieved and what is yet to be achieved and the strategies that are used in each case. In these examples, both women ended up with a particular global appeal in two alternative pathways to formal leadership.

The historical role of Shirley Chisholm as the first woman to run for presidency of the United States on a leading party ticket, is developed in chapter 5: "Black Women Lead the Desire for a Transformed United States: The Pivotal Role of Shirley Chisholm." It takes us through the origins of Black women's leadership in the United States as represented in the emblematic Harriet Tubman up to the contemporary placement of a Black woman of South Asian and Caribbean descent as the Vice President of the United States in 2021. We see this as only a beginning as the actual process of leadership of Kamala Harris will be studied and examined from multiple angles in and out of the United States, in popular media as in academic political science and historical texts.

While the Caribbean is often literally erased in larger world cartographies, it nonetheless has a much larger historical footprint in the larger African world than is recognized in mainstream considerations. Chapter 6: "Advancing Global Leadership Paradigms from the Caribbean" is informed by the bold claim that the Caribbean intellectual tradition has always offered advanced models of political and intellectual leadership. The relatively small size of disparate islands often masks the cumulatively larger demographic and spatial relationships that exist in reality. Based on the abolitionist models advanced in several anti-slavery campaigns and actions for reparative justice, the political leadership of several Pan-Africanists, stellar literary and theoretical advancements of scholars and writers and feminist activists and thinkers, it is not unusual then to see the current model of Prime Minister Mia Mottley of Barbados as also advancing new leadership models.

Finally, chapter 7: "Marielle Franco and Black Left Feminist Leadership in Brazil" establishes a continuity with African diasporic leadership models in the United States, the Caribbean and Africa as expressed in the political example of Marielle Franco but also provided earlier in the work of Lélia Gonzalez. We recognize nonetheless that the political leadership of Black women in Latin America is a book still to be written, even as we mark here the fact that Ana Irma Lassén became the first Black lesbian to become a senator in Puerto Rico in 2020. Beyond the coda, which concludes this work, the advanced role of women and leadership in Cuba has to be studied on its own as it pertains to Black women. *Black Women's Rights: Leadership and the Circularities of Power* in this writer's view offers an opening rather than providing hard conclusions. It provides instead a theoretical or conceptual window or door as one needs it, and if we imagine a larger opening, a portal perhaps, through which we can imagine many other studies and analyses of Black women's leadership and the ways we interact with power in a variety of related fields. This in my view will continue to be filled in with specific details and advances as women, representing half the world, also assume leadership as a right, for a more equitable and transformed world.

Black Women's Rights: Leadership and the Circularities of Power uses the language of "rights" and "power" precisely because it claims that the standards by which we assume and access leadership (from "bottom power" to working diligently towards one's goals) suggest women have always been in the process of finding transformative strategic alternatives to the male-dominated leadership status quo. The creative use of power does not have to assume dominance but require the ability to make decisions that advance our communities for a better passage through this world. Anecdotally we learn that mature (post-menopausal) African women refer to themselves as receiving "power surges" as opposed to "hot flashes" which they welcome as enhancements of their ability to navigate the world confidently. And as this work will show, the issue of "rights" has continued to be articulated by women in a variety of contexts. Called The International Bill of Rights for Women (CEDAW—the Convention on the Elimination of All forms of Discrimination Against Women) along with various regional versions such as the Protocol on the Rights of African Women, continue to assert women's rights as human rights. Still we go beyond the United Nations functional definitions of human rights, still informed by European constructions of rights, to think of the "beyond," that is of the Wynterian discussions of how the human itself was constituted as white and male propertied subject in the wake of European "enlightenment" which ushered in modernity and its expansions to the "New World." Thus, the assumptions were/are always that the Black woman was/is absent in any claims to full recognition and definitely not participation. Still we reclaim and re-assert our own "Third Event" full belonging.[48] Wynter is deliberate in her "Un-settling the Coloniality of Being/Power/Truth/Freedom: Towards the Human, after Man, Its Overrepresentation" (2003) that we cannot accept the histories, time-lines, framings and theoretical presuppositions of many of these Western Enlightenment-derived structures and academic definitions, since they are so marred by European man's conception of himself as subject.[49] We note that she includes "power" in her assemblage of dominant frameworks which populate all Western theoretical models.

This work is a culmination of several intellectual threads that I have pursued in related fields of literature and social and cultural politics, Black Women's Studies, African Diaspora Studies throughout my academic career. Theoretically, my articulation of a conceptual framework for developing and thinking through this work is also guided by Claudia Jones's assertion of rights for "half the world" and her admonition that: "we must multiply a thousand-fold the leadership of [Black] women in the fight for peace (111). . . . to work among and earn leadership among, the masses of women in order to help dissolve the foul tissue of lies about women's capability and leadership in women's struggle for peace and progress (115)."[50]

NOTES

1. "I think that 'twixt the negroes of the South and the women at the North, all talking about rights, the white men will be in a fix pretty soon" (1851, Women's Rights Convention, Akron, Ohio).

2. University of Illinois Press, 229.

3. Ibid., Epigraph, p. 334.

4. Ibid., p. 334. The larger framework of a National Woman's Rights Committee by first generation women's rights activists is identified here but not without the assertion that came through the voice of a Black woman asserting her rights as well.

5. *The Constitution of the United States of America.* Fifteenth Amendment (Passed 1869, ratified, 1870), Section 1: "The right of citizens of the United States to vote shall not be denied or abridged by the United States or by any State on account of race, color, or previous condition of servitude" https://constitutioncenter.org/interactive-constitution/the-constitution (Accessed 11/16/2021).

6. See Michael G. Hanchard's tabulated listing in his appendix to *The Spectre of Race. How Discrimination Haunts Western Democracy* (Princeton and Oxford: Princeton University Press, 2018): 217–223. Though he was focused on "Political Prohibitions on People of African Descent in Latin America and the Caribbean," the information indicates in detail who was accorded those rights and as a rule these were limited to free and propertied white men.

7. DuBois's legendary call at the First Pan African Conference in London in 1900 is an oft-repeated reminder of the fact that race remained a central concern throughout the 20th century and still continues as major issue into the 21st century.

8. See Tiffany Magnolia discussion, "A method to her madness: Bessie Head's *A Question of Power* as South African National Allegory," *Journal of Literary Studies,* 18:1–2, 154–167, which makes a similar argument.

9. The ratio of women to men continues to hover around 50%, with most countries having between 49 and 51%. For example, according to *The Worlds Women,* 2015, population projections estimate that there are 3.6 billion women and 3.7 billion men worldwide. In other words, women constitute slightly less than half of the global population (49.6%). The ratio of males to females (sex ratio) indicates that there are 102 men for every 100 women. In 2017, according to "Gender Ratio" by Hannah Ritchie and Max Poser, https://ourworldindata.org/gender-ratio https://ourworldindata.org/gender-ratio: "The sex ratio—the share of the population that is female—varies across the world. And globally in 2017 the share of women in the world was 49.6%." However, there is variation across age groups as women tend to live longer than men which increases the balance over age 60. See also United Nations Popular Fund https://www.unfpa.org/data/world-population-dashboard They offer a scale assessing world population from 2015–2020.

10. "Women's Political Future," May 20, 1883. Address before the World's Congress of Representative Women at the Chicago Columbian Exposition of 1893.

11. Gloria J. Browne-Marshall, *She Took Justice. The Black Woman, Law, and Power 1619 to 1969* provides a chronological listing of Black women from Queen Nzingha to the Civil Rights Era, a list of cases advancing her themes of how Black women used a variety of means to attain social justice to challenge and also to claim power.

12. See chapter 2 of Carole Boyce Davies, *Left of Karl Marx. The Political Life of Black Communist Claudia Jones* (Duke, 2008): 65–98.

13. Titled "From 'Half the World' to the Whole World: Journalism as Black Transnational Political Practice" (69–98), this chapter explored the range of her journalistic

contributions but centered her "Half the World" assertion as capturing her Black left feminist position.

14. *Political Affairs,* 27 (August, 1948): 738–743.

15. See chapter 2 of *Left of Karl Marx. The Political Life of Black Communist Claudia Jones* (2008) for discussion. See also her essays in *Claudia Jones. Beyond Containment* (Ayebia, 2013).

16. http://www.un-documents.net/mex-dec.htm "Gathering a Body of Global Agreements" (Accessed 3.8.2022)

17. Aidoo, A.A. (1984).

18. Conversation with Ellen Johnson Sirleaf, Uniondale, New York, November 9, 2018.

19. While there are debates about the application of human rights discourses in the legal and political fields and even who qualifies as "human" as in the Wynter position in the humanities (i.e., and therefore which humans are worthy of the receipt of these rights), James offers a basic understanding: "Human rights are an affirmation of how and why all women, men, and children are entitled to live their lives in freedom and with dignity. And these basic rights include a commitment to the formulation and protection of fundamental, universal, and inalienable rights despite such boundaries as national borders, religious affiliation, and political alignments" (10). For discussion of some of these positions see Elizabeth Anker's, *Fictions of Dignity. Embodying Human Rights in World Literature* (2012).

20. Aminata Diaw was honored at the CODESRIA assembly in Dakar in 2018 for these and other intellectual and political contributions. See https://codesria.org/spip.php?article2843.

21. Sankara, Thomas. "The Emancipation of Women, and the Liberation Struggle of Africa: On the Liberation of Women." March 8, 1987. Also available as *Women's Liberation and The African Freedom Struggle.* Pathfinder Press, 2007.

22. See appendix.

23. Krook offers a pretty extensive listing of the application of quotas in different countries in various decades, pp. 312–313. See also the Global Data Base for Quotas which has a country by country listing https://www.idea.int/data-tools/data/gender-quotas/country-view/68/35

24. Local Government Act, Schedule 1, Section 11.

25. https://www.idea.int/data-tools/data/gender-quotas/country-view/310/35 (Accessed 11/23/2021).

26. Some analyses indicate that Wade who was not very popular at the time used this to get increased support of women voters but that it did not work to his benefit in the end.

27. https://www.cmi.no/publications/6230-gender-parity-in-senegal-a-continuing-struggle

28. Halima Diallo, M.A. Thesis, 2019. I interviewed Halima in 2019.

29. Ibid.

30. See "Facts and Figures: Women's Leadership and Political Participation" for 2021, https://www.unwomen.org/en/what-we-do/leadership-and-political-participation/facts-and-figures [Accessed 2/2/2022].

31. Conversation with Senegalese cultural exponent Babacar Mbow, Curator of the exhibition on Black Women and the Production of Knowledge at the Museum of Black Civilizations, Dakar, Senegal, March 5, 2020.

32. Cited in Liv Tonnessen and Samia al-Nagar, "Patriarchy, Politics and Women's Activism in Post-Revolution Sudan," CHR Michelsen Institute, University of Bergen, Sudan Brief, June 2020.

33. Ibid.

34. London: Biteback Publishing, 2020.

35. Da Silva, Benedita, *Benedita da Silva: An Afro-Brazilian Woman's Story of Politics and Love* (Monroe, Oregon: Food First Book, 1997).

36. https://www.aaihs.org/the-persistence-of-institutional-sexism-in-africana -studies/

37. All-male search committee in 2022 at Cornell's Africana Studies Department created by the current director, a philosopher of African Studies, still had to be escalated to Provost of Diversity level and challenged before one lone woman was added with all the difficulty of representation involved.

38. Moya Bailey, *Misogynoir Transformed. Black Women's Digital Resistance* (NYU Press, 2021).

39. In part generated by a paper which I contributed to their first conference and curated by Babacar M'bow.

40. A palpable revision of the Marxist byline: "Workers of the World Unite" offered by women in left feminist contexts.

41. See *Encyclopedia of the African Diaspora* (2008) for which I served as the general editor for the global breadth of the African Diaspora.

42. There are seventeen interlinked sustainable goals as set in 2015 by the United Nations, with gender equality being goal five, to be achieved by 2030.

43. Michel Foucault, "The Subject of Power," 1982, 779.

44. See Carmichael and Hamilton, 1967.

45. See especially chapter 15, pages 149–165 for discussion also the unpublished honors thesis of Tia Hicks.

46. I address this in an earlier work on the participation of Condoleezza Rice in a leadership role in US right wing politics, including the War on Iraq. See: "Con-di-fi-cation: Black Women, Leadership and Political Power," *Feminist Africa*, March, 2007.

47. Nadia Brown has a variety of ongoing projects on this issue in the US election cycle of 2020 such as her "'If Not Now, When?': Black Women Seize Political Spotlight" *US News and World Report*, August 3, 2020 https://www.usnews.com/news/ politics/articles/2020-08-03/if-not-now-when-black-women-seize-political-spotlight

48. See my "Occupying the Terrain: Re-Engaging Beyond Miranda's Meanings: Un/Silencing the 'Demonic Ground' of Caliban's Woman," *American Quarterly.* Forum on Sylvia Wynter, 70: 4 (December 2018): 837–845 for discussion.

49. *CR: The New Centennial Review* 3:3 (Fall, 2003): 257–338.

50. "For the Unity of Women in the Cause of Peace" (1951) in *Claudia Jones. Beyond Containment* (Ayebia, 2011): 103–120.

Chapter 1

Assuming the Right to Leadership

Black Women and Political Power

In 1901, Catherine McKenzie, a Black and women's rights activist in Jamaica, asserted that "[T]he subject of 'Woman's Rights' is before the world . . . a subject which is here to stay, to be discussed, and to be settled. It may be said to be the progeny of the nineteenth century; but it is to grow and develop into full maturity during the century upon which the world has just entered."[1] Here we have a fitting women's rights counterpart to W. E. B. DuBois's parallel assertion on the prominence and permanence of the color line made a year before, at the first Pan African Conference in 1900 in London (i.e., "The problem of the 20th century is the problem of the color line"), meaning that the problematics of race would be the issue dominating the 20th century. The fact that we know only DuBois's assertion speaks to the issues that concern us in this work which describe how women's rights are rarely represented in male supremacist world culture. Retrospectively, we can just as easily see, through this lens, the 20th century as one in which women's rights were going to be centrally positioned and indeed they were. Speaking directly on the issue of rights, McKenzie, in her speech at the 1901 People's Convention titled "The Rights of Women," according to Reddock, "defined a legal right as something to which one was entitled based on divine justice. She argued for equal rights for women and for women's access to education and to professional positions."[2]

Framed in this work as a Black women's rights discourse, we note as well that the whole discourse of rights[3] also reveals the ways that human rights are monopolized by the nation-states we inhabit and the international agencies that define them. As such, we can assert from the outset that Black women remain among the groups least likely to receive those basic rights that mark modern citizenship, thus the converging in this work of Black rights and women's rights as both pertain to Black women. Indeed, following Sylvia Wynter's theoretical positions[4] on this, the entire construction of the human

functions to represent only Western bourgeois man, *homo economicus,* following his violent self- instatement codified with the dominance of Western
modernity. This leaves all those constructed as others outside of the pole of
recognition, having to consistently claim rights to live as full human beings
in the world.

The assertion of Black women rights to leadership suggests as well that
Black women have the capacity, capabilities, skill, knowledge to lead in the
contemporary as they have in the past. It does not assume that every Black
woman provides transformative leadership but that they also have a right
to assume that leadership as members of a given society or organization.
Additionally, we can assert that their leadership can enact alternative strategies to the given normative models of traditional male leadership. In this
framing, Black women are not secondary in the temporal sense, nor are they
a monolithic group, but possible and alternative leaders in that they can, if
they choose, practice leadership differently, offer new models in the face of
the combative models that manage our world today. The idea is not that they
are only alternatives to leaders in the place of men, but that they often can
enact different forms of leadership outside of these official structures in local
and global contexts.

My central concerns in this study are women's participation in, and/
or transformation of, leadership paradigms and the way women navigate
masculinist leadership constructs and redefine and/or work to create new
pro-women or pro-feminist leadership. I will explore these issues through a
study of some of the thoughts and practices of African women, on the continent and in the African diaspora, who have exercised leadership in a variety
of spheres, largely political and creative.

Generally, political leadership is still seen as a masculine prerogative, corrupt practices or incompetence notwithstanding. Leadership in many countries is understood through a series of so-named "founding fathers," a history
in which women always play an ancillary or subordinate role, and sometimes
no role at all. In most countries of the world, political representation is still
overwhelmingly male. For this reason, new and continuing questions have
arisen about the nation as a masculine construct, created for the benefit of
male leaders.[5] This masculinized notion of leadership has a direct impact not
only on the representation of women's issues but also on patterns of governance, including war and conquest. Normalizing this view maintains the
gendered nature of social organization in which men dominate.

Assertions of women's leadership as possibly being or informing transformative models of governance have contested the stereotypical equating of
leadership with masculinity. Also contesting these assumptions by their very
presence are women who are deliberately assuming leadership in political

and other institutional sectors. The impact of women's leadership, and more specifically feminist leadership, challenges a normative model of charismatic leadership as the dominant, or only, model of political power.

Classic definitions of leadership have often linked a Weberian notion of charisma to leadership, assuming a variety of interpretations of how one is born with or acquires this illusive quality. The leader is usually a man, a hero, the major decision-maker, speaker, and motivator.[6] Generally, in this model, power arises when the individual charismatic leader develops the personal and oratorical skills to attract loyal followers. A dialectical relationship is established between leader and followers that endows the leader with the ability to move masses of people into acquiescence or action.

Consider Cedric Robinson's *The Terms of Order. Political Science and the Myth of Leadership* (2016), which offers a reasoned and careful analysis of political leadership. In its new foreword, Erica Edwards confirms that the work was organized to offer a "devastating critique of politics and its reorientation of intellectual and social energy toward antipolitical, radical transformation," especially since "the mythos of leadership, masquerading as order, covers the most hideous forms of violence against those who interrogate the status of the political both in explicit acts and in their very being" (ix–x).

Robinson's work explicitly challenges the entire intent of political leadership (5–6). Much of this construction of leadership, which in this orientation is explicitly male leadership, lies within the formation of the "state as an administrative apparatus" (1). Robinson examines "The Parameters of Leadership," "The Question of Rationality," and "The Messiah and the Metaphor" with a focus on the constructions of the leader as a manifest idea, as messiah, and ends with an exploration of anarchism. One of his key definitions is that: "Political leadership is then the reified expression of a tradition of meaning which authorizes and determines the loci, forms, and styles of social and economic resolution, and presents the means of their ultimate legitimation or illegitimation" (45). For Robinson, the entire apparatus of leadership is a myth, an "ordering principle" meant to control. Thus, the political is associated with "power, authority, order, law, the state, force and violence," but it also "presupposes the possibility of continued action" (7).

Still, all of these concepts of leadership have a masculine equivalence. In the rest of his work, Robinson mounts an interesting argument about issues in leadership, so relevant to a contemporary time frame. We now recognize how Eurocentric democratic systems hide and thereby maintain a range of inequalities within nations, gender being one of the most salient factors in leadership. We also see confirmation in D'Weston Haywood's 2018 study *Let Us Make Men: The Twentieth-Century Black Press and a Manly Vision for Racial Advancement* a point that has been asserted by Black feminist scholars that Black male leadership dominated 20th century Black freedom struggles which saw the fight for racial justice as coterminous with the fight to assert Black manhood.

The "myth of leadership" becomes central to any study of political leadership when women, realizing their exclusion from state centers of power, make moves toward acquiring and exercising that power. In African and Caribbean nations, as well as in the United States civil rights movement, beginning in the 1950's, with Ghana being the first to achieve independence in 1957, after having experienced enslavement and other subordinations of their populations via European forms of colonialism, the structures of political organization already in place derive from European structures of leadership, which are then mimicked (in the full sense of that term) and applied structurally as their parliamentary systems. Because in African contexts, whatever parallel political power women had prior to colonialism was superseded and often removed with the arrival of colonial order, returns to power in contemporary African societies follow the "terms of order" already established in these colonial contexts.[7] In these spheres, masculinity remains dominant even when the activism of women led to the attainment of that leadership. This is consistent in all post-colonial African and Caribbean nation-states. The Haitian paradigm is also worth considering in this context as well. With their independence though in 1804 following the Haitian Revolution they also similarly repeated the dominant political apparatus of Black male leadership though there is growing evidence of women's participation in their struggles for liberation. A similar situation exists in all new Caribbean nations, where independence movements and efforts toward neo-colonial leadership also repeated the embedded logics of the European nation-state. In each case, leaders utilized the same structures already in place, generally without any major changes in these structures, under the guise of maintaining orderly transfers of power.

The United States' electoral context offers another interesting example, particularly in the 2020 presidential race which will be studied by political scientists as a textbook example of what happens when the "gentleman's agreement" for running a country and an assumed orderly transfer of power from one male leader to another, following an antiquated and disjointed electoral system, did not work smoothly and revealed a number of troubling gaps culminating in an insurrection on January 6, 2021. Former United States Secretary of State Madeline Albright (1997–2001) in *Fascism: A Warning* (2018), had sounded cautionary notes, using examples from Europe, to indicate that without care about the erosion of democratic norms, the United States can easily be in the twilight of democracy.

In this introductory chapter, I explore some of these meanings of national leadership, as masculinized, applicable to African, Caribbean and African-American contexts, using some contemporary examples to examine

the issue of leadership as it pertains to women. I will consider (1) some definitions of leadership as proposed by women, (2) the nature of women's participation in political organization, and (3) current trends in political leadership.
I discuss these three areas, with a focus on women of African descent, from
a selection of global communities and ethnic-racial identities. Significantly,
because ethnic and racial minorities in mainstream countries and women in
the Global South have had to contest a variety of intersecting oppressions,
including colonialism and other forms of discrimination, the challenge to
remove gender disparities attains heightened importance in these locations
and therefore allows opportunities for substantial gains worldwide. This work
does not only argue for women's rights. Instead, it assumes them as normal
rights and responsibilities of living in a given society.

WOMEN'S DEFINITIONS OF LEADERSHIP

I begin deliberately with a definition of leadership supplied by an African
writer from Ghana, Ama Ata Aidoo, who said, "'Leadership' in this context
does not refer to political leadership exclusively. We speak of the entire spectrum of the intellectual, professional, and commercial elites in positions to
make vital decisions on behalf of the entire community." Aidoo thus expands
the framing of leadership to ensure that it is not just political leadership that
counts; rather, the range of leadership possibilities in a given society should
be assessed.[8]

A more traditional definition of leadership comes from Hillary Rodham
Clinton in her book *Hard Choices* (2014): "Leadership, by definition, means
being out in front of your people when it is called for. It means standing
up for the dignity of all your citizens and persuading your people to do the
same" (583). As a definition from the first woman candidate to make it to the
final round of the contest for presidency of a world superpower, the United
States, this quotation highlights some of the important understandings of the
contradictions, impacts, and challenges of women in leadership positions at
the highest level. Clinton indicates that her definition was developed and
stated in the process of asserting human rights for gay, lesbian, bisexual, and
transgender people at a forum in recognition of International Human Rights
Day at the Palace of Nations in Geneva, Switzerland, on December 6, during
her term as Secretary of State.[9] Yet, in this framing, leadership, for Hillary
Rodham Clinton, meant that the person who claims such a position has an
obligation to represent and advance the needs of all of his or her people. After
losing the election although winning the popular vote, Clinton cited the "shat-
tering of the glass ceiling" metaphor as her process: "I know we have still not
shattered that highest and hardest glass ceiling, but some day someone will

and hopefully sooner than we might think right now."[10] Still it is worth contrasting this with New Zealand's progressive young prime minister Jacinda Ardern (2017 to present) who became the youngest head of government at the age of thirty-seven and who defines an empathetic leadership as "kindness," has no room for racism, and indicates that the "true measure of leadership is the ability to confront the anxiety of the people of their time." Thus, analysis of her leadership style concludes "that Ardern's kindness is an important component of the necessary exercise of her political control that derives from her formulation of her political persona, the delineation of her relationships with others, and her navigation of the exigencies of the political field."[11]

Women in public leadership positions express a variety of responses to the term "leader." In the introduction to *Talking Leadership: Conversations with Powerful Women,* Mary Hartmann indicates that many of the thirteen women she included, already identified as leaders, cited "negative associations with traditional leadership systems or styles" largely because of the practice of the term. Significantly, there is now a recognition that women have a "comparatively longer history of leadership in their home and communities" (3), and that leadership in the national public sphere is more recent, and still insufficient in terms of numerical representation when compared to the actual proportional population of women in the world and the importance of local community impact. Indeed, the sense now among women is that local impact is able to effect more change than national level politics.[12]

Authors of the report "Transformative and Feminist Leadership for Women's Rights" (2017) found that "leadership theory was shaped within a gendered system" (8). As a result, a newer model was needed:

> [The] conceptualization of transformational leadership theory was an important one in this regard, where leadership is not defined as an individual exercise but rather is an ongoing, collaborative process, whereby leaders come to understand the motives of followers and prioritize satisfying their higher needs and engaging the full person for mutual benefit. (8)

Nevertheless, transformative leadership[13] itself has also been faulted as being limiting unless it benefits from concepts emerging from feminist leadership but not without a recognition that gender creates a fundamental difference. According to "Feminist Leadership for Social Transformation: Clearing the Conceptual Cloud"[14] a range of definitions of feminist leadership exists, generally from women in practice, that assert feminist leadership as emphasizing collaboration, power sharing, and advancing women in general (10–12).

Caribbean feminist leadership activist Peggy Antrobus in "Transformational Leadership: Advancing the Agenda for Gender Justice,"[15] provides an approach to two principles—transformational leadership and feminist leadership—that are useful in advancing this discussion. She indicates that "women's leadership is a different concept from transformational feminist leadership—being a woman does not make one a feminist" (55). Here she makes a distinction between "transformational leadership" and "transformational feminist leadership," the latter pertaining to economic, political, and social transformation and a "commitment to an agenda for social change" (55). In transformational feminist leadership, remedying gender inequities is paramount for it also empowers all women.

Much work on leadership has come from the corporate management sector. Noel Tichy's *The Cycle of Leadership. How Great Leaders Teach Their Companies to Win* (2002) offers a range of practices that companies and individuals can envelop, often with "winning" being the imperative. Still, the economic practices of corporations and their approaches to leadership, even when they have a record of advancing women, are often in contradistinction to the interests of people around the world, even as world leaders seek global partnerships. Thus, leadership in corporate contexts bears multiple historical layers that do not accommodate a flattened or neutral understanding of how leadership for men or women is acquired. Often, leading and winning in corporate contexts mean that most women in the world are still subjected to exploitation; the corporate goal is maximizing profits, even if corporate social responsibility statements and practices are in place. What happens to women in these leadership cycles is still material for ongoing discussion because the qualities asserted tend to challenge the ways that women continue to be represented. In the most recent statistics, equitable representation of women in corporate life remains at a standstill. According to *The World's Women, 2020*, women held only 28% of managerial positions globally in 2019—almost the same proportion as in 1995. And only 18% of enterprises surveyed had a female Chief Executive Officer in 2020. Among Fortune 500 corporations only 7.4%, or 37 Chief Executive Officers, were women.[16]

In the United States, even with an increasingly higher rate of professional qualifications, women still lag behind men in terms of ability to access higher level professional positions. The Global Gender Gap Report for 2020 indicates percentages are around 25% in most fields, from academia to the corporate world. For women of color the figures are even lower. Thus, in relation to the rest of the world, if we examine differences within the last five-year period, the report indicates:

The United States ranks first in women's educational attainment on the World Economic Forum's 2016 Global Gender Gap Index of 144 countries. But it ranks 26th in women's economic participation and opportunity and 73rd in women's political empowerment.

In fact, in the public sector—and in the percentage of female legislators in particular—the United States lags far behind many countries:

The world average for the share of women in the lower houses of national parliaments is 23.4 percent—slightly above the 19.3 percent in the U.S. House of Representatives.

At the current rate of change, it will take until 2117 for women to reach parity with men in the U.S. Congress.[17]

By 2020, despite some movement toward parity, "[A]t the other end of the scale, it is forecast to take just 12 years to attain gender parity in education, and in fact, overall, gender parity has been fully achieved in 40 of the 153 countries ranked." Yet, the report asserts that based on current patterns and rates of movement, "it will take 95 years to close the gender gap in political representation, with women in 2019 holding 25.2% of parliamentary (lower-house) seats and 21.2% of ministerial positions."[18]

The nomination of then senator Kamala Harris to the vice presidency in 2020 by candidate Joseph R. Biden, Jr., keeping a promise that he would nominate a woman of color if he won the primaries, was seen as an advance of women to leadership positions at the highest levels. Nevertheless, the United States is ranked 53rd of 153 countries in terms of women leaders, having no woman ever elected the head of state and with women constituting only 25% in political representation. In my 2020 essay, "The Promise of Kamala Harris," I indicated that

> the United States, regardless of its international pre-eminence, has lagged behind the world in having women attain political leadership. Harris is the only Black woman who is a U.S. senator and the second in its history after Carol Moseley Braun and once she becomes vice president there will be no Black woman in the senate. While this is scheduled to change with the Harris Vice Presidency, those of us studying and observing this anomaly wonder how the "most advanced country in the world" could still be so behind in having women in the highest rungs of political leadership.[19]

However, women before Harris have made a bid for the United States presidency, notably the legendary Shirley Chisholm, who ran on the Democratic Party ticket in 1972. Chisholm however was preceded by Charlene Mitchell on the Communist Party ticket in 1968. Lenora Branch Fulani with the New Alliance Party ran in 1988, Elaine Brown in 2008, and Cynthia McKinney of the Green Party in 2012 also contested the American presidency. Before Kamala Harris, Charlotta Bass ran for the vice presidency on the Progressive Party ticket in 1952; professor and activist Angela Y. Davis in 1980 and 1984 on the Communist Party ticket; Geraldine Ferraro in 1984 was the Democratic Party VP candidate, and Rosa Clemente VP for the Green Party in

2012. It is important to insert here that the dominance of the two-party system in the United States means voters' choices are reduced to primarily between the Democratic or Republican parties, and this has groomed the population to accept only two alternatives and thereby has limited the avenues and range of choices for women to enter politics. In addition, the structural racism and sexism built into the political system has deterred women from full participation in the political process.

The absence of women in the leadership of political organizations and movements provides a correlation with the limited accession to political power. Again, according to "Power and Decision-Making" of *The Worlds Women* (2015), the role of women in political movements and organizations provides another important context for understanding the nature of women's leadership. The role of women in mainstream political parties has consistently advanced from constructed absence to more visibility, following the charges and claims of the second wave feminist movement of the 1970's and 1980's. Still according to 2021 figures, while "women are underrepresented at all levels of decision-making worldwide, and achieving gender parity in political life is far off . . . women demonstrate political leadership by working across party lines through parliamentary women's caucuses—even in the most politically combative environments—and by championing issues of gender equality, such as the elimination of gender-based violence, parental leave and childcare, pensions, gender-equality laws, and electoral reform."[20]

Assessing these developments against an international benchmark reveals the difficulties as well as the gains to date. An interesting study which does some of this work is Sylvanna Falcon's *Power Interrupted. Antiracist and Feminist Activism Inside the United Nations.*[21] She argues, interestingly, that the anti-racist forums offered more "strategic context" for activists than those focused on women even as the limitations remained (163). For the purposes of this work, CEDAW—the Convention for the Elimination of Discrimination Against Women, Called the International Bill of Rights for Women—is identified as an international instrument for understanding how principles of women's rights have been challenged and therefore what the patterns of achievement have been over the years.[22] The Convention defines discrimination against women in Article 1 as

> any distinction, exclusion or restriction made on the basis of sex which has the effect or purpose of impairing or nullifying the recognition, enjoyment or exercise by women, irrespective of their marital status, on a basis of equality of men and women, of human rights and fundamental freedoms in the political, economic, social, cultural, civil or any other field.

To remedy this discrimination, Article 7 of the convention indicates:

States Parties shall take all appropriate measures to eliminate discrimination against women in the political and public life of the country and, in particular, shall ensure to women, on equal terms with men, the right:

(a) To vote in all elections and public referenda and to be eligible for election to all publicly elected bodies;

(b) To participate in the formulation of government policy and the implementation thereof and to hold public office and perform all public functions at all levels of government;

(c) To participate in non-governmental organizations and associations concerned with the public and political life of the country.[23]

Recall that Article 7(a), the right to vote, like the abolition of slavery in the 19th century, took the entire 20th century to be realized, beginning with Suffragist movement in the United Kingdom and the United States, which organized to challenge this blatant inequity. In the United States, the landmark case of *United States v. Susan B. Anthony* (1873) is recognized as beginning this challenge to the absence of women from any political participation.[24] My point here is that the right to vote is seen as the most fundamental of democratic citizenship rights, but it also portends a participation of women in the policy arena (i.e., political leadership in the policy of a given country as indicated in Article 7(b) of CEDAW). The problem is often application or enforcement at the local, state, and national levels. The CEDAW Committee of Trinidad and Tobago, an organization formed in that country in 2018, explicitly created to monitor the application of CEDAW, issued its statement of intent:

The CEDAW Committee is made up of a diverse group of individuals representing organizations, communities, cultures, genres and perspectives with the common goal of Collaboration, Education, Development, Advocacy, Wisdom and oversight of the convention of which the state is a signatory.[25]

But we repeat that the United States has never ratified CEDAW. In 2019, the statistics for women in political leadership in the United States revealed a rise to 19.3% of women in the U.S. House of Representatives and 24% in state legislatures. The Center for Women and Leadership at Rutgers University indicates that "In 2020, 127 (105D, 22R) women hold seats in the United States Congress, comprising 23.7% of the 535 members; 26 women (26%) serve in the U.S. Senate, and 101 women (23.2%) serve in the U.S. House of Representatives. Four women non-voting delegates (2D, 2R) also represent American Samoa, the District of Columbia, Puerto Rico, and the Virgin Islands in the United States House of Representatives."[26] In 2022, U.S. president Biden finally appointed a Black woman to the US Supreme Court, as fulfillment of a campaign promise that he had made.

WOMEN AS LEADERS IN SELECTED BLACK
POLITICAL MOVEMENTS AND ORGANIZATIONS

It is important to assert that women have consistently played a role in political movements, even when their leadership has not been perceived. One example comes from the organization which, until the international reach of the Black Lives Matter Movement in 2020, was generally understood as the largest international racial/ethnic organization in history. The Universal Negro Improvement Association and African Communities League (UNIA-ACL), an international political organization, is recognized as having been led by charismatic leader Marcus Garvey; his name often given to the organization in several contexts referring to the organization colloquially as "The Garvey Movement." Yet, research such as Tony Martin (2007), Keisha Blain (2018), and Natanya Duncan (2022) demonstrate that women's leadership also took the movement forward with re-assertions that Amy Ashwood Garvey, Marcus Garvey's first wife, was a co-founder and co-builder of the UNIA and that she was recruited by him for this purpose. This had been already asserted by political theorist Cyril Lionel Robert James, who in *A History of Pan-African Revolt* (1938) confirmed this collaboration: "In August 1914, Marcus Garvey, a Jamaican Negro printer, and Amy Ashwood, his friend, almost a schoolgirl, founded the Universal Negro Improvement Association in Kingston Jamaica" (197).

Besides her early work advancing the Black Cross Nurses in the New York establishment of the UNIA, Amy Ashwood Garvey would later develop a proposal for a major project for studying the Black Woman in historical and still relevant contexts[27] which we will highlight later and advanced the formation of Caribbean feminist movements through a series of tours throughout the Caribbean. Amy Jacques Garvey, the second wife of Marcus Garvey, is also identified as the major leader of the movement during Marcus's incarceration.[28] Impressively, she is credited with critiquing W.E.B. DuBois about his use of the word "negro" in a letter which begins by saying: "I am bottled up here in this small island with two small boys to support etc." She advised the famous Dr. DuBois not to use the word "negro" in his writings and provided a variety of references to the word "African" as preferable, ending with: "No, don't use it. Except where an Organization bears the name."[29] Amy Jacques Garvey was for years the primary UNIA documenter and archivist, being the compiler and editor of *The Philosophy and Opinions of Marcus Garvey* (1986). Further, Amy Jacques Garvey's "Women as Leaders Nationally and Racially" (1925) asked Black women to "push forward, regardless of the lack of appreciation shown you [and] strengthen the leadership of vacillating Negro men" (110). Like Maria Stewart (1803–1879)[30] abolitionist and women's rights activist, the first Black woman identified as speaking publicly on these issues, she saw Black women as potential future leaders: "Be not discouraged Black women of the world, but push forward, regardless of the lack of appreciation shown to you. A race must be saved, a country must be redeemed . . ." (110).

A recognition of the leadership role of women in the UNIA takes nothing away from the historical significance and prominence of Marcus Garvey. Indeed, the entire collection edited by Veronica Gregg, *Caribbean Women. An Anthology of Non-Fiction Writings, 1890–1980,* provides the thought of a range of Caribbean women in activist-political contexts, the earliest by Catherine McKenzie, specifically on "Woman's Rights" as indicated at the start of this chapter. So, given the work that the two Garvey wives did to advance Marcus Garvey's projects and political movements, "Garveyism" can also be read as the entire package of activities created by Marcus Garvey, Amy Ashwood Garvey and Amy Jacques Garvey as I have argued in "Pan-Africanism, Transnational Black Feminism and the Limits of Culturalist Analyses in African Gender Discourses."[31] Furthermore, new work such as Natanya Duncan's *Crossing Waters and Fighting Tides: The Efficient Womanhood of the UNIA in the Black Global World* (2022) and Keisha N. Blain's *Set the World on Fire. Black Nationalist Women and the Global Struggle for Freedom* (2018) reveal a variety of "women leaders who were actively involved in the UNIA and subsequent Black political organizations it spawned in the post-World War I period and in particular how these women made their way to the "forefront of political movements for global black liberation" (10).

In my research on political activist Claudia Jones[32] who was the only Black woman elected to the central committee of the CPUSA, I found that the creation of a Women's Commission under the leadership of Elizabeth Gurley Flynn (1890–1964) fostered the advancement of women in the Communist Party USA. In 1945, Claudia Jones championed the idea of the triple rights of Black women—as workers, as women, as Black people—in her essay, "An End to the Neglect of the Problems of Black Women" (1949).[33] Jones described the ways in which many institutions, including progressive ones, discounted Black women, either as participants or as leaders. Thereby these groups replicated the dominant notions of society as they avoided consideration of Black women as thinking and acting subjects. Until her deportation to London in 1955, Claudia Jones had also titled her column in *The Daily Worker,* "Half the World," using a framework that is now commonplace post-Beijing United Nations' language to describe the disproportionate representation of women in leadership when viewed against their actual numbers as citizens of various countries worldwide. The "half the world" concept provides one of the theoretical frames for this present study.

From the "We Charge Genocide" petition to the United Nations in 1951, signed by several women, including Charlotta Bass, Dorothy Hunton, Claudia Jones, Louise Thompson Patterson, Eslanda Goode Robeson, Maude White Katz, through the contemporaneous 2020 actions protesting the killing of Breonna Taylor, women appear at the forefront of political leadership. A 2020 essay, "Black Women Are Leading the Movement to End Police Violence," identifies a range of past and contemporary actions by Black women throughout the 20th century and into the present in challenging state-supported oppression in the United States.

Indeed, while the Blain's essay centers on Breonna Taylor killing during a botched drug raid in her own apartment in Louisville, Kentucky, it concludes, "Together, the nationwide efforts of Black women—as writers, organizers and activists—have shaped a national movement against state-sanctioned violence and anti-Black racism."[34] She asserts further that "Black women have taken the lead in finding alternate routes to obtain justice and achieve systemic change due to the inability of the criminal 'justice" system to administer punishment in cases of police shooting." However, she suggests this as not a new phenomenon, citing the support of Audley "Queen Mother" Moore in 1945, through Fannie Lou Hamer and her critical role in voter registration in the formation of the Mississippi Freedom Democratic Party and the 1964 Democratic Party Convention.

Still less known is Pauli Murray's biography *Song in a Weary Throat. Memoir of an American Pilgrimage* (2018) supported by the documentary "My Name is Pauli Murray" (2021). Her work as women's rights legal activist (1910–1985) is identified with gendering the language of Jim Crow to "Jane Crow" to account for the gendered and racial implications of Black women in United States facing structural racism and sexism, but is less prominently recognized in the stream of leadership identifications. Further in the legal field, the work of Constance Baker Motley is often not as publicly recognized as are comparable men as revealed in a recent study by Tomiko Brown-Nagin, *Civil Rights Queen. Constance Baker Motley and the Struggle for Equality* (2022) even though she was the first Black woman to serve as a federal judge. Indeed, the author details several cases in which Baker Motley's legal work was absolutely central throughout the 1950's and 1960's to providing the delivery of critical legal gains for African Americans in the United States. Additionally, Baker Motley who in many ways is a compendium of firsts, serves as an inspirational precursor for the first (2022) Black woman nominated and confirmed to the Supreme Court, Ketanji Brown Jackson.[35]

Scholarship on women's leadership in US Black Freedom Movements grows exponentially with each addition. Full length studies devoted to the contributions of various activist women such as Keisha N. Blain's *Until I am Free. Fannie Lou Hamer's Enduring Message to America* (2021) add substantially to the growing library of Black Feminist Biographies which for a long time was limited to Barbara Ransby's *Ella Baker and the Black Freedom Movement. A Radical Democratic Vision* (2004).

The dialectic between local/grassroots activism and what she terms the "localizing of international human rights" of Black women across a variety of spectra but mostly in the United States is the central framework of Stanlie James in her *Practical Audacity. Black Women and International Human Rights* (2021). The work becomes thereby a collective biography of women engaged contemporaneously in community work to advance the communities in which they live as they also build global connections. Her interesting conclusion asserts that "although all women featured in this book are leaders in their own right . . . they have also come to rely upon each other, to learn from each other, to mentor each other and to share information about funding resources informally" (202). She sees them as creating both national and international networks of human rights practitioners . . ." (202). Here are women who are known in their communities but are often with limited exposure on a national and international stage. These are also the women who like Ayesha Imam and Jaribu Hill have kept working for social justice in the intervening years before contemporary Black Lives Matter activism.

Full historical assessment will be done about the pathways and the work that moved Black Lives Matter from being an online hashtag group to an international movement. Currently, the activism by Black women, we again acknowledge here, created and sustains the Black Lives Matter movement. Founded by Alicia Garza, Patrisse Cullors, and Opal Tometi, Black Lives Matter gained prominence after the killing of Trayvon Martin in Sanford, Florida, and the exoneration of his killer George Zimmerman in July, 2013. However, The Black Lives Matter Movement reached its international apogee in May 2020, after the public killing of George Floyd with the unrelenting suffocation via a knee on his neck by a policeman in Minneapolis, Minnesota in the United States, for almost ten minutes while he screamed in pain and died in full public view recorded by mobile phone and circulated on social media. Black Lives Matter then became an already-created and therefore usable structure and so was able to galvanize a mass response, as social movements often do. In this case, a particular conjunction, with its iconic symbolic implications of a Black man's life being suffocated by white state actors resonated historically and symbolically with numerous prior examples. This has led to Black Lives Matter, because of social media, surpassing the Universal Negro Improvement Association in its international reach and subsequent local organizing to end police brutality and to continue other unfinished decolonial movements around the world with the help of the global uses of social media and the recognition that similar "knee on the neck" practices occur in several locations.

The role of women in Civil Rights and Black Power movements in the United States is being substantially clarified as well.[36] An entire library of materials on Black women's activism is developing about the period between the 1930's and the 1950's, documenting the rise of the Civil Rights Movement and the activism of Rosa Parks and the women before or along with her such as Claudette Colvin (1939 to present). Here the work of Mary Fair Burks who co-founded the Women's Political Council in Alabama in 1946 and became a close friend of Martin Luther King Jr. and Coretta Scott King has to be acknowledged. The Women's Political Council itself is one of the under-explored histories of women's leadership in that period, identified as the "driving force behind a municipal bus boycott in 1955 that focused national attention on the day-to-day indignities of segregation in the Jim Crow south."[37] Burks's activism preceded and served as one of the major organizing forces behind the Montgomery Bus Boycott which led to the now-historically recognized action, subsequent arrest of Rosa Parks and her entry into Civil Rights History.[38]

The stellar leadership of Fannie Lou Hamer documented in *"Until I am Free"* (2021) by Keisha Blain, provides another example of the ways that often movements take for granted the work of major contributors if they are women, if they are not ministers of the gospel, even if they do engage in major leadership roles. "We Want Leaders" is the title of a chapter devoted to this question including this relevant summary: "Fannie Lou Hammer's ideas on leadership—especially the qualities that make a good leader versus an ineffective one—grew from personal experience" (43) but also indicates the influence of Ella Baker's leadership style, particularly since Baker resisted the "charismatic leadership" model of leadership which emanated from the male ministers of the Black church. Ella Baker's "group centered leadership" model included giving youth the opportunity to participate fully in political decisions that advanced community as a whole. Additionally, she too learned from her involvement with the Student Non-Violent Coordinating Committee (SNCC) particularly because of "their commitment to allowing local people to lead in their own terms . . ." (45). Thus, Fannie Lou Hamer developed comradeship with the younger Stokely Carmichael (Kwame Ture), even visiting Guinea in 1964 which allowed her to see the African continuities in her Mississippi community and engage directly with independent African leadership. Clearly the feeling was mutual as she felt that they actually listened to her and took her ideas seriously and simultaneously ignited "the spark in her political activism simply by granting her the opportunity to lead" (45). It is important for us to note how Stokely describes Fannie Lou Hamer's leadership style in his 2005 auto/biography *Ready for Revolution*:

She did not merely represent an *idea,* some SNCC *theory* of grassroots leadership . . . She was smart and really funny, and by virtue of her history and experience, politically very astute. Unlettered though she was politically, she had a
shrewd understanding of political and economic power and the injustices of its
effects on poor folk in this country because she had lived it . . . More than a
symbol, she was day to day a real leader in her community, and as real to us as
member of the family. And if she was also a symbol, she was a symbol of the
best in our people, and the best of what SNCC wanted to think the struggle was
all about. (315–316)

Specific to the Black Panther Party, Robin Spencer's *The Revolution Has
Come: Black Power, Gender, and the Black Panther Party in Oakland* (2016)
offers some further details in relation to the gendered aspect of the Black
Power Movement. Elaine Brown's role as head of the Black Panther Party in
its last years is recorded in her memoir, *A Taste of Power* (1992). Tia Hicks
honors thesis for Africana Studies, Cornell University, which I supervised, on
Women of the Black Panther Party titled "Revolution From The Ground Up:
Centering the Activism, Leadership, and Experiences of Women in the Black
Panther Party" (2012) included a variety of interviews she conducted with a
range of women in the Party's leadership.

The continued silencing of the work of women in Civil Rights and
Black Power activity for example is documented by the trajectory of Gloria
Richardson during the March on Washington which relegated women like
her to a simple "Hello" or to singing as did Mahalia Jackson but not ever
giving a full address. An essay by Barbara Smith, "The 'Creative Chaos' of
Gloria Richardson" (2021) summarizes the silencing of this iconic activist
even in recent coverage which privileged the image of Martin Luther King Jr.
as it announced her passing. Joseph R. Fitzgerald's *The Struggle is Eternal.
Gloria Richardson and Black Liberation* (2018) develops well the history of
this activist's childhood and her development into grassroots activism and
the founding of the Cambridge National Action Committee in conjunction
with the Student Non-Violent Coordinating Committee (SNCC). In this way
Gloria Richardson became one of the significant leaders in the movement
who would be identified for her more progressive leadership by Malcolm X
in his famous "Message to the Grassroots" speech in Detroit in 1963. She
described her organizational method as creating a list of items by having surveyed community on their needs, using a model she developed based on her
Howard sociology training from E. Franklin Frazier. The survey revealed as
critical issues the end to racist segregated hospitals, housing, jobs, and other
economic aspects of segregation in the delivery of basic services to the Black
community as opposed to wanting only the classic voting rights as more acute
and immediate needs than the latter.

We can conclude then that activist work by Black women for women's rights has existed from the Suffragist movements at the turn of the 20th century to the more recent Black Lives Matter, #MeToo, and #Time'sUp movements in 2006. Women have been consistently involved in local political party organizing, and some have sought national office, with seemingly more opportunities in left-leaning organizations than in mainstream parties. How this impacted national political participation for all is another research-generating question to which this study contributes and which is already producing a steady stream of journal articles which describe the many Black women who contributed even under white supremacist policing. DeNeen Brown's "The Black Women Who Paved the Way" (2021) describes several experiences in the 1960's of abuse suffered by Black women attempting to register to vote but also describes them as consistently organizing and planning "resistance movements." The premise which underscored their actions were supported morally by the fact that the United States claims to be a democracy while denying Black people the right to vote and thus contradicted any lofty moral political principles it advanced globally; the right to vote being the most fundamental principle of a democracy.

TRENDS AND MODELS IN WOMEN'S LEADERSHIP

Dessima Williams's "Bringing More Women into Leadership," serves as a benchmark for this study, beginning the call, at the turn of the 21st century, for the advancement of Black women's leadership.[39] Published in 2000, it described the abysmally low representation of women in political office as we entered the 21st century, to which the gains twenty years later can be compared. In 2000, it was inexcusable to her that women who made up 50% of the world's population held only 6% of seats in national cabinets and 13% of seats in world parliaments. In 2022, women in political power globally wavers between 24% and 25% in most governments and parliaments and as heads of state, though in this latter category it is even less, resulting in the conclusion that "women are underrepresented at all levels of decision-making worldwide, and achieving gender parity in political life is far off."[40] Between 1995 and 2015, there was an approximately 10% increase (from 12 to 22% in parliaments; 12 to 19% in the executive branch, and 6 to 18% cabinet ministers).[41] *The World's Women* report concludes:

> A few factors contribute to this blatant underrepresentation. Women are seldom leaders of major political parties, which are instrumental in forming future political leaders and in supporting them throughout the election process. Gender norms and expectations also drastically reduce the pool of female candidates for

selection as electoral representatives, and contribute to the multiple obstacles that women face during the electoral process. The use by some countries of gender quotas has improved women's chances of being elected. Yet, once in office, few women reach the higher echelons of parliamentary hierarchies. (https:// unstats.un.org/unsd/gender/chapter5/chapter5.html)

As in the centuries-long abolition movement, women's political power has gradually increased, but clearly it has not been substantial enough to get even close to parity. In some countries, the numbers are higher. For example, Rwanda, which is still recovering from horrendous internal strife and genocide, has a parliament in which 64% of its members are women.[42] In 2018, Bolivia had 53%; Cuba, 49%, Seychelles and Sweden, 44%; these countries are indicated as the leaders in women's participation in government and by 2020 it is indicated as follows: "Only four countries have 50 per cent or more women in parliament in single or lower houses: Rwanda with 61 per cent, Cuba with 53 per cent, Bolivia with 53 per cent, and the United Arab Emirates with 50 per cent."[43] In the Cuban case, because of the ongoing US-led blockades, it is difficult to get a popular sharing of any of this information. Much of the Rwandan success in developing women leaders includes promoting debating and other empowerment skills that lead to political access but also the hard work of women activists who helped shape women's involvement following their experience of genocide.

Again, according to *UN Women, 2015*, "The most substantial progress between 1995 and 2014 was made in sub-Saharan Africa, where women's representation increased from 9.7 percent to 24 percent" (30). Still, for political scientist Paul Tiyambe Zeleza (2006) who served on the Advisory Group which produced the report "Gender Equality: Striving for Justice in an Unequal World" (2005), the record in 2006 was still dismal or "dreadful for much of the world" and even in Africa where there has been relatively more movement, women often served short periods sometimes for less than a year. We note as well the unevenness he described as some countries like Nigeria are surprisingly listed still as having only 5.6% representation in January 2019. Women presidents or heads of state remain the lowest represented with a 6.6% equivalence and includes the following countries: Germany, Bangladesh, Barbados, Croatia, Estonia, Ethiopia, Georgia, Marshall Islands, Lithuania, Malta, Nepal, Norway, New Zealand, United Kingdom, Serbia, Singapore, Trinidad and Tobago, and Tanzania in 2020. Some of these positions we know are ceremonial, as is the presidency of Paula-Mae Weekes in Trinidad and Tobago. In Britain, Theresa May (2016–2019) who was the second woman in this leadership position after Margaret Thatcher (in office from 1979–1990) was replaced by Boris Johnson in 2019. Liz Truss, a white woman, replaced him in 2022. Percentages of women leaders are somewhat larger for parliamentary positions, narrowing considerably at the highest offices (prime ministers or presidents) in each country.

So, following the benchmark year 2000 assertion by Dessima Williams, the year 2020 serves as another important benchmark, twenty years later, and therefore useful for examining some of these accomplishments and movements. Although education of girls through primary education has increased worldwide, "women's representation in parliament has more than doubled globally, it has still not crossed the barrier of 25% of parliamentary seats in 2020. *The World's Women 2020* reports that women's representation among cabinet ministers has quadrupled over the last 25 years, yet remains well below parity."[44]

Many of the gains made in 2020 are only expected to solidify the 21st century. Yet after the pandemic of 2020, preliminary predictions indicate that women's representation in the workforce will regress, prompted by changes in the needs of child care, homeschooling, which often falls to women and other retrenchments. Above all, women's labor is still highly exploited; women are still doing the bulk of unpaid domestic work as compared to men.

An article by Reneva Fourie, "Deepening the Participation and Representation of Women in Politics in Africa" (2017) offers a range of practical steps that governments in Africa should continue to take to enhance women's participation even further. These include:

> "enabling legislative frameworks . . . so that statutory provisions interface between constitutional, traditional and religious law" are interpreted "in a manner that not only guarantees women fundamental political rights, access and opportunities; but also ensures the promotion, protection and enforcement of human rights, social and physical protection of women, and equality in the economy and the workplace." (67)

Developing examples of women's leadership following the Joseph Biden election win in 2020 in North America still must be studied as the actual practice is just as significant as simply inserting women in leadership roles. This is especially significant since countries like Canada and the United States claim leadership in the practice of democracy and are consistently seen as setting examples. The Canadian government led by Justin Trudeau for example made the decision to have equal female and male representation in his cabinet. Campaigns like "Ask Her to Run" capture one of Trudeau's strategies.[45] Alter finds explicit identifications of the need for women's leadership is a timely move since "The countries with the most female lawmakers have made major strides on issues such as education, labor-force participation and paid leave. Each of the countries below has either a parliament or a ministry that is at least 50% female, while women make up only 19% of the U.S.

Congress and only four of Obama's 15 Cabinet members" (Ibid.). However, much of the momentum of Trudeau's early assertion failed in its execution. The "Put a Woman" campaign in Trinidad and Tobago and the activist work of organizations like Emily's List and the National Women's Political provide an important opportunity to witness the need for parity in actual administrative positions though promises and preliminary nominations have so far definitely altered the expectations of women's leadership in the United States in relation to the rest of the World.

Women's involvement in formulating and implementing government policy, as well as fully holding public office still is the next movement towards balanced representation for half the world. We remain still at the point of pointing out exceptional firsts, whether Golda Meir of Israel (1969–1974), Margaret Thatcher of the United Kingdom (1979–1990), Indira Gandhi of India (1980–1984), Angela Merkel of Germany (2005–2021), or Kamala Harris (2021–present) with only a few other progressive models. And sadly, many of the first generation of women in highest offices of leadership adopted very heavy political approaches more typical of traditional male paradigms. It is also significant that this brand of political leadership reached its zenith in Margaret Thatcher's tenure, prompting cultural critic Stuart Hall (1988) to coin the term "Thatcherism" to capture her particular brand of gendered neoliberal leadership, or the "Condification" of Condoleezza Rice in the Bush II administration for her role in the war on Iraq.[46] There is a new possibility however in Jacinda Ardern (New Zealand) who is explicit about having a no tolerance of racism or open access to guns in her country, and demonstrates advanced human values in her own life, having a baby while in office and bringing her on the floor of the United Nations general assembly.

So how are concepts of leadership informed by or advancing feminist theory? The past and contemporary model of male leadership tends to be the charismatic leader.[47] How do women compete with that political model while developing some of those necessary skills but also applying the community leadership techniques honed in women's communities and organizations? This study will pursue some of these questions by examining the stories of women in leadership in a variety of locations across Africa and the African Diaspora.

The availability of autobiographical texts for some readers aids this process as the "leadership stories" that women tell are significant to the understanding of the pathways that they take as they get to political positions with some power. A number of stories will therefore populate this text. I offer then not a political science examination in terms of policy and process but one which brings together a number of analyses in order to witness these movements through time and contemporaneously. Chapters will focus on women in Africa, the Caribbean, Brazil and the United States who in my view occupy the role of alternative and transformative leadership even when never formally occupying official positions. Therefore, we can assess what their strategies are as they acquire and exercise leadership and hopefully offer an alternative to the classic male leadership paradigms.

Older models of attaining leadership through one's husband or father (Indira Gandhi, Benazir Bhutto, Hillary Clinton) even when the woman is capable in her own right, are neither ideal nor desirable going into the future. That model, in this writer's view, operates still on the logic of patriarchal privilege. It also suggests a certain dependency on men (fathers or husbands) for name recognition and their political networks to attain and maintain their leadership.

As Reshma Saujani noted in *Women Who Don't Wait in Line. Break the Mold*, even in women's organizations women are sometimes cautioned to take time before aspiring to leadership. For men, this is never an option. Thus, she concludes: "The old, last century paradigm urges to go slower, to be careful and cautious, and to wait our turn. But that paradigm is broken. We need to change it, or women will never achieve full parity and equality in American society" (li). Hillary Clinton's advice about "being out in front of your people" and "standing up for the dignity of all your citizens" and "persuading your people to do the same" are all classic tropes of traditional leadership. However, Hillary Clinton had worked actively for women's rights in a variety of organizations, advancing some of the issues she articulated in her speeches at the Fourth World Conference on Women, Beijing 1995.[48] Many of these experiences were downplayed, also by the candidate herself, in her political run for the US presidency.

This work nonetheless reclaims the fact that a Black woman, Shirley Chisholm, had run for the Democratic Party's nomination "unbought and unbossed" in her words in 1972. The overarching question remains: How does a woman navigate these histories and at the same time chart a different model of leadership? How this is played out will be discussed in the following chapters. The assertion of feminist transformative leadership has been indicated as the model that brings together feminist theory and transformative leadership, but feminist theory has also informed transformational leadership itself.

One significant tendency is that much of the work on women's leadership has been generated and done by feminist organizations working in activist modes on leadership for social transformation and/or the ending of inequalities. The studies of CREA-Creating Resources for Empowerment in Action reports, coming from an actual meeting "Building Feminist Leadership—Looking Back, Looking Forward" and with input from women from a variety of global locations is a useful document. The introduction to *Talking Leadership* indicates that scholarship on leadership is also very specific to

certain fields, mostly in management and some now in educational administration. In the field of psychology for example, *Women and Leadership.
Transforming Visions and Diverse Voices* (2007) chapters address Models
of Leadership and Women; Collaboration and Leadership; From Margin to
Center: The Voices of Diverse Feminist Leaders. Its introduction begins by
describing the "paucity of literature on feminist leadership" and indicating the
need there to "deconstruct existing theories and principles of feminism and
leadership to understand effective leadership styles among women, and their
intersection with feminist principles" (4).

The common research approach is to garner information from women leaders, as was done in *Women at the Top. What Women University and College
Presidents Say About Effective Leadership.* The authors of that work interviewed ten women; the authors of *Talking Leadership* interviewed thirteen
women. In both works, the goal was to record their stories, document their
experiences, and perhaps teach some best practices. The difficulty of getting
beyond celebrating the first few women leaders has to give way to more substantial study of women in politics. Interest in what happens to women once
they attain leadership in certain countries and how they navigated the path to
leadership is one path of entry into this subject.

Much of the available work on leadership has been available in journal
articles, or organizational reports as this study discovered. Newspaper articles
and online interviews and speeches are also another source particularly in the
contemporary period. Some edited collections from conferences have begun
to provide additional studies. *JENDA: A Journal of African Women's Studies*
devoted two issues in 2006 and 2007 (issues 9 and 10) to studying women and
political leadership in a number of spheres but also issue 19 (2011) was dedicated to the three women who won the Nobel prize that year.[49] Additionally
the issue of women and leadership would run through several other themes
in other issues of this journal. Organizations such as the African Women's
Development Fund and DAWN (Development Alternatives for a New Era)
have been the catalysts for advancing women in political leadership on the
continent of Africa. Several women, including Aminata Dramane Traoré,
former Minister of Culture of Mali, have developed their feminist leadership
positions from assignments in international organizations for development in
particular sectors like agriculture.[50] Through those experiences, the women
leaders realized how women were disadvantaged and/or not represented in
these sectors. Studies reveal that deficiencies in women accessing leadership
exist in all fields: media, law, the corporate world, and definitely academia.[51]
An increase in the numbers of women's leadership centers and institutes[52]
with specific missions geared to women's empowerment is still necessary,
as these have provided the critical literature, the skills, and the assessment
of the gains women have made in and through political power. And if and

when women get to leadership what will be the chosen or practice model especially since we have several examples. This work will pursue several of these articulations of leadership.

FROM GETTING THE RIGHT TO VOTE, VOTING AND THEN LEADING

Still keeping in mind that Article 7 (a) of CEDAW focused on the right to vote as indicated above: "(a) to vote in all elections and public referenda and to be eligible for election to all publicly elected bodies" one can say that the entire 20th century was technically dedicated to ensuring enfranchisement. The second item "(b) to participate in the formulation of government policy and the implementation thereof and to hold public office and perform all public functions at all levels of government" still awaits full revelation everywhere.

In the United States, for example, Suffragist activity led to the right to vote and the passage of the 19th Amendment (passed in 1919 and taking effect in August 1920) beginning with the 1848 Seneca Women's Rights Convention. This was not clearly even as a few states had prior to this provided the right to vote. However, Black women in the United States could not be considered getting the right to vote until 1965 with the post-Civil Rights Voting Rights Act. Stories of discrimination as Sidney Trent's "The Black Sorority That Faced Racism in the Suffrage Movement but Refused to Walk Away"[53] describe that even in the quest for women's rights, as demonstrated in the organization of the suffragist marches as have been recorded in the actions of the Black sorority, Delta Sigma Theta Sorority (all Howard University students) its founding coincided with the idea of marching for women's rights.[54]

Michael Hanchard in *The Spectre of Race. How Discrimination Haunts Western Democracy* offers an important detailing of the various countries in the Americas and in his Table A.1 lists the "Political Prohibitions on People of African Descent in Latin America and the Caribbean." These prohibitions included literacy requirements, property ownership and professional occupations and exclusion of Servants, Day wage Laborers and/or Debtors. What is even more fascinating for the purposes of this book is his Chart A.1, Countries of Latin America and the Caribbean from 1805 to the end of the century that created literacy, property, and other laws specifically designed to limit or prohibit voting and other forms of political participation of freed Blacks, slaves, and their descendants. This Hanchard table provides a useful country-by-country listing of who was accorded citizenship and who was denied. Basically, all countries in the Americas denied full citizenship to women, slaves, illiterates, servants, wage workers, line infantry men, and debtors. Generally, at the same time they limited public office-holding to white male citizens with property or in professional occupations (217–224).

The link between the denial of the right to vote and the denial of participation in the political process are consistent. We hasten to add as well that these exclusions were not the same ones that were in effect in European countries, and that with colonialism the structures of exclusion were exacerbated and triangulated perhaps as it relates to Black women who were enslaved and/or colonized and therefore far away from accessing those rights without struggle. Hanchard's "Colonialism Reconsidered" makes the point that "[M]any of the politics, norms, and attributes associated with non-Western political systems and governance could be found within Western polities and societies, especially among marginalized populations and the spaces they inhabit" (186). In short, the Western European powers defined as democracies their own societies which were inherently already unequal. And as African feminist scholars have shown once they began the colonial processes, they transported these inequalities to these territories they now controlled.

Robert Buddan's "Universal Adult Suffrage in Jamaica and the Caribbean Since 1944" begins with the sentence "The right to vote is the basic principle underlying democracy" (135). The rest of the paper though examines the pathways towards acquiring this fundamental of democracy and how it was negotiated. Thus: "Adult suffrage began in Jamaica in 1944 and spread to the other islands between then and 1962. In that eighteen-year period, it created a democratic revolution among twelve small Caribbean countries and among eleven of those countries between 1944 and 1954. This period inaugurated mass politics in the Caribbean" (135).

His key point though is that there was a significant advancement of rights following the 1930's labor riots which led to the Moyne Commission and at a time when few Caribbean people had the right to vote. Studying this relationally then, we can see that for people of African descent in the Caribbean and Africa, as in the United States of America, these fundamental rights of citizenship had to be fought for in various ways and are still, particularly delayed in the United States, or are very fragile gains, threatened to be withdrawn in various ways, based on the benevolence or malevolence of who is in power. African Americans in the United States are still subject to a variety of voting irregularities and an absence of uniformity in how voting is handled from state to state.

It is significant as well that in the UN Sustainable Development Goals to be achieved by 2030, ten years from the beginning of this writing in 2020: Goal 5 is indicated as: "Achieve Gender Equality and Empower All Women and Girls." Its descriptive premise assumes the inequalities which exist and asks for equality which in this case is read as parity in political representation.

Black Women's Rights: Leadership and the Circularities of Power resists the tendency to celebrate (even as we acknowledge them) by reveling in exceptional firsts whether it is Eugenia Charles in Dominica (1919–2005); Ellen Johnson Sirleaf, first African woman president of Liberia (2006–2018); Samia Suluhu Hassan as the first woman to be president of Tanzania (2021–present); Mia Mottley, prime minister of Barbados (2018–present) with Sandra Mason, formerly governor general in the British colonial system (2018–2021), as president (2021–present). The earliest of these "first women in leadership" often have to adopt very heavy political approaches more typical of traditional male paradigms. Even so, it reveals that there has been a consistent pattern of women contesting their exclusions, avoiding the detour of the first lady pathway, and asserting the parallel right to occupy leadership positions, particularly when they have the credentials, experience and ability to lead, some using traditional male leadership models.

When asked in an interview with Paul Vallely about women's capability to be better or less-corrupt leaders Ngozi Okonjo-Iweala who in 2021 became the first African woman to direct the World Trade Organization but before that when she served as Minister of Finance in Nigeria and had in the process received death threats as she attempted to rid Nigeria of corruption replied: "Seriously, as an empirical observation, women tend to be more honest, more straightforward, more focused on the job, and bring less ego to it. I don't know if it's a feminine instinct but running an economy is sometimes akin to running a household which is after all the smallest unit of production and consumption in the economy" (16).

Still, we watch these developments unfold as women enter the political field. This work assumes that we have entered a new period in women's political leadership which has to be marked, studied and analyzed in various ways as the years progress. Yet, we move from cautious optimism at these victories to an assumption that leadership is a demographic right. But we also provide a necessary critique of the shortcomings or failures of women's leadership. Even as we examine some of the gains and struggles of women in political leadership, to keep open the series of generating questions, we indicate, which can hopefully serve as cautionary pauses as one assesses the choices which come with political power. What happens when members of a subordinated group rise to power within an oppressive system? Who do these people end up representing? How does a woman manage the political demands while understanding her location in history? How do class, socio-economic status and political affiliation affect the nature of one's participation in the political and intellectual process? How do we begin to subject the rise of women to leadership positions to the kind of internal critique that is fair and necessary?

NOTES

1. Paper included in Veronica Gregg, ed. (2005) *Caribbean Women. An Anthology of Non-Fiction Writing 1890–1980*: 98–103, which includes her definition of rights.

2. According to Rhoda Reddock in the *Dictionary of Caribbean and Afro-Latin American Biography,* Catherine McKenzie "was probably the first of a number of Afro-Caribbean women who championed the rights of women within and through Pan-Africanism during the first half of the twentieth century. McKenzie made her demands for women's equality and human rights in numerous public appearances."

3. See for example, Aragon Eloff, "The Very Idea of Rights: A Critique of Human Rights Discourse." https://medium.com/@aragorneloff/the-very-idea-of-rights-a -critique-of-human-rights-discourse-84706f002c85

4. See for example her "No Humans Involved" and several other related works. "'No Humans Involved': An Open Letter to My Colleagues." *Voices of the African Diaspora* 8:2 (1992) and much later clarification in "Unsettling the Coloniality of Being/Power/Truth/Freedom: Towards the Human, After Man, Its Overrepresentation—an Argument," *New Centennial Review,* 3:3 (Fall: 2003): 131–149.

5. See Parker et al., 1992; Wendt and Andersen, 2015.

6. For an extensive overview of traditional and contemporary definitions of leadership see "Feminist Leadership for Social Transformation: Clearing the Conceptual Cloud," by Srilatha Batliwala (CREA, May 2010) and on charisma arising from sociologist Max Weber (1864–1920) see the "Charisma and Populism" introduction to *Caribbean Charisma,* ed. Allahar (2001).

7. See Nwando Achebe (2020) and her other work on this subject. See also the special issues of *JENDA: A Journal of Culture and African Women Studies* edited by Nkiru Nzegwu (Issue 9 & 10, 2006 & 2007) which provides a nice range of timely statistics and historical information on African women and leadership. Paul Zeleza's essay on the significance of Johnson Sirleaf's Victory, asserting nonetheless that the "global record of women's political representation among heads of state and government is dismal." He indicates in 2006, 46 female presidents and prime ministers worldwide, many serving for short periods, some less than a year.

8. Aidoo, 1984, 321.

9. Speech available as "Remarks, Hillary Rodham Clinton, Secretary of State, Palais des Nations, Geneva, Switzerland," December 6, 2011, at https://2009-2017.state .gov/secretary/20092013clinton/rm/2011/12/178368.htm

10. https://www.cnn.com/2016/11/09/politics/hillary-clinton-concession-speech/ index.html Accessed 11/19/2020

11. Geoffrey Craig, "Kindness and Control: The Political Leadership of Jacinda Ardern in the Aotearoa New Zealand COVID-19 Media Conferences," *Journalism and Media* 2, no. 2: 288–304, 2021. https://doi.org/10.3390/journalmedia2020017

12. Presentation by Siga Fatime Jagne, Commissioner, Social Affairs and Gender at Economic Community of West African States (ECOWAS) to Black Women and Political leadership Class, Cornell University, 2020.

13. Many scholars have pursued definitions of transformational leadership. The Oxfam report provides a discussion of some of these positions, their limitations and their contributions.

14. Batliwala, 2010.

15. *Gender & Development*, 8:3 (2000): 50–56.

16. *The Worlds Women 2020: Trends and Statistics* https://www.un.org/en/desa/worlds-women-2020 (Introductory page of online version).

17. "The Global Gender Gap Report." http://www3.weforum.org/docs/GGGR16/WEF_Global_Gender_Gap_Report_2016.pdf.

18. www.weforum.org/reports/gender-gap-2020-report.

19. https://www.thecrisismagazine.com/single-post/2020/08/27/THE-PROMISE-OF-KAMALA-HARRIS

20. UN Women, "Facts and figures: Women's Leadership and Political Participation" for 2021. https://www.unwomen.org/en/what-we-do/leadership-and-political-participation/facts-and-figures#_edn14 [Accessed 2/23/2022]

21. Seattle and London: University of Washington Press, 2016.

22. Preamble to "Convention on the Elimination of Discrimination against Women" United Nations Website. www.un.org/womenwatch/daw/cedaw. Accessed 3/31/2020.

23. http://www.un.org/womenwatch/daw/cedaw/states.htm

24. Timelines of the right to vote are now available, indicating places and years when the right to vote was won. See for example The Nellie McClung Foundation statistics on www.ournellie.com/about-us Accessed 3/31/2020

25. Taken from the public organizational posting https://www.facebook.com/TTCEDAWChamps/

26. https://www.cawp.rutgers.edu/women-us-congress-2020 Accessed 3/31/2020

27. Published as an appendix to Tony Martin's *A Tale of Two Amies* (2007).

28. Ula Taylor, 2001.

29. Gregg, 2005, 210.

30. "African Rights and Liberty," February 27, 1833. https://www.womenhistoryblog.com/2013/02/maria-stewart.html.

31. *Feminist Africa* 19 (2014): 78–93 a version of which was presented first on a panel on Panafricanism and Feminism at the Caribbean Studies Association, San Andres Island, Colombia conference 2008.

32. See my *Left of Karl Marx. The Political Life of Black Communist Claudia* Jones (Duke, 2008). Sometimes referred to as the triple jeopardy or triple oppression thesis, this reappears in the work of Angela Davis such as *Women, Race and Class* (New York: Random House, 1981).

33. *Claudia Jones Beyond Containment, 75–85.*

34. *The Washington Post* October 1, 2020.

35. In "Black Supreme Court Nominee Finds Inspiration in Black Caribbean American Justice," Baker Motley is identified as "the first Black woman to argue before the Supreme Court and went on to win nine out of ten cases. She was the first Black woman to serve in the New York Senate, the first Black woman in history to serve as a federal judge. In 1965, she became first woman and first African American to be the Manhattan Borough President." *Caribbean Today*, March, 2022: 15.

36. See Ashley D. Farmer's *Remaking Black Power. How Black Women Transformed an Era*, 2017.

37. Cited information from Paula Giddings and my own relationship with Mary Fair Burks who was my literature professor is identified in *Caribbean Spaces*, pp. 49–50. See also "Mary Fair Burks. An Old-School Professor Who Shaped the Civil Rights Movement." March 13, 2019. https://bit/ly/3c004L1

38. Jeanne Theoharis, *The Rebellious Life of Mrs. Rosa Parks.* Boston: Beacon Press, 2013 details her trajectory.

39. *Boston Globe,* March 8, 2000. Williams was Grenada's ambassador to the United Nations in 2008.

40. UN Women 2019. 2020 stats indicate 10 women as heads of state.

41. *The World's Women 2015.* https://unstats.un.org/unsd/gender/chapter5/chapter5.html

42. Gregory Warner, "It's The No. 1 Country for Women in Politics—But Not In Daily Life" NPR, July 29, 2016.

43. https://www.unwomen.org/en/what-we-do/leadership-and-political-participation/facts-and-figures#_edn1

44. https://www.un.org/en/desa/world%E2%80%99s-women-2020

45. Charlotte Alter, "Here's What Happens When You Put More Women in Government," November 5, 2015. https://time.com/4101749/justin-trudeau-women-cabinet-parliament-government/ https://www.elitedaily.com/news/politics/justin-trudeau-talks-feminist-cabinet/1853014. Studying how this is activated in real time will be a project that reveals how policy promises are activated or not realized as it pertains to male leadership that begin with an assertion of empowering women.

46. "Con-di-fi-cation. Black Women, Leadership and Political Power." *Feminist Africa* (6: March): 67–84.

47. Edwards, 2012.

48. "N'dri Assie Lumumba has a good overview of the speeches delivered in Beijing, their impact and the way she addressed the common history of marginalization and current locations in society of women across the globe" (85).

49. https://www.africaknowledgeproject.org/index.php/jenda/issue/archive

50. From interview conducted with Aminata Dramane Traoré in Bamako, Mali, 2018 (see appendix).

51. Even as we have considered political leadership, in academic institutions, some departments of universities have never had women as chairs or directors, even though there are qualified women on their faculties and often for those women who attain leadership it is sometimes a difficult and contested term of office. The numbers of women presidents is still relatively low. Studies of inequities in universities are conducted but filed without concerted attempts at implementation.

52. The Georgetown University Women's Leadership Institute is one of these, offering leadership programs in business and political sectors. The Institute for Women's Leadership and the Center for Women's Global Leadership at Rutgers University provide useful resources.

53. *Washington Post*, August 8, 2020.

54.   https://www.washingtonpost.com/graphics/2020/local/history/suffrage
-racism-black-deltas-parade-washington/?fbclid=IwAR1o69gAUFeG_
IITJ5bBObvKFy2g44-e4N5wuoIRVGdKn2KrR1GQhH6Vb3c

Chapter 2

Feminist Literary Leadership in African Women's Writing

"Towards Feminist Pan-Africanism and Pan-African Feminism," a 2019 lecture by Sylvia Tamale, is a tour de force examination of the politics of African women's creative and theoretical praxis on the continent itself and in the larger African world, with a final call for a "Pan-African movement divorced from statecraft and patriarchal politics" (61).[1] In this assessment, Tamale asserts "the kind of patriarchy we are fighting is borne out of the Western hegemonic worldview that constructs the generic human subject as male. It's institutions and ideologies are male-dominated, *pushing more than half of the continent's population* (my emphasis) into the margins of social existence" (58–59).

This chapter demonstrates that feminist leadership had been provided already in the literature by African women writers when it was not yet apparent in other fields, already contesting some of these patriarchal assumptions. Women writers of the generation of African writers making the anti-colonial critique, of which Achebe was the leading exponent, had advanced some of these positions without the major international recognition that a writer like Chimamanda Adichie is now afforded.[2] Writers such as Mariama Ba (Senegal, 1929–1981), Ama Ata Aidoo (Ghana, 1942–present), Buchi Emecheta (Nigeria, 1944–2017), Nawal el Saadawi (Egypt, 1931–2021), Flora Nwapa (Nigeria, 1931–1993), and Bessie Head (South Africa, 1937–1986) had consistently articulated advanced feminist positions on women's experience in African contexts, were often critical of aspects of African traditions that disadvantaged women, but also of looming problems in the rising post-independence states. They were also often ignored, embattled, challenged, declared controversial, and excluded from major literary canons until the rise of a comparable African feminist literary criticism.[3]

The fact is that even as we celebrate the contributions of Chinua Achebe, with the kind of well-deserved world renown that he received, his early and

53

representative *Things Fall Apart* (1958) rapidly came to be defined as the "archetypal African novel" which focused on some specific targeted challenges of the African encounter with European colonialism. Still, in that approach, African women were not given the full range of possible historical representations. Additionally, African masculinity was posed as the response to European colonial dominance. Much of the writing in that modern African literature period, nationalist in orientation, did not include women as leading figures in its thinking about the construction of new nations. And even in the documentation of that literature, a standard text such as *A History of Twentieth-Century African Literatures* (1993) had to be pushed by its publisher to include women writers, resulting in one chapter describing the place of women in African literary history.[4] Meanwhile, an entire body of writing by African women created a more nuanced examination of African realities, which included critiques of some of the limitations of the postcolonial state, and therefore of male leadership. Thereby, the presentation of the other side of the story, the one in which women lived complex lives of "joys" (*The Joys of Motherhood,* 1979) by Buchi Emecheta and "pains" (*Woman at Point Zero,* 1975) by Nawal el Saadawi, was made significant.

In our contemporary 21st century experience, after the migration of a generation of African professionals of all classes and their families to American and European locations, documented as *The New African Diaspora*,[5] a different reading of African literatures reveals a variety of other narratives. These include recognition of the contributions of African women writers to the larger field of African writing *and* the rise of young writers who are living the experience of migration to major world countries. This new generation of writers is pursuing a variety of different angles, often ushered in by a series of diasporic realities, living thereby a kind of trans-African reality. This generational shift presents the need for a complete rethinking of the contours, nature, themes, and concerns of African literature today, one in which women writers are central and no longer marginal. Nobel laureate Wole Soyinka for example indicated in an interview in *The Guardian* at the publication of his recent work, *Chronicles from the Land of the Happiest People on Earth* (2021)[6] in response to a question on contemporary African literature: "There is a marvellous crop of young writers, particularly young female writers who have become a pride of the continent."[7] Writers such as Chimamanda Adichie, who herself has been criticized by another generation of writers,[8] in my reading, combine and exemplify the convergence of these new realities.

Thus, one can identify new generations of African writers[9] making another type of political intervention at a different historical juncture, each producing different articulations of African literature outside of those frames set by earlier writers in the heyday of formal European colonialism and the anti-colonial critique which led to political independence. Within the succeeding generations of African writers who are recognized, being born outside of Africa to Nigerian parents as is Tope Folarin who won the 2013 Caine prize for his short story "Miracle"[10] and the author of *A Particular Kind of Black Man* (2020) is not unusual. The experience of studying in Europe or the United States represents another point of access to publishing apparata. Thus, their writing tends to address a wider range of concerns, including the role of the United States in a different kind of coloniality or imperialism. Folarin's representative story "Miracle" as does the novel centers a Nigerian community living in the midwest United States. A key protagonist is a blind prophet visiting a small church community of Nigerian migrants who in the end is unable to produce the expected miracle of giving perfect vision to a young boy who merely needs glasses while he himself cannot see. Folarin revealed in 2013 that he had, by the time of his writing, never traveled to Nigeria, largely because his working-class family could not afford to purchase tickets for the family for such a journey.[11]

One can perhaps make a similar case for placing Bernadine Evaristo who as co-winner of the Booker Prize for 2019 for *Girl, Woman, Other* (with titular echoes of Trinh T. Minh ha's *Woman, Native Other,* 1989) as also a product of that migration of Africans to the centers of former colonial powers. A structurally innovative novel with multiple characters, it has propelled the writer into a much larger platform which included the space to describe her experience of growing up with a Nigerian father and British mother.[12] In the Evaristo and Folarin cases, which are representative of a critical aspect of the continuing diasporization of Black communities, one has to think now of a series of overlapping categories of belonging such as Black or Afro-British or be able to place their work within the larger African Diaspora Literature as does Margaret Busby in her *Daughters of Africa* (1992).[13] Bernardine Evaristo, though she would prefer a more fluid sense of her position as a writer, then can be seen as an African woman writer as well. Indeed, her constellation of characters includes an African woman who migrates to London with her partner who dies and is bereft of intimacy finding it at one point in a same-sex relationship, a subject explored only tentatively by an earlier generation of African women writers. Questions of labor and finding employment or developing alternative means of making a living, and of raising children dominate Bunmi's experience in London, particularly when her daughter Carole does not follow the traditional family prescriptive after she gets an education in one of England's major universities.

Many writers of this current post-colonial generation had traveled out of the African continent before becoming recognized, unlike the Chinua Achebe, Ngugi wa Thiong'o or Ousmane Sembene generation, who were often writing at home in their various countries (Nigeria, Kenya, Senegal) before gaining international acclaim. Still, their publications, written in Western languages (English and French mostly), were for global audiences.[14] The following generation, diasporically literate, navigate home and abroad conceptually as they do personally. Still, choosing to return home or to write in their African home space, as Binyavanga Wainaina's experience indicates, meant having to face the issue of recognition at home while developing international readerships. Wainaina, who won the Caine prize in 2014, "came out" to publicly claim his non-conforming sexual identity in *The Guardian*[15] in response to repressive anti-homosexual laws in some African countries.

For the international audience though, Chimamanda Adichie is perhaps the most well-known and acclaimed of the writers of her generation, winning numerous literary awards and celebrity status and its accompanying rewards and criticisms. She too indicates that she lives both experiences, continental and diasporic and writes confidently about both. In many ways her novel *Americanah* (2014) has become the "archetypal novel" of its generation. But, her *New York Times* story of her father being kidnapped in Nigeria poignantly captures this new experience of being a writer with international acclaim who has to navigate difficult experiences at home as well (Adichie, 2015). The recent critique she received for not being sensitive to transgender issues though saw her push back at being typecast as unsupportive of these positions.[16] For Chimamanda, however, her life as a writer has provided access into a series of prominent "red carpet"[17] recognitions with a parallel ability to wear and represent African high fashion, while being critical of gender on both sides. Her critique of Hillary Clinton[18] for having "wife" as her first designation in her professional description was a timely one which led the former first lady and presidential candidate to change this limiting identification, which may have cost her the presidency, as I argue elsewhere in this work. Interviewing Michelle Obama in London at the South Bank Centre's Royal Festival Hall, on her autobiography *Becoming* (2018), Adichie asked directly whether Michelle and Barack have any rivalries, in the background of which one can hear echoes of her position articulated on sexism in "We Should All be Feminists." Adichie is also conscious of the issues of Black women and representation, as on the issue of natural hair grooming styles, demonstrated in her having set the opening chapter of *Americanah* in an African hair braiding salon in the United States and her own personal presentation of a range of African hairstyles. Thus, her response indicating the link between African self-representation and the domination of the European aesthetic, with the example of what would happen if Michelle Obama wore her hair in a natural style: "Barack Obama would not have won," she says emphatically.[19]

The first generation of African women writers had to earn critical recognition with much support from African feminist critics and make those claims assertively to the authority of being writers for themselves as did Buchi

Emecheta or Ama Ata Aidoo. Chimamanda, to her credit, does recognize the pioneering work of writers like Ama Ata Aidoo[20] who she too identifies as setting some of the early themes and arguments for a more gender-balanced modern African literature.[21] Writers of Adichie's generation are able now to articulate confidently these and other related issues raised by Ama Ata Aidoo, because writers in that earlier cohort had already done "daily battle." For example, Fatima Mernissi's *Doing Daily Battle* (1989) described her process, as does *Dreams of Trespass: Tales of a Harem Girlhood* (1995) as she also claimed a place for African women's writing in Northern Africa. Chimamanda is very clear about this history, and specifically about Achebe's place in the hierarchy of African writing and African women's location in these historically patriarchal structures.[22]

Despite this patriarchal inheritance in African writing, the gap between these writers in terms of age, influence, concerns, gender, and time create a wholly different set of representations. Adichie's "The Headstrong Historian" in her short-story collection, *The Thing Around Your Neck* (2009), is clearly a rewriting of the Okonkowo narrative in *Things Fall Apart*, even with the word play on "Thing" in the book's title. Things have already fallen apart; we assume from her narrative. In "The Headstrong Historian" the person affected by colonialism is a woman, the grandmother, who develops as a resisting subject, but who importantly is able to take the fight forward via the female line. It is the granddaughter who becomes a thinker and a scholar of African history. Interestingly, Adichie mentions the presence of such a dynamic and resisting grandmother in her own life. Thus, "The Headstrong Historian" harkens back to Achebe by reworking some of the same turf that he had covered: timeframe, names, traditional cultural practices that maintained inequality, colonial incursion, and the arrival of the white man, Christianity and its effects, and colonial schooling. She even re-writes Achebe's imagined colonial text, which ends *Things Fall Apart*, entitled *The Pacification of the Primitive Tribes of the Lower Niger*, with the title *Pacifying with Bullets: A Reclaimed History of Southern Nigeria*.

In the context of this discussion, what is significant about "The Headstrong Historian" is that Adichie focuses on a more elaborated set of positions for women via a grandmother who was wronged by both family (tradition) and colonialism. She presents a granddaughter who re-writes her grandmother's power of creativity and political sensibility. In this story, she makes the person affected by colonialism (the grandmother) a proto-feminist from childhood, and bypasses the colonized son for a new generation, the granddaughter who becomes a thinker and a scholar of African history and re-captures her grandmother's innate resistance and unfulfilled quest for justice. Thus, the grand-daughter, takes back her African name, resists colonial educational tendencies in the academy, and writes books that reclaim African history.

Chimamanda Adichie's TED Talk, "We Should All Be Feminists," is loaded with anecdotes about gender inequality in contemporary Africa that span class, age, and circumstance and that range from her childhood experience of being denied being the class monitor in elementary school, the challenge to adult privileges like walking into a hotel unaccompanied, because, as a woman, she would be assumed to be a sex worker, or being rendered invisible when in the company of men. Claiming her own feminism and asserting that her grandmother was also a feminist in practice, she highlights the ridiculous conclusions of men and women (some of them university-educated) in her community that attempt to return her to a place of acceptance of gender inequality. From Adichie's point of view, we have evolved but our ideas about women have not.

Adichie provides for her audience a simple definition of feminism, advanced a bit beyond the definition she found in a dictionary in her childhood search, but limited nonetheless: a man or a woman who says "yes there is a problem with gender and we must fix it." For scholars it is a much more complicated set of definitions with a body of scholarship to match.[23] Adichie is clearly aware of the variety of feminist positions, for in the same TED talk she indicates that she is very familiar with the "systems of oppression" approach, which is one of the hallmarks of Black feminism. The most advanced articulation of African feminist positions carries the class/race/gender articulation of African women's rights, using an interlocking "systems of domination" approach, challenged by the development of a full humanity in which political and economic power is shared. An editorial to a special issue on women, titled "Women on the March" in 1986 proposed an economic/class-based feminist approach to the democratization of African women's rights that is always worth citing for its timeliness and concise articulation of what still remains an advanced position on women's rights.

> Our vision of feminism, born of our experience as activists and analysts, has at its very core a process of economic and social development geared to human needs through wider access to economic and political power. Equality, peace and development by and for the poor and oppressed are inextricably interlinked with equality, peace and development by and for women.[24]

Of relevance to this study, Adichie cites Wangari Maathai's claim that women appear infrequently in leadership in Africa. She engages a range of feminist issues anecdotally and descriptively by asserting that equal pay for equal work is a fundamental right and that rape reveals the depravity of men and not women's lack of inhibition. Adichie pays significant attention to the issue of sexuality in this talk and challenges the assumption that women are raised to marry while men have choices. She describes a woman she knows who pretended domesticity in order to get married and critiques the idea that women must silence themselves and not express their sexuality.

In Chimamanda Adiche, then, we see an assumption that feminist issues, are normal human rights, related to living in the contemporary world. Thus, in a CNN "African Voices" (2009) presentation, Chimamanda spoke casually of key themes that preoccupied her. One of these salient themes she indicates is "the idea that marriage is not set up for the benefit of women and indeed can be dangerous for women, but that women are conditioned to behave 'as though marriage is a prize.'" Another contemporary issue for her is the hypocrisy concerning the denial that same-sex relationships existed/exist in Africa. Chimanda Adichie sees the need to challenge these as assumptions of the requirement for equality in the treatment of men and women as human beings and as basic human rights appropriate to all.

Thus, besides dealing with the issues of international migration of Africans to the United States and the United Kingdom and the related issues of navigating these systems through education, Adichie's novel *Americanah* also offers an unabashed engagement with all salient aspects of sexuality, in and out of Africa, for her generation. The lead character, a young Igbo woman, reveals a range of tentative sexual escapades as a teenager in Nigeria, her migration to Lagos then to the United States as a student, where she experiences a level of poverty that leads to an encounter in which her dignity is compromised. She ends up living in long-term relationships with white and Black American men before returning to Nigeria where things have indeed fallen apart, way beyond even Achebe's version. *Americanah* is about sexuality as much as it is about transnational migration, and about the full realization of the African woman as literary subject, but it is also a critique of life in the post-colonial state in which American narratives dominate.

In contrast to Achebe who documented the period of the British colonial incursion into Africa and the difficulties of a concerted and organized response, Adichie is aware of the colossal importance of the United States as a world hegemon. The titling of the book, while a play on the way Nigerians referred to those who had gone abroad to the United States and returned with affectations, is also about the Americanization of the world, which renders Africans and others around the world at times totally dispossessed both at home and abroad and having to make their way in this world of American dominance which has impact everywhere. Our protagonist returns home to Nigeria, but it is not an idyllic return and instead is one fraught with myriad cultural adjustments along the lines of the critique-of-independence genre of novels.

Additionally, taking Chimamanda's recognition and her version of feminism to another generation and reading demographic, popular singing icon Beyoncé sampled Adichie's TED talk, "We Should All Be Feminists" which in many ways fulfills perhaps a more elaborate marketing and recognition model than had been seen before.[25] That the Adichie's TED talk on feminism ended up being sampled on artist Beyoncé's popular self-titled album's 11th track, "Flawless" (2013) provided one of the major ways that an African writer's work was able to circulate via popular media. Textually, it carries many of the themes and assertions that run through the work of African feminist literary and theoretical writers: "Feminist: the person who believes in the social, political, and economic equality of the sexes."[26]

FEMINIST LITERARY LEADERSHIP POSITIONS AND SMALL "f" ASSERTIONS

Perhaps most representative in asserting feminist literary leadership positions about forty years ago, Buchi Emecheta published several books that challenged the assumptions about woman's place in African societies. Emecheta, who died in 2017, produced an array of writings with the centerpiece being *The Joys of Motherhood* (1979).[27] Collectively, these works provide enough themes in a substantial body of work that will be read and studied by future students and critics.[28] Although Emecheta's works advanced many women's rights or women's conditions, her statement: "I work towards the liberation of women but I'm not feminist. I'm just a woman" generated quite a bit of debate, at the time, on this rejection of what then was an exciting political moment. Many indicated that her creative works spoke to feminist issues, even if she did not claim that ideological position rhetorically, as they addressed a range of relevant topics: child marriage, motherhood, life as a single mother, violence against women, the woman's right to economic independence, and above all the freedom to be a writer. Emecheta then had consistently foregrounded her professional status as a writer:

> Being a woman writer, I would be deceiving myself if I said I write completely through the eye of a man. There's nothing bad in it, but that does not make me a feminist writer. I hate that name. The tag is from the Western World—like we are called the Third World. I work toward the liberation of women, but I'm not just a feminist. I'm just a woman.[29] [Additionally, and more relevantly to this discussion is that famous declaration]:
>
> Being a woman, and African born, I see things through an African woman's eyes. I chronicle the little happenings in the lives of the African women I know. I did not know that by doing so I was going to be called a feminist. But if I am now a feminist then I am an African feminist with a small f.[30]

Those familiar with African feminist theoretics can recognize many feminist themes even within such denials at the linguistic level. But several other analytical possibilities loom when viewed retrospectively. In some views, perhaps Emecheta comes closer to Alice Walker's "womanism," which was developed precisely to have a space for Black women to claim a rights discourse without being subject to Western bourgeois understandings of gender.[31] Thus, womanism which Walker used as an equivalent to a kind of cultural Black feminism became coopted by Afrocentric feminists as being more relevant to the Black woman's experience and used as well by some African feminist critics.[32] One could also immediately think of all the qualifi-cations that were offered to challenge monolithic understandings of feminist movement as always European-American generated. Thus, African feminism by Filomina Steady (1981) similarly offered a major redefinition of main-stream feminism.

Beyond the culturalist readings, the explorations of class/gender systems, as these pertain to African societies, continue with renewed emphasis. Given the social science research by African women scholars, which addresses[33] the intricacies of class and gender dynamics, particularly as these engage women's contemporary realities, the overemphasis on cultural studies in the US academy tends to overshadow the political economy work, in which some of these questions are inevitably raised. Thus, we can pose as ongoing ques-tions: what are the continuing class/gender relationships in African societies that continue to position poor women in contemporary economic structures as always at a disadvantage? What is the nature of the acquisition of those rights that are owed to African women as citizens of their various nation-states. The example of Audre Lorde, who claimed all of her political and personal identities, is also relevant.[34] The theoretical position of Sylvia Wynter in "Beyond Miranda's Meanings"[35] also offered a challenge to the absence of the experience of Black women in the understanding of the primary feminist positions but, further, that gender is but one of the ways that Black people are subordinated under the Western definitions of "man" or the human.

In her essay, titled "Feminism with a Small 'f,'" Emecheta offered then a controversial position which now can be seen clearly as an advanced posi-tion on women and leadership that seems more attuned to current feminist framings and therefore relevant to this book's project. There she asserted, on women's political leadership, that she came from a tradition of women's empowerment. She also recalls in that essay, the Aba Women's War of 1929 in which African women pushed back against fines imposed by the British colonial apparatus. Even more relevant to our current discussion of leader-ship, she offered a commentary on the then available models of women's leadership, though subject to critique since a Black female version of

Margaret Thatcher is also a highly oppressive political model. There is then a dated class-based contradictory assertion implicit in her conclusion that:

> There should be more choices for women, certainly women who wish to be like Geraldine Ferraro should be allowed to be so. We need more of her type, especially among the black women. We need more Golda Meirs, we need more Indira Gandhis. But those who wish to control and influence the future by giving birth and nurturing the young should not be looked down upon. It is not a degrading job. If I had my way, it would be the highest paid job in the world. We should train our people, both men and women to do housework. A few privileged African women are now breaking bonds. They live at home and work outside. Most of these women were lucky enough to come from families where the girls were allowed to go to school and to stay there long enough to acquire knowledge to equip them to live away from their families and to rub shoulders with men. Black women are succeeding in various fields along these lines. (182)

Still, for Emecheta, the African feminist position is revealed in a consciousness of "political oppression of colonialism, Western domination, and societal domination of a sexist nature" (255), but also in some internal contradictions in African society as expressed in *The Slave Girl* (1977). Yet, she was unable to make the critique of women who get to leadership but use the masculinist leadership paradigm as did Margaret Thatcher or Golda Meir. Still, Emecheta's time and location in London offered her a global vision of African women in the continent and in the African diaspora that is more current with the next generation of writers. In one of her interviews, she says: "Black women all over the world should re-unite and re-examine the way history has portrayed us."[36]

Presenting the African immigrant experience from the woman's point of view, the autobiographical novels *In the Ditch* (1972) and *Second Class Citizen* (1975) reveal her protagonist's Adah's struggles with both the domination of a difficult husband and the realities of living in the colonial center and encountering racism and British racial condescension. *Head Above Water* (1986) provides the full autobiographical experience which informs both. But they become testimony cumulatively on the impact of British colonialism on African subjects which led to the same migratory experiences of Africans attempting to make lives in Europe.

The critique of feminism as an overarching monolithic ideology and politics has already come from a variety of locations—all challenging the assumption that women experience oppression in the same way or have access to power in a unilinear way; all providing counter versions, revisions, new combinations, expansions often rather than limitations. African feminism has been one of these counter versions. However, it may be useful to briefly here delineate a series of lines of African feminist[37] inquiry, following a genealogy of work by scholars of African gender systems, such as with the generation of Omolara Ogundipe, (1940–2019), the author of "Not Spinning on the Axis of Maleness" and "Sitwanism" moving to the following generation of African feminist scholarship, such as Obioma Nnaemeka's[38] contributions, and definitely the work of the feminist legal theorists who worked on bringing the Protocol of the Rights of African Women in force in 2006. These meet another generation of women who like Bibi Bakare Youssef, the founder of Cassava Republic Press, or Lola Olufemi, *Feminism Interrupted* (2020), who asserts the need for a radical feminism. Thus, continue to challenge gender inequities, the latter asserting a radical feminism.

Thus, in the same generation and timeframe as Emecheta, another conceptualization of the position of women in an African context was Molara Ogundipe's "African Women, Culture and another Development"[39] (1984) acutely aware of this difference, as she located women within socio-economic realities. Using deliberately a Maoist "mountain" metaphor, Ogundipe provided an assessment that illustrated a range of oppressions: colonialism, tradition, neo-colonial realities of underdevelopment and poverty, male power, and race which she divided along class and racial lines. The class/race/gender articulation of African women's rights, linked the critique of economic/class systems that disempowered most women in contemporary Africa, dominated the discourse subsequently. The *Feminist Africa*[40] journal collective, the work of Pat McFadden in Southern Africa and other contributors from across the continent offered feminist social science analyses. African feminist legal work in Nigeria, Ghana, Liberia, Kenya, Uganda, South Africa, Gambia and ongoing work among women in the Arab world and Francophone national communities like Senegal[41] provided steady challenges of male dominant systems.

Yet, in the midst of this academic theorizing of gender, we can locate a conscious women's rights positioning, culturally and experientially generated in Emecheta's early literary critique of issues that were of concern to African women. In Emecheta's version, articulated creatively, marriage and motherhood could mean the destruction of one's creative spark, a willful enslavement to cultural norms. Thus, in one of her last interviews, she asserted that, "Women are capable of living for so many other reasons than [just] men."[42] In my reading, the creative texts carry forward the intellectual African feminist concerns, and can be analyzed on this basis as doing the kind of creative-theoretical work that she herself countered in her small "f" feminist assertion. Still, we can also factor in Emecheta's clarification in the same feminism (with a small "f") paper she presented at the 1986 Second African Writers Conference in Stockholm, Sweden, for she actually had claimed an African feminist position, though the small "f" is what was circulated titularly (i.e., ". . . But if I am now a feminist then I am an African feminist with a small f").[43]

In this reassessment, I see her as claiming still an assertive woman's rights position even in that language which had prompted Nigerian poet, Niyi Osundare to refer to Buchi Emecheta as "The Unintended Feminist."[44] For Osundare, this is what makes Emecheta the African feminist who "taught the world other ways of looking at gender from the African perspective." For clearly, Emecheta had offered an African women's rights position not identical to Western bourgeois feminist articulations; hers was specific to the African women's realities that she had experienced and described and for those bereft of those rights. The logic of the small "f" which has received a much attention, however allows the articulation of a woman rights discourse. Its use subordinates the larger movement or political position to specific geographical, cultural, or other political interests, or it qualifies or limits the meaning of feminism as deployed in Western formulations. The same would also apply to "socialism" (small "s") for example. In a sense the logic of the small "f" is what has been sustained.

Discussion of African women's rights has had much more mileage than have African feminist discourses; that is, an economic/class-based feminist approach to "the democratization of African women's rights" seems to carry more momentum. The "systems of domination" approach, linked to the development of a full humanity in which political and economic power is shared remains the preferable ideological framing for most African feminists. For example, Sylvia Tamale's *Decolonization and Afro-Feminism* defines "Afro-feminism" as working "to reclaim the rich histories of Black women in challenging all forms of domination, in particular as they relate to patriarchy, race, class, sexuality, and global imperialism" (xiii) while citing the Charter of Feminist Principles for African Feminists of 2016.

VISIONS OF AFRICAN WOMEN'S INTELLECTUAL AND POLITICAL LIVES

What becomes clear immediately in this analysis of past and present generations of African women writers is that global citizenship, new identities and subjectivities, sexual orientation, and experiences at home and abroad were and still are clearly part of intellectual and artistic frameworks. In that same generation of women writers as Emecheta, Ama Ata Aidoo had defined herself explictly as a feminist. As early as 1984, Ama Ata Aidoo had also offered a theoretical/experiential articulation of issues that African women needed to have addressed if there was going to be a post-independence reshaping of social and economic conditions. Thus in *The Dilemma of a Ghost* (1965),

Anowa (1970), and *No Sweetness Here* (1970) we have clear framing in the literature of what could easily be called the "African woman question."

We can also identify a conscious women's rights positioning, in her early affirmative critique of issues of concern to African women. Indeed, these political issues raised by Ama, as by other women writers provide an operational context for what followed and have become useful information for those wanting to embark on some form of women's rights analysis. We recall Ama Ata Aidoo's summary which also includes a "half the world" assessment:

> [. . .] marriage has proved singularly effective as an instrument of suppression. It has put *half (or often more than half) of humanity* through mutations that are thoroughly humiliating and at best ridiculous. (263)[45]

For Aidoo, the emancipation of women was political and the "last possible hope for ourselves and for everyone else on the continent."[46] In this classic essay in *Sisterhood is Global*,[47] Aidoo had offered one of the first available sociological articulations of some of the realities of African women in the early "post-colonial" period. Her short reflective essay, "To Be a Woman," used some of the writer's own experience and followed the statistical information on the republic of Ghana on the condition of women in key areas like sexual harassment, marriage policy, divorce, herstory, and rape. Particularly striking was Aidoo's assertion that she came of age with a recognition that it was taken for granted that a woman fulfilled a catalog of service roles but stressed that this condition was no "less ridiculous than anywhere else" (259). From there she went on to enumerate the challenges of being a writer when societal expectations instead demanded domestic service. One of her conclusions: that "the criteria for judging human accomplishments, if they are exclusively masculine" (261), render women outside of the prevailing definitions of what constitutes a full and functioning human being.

A critical contribution in this vein is her novel *Anowa* (1970/1985),[48] which can be read as one of the most important creative-theorizings of diaspora and middle-passage textualities with reference to the struggles of African women. Ama Ata Aidoo, then, remains one of a small group of African writers who actually engaged some of the historical, personal, and ideological issues on the African side that ushered in the forced displacement via trans-Atlantic slavery that helped shape the "New World" side of the African Diaspora. Anowa is that talented, creative, and ambitious woman as not at all complicit. Aidoo's character Anowa navigates outside of traditional inequities and heads toward independence and full partnership—until stymied by corrupt male dominance and complicity with enslavement, which is also read as male impotence. Anowa is that talented, creative, and ambitious woman whose leadership potential seems to be derailed by her male partner Kofi Ako with whom she had imagined creating a new model of relationships. Anowa navigates outside of traditional inequities and is literally on the road to independence and full partnership only to be hampered by a new, colonially derived version of male dominance. Like Janie in Zora Neale Hurston's *Their Eyes Were Watching God* (1938), who becomes the mayor's wife to be placed on a symbolic pedestal in the Big House, Anowa also rejects that form of marriage and prefers to remain outside of the trappings of a new oppressive colonial power that enriches itself in the beginnings of economic globalization.

As we see, by way of comparison, these questioned speculations on what it means to be an intellectual as a Black woman, are less relevant, it seems, to the second generation of African women writers and scholars because a writer like Ama Ata had already taken on some of these challenges directly. It is worth reiterating here that Aidoo's essay while it was one of the first available articulations of some of African women's realities in the early "post-colonial" period, she wanted it clear that these subordinations applied to women everywhere (259). For Ama Ata, the then contemporary and still gender-reactionary positions of African men owe some of their origins to the European Victorian notions of women's place, which were imported with colonialism.[49]

What are now fundamental rights in an international law instrument like the African Union's Protocol on the Rights of Women in Africa (2005) were issues that a writer/activist like Ama Ata Aidoo had already challenged as providing for the full possibilities of African women. Article 6 of the Protocol, for example, concerns marriage, with ten (10) items pertaining to women's rights in marriage—from rights to property to fair treatment and relations to children. Article 5 discusses the elimination of harmful practices, defining these as "all behaviour, attitudes and/or practices which negatively affect the fundamental rights of women and girls, such as their right to life, health, dignity, education and physical integrity."[50] Article 7 discusses separation, divorce, and annulment of marriage; Article 12 is on the right to education and the removal of barriers that discriminate against women in educational settings.

A subsequent work by Aidoo, *Our Sister Killjoy or Reflections from a Black-Eyed Squint* (1977), also dealt with the African woman's appearance in the West as sexualized and racialized, relatively earlier than this theme's current appearance. The larger narrative structure, experimental in form, engages the African student abroad and signifies what we begin to see as the development of the second-level African diaspora.[51] The character Sissie does return home, having navigated Europe, with a surprised recognition of the inherent limitations of those who had colonized others. Aidoo also cleverly presents a layered reading of same-sex sexuality and desire but locates the white woman's desire for this African woman within a predatory desire of Europe for Africa. The textually-expressed desire of Marija for Sissie appears as a subtext at the level of desire of the German woman for the African woman's blackness and sensuality, using the seductive metaphor of the plums. Through an erotic use of language, our sister flirts with a series of possibilities across gender and place (40).

Sissie for her part is well aware of the seduction of Europe, and while the men stay off the center of this portion of the text, it is the white woman and Black woman who engage what their encounters mean. Sissie herself ruminates on some of the spoils of Black male privilege, that is, that this would have been an interesting European romance if "she Sissie had been a man: "That was a game. A game in which one day, she became so absorbed, she forgot who she was, and the fact that she was a woman. In her imagination, she was one of those Black boys in one of those involvements with white girls in Europe" (61). The opening section, deliberately titled "Plums," reveals that "Our Sister" is also well aware of same-sex sexuality at the precocious girls' school level (67), but we get a combination of horror and desire in the encounter when she felt Marija's hands on her breasts (64) during a tour of the more intimate spaces of the house. It is significant that the hands are described as white and cold. This same-sex desire story, we have indicated, is layered within the larger narrative structure, and is experimental in form particularly for its time. For the larger narrative is of the African student abroad and therefore at the beginning of what has been called the development of the second-level African diaspora. But it also layers those stories, palimpsest-like, over the larger narrative of European colonization of Africa and the anti-colonial response. Sissie's reflections on Europe's predatory nature occur in the text as poetic reflection, often directly following the narrating of textual events, within the larger journal-like structure throughout the entire text. The logic of reflections guides the text titularly and structurally. Resolution of this same-sex white woman/Black woman encounter occurs then as a kind of flirtation, from which "Our Sister" extricates herself, as in the end she returns home. The meanings of Africa in this relationship with Europe remain Fanonian and clear about expropriation.

Traveling through Europe then is an exercise in clarification, seduction, and repulsion, treats and their costs, a kind of journey into the belly of the beast, from which she must always exit emotionally and physically. Thus, in the second half of the book, as she confronts the settling "new" African diaspora, the absence of a commitment to a return is the primary concern. In the end, Sissie returns to Africa full of idealism, for the possibilities of the new African nations. A variety of contrasting emotions occupy the narrator, exile and return for self and larger group, colonialism, racism, and economic exploitation, the white woman's role in this larger pattern. The story is confessional and conversational, containing poetic sections that carry thoughts, responses, and conclusions. The author uses the epistolary form, through a love letter, which allows further space for final reflection.

Aidoo demonstrates in several ways her ability to move away from the "or" offered by political theorist George Padmore between Pan-Africanism and Socialism.[52] Instead, she operates with the conjunctive "and" between feminism and Pan-Africanism, able to navigate these intersections using a sophisticated conjoining of African political issues. Thus we have an example in Sylvia Wynter's critique of western feminism, that is, that "in the wake of the sixties, women activists had ceased the earlier 'echoing' of Marxist thought and had redefined the Woman Question into an issue that was specific to their own concerns, rather than being, as before, a subset of what might be called the Labor Issue"[53] while the "multiple movements related to these questions had most forcibly erupted in concrete political and social struggles all over the globe . . ." (Wynter, 2003: 312).

As demonstrated, writers like Ama Ata went beyond a limitation to culture and class, to offer an explicit critique of African male opportunism even when claiming radical positions: "the fact that a colleague understands the finer points of Marxism or is the most fearless fighter in the bush does not automatically mean that he has the haziest notions of woman's capabilities" (1984: 265). Thus, for Aidoo, the issues of organization and social transformation must include "visualizing a world in which the position of women has been revolutionized" (263). The issue of women's rights in marriage remains as she moves the characters into the contemporary, where we find *Changes*.[54] Set in contemporary urban Ghana, its protagonist a young woman, Esi, names her experience of marital rape, rejects an unsatisfactory marriage, but as she opts out of this marriage, is seduced into being the second wife in a polygamous marriage, which also ends up being not a satisfying option. But unlike in the Anowa example, this critique of marriage is pursued without the losses being assigned to the woman; this time sexual partners and sexual pleasure are assumed as a woman's right, not just a man's. Here are women living as professionals in a contemporary world in which mobility is critical. Motherhood is not an essential, defining identity, as it was in the earlier Emecheta framing, even though it is an option. Ultimately, Esi claims herself under these conditions as she continues to find answers to difficult questions.

In a related essay, "The African Woman Today,"[55] Ama Ata had offered a larger critique of the entire construction of African women particularly as they were often presented in dominant media representations in the timeframe of her writing (the 1990's), perpetually begging for aid. Instead, she begins by providing a listing of African women who transcended constructed gendered limitations. She makes the point that one should reassess indigenous African societal patterns, the conquest of the continent by Europe and put into context therefore "the apparent lack of vision or courage in the leadership of the post-colonial period." Here is where she makes her famous assertion: "... it is not possible to advocate independence for our continent without also believing that African women must have the best that the environment can offer. For some of us this is the crucial element in our feminism" (1992: 323).[56]

NEW AFRICAN FEMINIST POSITIONS

The African Union's Protocol to the African Charter on Human and People's Rights on the Rights of Women in Africa (2005) (signed by 49 countries and ratified by 43 out of 55 countries in 2021)[57] can be seen as offering a major benchmark because it has enshrined many of the advances that African feminists writers, scholars, politicians, and legal practitioners have been asserting as rights over the years as seen earlier in the literary description. The claim has been for women's rights as human rights consistent with international assertions which continue to make that a reality. In an often war-plagued post-colonial Africa under male leadership, issues of violence have remained prominent. According to the Protocol:

> "Violence against women" means all acts perpetrated against women which cause or could cause them physical, sexual, psychological, and economic harm, including the threat to take such acts; or to undertake the imposition of arbitrary restrictions on or deprivation of fundamental freedoms in private or public life in peace time and during situations of armed conflicts or of war.

New challenges, new media, different forms and different audiences than were available to earlier generations present novel approaches to textualities and to political realities, beyond the timely Fanonian colonial experience for young women in *Nervous Conditions* (1988) of Tsitsi Dangarembga. In *Sensuous Knowledge. A Black Feminist Approach for Everyone* (2020) Minna Salami offers a novel approach to doing feminist analysis, challenging the nature of the rhetoric of academic presentations, using a bell hooks challenge to standard citational practices and showing a deft ability to move through a range of feminist knowledges while still grounded in her beginning Nigerian grandmother's orientation. Thus, for Salami, the color blue becomes representative of liberated women, and her work is framed in chapters which deal with key issues like Knowledge, Liberation, Decolonization, Identity, Blackness, Womanhood, Sisterhood, Power and Beauty. Written for a general audience, explicit in its titling, it is a clear distilling of knowledge generated from literary texts like Toni Morrison's to the left theoretics of Noam Chomsky. Her actual history of blogging via *Ms Afropolitan* (2010), identify her as explicit about her multiply identified ethnic formation but puts value in the ability to engage the world from these positions, while maintaining an explicit African feminist political orientation.

Relevant to this work as well is that Minna Salami organizes her book chapters by using very specific theoretical categories like "Power," "Knowledge" "Beauty" and deliberately goes into detailed explanations of these drawing both from the academic-theoretical pool as from indigenous women's knowledge and personal-lived experience. Thus the chapter on "Power" offers important background information on Queen Hatshepsut who served as a Pharoah in Egypt but who was wiped out deliberately from historical record. She offers a variety of versions of these past examples of leadership in Africa and the African diaspora, cites from Audre Lorde's definitions of "power" in the same framework as she does from Hannah Arendt's theoretical exegeses on power. Additionally, she is deliberate in her reassertions that once we enter the language of the academic community, we are already embedded in Euro-patriarchal systems of thought; that since men assume politics as theirs women need as well to re-define the nature of politics for their purposes.

This chapter has argued that feminist leadership had been provided already in the literature by African women writers when it was not yet apparent in other fields. This led to subsequent writers like Chimamanda Adichie attaining prominence with work which centers transnational migration, sex and sexuality, class, education, and race, as the African experiences them in the United States as women try to find ways to enhance their struggling economic lives. A parallel reference to the form of the work is presented as a movement between "blogging" and "traditional narrative" as writing strategies. Adichie frames her character Ifemelu as a blogger who uses this medium to express her thinking on race and identity in America. Using social media familiar to her generation, a series of blogs are placed directly into the text, as indicated by a different font; the blogs are used to advance the narrative, as proverbs or stories would have been used by Achebe. At the same time, the novel's more traditional narrative structure explores the experiences of its protagonist in the new African diaspora.

Contemporary African women's writing demonstrates a decolonial assumption across Africa and the African Diaspora. A prominent feminist sensibility is also assumed in essays, as in creative writing (poetry and prose), but also as engagements with the problematics of exile, of migration in multiple directions, and the implications of engaging a larger world with eyes wide open to multiple axes of domination. A cautionary note, though, is expressed in 'Beauty, Mourning and Melancholy' in a review essay by Mukoma Wa Ngugi, living this generational meaning both autobiographically and in his creative and intellectual work. Mukoma identifies the meaning of the second generation, those migrated and those at home, as having already lost any connections with traditional "practices." While the older generation of Ngugi wa Thiong'o could write about the loss happening in their childhoods, the loss has already happened by the time the postcolonial generation appears, sometimes violently through destruction by the colonial state. So for him, it is no longer about mourning that which has been taken away by colonialism but about not even being aware that it had been taken, while somehow feeling the melancholy of separation and absence in diaspora. He describes Tope Folarin's father as "mourning things he has lost—country, wife, culture and so on." The son, meanwhile, raised in Utah by Nigerian parents, with no knowledge of or trips to Africa, can only write about their experiences in diaspora. Thus, significantly, Mukoma also argues for a new genealogy of African writing.

In this chronology the writer Phillis Wheatley (c. 1753–1784), who was transported to the United States transatlantic slavery from the Senegambia region to New England, should be placed at the head of that tradition.

In this context of mourning, Taiye Selasi's *Ghana Must Go* (2014) begins with the death of the father, literally, the death being the catalytic event in the novel that triggers his family's return to Ghana and their engagement with all the missing history and related difficult experiences of his children in the African diaspora as well as on the African continent. The death of the father has of course symbolic implications in the removal of a patriarchal ownership allowing the family to work out his own failings as their own contemporaneous issues of class and place and transnational identity.

Several members of this new generation of African writers have lived in the United States or Europe, even given rise to a short-lived identity of Afropolitanism.[58] NoViolet Bulawayo, hailing from Zimbabwe, and having studied in the United States and with an MFA from Cornell University, wrote about these two experiences (African urban realities and racialization following US migration) in her book *We Need New Names* (2013). Hers is a stark portrayal of the world from the point of view of a young girl who is wise beyond her years, due to having to confront all the ills of the postcolonial state and later to manage life in the United States and all that this entails as an immigrant.

One of the most striking examples of a contemporary literary African feminist framework is *A Girl is a Body of Water* (2020) by Jennifer Nansubuga Makumbi who actually had studied for a Ph.D. on African indigenous feminisms which clearly, in her words, informs her novel. It is a wonderfully engaged coming of age story of a young girl in Uganda moving her through the ways that she learns about issues that separate and subordinate women through lessons she gets from stories told by the purported "witch" of her village, but which actually gives her the woman's oral history of her people. We learn that "Makumbi introduces readers to the indigenous feminism rising out of the experiences of *mwenkanonkano*, a Ugandan movement that predates Western feminism."[59] In this available interview with the author she indicates:

> I wanted to explore two things. One was the idea that feminism comes from the West, and therefore, feminism is destroying our culture. So I needed to locate feminism in my culture. For me, I had to start from the beginning. When did women start to get oppressed? I needed to look at my people, my culture, from the moment it happened: Why did it happen, and how did it happen? (6)

To do this, she allows the oral narrative which indicates that the first woman came from the sea as told to the young Kirabo in order not to dampen her ability to fly. Significantly the young girl prior to narratives and rituals of domestication had already constructed herself as having that ability to do so. Like Toni Morrison as well, she indicates that her writing audience is her own people, in this case her Ugandan audience first. She describes a certain confidence in having studied African creation mythology which she claims are among the oldest in the world and therefore a good place to see African women's empowerment as constructed before European involvement. Even so the quotidian complications of marital demands and competitions impede but do not completely extinguish this initial creative imagination.

With Boko Haram's 2014 kidnapping of over 200 young Nigerian girls from school, which generated the Bring Back Our Girls Movement, we witness a different engagement with some of the failures of the post-colonial African state. We see that the lives and conditions of women cannot remain marginal issues as they were presented in the past. A new generation of African writers, many having already been through the migratory experience before writing, is engaging a range of issues that are no longer identical to those that concerned writers of the immediate colonial experience.

It is fitting to end this discussion of literary constructs of feminist leadership in African women's writing with Maaza Mengiste *The Shadow King* (2020), an interestingly structured and scopic text in which the author creates women, such as Hirut through whose memories in 1974, on the verge of the youth uprising which claimed to want to create a new model of government, we are told the story of the resistance to the Benito Mussolini invasion of Ethiopia in 1935 through the eyes of women who had to resist multiple levels of subordination to finally embody the public personae of soldiers. "As if the ground beneath their feet had not been won by some of the greatest fighters Ethiopia had ever known, women named Aster . . ." (4), she says, the latter described as another type of resisting woman, like other courageous women in the past who also claimed the right to wear military clothing generally worn by men and to reclaim the right to own and bear arms, in order to enter battle in the face of public censure. At the same time these same women became the subject of legendary stories and songs heralding their bravery. The textual action operates on multiple levels to reposition women in leadership as the women of the Haile Selassie royal household are also given space to call women out to defend their country. While the narrative about Emperor Haile Selassie's role in soliciting the League of Nations during Mussolini's invasion of Ethiopia is dominant in most accounts of this period, the parallel role of women is rarely part of the dominant public mythology. Thus, in *The Shadow King,* we are given an entire speech from Empress Menen on September, 1935 (71–74) calling women to defend their country. Relevant lines included are: "We are confident that women everywhere have the same desire in maintaining world peace and love" (73) and ". . . we would like to bring this to the attention of all women through the world, that it is their duty to voice and express solidarity against such acts" (74).

In *The Shadow King* we have a full exploration of women who fought as soldiers and did the supportive work, two decades ahead of the women documented by Frantz Fanon in "Algeria Unveiled"[60] who also fought in the Algerian Revolution, in the 1950's, to liberate their country from French colonialist violence. In this text, violence against women operates in both the domestic and public sphere. The centering of Ethiopia remains significant as the conjunction of transcendence and the vicissitudes of war continue to plague Ethiopia even in 2021. There is no doubt about authorly intent to foreground and re-present women's leadership in Ethiopian military endeavors and in particular the defense of the country from European invasion as the writer provides an "Author's Note" at the text's closing which says:

> My great-grandmother represents one of the many gaps in European and African history. *The Shadow King* tells the story of those Ethiopian women who fought alongside men, who even today have remained no more than errant lines in faded documents. What I have come to understand is this: The story of war has always been a masculine story, but this was not true for Ethiopia and it has never been that way in any form of struggle. Women have been there, we are here now. (425)

The advancement of the position of women in society, including the epistemological challenge to erasure, remains fundamental in each of these scenarios. Issues raised by an earlier generation of women writers whose works paralleled that of the generation of male writers in the immediate colonial period, remain current, as a new generation confronts at times more insidious forms of fundamentalisms and the incomplete politics of decolonization. The possibilities of advancing beyond more recent received notions of women's rights assumed to be absent, unfulfilled and unnecessary are often juxtaposed with histories of women who exercised leadership throughout history at local and national levels. The conjunction of these past paradigms with current political demands advance new models for the future.

NOTES

1. Sylvia Tamale, "Towards Feminist Pan-Africanism and Pan-African Feminism" was a lecture given as part of the Nyerere Dialogue Lecture Series on September 25, 2019, and indicated as a chapter in a forthcoming book to be titled *Decolonizing and Reconstructing Africa: An Afro-Feminist-Legal Critique* which became when published *Decolonization and Afro-Feminism* (2020).

2. "Women on the March" in the *Journal of African Marxists* proposed an economic/class based feminist approach to the democratization of African women's rights, Ogundipe (1984: 3).

3. See for example Aidoo's "Ghana—To Be a Woman" in Robin Morgan, *Sisterhood is Global* (Feminist Press, 1984, 1996) and Obioma Nnaemeka, "Feminism, Rebellious Women, and Cultural Boundaries: Rereading Flora Nwapa and Her Compatriots." *Research in African Literatures* 26:2:1995: 80–113.

4. See Boyce Davies and Fido, 1993. The editor of this volume came to us at an African Literature conference to indicate that this was a request from the publisher for which he needed our contribution.

5. See Isidore Okpewho and Nkiru Nzegwu, *The New African Diaspora* (Indiana, 2009).

6. Pantheon, 2021.

7. *The Guardian* (London). Interview with Chibundu Onuzo, "Wole Soyinka: 'This Book is My Gift to Nigeria'" September 25, 2021.

8. https://www.npr.org/2021/06/17/1007350665/chimamanda-ngozi-adichie -directs-fiery-essay-at-former-student-and-cancel-cultur

9. A panel discussion on Africa's Literary Identity was dedicated to this question of identifying the new generation of writers, Moderated by Uzodinma Iweala, award-winning author of *Beasts of No Nation*, it featured this author, TMS Ruge, Hannah Pool and Tope Folarin and was held at Pace University, New York, on September 27, 2013. Podcast available: http://bit.ly/16CWGBN

10. www.caineprize.com/pdf/2013_Folarin.pdf and author of the more recent *A Particular Kind of Black Man. A Novel* (Simon and Schuster, 2019) about the Nigerian-American experience.

11. At a panel discussion organized by Africare at Pace University on Africa's Literary Identity, September 27, 2013, New York City, Tope Folarin indicated that his father sold ice cream and cleaned buildings, and his mother worked as a nursing assistant in the Midwest United States where he was one of only a few Black children in the school he attended and that he had not yet traveled to Africa.

12. See her interview on Sky News, The South Bank Show, November 28, 2020.

13. Its title coming as indicated from Maria Stewart who we discussed in the last chapter. A new edition was published in 2019.

14. See Mukoma wa Ngugi's study *The Rise of the African Novel: Politics of Language, Identity and Ownership* (University of Michigan Press, 2018) on the genesis of the African novel on this point. It was gratifying to witness the writers of the Mbati Cornell Swahili Prize for Literature in Dar es Salaam, January, 2022, the only African language literary prize anywhere.

15. Kenyan writer Binyavanga Wainaina (2014) declares: "I am homosexual" http://www.theguardian.com/world/2014/jan/21/kenyan-writer-binyavanga -wainaina-declares-homosexuality (Accessed 6/23/2015). This important interventionist writer sadly passed in 2019.

16. https://www.theguardian.com/books/2017/mar/13/chimamanda-ngozi-adichie -clarifies-transgender-comments. See also https://www.vox.com/22537261/chimamanda-ngozi-adichie-transphobia-cancel -culture-jk-rowling-akwaeke-emezi-olutimehin-adegbeye

17. Tina Mfanga (2021) a Tanzanian activist, has defined what she calls "red carpet feminism" to describe this particular location accorded some women of status.

18. https://www.youtube.com/watch?v=tz8MHG-IIYM (Pen America, April 24, 2018). But, see also Mukoma wa Ngugi's "Chimamanda let Hillary off. But my father showed how to stand up to power" in *The Guardian,* December 1, 2018, https://www .theguardian.com/commentisfree/2018/dec/01/writers-power-chimamanda-ngozi -adichie-hillary-clinton-pen Accessed 5/28/2020.

19. https://www.youtube.com/watch?v=tz8MHG-IIYM (May, 2014). Accessed 5/28/2020

20. Chimamanda Adiche, in an interview on CNN "African Voices" (2010), described the themes that preoccupied her in her then most recent collection of short stories, *The Thing Around Your Neck.*

21. Adams, 2012, offers a collection of essays on various aspects of the work of Ama Ata Aidoo.

22. Adichie was interviewed in *The Times of India* in 2011.

23. The journal *Feminist Africa* for example names itself as such an offers a range of positions in a variety of fields. More recent examples include Sylvia Tamale's *Decolonization and Afro-Feminism.* Ottawa: Daraja Press, 2020.

24. See, for example, Ogundipe (1984). "Women on the March" to the *Journal of African Marxists* and the introduction (1986).

25. Achebe's *Things Fall Apart* was used in classes from anthropology to political science, and of course a literary staple, making its way onto high school international baccalaureate reading lists as well.

26. According to reports, a huge leap in sales of *Americanah* occurred simply from this placement, with a staggering rise up the rankings. See Robinson Meyer, "When Beyoncé Samples Your TED Talk, This Is What Happens to Your Book," *The Atlantic,* December 23, 2013, https://www.theatlantic.com/technology/archive/2013/12/when-beyonc-samples-your-ted-talk-this-is-what-happens-to-your-book/282610 (accessed August 11, 2022).

27. Her children's fiction: *The Moonlight Bride* (1980), *Titch the Cat* (1979), and *Nowhere to Play* (1980). *The Wrestling Match* (1980) and a variety of novels on African women's experience in her time include *Adah's Story* (1983), *A Kind of*

Marriage (1986), and *Gwendolen* (1989) are other less known texts. Her subsequent novels include *Double Yoke* (1982), *The Rape of Shavi* (1983), *Naira Power* (1982), *Destination Biafra* (1982), *Kehinde* (1994), and *The New Tribe* (2000).

28. See for example Katherine Fishburn, *Reading Buchi Emeceta. Cross-Cultural Conversations.* Connecticut: Greenwood, 1995.

29. "Beyonce and Chimamanda on feminism with a small 'f,'" https://medium .com/@damikazeem/beyonce-and-chimamanda-on-feminism-with-a-small-f -a41f196c0994. See full article here: https://www.encyclopedia.com/social-sciences /encyclopedias-almanacs-transcripts-and-maps/emecheta-buchi-primary-sources

30. Buchi Emecheta, "Feminism with a Small 'f'!" In *Criticism and Ideology: Second African Writers' Conference*, edited by Kirsten Holst Petersen. Scandinavian Institute of African Studies, 1988, pp. 173–185.

31. Alice Walker, "Womanist" (A Definition) Frontispiece to In Search of Our Mothers' Gardens. Womanist Prose (1983) and Ogunyemi, C (1985).

32. Chikwenye Ogunyemi's "Womanism: The Dynamics of the Contemporary Black Female Novel in English," *Signs,* 11:1 (1985): 63–80.

33. See for example Akosua Adomako Ampofo, "My Cocoa Is Between My Legs: Sex as Work among Ghanaian Women," and "Work as a Duty and as a Joy: Understanding the Role of Work in the Lives of Ghanaian Female Traders of Global Consumer Items," in *Women's Labor in the Global Economy. Speaking in Multiple Voices.* Edited by Sharon Harley (New Brunswick, NJ: Rutgers University Press): 182–220.

34. Her essay "Age, Race, Class, and Sex: Women Redefining Difference," *Sister Outsider* (1984) is a good place to study her approach where she claims a more expansive listing than the woman, race and class triumvirate. "As a forty-nine-year-old Black lesbian feminist socialist mother of two . . ." (114).

35. After/Word to *Out of the Kumbla,* 1990: 355–372.

36. http://www.pulse.ng/books/buchi-emecheta-on-feminism-id5030332.html

37. Filomina Steady, "The Black Woman Cross-Culturally: An Introduction" in *The Black Woman Cross-Culturally* (Cambridge, MA: Schenckman, 1981): 7–41. Some of these positions influenced my early articulation of this in literature, a cultural product, as expressed in the introduction "Feminist Consciousness and African Literary Criticism" to *Ngambika. Studies of Women in African Literature* (Africa World Press, 1986): 1–23.

38. Nnaemeka (1998) describes her work as "Focusing on the pluralisms of feminisms, these essays address the conflict between indigenous African feminisms and the radicalism of variants of Western feminism with their emphasis on sexuality and seeming oppositions to motherhood. They collectively argue that the African environment specifically should provide the context for any meaningful analysis of feminisms on the continent."

39. *The Journal of African Marxists* 5 (February, 1984): 77–92. At this point, Molara Ogundipe was perhaps one of the few beginning to offer a socialist-feminist reading of African gender systems.

40. *Feminist Africa* 12 (2009) has a wonderful range of essays on various locations from Ghana to Kenya, looking at issues like the gendered politics of farm household production. A survey of the journal *Feminist Africa* for the last ten years is illustrative.

More issues were devoted to culture, a few with the role of the universities and with activism, one dealt with the diaspora. But a special issue on "Land and Labour" is exemplary in that it pursues some of these discussions as they relate to women's work in the various modes of production.

41. The African Women's Leadership Conference at the Museum of Black Civilizations in March, 2020, accompanied an exhibition of African women sponsored by UN Women in Africa.

42. Interview with Julie Holmes in The Voice July 9, 1996.

43. Emecheta, 1988, 173–185.

44. *Sahara Reporters,* January 29, 2017.

45. Aidoo, A.A. (1984).

46. Ibid.

47. (New York: Anchor Press, Doubleday): 258–265

48. See chapter 3, of Carole Boyce Davies, "Deconstructing African Female Subjectivities: Anowa's Borderlands" of *Black Women Writing and Identity. Migrations of the Subject* (Routledge), 59–79.

49. She makes this point in a bit more detail in her essay, "That Capacious Topic: Gender Politics," which appeared in the book ed. By Philomena Mariani, *Critical Fictions. The Politics of Imaginative Writing* (1991). Seattle, WA: Bay Press, 1991.

50. http: www.african-union.org/root/au/documents/treaties/documents/test/protocol (Accessed February 14, 2011).

51. See for example Paul Zeleza's essay in Okpewho and Nzegwu, eds. *The New African Diaspora* (Indiana University Press, 2009).

52. George Padmore who was one of the major advisors of the first prime minister of Ghana Kwame Nkrumah had written a text titled *Panafricanism or Communism? The Coming Struggle for Africa* (London: Dobson, 1961).

53. Wynter (1982). Intellectual/activist women, in the time in which Claudia Jones worked (the 1940's and 1950's), the Caribbean leftist who has been my focus in recent years pursued the socio-economic status of working-class Black women.

54. New York: Feminist Press, 1993.

55. *Dissent* (Summer, 1992): 319–325.

56. This is a position on women that some of the most progressive developers of Africa had come to articulate and she cites Dr. Kwegyir Aggrey on this ["If you educate a man, you educate an individual. If you educate a woman, you educate a nation" ("To Be a Woman," 259)] though it is often attributed to Nkrumah. But also, the late Thomas Sankara of Burkina Faso is also credited with a similar articulation as well.

57. African Union website Accessed 11/25/2021. With 2020 as the year of ratification, domestication and implementation, called as well the Maputo Protocol on Women's Rights in Africa, the number of states ratifying the protocol increased substantially.

58. Often identified with Taiye Selassi author of *Ghana Must Go: A Novel* (2013) but perhaps better known as the author of "Bye Babar" *Lip Magazine*, March, 2005. http://thelip.robertsharp.co.uk/?p=76 But see also Alpha Abebe, "Global Citizenship with African Routes," April 10, 2015 https://blog.politics.ox.ac.uk/afropolitanism -global-citizenship-with-african-routes/ Accessed 5/27/2020

59. See for example Khadija Abdalla Bajaber, review in *The New York Times*, "Set in Uganda, This Coming-of-Age Story Contains Universal Themes," September 1, 2020.

60. *A Dying Colonialism* (1959) (New York, Grove Press, 1965).

Chapter 3

Alternative President! Nomzamo Madikizela-Mandela's Challenge

The political leadership of Winnie Nomzamo Madikizela-Mandela[1] in South Africa, in and out of the African National Congress (ANC) leading to the end of her paternalized relationship with Nelson Mandela, is instructive. Throughout Nelson's twenty-seven-year incarceration, she exercised leadership and created a liberatory political movement. Yet it was this same leadership which threatened to destroy her, given her activism in the face of the world's last and most blatant horrendous system of racial oppression—South African *apartheid.* As such, she was heavily castigated for the demise of the marital relationship and constructed by the androcentric state media in multiple negative ways. This chapter argues, instead, that what unfolded was a direct trivialization of her leadership based on her gender and sexuality and not at all on her actual political contributions to the ending of apartheid.

Generic organic leadership of activist women like Nomzamo Madikizela-Mandela often escapes recognition and tends to be misrecognized, under-appreciated, and taken for granted. Still, we can assert that Nomzamo Madikizela-Mandela created another leadership paradigm than what was expected and actually became the *de facto* leader of South African resistance to apartheid during the incarceration or exile of the ANC male leadership which included her husband. Her trajectory without Nelson charts the activism generated by an understanding that the rights of women are fundamental to national rebuilding after the ravages of corrupt and violent white male leadership. This discussion highlights the ways in which Nomzamo Madikizela-Mandela brought a different type of political leadership into existence and thereby contributed to an ongoing understanding of some of the world's current social problems as she also pursued a range of cultural and intellectual advances.

The nation as a masculine construct, created for the benefit of male leadership is revealed again in this context. A central and relevant question here is:

What new institutions and leadership models, especially in Africa, have been created to take us into the future? This chapter argues that Winnie Nomzamo Madikizela-Mandela offered a distinct leadership model that made her an alternative president. Her work challenged the male paradigms that began with Nelson Mandela. In this case, he was the one who was presented as the charismatic leader given the historical conjunctions of his resistance to South African apartheid. In the post-apartheid/new nation period, he inevitably became a global iconic statesman given the nature of constructed leadership narratives and his own towering persona.

To put this in context, we recall here our earlier discussion (see chapter 1) that the average representation of women in political leadership globally still hovers around 20% in most governments, parliaments, and heads of state. During the time of Winnie Mandela's activism (1960's–1980's) that figure would have been below the 6% recorded at the turn of the century.

Thus, in the South African context, applying Dessima Williams's term "global gendered apartheid" has actual meaning for it describes directly the extreme imbalance in representation and signaled the need for correctives to the situations of gendered inequality that still exist. For South African women "gendered apartheid" was real, as they were defined as "minors" in the law. Writer Ellen Kuzwayo (1914–2006) a women's rights activist, politician who with Audre Lorde and her partner Gloria Joseph were founders of a Global Women's Support Network called SISA—Sisterhood in Support of Sisters in South Africa[2] described this extreme social positioning during the heyday of apartheid in her autobiography *Call Me Woman* (1985). Happily, Kuzwayo was finally able to serve on the first truly representative parliament in South Africa, at the end of apartheid. This is how Gloria Joseph describes their collaboration:

> As the founder of SISA (Sisterhood in Support of Sisters in South Africa), I worked closely with two women's self-help groups, the Zamani Soweto Sisters and the Maggie Magaba Trust. These two groups, led by Ellen Kuzwayo, known as the unofficial mayor of Soweto, were outstanding examples of women as reason and force. Their work was concerned with developing skills to be utilized in a new South Africa while simultaneously resisting the sordid practice of apartheid.[3]

Thus we see in operation the leadership activities "unofficial mayors," who functioned almost as a shadow to the dominant structure described, that is, women exercising alternative leadership in their own communities when excluded by state practices. Because of continuous activism, in the South African context, we witness a gradual rise of Black women to political leadership so that by 2020, "women ministers comprise 41% of the cabinet, women deputy ministers make up 47% of the total number of deputy ministers and there is a 41% representation of women in the National Assembly," says the South African government website.[4] This advancement had been aided by the existence of a "Women's Charter" in 1954,[5] a document enshrining women's rights, which led to early anti-apartheid and pro women's struggles, such as the *"Now you have touched the women, you have struck a rock"* anti-pass campaign of 1956, in which Lilian Ngoyi was a major leader. The "Women's Charter" was later adopted by the Women's National Coalition campaign in 1994 and helped create better conditions for women in modern South Africa. Winnie Madikizela was active in all of these movements.

The generating questions raised in the introduction of this work, when applied to South Africa allow us to ask: how does Nomzamo Madikizela-Mandela fit into this absence/presence of women in a political leadership framework? This chapter seeks to address this issue in a few ways, by studying her own articulations on this and the surrounding oppressive political and lived reality against which she operated. Clearly, she was a leader, though not formally identified, of her political party, the African National Congress, but more significantly an organic leader of the people in general.[6] And because "gender norms and expectations also drastically reduce the pool of female candidates for selection as electoral representatives," as *The World's Women* report indicates as one of the ways that women are kept from leadership, she was betrayed by that same political process at the highest level, from gaining the political power to make changes at the state level. However, in my view, Winifred Nomzamo Madikizela-Mandela functioned as an alternative president in that period before Nelson's release, and definitely was seen in this light in the Black South African popular imaginary. Her position as an organic leader operated in two senses: She definitely rejected the mythical "First Lady" paradigm with its expectations of a certain compliance; she maintained a political presence that consistently provided alternative leadership and service to her immediate and larger national communities.

Women like Nomzamo Madikizela-Mandela who resist that compliant "First Lady" construction make a deliberate decision and instead become "resistant to colonial/patriarchal order."[7] This choice is resonant in the idea of leaving (or staying with) the "Great Man." As other women who were married to world leaders reveal, such a decision is always fraught with drama, as their subsequent activities are still always carried out with public media documentation and curiosity. Although the formal Winnie and Nelson marital relationship ended after his release from twenty-seven years of imprisonment as a political prisoner, Winnie had, in my view, already left the "Great Man" emotionally. Their long separation had already been created by South African state practices. Further, the government's demand for a compliant and safe leadership after his release further cemented this marital split.

The end of that relationship and the later political life of Winnie Nomzamo Madikizela-Mandela are illustrative of my "alternative president" assertion. Although Madikizela-Mandela had waited twenty-seven years, it was not a passive period for her as during this time she tirelessly advocated for his release but above all, created a Free Nelson Mandela movement and served as a leader in his stead. This meant making deliberate public activist/resistance choices in the face of South African apartheid's ideological structures.

Recent documents from agents and operatives for South African government intelligence agencies, as revealed in the documentary *"Winnie"* (2017), describe that the state and its transitional government wanted her as far away from Nelson as possible during that period of his preparation for release, when he was separated from his other incarcerated colleagues and kept in a minimum residential accommodation as he was being groomed for the presidency. Officials, we learn, wanted her even further away once he became president if she was not willing to perform the United States' First Lady stereotype they wanted. According to the documentary *"Winnie"* by Pascale Lamsche,[8] the apartheid state launched a disinformation campaign, creating and placing horrible stories to malign her in the media. These stories were then circulated worldwide. Worse still, they placed their agents inside her security service who committed criminal acts which were then attributed to her.[9]

For her part, Nomzamo aided the military wing of the African National Congress (ANC) as one of its soldiers, providing support for those engaged in armed struggle. At the same time, she became the voice of resistance and consistently grew in confidence, in service, and in articulation of the goals of South African liberation, as outlined in its Freedom Charter.[10] We note relatedly that The Freedom Charter was a forward-thinking human rights document, asserting that "people" included both men and women. Thus, attempts to discount or trivialize Nomzamo's contributions on the basis of her gender provide proof that women as leaders are more often evaluated in terms of their sex than by their political contributions.

Since patriarchy is so entrenched in societal thinking about women's roles in political leaders' lives, one of the ways that women have accessed power is through marriage to a man with potential for leadership. Often, they are ones who help to cultivate these "great men" along the way. Still, these women's contributions are always minimized in order to reduce them to the role of appendages. However, in most professional-political marriages, the wife has a particular skill set that allows the husband to take his leadership to the next generation. For example, Winnie Madikizela-Mandela reported that Nelson called on her to help fundraise for his political movement, in a way reminiscent of how Marcus Garvey approached Amy Ashwood Garvey the first time with the request that she help him build and found the movement which became the Universal Negro Improvement Association. Although Nelson's request to Winnie was clearly his ulterior motive for getting to meet this then beautiful young woman, he clearly recognized a certain sophistication, beauty, and competence in her bearing and in her delivery of social worker services to her community, which he realized right away would make her the ideal partner for someone in his situation.

Winnie Nomzamo Madikizela-Mandela's story reveals the fact that Black women have continuously exercised leadership in many ways. Yet, their leadership has tended to be subject to historical erasure, given the ways that histories have been written to privilege white/male power. So, in the period of the African National Congress's accession to power and until her death in 2018, some members of a new generation in South Africa indicate that they were not taught about her contributions to the ending of apartheid.[11] As in the African American context, men who were leaders of major nationalist movements in throughout the 20th century often had wives/women who were ideologically in tune with their various projects. Winnie was clearly one of these women, and she excelled beyond Nelson's expectations, foregoing the life of the young protected bride and knowing in the process that when she married him she had married the struggle against South African white supremacy.

Historically there has been a consistent pattern of women contesting their exclusions, challenging attempts at dispossession, and asserting the parallel right to occupy leadership positions, particularly when they have the credentials, experience, and ability to lead. Since women's contributions in twentieth-century activist movements were often taken for granted, it was easy for them to be written out of history in relation to the men in their lives. But with Winnie Nomzamo Madikizela-Mandela, we see a deliberate set of actions, taken by her to defy being written out of history: an awareness of the place of Black women in society; a conscious assumption of a political role in the liberation of her people.

DETOURED PATHWAYS: NATIONAL
WIVES/POLITICAL WIVES

The recent 2021 election of Xiomara Castro in Honduras, the spouse of a former president Manuel Zelaya, and therefore one who served as first lady from 2006–2009 to becoming the first woman president of Honduras provides one version of the detoured pathway of women to the presidency.[12] Significantly Xiomara is identified as a democratic socialist, who had contested elections twice before and would have in the process developed her own political following. Besides a popular perception of the role of first lady as wife of the nation or a national wife, there is also the logic of the partner or comrade-in-struggle, who already had used her knowledge and skill in the advancement of her partner's political trajectory and can now apply these to her own leadership pathway. Still, such a move while it provides one of the essential ingredients of name recognition and prior visibility, for political office also means the accompaniment of a similarly generated political baggage which the candidate has to negotiate carefully.

The stunning defeat of Hillary Clinton in her quest for the American presidency in 2016 has been identified as heavily weighted toward "unlikeability" and represents another distinct model of the spouse to presidency pathway. Fuller analyses and feminist readings reveal that her defeat was also caused by the nature of the American electoral system or the way that "democracy" is practiced in the United States. Several other factors, include the conservative, white supremacist backlash against the first Black president, Barack Obama, from the predominantly white working class's economic losses. According to most polls, 55% of the electorate viewed Hillary Clinton unfavorably. Many critics attributed Hillary's loss to her political judgment, past decisions during her husband's presidency, and a tendency to not be fully honest about past errors. However, no similar ills seemed to beset the candidate who became President (2016–2020), despite his more egregious errors, sexist and racist statements, and myriad *faux pas.*

My position still is that using the first lady to president route to leadership is a detoured pathway and a classic and major pitfall for which Hillary Clinton paid the price. Historically, one of the ways that some talented women made it to leadership was through being married to, or being the daughter of, a famous man. That model I suggest here ended with Hillary Clinton. In many professional-political marriages, the wife has a particular skill set that allows the husband to assume leadership as he counts on his wife's support. This is clearly evident in many American presidencies, including the visible first lady profiles of Eleanor Roosevelt, Nancy Reagan, and Michelle Obama. Well-documented examples exist of their public support, enhancement projects, and public demonstration of the emotive side of the presidency. Public-approval ratings intensify once those women indicate they are either "mom in chief," as Michelle Obama did, or smiling, adoring wives, as was Nancy Reagan.

But Hillary Clinton's political career using that older model contrasts starkly with those of other women, such as Shirley Chisholm, who ran "unbought and unbossed" for the presidency and in the same Democratic Party in 1972, or Charlene Mitchell who ran on the Communist Party ticket in 1968.[13] During Hillary Clinton's days as a first lady, once she veered from that expected emotive role and demonstrated her intellectual and political skill, her "likeability factor" plummeted. This was evidenced during the first term of William Jefferson Clinton (1993–2001) when she was put in charge of health care reform and later when she became the supportive wife during the revelation of his sexual transgressions. Her run for the presidency in 2016 became a more heightened example of precisely that challenge to "first lady-hood" that reveals her attempt to access power on her own terms but still with ties to his personal and political history.

Additionally, Hillary Clinton throughout her campaign cultivated the "my husband" approach to running for president, using that language consistently. Indeed, as we noted earlier, Chimamanda Adichie in a videotaped interview with the former first lady asked her why "wife" was her first descriptor in her range of self-descriptions.[14] Hillary responded that she was going to change that right after the interview. Even as she staked out an independent claim, she constantly referred to Bill Clinton as "my husband" in several responses and speeches and not as "President Clinton," which would have been the appropriate address. Bill Clinton was a fixture on her campaign trail as a surrogate, rekindling the historic ways that he was seen, both positively and negatively. I see this engagement with her husband's history as her deliberate attempt to maintain the wifely/first lady posture, which ironically positioned her as not running in her own right in these instances but as the wife of a former president. This left her totally open to the Trump campaign's enhancing of precisely that link.

It is significant to indicate though that at that same time, there was a steady rise of women to various positions of leadership, outside of the United States, heightened between 2005 and 2012 and up to the present with Theresa May becoming the 2nd woman Prime Minister of the United Kingdom in that same year that Hillary ran for the US office (July 2016), following Margaret Thatcher (1979–1990). Others include Angela Merkel as the German chancellor from 2005 to 2021; Mary Robinson, President of Ireland, 1990–1997. So, there were several contemporaneous historical contexts and models which allow us to see some of these trends in women's international leadership, with women running as heads of government, in their own right. In Africa, beginning with Ellen Johnson Sirleaf who became the president of Liberia in 2006 and again won a hard contested second term in 2012, four other women were then heads of state. And in the Caribbean, Portia Simpson Miller served as Prime Minister of Jamaica (2012–2016), as did Kamla Persad-Bissessar in Trinidad and Tobago (2010–2015); in Brazil Dilma Rouseff (2011–2016). In other words, there has been a consistent pattern of women contesting their exclusions, avoiding the detour, and asserting the parallel right to occupy leadership positions, particularly when they have the credentials, experience, and ability to lead.

We can assert that several of these women have been intellectually superior to their husbands, who were able to attain leadership largely because of the cultural assumptions of leadership with masculinity and male power. Still, the evidence so far reveals that pursuing leadership in one's own right and not as a wife has produced more positive results. Minus the baggage of a former president as partner; with an ability to pursue one's own directions to leadership in a solidly independent way, a woman has a better chance of accessing state power.

CONTRADICTIONS OF LEADERSHIP
IN BLACK FIRST LADY STATUS

Representing an interesting blend of political power and wife as helpmate status, the first Black first lady of the United States, Michelle Robinson Obama (2009 to 2016) manifested unparalleled dignity as the first Black woman to occupy this highly visible position. With Michelle Obama, we see the beginnings of a different model being crafted. But in my view, Black communities have been practicing for this model for quite a while. Many Black churches have an identified "first lady," the wife of the leading minister, who often dresses the part, wearing stunning hats and beautiful suits. She is addressed as and referred to by that title. Her role in the church is akin to that of the presidential first lady: to establish her presence via her projects and her leadership in the church and to impart a certain dignity to match the lead minister's power in that community.

The historical presidential first lady is usually an economically privileged and racialized white female subject who supports her husband's execution of the presidency and figures in the national imaginary as the ideal model of the supportive wife. While this mythology was substantially confronted by the presence of a Black woman, historically the antithesis of that construction, Michelle Obama presented images of strength in her physicality, an unabashed sense of personal style, and clearly defined love for family, community, and other people. Her task was not easy, as the construction of what is considered beautiful in various cultural imaginaries was challenged by her very presence and self-presentation. Her self-constructed role as "Mom-in-chief" after being maligned by negative criticism, became a giveaway to that American imaginary of what a first lady should be, a subtle recognition of what American cultural values are said to be, like "mom and apple pie."

But there is another trajectory, through which one can identify an intellectual Michelle Obama. Ms. Obama has maintained that getting an education was necessary to her empowered self-definition. Her critical thought began to develop during her undergraduate years, beginning with her work as an African American Studies minor at Princeton University, where she wrote a thesis examining the nature of Princeton-educated Blacks and their relationship with community and argued for the responsibility of educated African

Americans to give service to the Black community. In her research project, she analyzed themes that continue to inform the nature of her work with Black communities at the intellectual and experiential level. These themes continue to be relevant to minority students and faculty on predominantly white campuses, including scholars in fields such as Black/Africana Studies. She has also challenged the elitism of academic institutions (especially the "ivy leagues"), choosing for her first presentation in 2009 a working-class university community, the University of California, Merced. In that commencement speech she noted that when she was growing up, the University of Chicago was inaccessible to neighborhood children, including the young Michelle, who lived in the surrounding community. She said,

> I grew up just a few miles from the University of Chicago in my hometown. The university, like most institutions, was a major cultural, economic institution in my neighborhood . . . Yet that university never played a meaningful role in my academic development. The institution made no effort to reach out to me—a bright and promising student in their midst.[15]

While at Princeton, she continued to struggle for full recognition, as she documented in her encounters with racism. In 2011, at Spelman College, an institution founded to create Black women as leaders in their professions, Ms. Obama described her own experience as a professional who chose community work instead of the corporate life. Describing some of her own professional pathways:

> So, much to the surprise of my family and friends, I left that secure, high-paying job and eventually became the Executive Director of a non-profit, working to help young people get involved in public service. I was making a lot less money—a lot—and my office was a lot smaller. But I woke up every morning with a sense of purpose and possibility. I went to work every day feeling excited—because with every young person I inspired, I felt myself becoming inspired. With every community I engaged, I felt more engaged and alive than I'd felt in years.

Even with training as a lawyer from one of the nation's leading institutions, and an executive/administrative career before coming to the White House, as a major orator on the campaign trail, Michelle Obama was a disorienting figure in the larger media world. Media outlets had to grapple with this new phenomenon, a Black woman as a leadership partner at the highest political office in the world.

It is important to assert too that the "wife" in patriarchal context, being reclaimed and reused in same sex-relations, though there are more favorable synonyms ("domestic partner" or "spouse") is also an economic identity that still connotes being the one subordinated, taken care of and in service to another, generally a male who holds the more powerful or lucrative occupation. Still, this mythology of the Black woman as first lady has been substantially challenged recently by the presence of many Black women in Africa who also as first ladies functioned historically as the antithesis of the idealized white female identity. Winnie Nomzamo Madikizela-Mandela, never becoming an official first lady like Michelle Obama in the United States, also presented herself through images of beauty, strength, and personal style, and above all an enduring love for family, community, and young people.

Women in earlier generations left relatively few autobiographies. As such, they ended up being constructed by those who chose to enter and describe their lives, often from the viewpoint of their husbands. Historical examples of the political wife abound, as seen in Marcus Garvey's life as we have described this earlier (see chapter 1), Tony Martin's *Amy Ashwood Garvey, Pan-Africanist, Feminist and Mrs. Garvey No. 1 or a Tale of Two Amies* (Majority Press, 2007) provided painstaking historical documentation that Marcus Garvey's first wife, Amy Ashwood Garvey, was identified as a co-founder and co-builder of the UNIA in official documents.[16] Indeed, subsequent work on women and the UNIA, Rupert Lewis and Honor Ford Smith (1988), Ulla Taylor (2001), and Keisha Blain (2018), Nydia A. Swaby's[17] ongoing work, reveal that both Garvey wives maintained substantial communication with a range of activist men, often intervening politically in the shaping of Pan-Africanism as a political movement. Women who were part of the UNIA movement also did other kinds of Black nationalist organizing in the United States, Europe, Africa, and the Caribbean.

A new group of self-narratives is emerging now in which women define their leadership pathways from their own angles of vision. Such a work is Michelle Obama's *Becoming* (2018). In this highly popular text and the surrounding media attention and promotional activities, Michelle Obama described many of the formerly untold stories that went into the development and sustenance of their relationship but also what it took to become First Lady while maintaining her own political commitments and personal and familial responsibilities. Still, critiques like the one provided by Keeanga-Yahmahtta Taylor describe the text's basic framing as the assumption of an ideological position that accepts "personal striving" as a substitute for broader programs that ensure racial equality, as opposed to the model advanced by activists for Black freedom rights like Ella Baker, who wanted ordinary people to "connect the dots of their oppression to a broader unjust social order" (11).[18]

Looking across the African diaspora (before Michelle Obama), Beverly Anderson Manley in Jamaica had challenged that same paradigm of the "national wife" by boldly calling her book *The Manley Memoirs* (2008) in the same spirit of reclamation. It is clear that for her time in that role in the

1970's and in the Caribbean, Beverley Manley occupied a similar presence, regionally and not as internationally visible as Michelle Obama. *The Manley Memoirs* operates then in the context of a national wife writing herself into history. First, Anderson Manley makes a deliberate construction of a "self in resistance to colonial/patriarchal order." Additionally, she claims with good evidence that several policies in favor of women were positions she pushed forward, using her influence. Although she describes the personal—her child-hood and relationship and marriage to Michael Manley—Beverly says that hers is a story about survival, particularly because she had dared to leave "the Great Man." She cites Manley as saying to her: "You will never make it without me" (225), motivating words for strong women all over the world. Leaving (or staying with) the "Great Man," as other women who were married to world leaders reveal, is always fraught with drama as their lives are always led in full public view.

In this context, the life of Winnie Nomzamo Madikizela-Mandela and the end of that relationship are also instructive. Popular masculinist responses to Madikizela-Mandela's experience demonstrate that it is expected that a woman should wait interminably, faithfully, and in the background while her husband is absent, and if not, public censure of the woman can be harsh. On the other hand, if a woman consistently exercises leadership during that time, her leadership can be discounted or trivialized because of her gender. Women still end up being defined more by their sexuality than by their political contributions, unless their work is perceived and made meaningful through a transformative feminist analysis.

WINNIE MANDELA AS NELSON'S WIFE

Winnie Mandela, in her earliest public identification, became known to the world, in this exact naming, as the wife of Nelson Mandela. But in that context, she also became the primary activist in South Africa from 1962 through 1990, during the twenty-seven (27) years of Nelson's incarceration. We can raise here a hypothetical question: What would have happened, in terms of delivering more progressive gains to Black South Africans, if Winnie Madikizela-Mandela had become the president of South Africa instead of Nelson? We will never know: Winnie Nomzamo Madikizela-Mandela died in 2018. Perhaps state power controls, limits, or corrupts, and one is never able to achieve all that is expected when one takes formal political office. This is one possible reading of what happened when, as an elderly man, Nelson Mandela became president after years of incarceration and what happened to Winnie Mandela relatedly. Although the world, and particularly South Africans, rejoiced at his release, South Africans and the entire Black world were technically cheated anyway since Nelson was denied this leadership for 27 years by the white power structure of apartheid. He was then groomed for leadership in a way that would ensure a compliant process of transfer. In the interim, during his long incarceration, the popular public sentiment was expressed in Hugh Masekela's "Bring Back Nelson Mandela" (1987) which became a kind of resistance anthem, circulating globally and mythologizing his absence and the dream of a triumphant return "walking down the street with Winnie Mandela."[19] This we know in the end actually happened, in the walk out of Pollsmoor Prison, but the ideological distance of the walk would be truncated.

Still, for those twenty-seven years of Nelson's incarceration, while Winnie Mandela, as a woman, was denied the formal recognition that she deserved as the leader of the anti-apartheid movement in South Africa by the African National Congress, it was accorded to her by the activist youth. In this capacity, she functioned as an alternative, organic president and as a consistent critic of the failures of leadership evident in South Africa before the end of apartheid and in its immediate wake. Recognized as perhaps the most significant woman who exercised leadership at critical junctures in her country's history, perhaps staying outside of the official political structures, while experiencing the same pattern of hardship, denials, pain, and many trials and tribulations that many Black South Africans experienced, gave her a different relationship to the larger community of South Africans and world citizens. A certain poetic justice exists then in her being formally named "Mother of the Nation" after her death.

Still, a clear distinction is available as one examines the political leadership of Winnie Madikizela-Mandela who grew from being "Nelson's Wife" (i.e., *Winnie Mandela*), into being one of South Africa's major leaders *Nomzamo Madikizela-Mandela*. In her first auto-/biography, *Part of My Soul Went with Him*, she states that one of her names, Nomzano,[20] means in Xhosa "trial"— those who in their life will go through many trials. In her life, she also went through a variety of trials (in law courts and in the court of public opinion) by the apartheid state and during subsequent attempts to create a South Africa free of its past struggles. A novel by Njabulo Ndebele titled *The Cry of Winnie Mandela* (2003) develops this paradigm around the discourse of the "waiting" that is expected of women: "Why shouldn't a woman-in-waiting begin to make permanent plans without her man?" (8). The novel ends with an imagined confession against a false reconciliation: "Nelson, the truth is I could hold your hand in public and walk with you out of prison, but I could not face the close proximity of your body in the privacy of our bedroom . . . It has more to do with the reality that you and I no longer lived in the same space of feeling, imagination, and desire" (133).

To challenge the accepted paradigm for women, *The Cry of Winnie Mandela* presents an interesting range of meditations on the concept of "waiting." Using stories of several South African women who were forced under apartheid to wait for men some of whom had been disappeared by the state, the novel also presents implications for women who do *not* wait. Under apartheid, Ndebele indicates, "Many never returned home, leaving behind waiting women. Some women followed their men, others simply waited" (6). He presents a variety of women waiting, calling them "Penelope's daughters" (from the Greek mythology), and the novel ends with a fictional version of Winnie Nomzamo Mandela's voice:

> Departures. Waitings. Returns. How right you are! Three pillars of a South African woman's life. I too saw my Nelson go. Then I waited for him. Then he returned. Yes. This is the story of hundreds of thousands of other women. Of course, my Nelson departed in a flourish. I waited with a flourish. Do you remember his return? There I was with him on every television screen in the world as he walked out of Victor Verster prison with a flourish . . . The war ends when the heroine triumphantly walks into prison, the entire world watching, to fetch her man. Winnie does not wait. She goes and gets what she wants. And there she was, coming out of the prison with her pride [*sic*]: Her Nelson. Holding hands. Waving. (104–105)

In early narratives Winnie was a queenly supportive presence to her iconic activist husband Nelson, both presented as the royalty of South African activism: Her various visits to see her incarcerated husband and her own imprisonment are described using that language: "Winnie approached the prison like the queen of Africa" (16) and alternatively as the "mother of the people." In "A Tribute to Nomzamo Winnie Madikizela-Mandela," which appears in *Part of My Soul Went With Him,* Bishop Manas Muthelezi describes Winnie in these terms:

> It is common knowledge that she has been subjected to systematic harassment, banning detention and imprisonment, an ordeal which even very few charged and convicted common-law criminals have been made to endure . . . In a very deep sense she qualifies for the title of being "The Mother of Black People." I am not saying this simply because she happens to be the wife of her husband who is one of the imprisoned leaders of black people, but also because of what she has become in her own right. (19)

He describes her experience as "a magnifying glass through which even the most uninitiated eye is introduced to the obscure, twilight existence of the banned and detained. Through her the invisible were made visible" (21). In her own words though, Winnie also describes her life as symbolic but adds the counter-narrative that she is also what the society fears: "I am a living symbol of whatever is happening in the country. I am a living symbol of the white man's fear" (27).

We learn in *Part of My Soul Went With Him* (1985) and in subsequent biographies like Anne Marie du Preez Bezdrob's *Winnie Mandela. A Life* (2003) that Winnie began her professional life as the first Black medical social worker in the country. She lost this position after her activism led to her being arrested but also to her joining South African women's protests against passes that the apartheid state instituted to control the mobility of Africans in their own cities. The women's protests became one of the most visible activist movements against apartheid. Documentaries like "You Have Struck a Rock" (1981) capture this aspect of the South African freedom movement, the full language being "Now You Have Touched The Women You Have Struck a Rock: You Have Dislodged a Boulder; You Will Be Crushed." That theme of strength and resistance symbolized in the rock and boulder metaphors defined the movement.

Winnie Nomzamo began married life as a young woman of twenty-two, when Nelson was forty-one, then almost double her age. She indicates a consciousness of the almost twenty-year "generation gap" between them, but she credits being raised by her father without female gender limitations which gave her a certain confidence. Additionally, she learned from her community of their history and the need to "fight the common enemy" (48). Her encounter with Nelson, which led to their marriage, is defined in her words as a "political marriage," with his proposal described in these terms:

> One day, Nelson just pulled up on the side of the road and said "You know, there is a woman, a dressmaker, you must go and see her, she is going to make your wedding gown. How many bridesmaids would you like to have?" That's how I was told I was getting married to him. It was not put arrogantly, just something that was taken for granted. I was madly in love with him at that stage, and so was he with me in his own way. (59)

She also indicates that they never completed the full ceremony, as in getting married in both places, both her family's and his. He paid *lobola,* (often referred to as "brideprice") and they got married in her home community, but he had to dash back without completing the whole ceremony. She concludes: "The day he comes out of prison, we must complete the wedding" (61), she had reflected in *Part of My Soul Went with Him,* including an imaginative description of how this was supposed to happen. We know now that this completion of the wedding in traditional terms never happened, and that there was never time to have a full and complete marriage, or time to discuss future plans and a life together. Still, the nature of their political marriage was already one that she understood: "I had so little time to love him, and that love has survived all these years of separation. I'm not trying to suggest that he is an angel. Perhaps if I'd had time to know him better, I might have found a hell of a lot of faults, but I only had time to love him and to long for him all the time" (72). Thus, very early she sensed that they were having a different kind of unconventional marriage, not really aligning with the romantic notion that she herself had and from which she had to grow and the larger assumptions of marriage and faithfulness that society assumes as well. In a sense their marriage was never conventional. In her words: "I think I am the most unmarried married woman. I look forward to some day—even if it will mean just a day—enjoying some kind of married life with him. I would be thankful for even that" (85).

After Nelson's arrest, trial, and conviction to twenty-seven years of incarceration, Winnie also suffered substantially and consistently from the harassment of the state while she remained outside. She endured home invasions by police, intense surveillance, incarceration, solitary confinement, and torture. She was banished to the rural area of Brandfort, where she was put in the same "waiting" situation of other South African women whose men were working and living elsewhere as described by Ndebele above. In direct challenge of the apartheid state's willing her to non-existence, instead, in Brandfort, she used her social work training to create creches to help with the malnutrition that she could see in the children in the rural community. She also created Women's Cooperatives to establish sewing projects to aid women and their children and maintain their homes in the midst of great need. Winnie described rural life under apartheid, with women in Brandfort marred by alcoholism and living in desolation in shacks, experiencing malnutrition and starvation. She used her internal exile as a means to understand the conditions of apartheid under which the entire country lived in a "Letter to Mary Benson" (45). Thus, helping community needs became a central framing of her political activity, which included raising funds and providing social work help to detained people.

The South African State under apartheid, like the United States in its time of legal segregation, ending officially with *Brown v The Board of Education*, 1954, though not in practice, instituted several processes to curtail activism. In both cases, they would use the threat of communism as the red herring under which they could prosecute those targeted. Creating a Suppression of Communism Act became one of the modes the South African apartheid state used to target activists (37). The Suppression of Communism Act, 1950 (Act no. 44 of 1950), renamed the Internal Security Act in 1976, was legislation of the national government in apartheid South Africa which formally banned the Communist Party of South Africa and proscribed any party or group subscribing to communism (repealed 2 July 1982). It defined communism and its aims broadly to include any opposition to the government and empowered the government to detain any one it thought may further "communist" aims (June 1950). It prohibited any action "calculated to advocate, defend or encourage any of the objects of communism (Marxist socialism); any act which aims at any political, industrial, social or economic change in South Africa . . ."[21]

There is an uncanny similarity (which clearly show a kind of partnership or at least an influence) with an identically-named version passed in the United States in September 1950 which targeted activists like Claudia Jones who would be prosecuted and exiled for having communist ideas. The McCarran Internal Security Act of 1950 (64 Stat. 987), Public Law 81–131, also known as the Subversive Activities Control Act of 1950 or the McCarran Act, was enacted over President Harry Truman's veto. The McCarran-Walter Act of 1952, or the Immigration and Nationality Act of 1952, revised laws relating to immigration, naturalization, and nationality (June 1952).[22]

In Winnie's case, the punishment was internal exile to a rural community and a banning order that forbade community contact and involvement in the normal activities of daily life. For her part, Winnie was realistically aware of the implications and difficulties her situation presented. She said: "I have been banned since 1962 . . . This one is under the Internal Security Act. It hardly makes a difference. All the other years I was banned under the Suppression of Communism Act. This one is a little more stringent than the other. That's the only difference really. It's exactly the same document I got in 1962. But, as I say, a little more stringent as the years go by. It has conformed to the pattern of the racist regime, stripping us of each and every human right" (37).

Banning was a tool of the South African apartheid state as it sought to curtail the lives of Black South Africans, used effectively against Winnie Mandela. It was heightened further by a more stringent act, The Internal Security Act of 1976, by which the Minister of Justice decided which activities could be seen as furthering the objectives of communism or endangering the security of the state. Thus, Nelson Mandela's statement on April 13, 1964, at his Rivonia Trial engaged this issue directly challenging the state's attempted equivalence of Black activism with communism as was also done in the United States, while simultaneously suggesting that Communist parties "had a common goal, the removal of white supremacy" and "had been the only political group prepared to treat Africans as human beings and equals, the only group prepared to work with Africans in their struggle to attain political rights and a stake in society. And in the international field [he added], communist countries have always come to our aid . . . [and they] often seem more sympathetic to our plight than some of the Western powers" (78–79).

During his incarceration though and having to create a political life on her own, Winnie gradually moved from being Nelson's wife to her own self as a Black woman leader with national and international visibility. We learn that this is reciprocated as the women composed songs to her once she joined the Women's Movement and became active. She describes her leadership positions in these words:

> I held the same position in the Women's Federation of South African Women as I had in the ANC Women's League. I was chairlady of our branch and I belonged to the provincial executive and the national executive. In 1958 we had been involved in organizing the anti-pass demonstrations under the leadership of Lilian Ngoyi. I among thousands of women were arrested throughout the country. I was pregnant at the time and Albertina Sisulu saved my first baby. She went out of her way in prison to look after me. (66–67)

However, it is in the period documented in the "Being Alone" chapter of *Part of My Soul Went with Him* that she becomes fully committed to South Africa's struggle and able to articulate herself outside of male dominance. She stayed outside of Nelson's attempt to dominate her, even while he was incarcerated, as is common for other women in similar situations, whatever the crime or reason for which the man is incarcerated. She admits that Nelson told her: "You will be vilified, you must expect that you will be told that you are responsible for my being in prison. You are young and life without a husband is full of all kinds of insults. I expect you to live up to my expectation" (83). Another example is when Winnie received Nelson's letter dated 15.4.76, in which he laments not being able to do as much as he should have when she was pregnant, and he wonders "what it'll be like when I return." He applauds her for going back to UNISA (University of South Africa) but warns her not to go to the public library in the evenings, for safety reasons of course, but still: "If on my return I found you away from home I'd seek you out and report to you first for that honour is yours, and yours alone" (94). Here is a mixture of distant love and desire, but nevertheless, control and the construction of Winnie as Nelson's wife, a location away from which we see she was clearly traveling.

Still, a sense of self presentation also accompanied a growing political awareness. *Part of My Soul Went with Him* thus begins by presenting a particularly constructed Winnie Mandela still in the space of a romantic "yearning" for a husband and marriage that would never be ever realized.

In a prior discussion of precisely this point, "Collaboration and the Ordering Imperative in Life Story Production,"[23] I describe this work as a "multi-authored text which was simultaneously the people's story of their collective surge to freedom, *and* the woman's (Winnie's) story of struggle over subordination." It was a "self" constructed by and contained with a larger struggle, as "synonymous with struggle." The narrative is framed by an editorial note and introduction, a tribute by Bishop Buthelezi, president of the South African Council of Churches and closes with letters from Nelson to Winnie and finally the South African Freedom Charter, copies of banning orders, petitions, and conditions under which she could visit her husband (8–9).

In many ways, *Part of My Soul Went with Him* reflects the construction of Winnie first as political subject as Nelson's wife and then her movement away from this subordinate identity. In the chapter where she describes being incarcerated and tortured, "No Human Being Can Go on Taking These Humiliations without Reaction. In Prison," we see another more mature version is evolving, a *self* that she made even more distinct in subsequent texts, speeches, and documentaries about her life, up until her passing in 2018. In her words:

> In the earlier years I was just a carbon copy of Nelson. I was no individual. If I said something, it was "Nelson's wife" who said so. When he was no longer in the picture . . . , the public began to say I wasn't just a carbon copy as such; I had ideas and views of my own. I had my own commitment and I wasn't just a political ornament. (83)

LEADERSHIP: FROM PRISONER NUMBER 1323/69 TO RADICALIZATION

In her 2006 speech titled "Being a Black Woman in the World," delivered in Chicago, Illinois, at the *V103's Expo for Today's Black Woman*, we see Winnie Madikizela-Mandela's ideological orientation, shaped by the Black Consciousness movement with a women's rights component and a clear understanding that what Black women faced in terms of discrimination was "multi-pronged, multi-sectoral and transgenerational." Thus, for her:

> Black women are discriminated by the white supremacy; they have to contend with male prejudice fed by patriarchal notions, they suffer abuse from white women who are also beneficiaries of white supremacy. At the same time, they are expected to form alliances with these women to defeat male privilege. They are expected to be in solidarity with their male folks to fight racial oppression. In this regard they have little choice. They cannot sit on the sideline and watch the Black male being reduced to an endangered species. After all, these men are the fathers of their children, the lovers, and their sons. In short, there is no other species that understand oppression as Black women do.
> By inducing pride and dignity in Black people, the Black Consciousness Movement demanded that Black people become their own liberators, thus expediting the subjective prerequisite for liberation. An important aspect of the Black

Consciousness Movement was its location of the possibility of change within the Black community. This lesson applies to Black women wherever they are.

But this was not just a popular Black feminist position acquired only in that context for an earlier assertion of this point had already appeared in *Part of My Soul Went With Him* as follows:

> Looking at our struggle in this country, the black woman has had to struggle a great deal, not only from a political angle. One has had to fight the male domination in a much more complex sense. We have the cultural clash where a black woman must emerge as a politician against the traditional background of a woman's place being at home! Of course, most cultures are like that. But with us it's not only pronounced by law. We are permanent minors by law. So, for a woman to emerge as an individual, as a politician in this context, is not very easy. (83–84)

Winnie Nomzamo Madikizela-Mandela was made aware very early in her various confrontations with the South African machinery about the process of the apartheid State's using the press to malign her. The position of the South African police machinery was a deliberate decision to destroy her if not physically then iconoclastically. This is also one of the tactics used by intelligence agencies such as COINTELPRO (The Counterintelligence Program) in the United States to create a groundswell of resentment and negative public opinion against a particular activist person or movement.

In *Part of My Soul Went with Him*, Winnie had anticipated and described the methods that the apartheid state used in creating her as sexually promiscuous in order to create a rift and provoke jealousy in her incarcerated husband Nelson and to besmirch and assault her character in national and world public opinion. Thus, she states: "If you read the court records of the time, you can see the systematic slandering of my name by the government: those affairs with just about everybody with whom I had contacts" (84). She refers to the use of the "gutter press" to malign her with stories about relationships with various men: "One such reporter—Gumbi was his name –would write an article in such a way that it becomes suggestive. Invariably, that type of article will find its way under the door of my husband's cell in prison . . . " (84). Meanwhile, after being subjected to actual banishment to a remote area, banning in order to reduce her contacts with community, she was eventually condemned to serve a period of solitary confinement (86) which she documents in *491 Days: Prisoner Number 1323/69* (2013) as the experience that fully radicalized her.

In several documentaries, such as the most recent *"Winnie"* by Pascale Lamache (2018), Winnie Madikizela-Mandela indicates that, after the long period of solitary confinement and torture that she was subjected to from

May 12, 1969, to September 14, 1970, she had become radicalized to execute self-defense against all who would intrude on her personal sanctity and that of the struggle for freedom. While she had discovered very early in her marriage that she had lost her identity and became Nelson's wife,[24] her personal struggle was also to reclaim her own identity as a woman and now as an activist. She recognized that Black women must fight both the larger political situation as well as "male domination in a much more complex sense" (83).

This desire to remain untamed by both Nelson (who had actually said that she needed a great deal of taming) (*POMS*, 88) and the larger political system before and after the ending of apartheid, by both the apartheid power structure and the Black male leadership of the African National Congress, however, ended up with Winnie's being respected and valorized by the larger South African Black community. That community began to see her as a political leader. Winnie described her 491 days of solitary confinement when she was charged, along with twenty-one others, under the Suppression of Communism Act as a period when in her words: "I got more liberated in prison" (*POMS* 105). She was described by fellow prisoner in this way: "Independent of her husband—she's a leader in herself" (*POMS*, 106).

In a generational shift from Nelson, the young people influenced by the Black Consciousness Movement according to Motlana, "related very well to Winnie Mandela; they never had problems accepting Winnie's leadership" (*POMS,* 115). In the 1976 Soweto Uprising, Winnie's leadership was evident in her making speeches to the youth, leading marches, and even serving as a pallbearer in one of the funerals. In the chapter titled "We Couldn't Stop Our Children. The Soweto Uprising, 1976," she describes her anger but clearly also her joy in seeing a new generation of South Africans unwilling to accept the brutalities of apartheid. While the state wanted to define the adults as directing the youth movement, as usual, it is the youth themselves who defined how things unfolded. Thus, was revealed " . . . her ability to bridge the gap between the youth and the adults and the different ideological factions" (*POMS*, 115).

Just as Nelson did with his incarcerated peers in Robben Island, in 1976 incarcerated in the Women's Prison in Johannesburg, Winnie also stood up for the rights of the other incarcerated women to get basic personal necessities. Sally Motlanta, who was detained with her, described Winnie's leadership in this way:

> To me a leader of that nature is a great leader. She would listen even to the smallest of us, and act. If you needed help in a difficult political situation, she knew which lawyers to go to and she would actually drive you there. Or if you got into trouble with the Pass Laws, anything—she wouldn't say, how much is it going to cost me to go to town to help this woman. She would jump into her car and

take you to a person who could give immediate help. I have worked with many leaders. Some are very self-assertive. But that girl was motherly, down to earth. To the young, to the old, she was the same. (117)

Winnie's *491 Days. Prisoner Number 1323/69* (2013), is a journal that documents the nature of that radicalizing experience. During incarceration, she experienced consistent interrogation and torture that produced dizzy spells and blackouts. Her secret journal, which she shared with her lawyer, became the material for this second book. She describes the nature of the cell in which she was incarcerated and the experiences of solitary confinement, providing day-by-day experiences of imprisonment: food poisoning, aloneness under confinement, and above all the permanent effects on her health. Several letters from Nelson to Winnie are included, all detailing that during this time Mandela was kept informed of and knew of the various conditions of his wife's situation, including the need for legal guardianship of their children, protection by security, and managing their home in his absence. An interesting letter from her on their twelfth anniversary recounts the details of their wedding and being forced to be on her own:

> We were hardly a year together when history deprived me of you. I was forced to mature on my own. Your formidable shadow which eclipsed me left me naked and exposed to the bitter world of a young "political widow." I knew there was a crown of thorns for me but I also knew I said, "I Do" for better or worse. In marrying you I was marrying the struggle of my people. (182)

Biographies of Winnie Nomzamo Madikizela's life are beginning to appear, generally detailing the well-known history, but often with the "Things Went Horribly Wrong" logic that came out of the Truth and Reconciliation hearings and President Mbeki's public slight, described in Bezdrob's *Winnie Mandela. A Life* (2003). In the end, we benefit from the resolution of a life in celebratory ceremonies which document how the community felt about her and honored her as "Mother of the Nation" and the numerous articles after her passing which indicate posthumously her significance to what became the country of South Africa. We can say as well that she believed in the realization of the ANC's Freedom Charter much of which has not been realized and her assumption that in many ways Nelson came out of prison compromised in ways that she could never accept. Additionally, she felt that if one spent "a quarter of your life in prison and still be prepared for the dialogue with your jailers that you called for twenty years ago, before they locked you up? The leadership would have to be involved in an entirely new kind of political thinking; perhaps a completely new basis for dialogue and negotiation"

(*POMS*, 127–128). Thus, in the end, Nelson Mandela's choice, as it was at the start, was always for the country of South Africa and not Winnie.

For this writer, the impasse between Winnie and Nelson to separate was ideological, much more than it was personal. She had imagined a socialist state: "It will be a socialist state—there is no other way of sorting out our starvation problems, the discrepancy between the population groups, the haves and the have-nots. Everyone will have a fair share of the wealth of this country" (*POMS,* 123). Basically, she offered a more socialist vision for South Africa than Nelson had by the time he left prison and in his succeeding administration of the state as its president.

Much of the malignment of Winnie was deliberate and constructed, as indicated by Vic Mc Pherson, director of STRATHCOM (Covert Strategic Communications) of South Africa's operations, who indicated that he had forty (40) journalists working to create negative stories about her and to strategically place them in papers in South Africa and around the world. He also indicated a number of Black agents who infiltrated the ANC and definitely her security service identified as the Mandela Football Club. Under President Botha, Operation Rumulus was put in place to directly target and malign Winnie Madikizela-Mandela.

As they contemplated the transition, we learn from the Head of National Intelligence that initially the path of the apartheid government was to make her into a kind of Jackie Kennedy first lady to accompany a Nelson presidency but since that in the end was not clearly Winnie's sense of herself, the approach shifted to malignment. Mandela was advised that, to become the leader of South Africa, he would have to separate himself from her. At the same time, a parallel plan was put in place to delegitimize her as a public icon via the charges of her involvement in the killing of Stompie Seipei by Jerry Richardson who was a registered informant for the Security Branch, placed in the Mandela Football Club and who killed Stompie to protect his identity. According to Niel Barnard, Head of National Intelligence, they told him what to say upon release.

It is also significant in considering this aspect of her leadership to see Winnie as a soldier for the liberation of her people as was Harriet Tubman identified in the United States. Throughout the 1980's she was identified as the most senior commander of the Mkhota wa Sizwe, the military wing of the ANC, with the highest authority in the 1980's of the guerrilla arm working both inside and outside of South Africa under the leadership of Chris Hani, who would be assassinated in 1993. Engaged also in guerilla activities for the resistance to apartheid, he would eventually be murdered as was Steve Biko ahead of him. This, combined with the recognition by the government that she had the power to mobilize large crowds of people rendered her a more direct target for government control than for Nelson. Her Black Power fist sign as she left the prison with Mandela at his release symbolically marked the difference. He would follow her in this signal only after she had posed it first. His attempt to see the world through her glasses becomes a failure.

THE POLITICS OF MEDIA COVERAGE OF WINNIE MADIKIZELA-MANDELA

When Winnie Madikizela-Mandela died on April 2, 2018, the post-apartheid South Africa she had served and helped usher into being celebrated her with ten days of mourning and a full state funeral in which she was described by South Africans as one of their most significant leaders. Here is one documented example of this posthumous recognition: "She was one of the most profound leaders of the ANC," said fifty-three-year-old mourner Brian Magqaza. "She fought from beginning to the end. Go well, Mama."[25]

One of my plans was to secure an interview with Winnie Mandela, and I approached this possibility from several angles. During one trip to South Africa, I met with a businessman who was a son-in-law and brought a letter indicating my interest, along with copies of all my books, so that she could see who I was and the kind of work I did. I left wondering if anything was delivered to her as I remember he kept asking me if I did not want to interview Graça Machel as well. Then, a few years later, a fortuitous meeting with Hugh Masekela in Trinidad provided me with direct contacts to her and the beginnings of a communication pattern leading to such a possibility. When I arrived in South Africa for an African Literature conference in 2015, during which time I hoped to get an interview, I was taken to her house by a poet from Soweto, Zanele Ndlovu (Novulakuvaliwe Za), a community member of her neighborhood in Soweto, who had direct contact with Mama Winnie, as she was referred to affectionately in Soweto. We went to the house and rang the bell and a very professional assistant came outside to tell us that Mama Winnie was still in the period of obligatory mourning for the recently departed Nelson. Still, she was happy to give me details so that I could arrange a time to come back and spend time talking with her. Sadly, work intervened and I delayed arranging a return trip to South Africa, so this interview never materialized. When I learned sadly of her passing, saddened at a missed opportunity and her loss, I organized a forum in her honor at Cornell University's Africana Studies and Research Center that included the showing of the film "Winnie" and a panel discussion with faculty members, students, and community.

New media assessments such as "Five Ways Winnie Madikizela-Mandela Influenced the Lives of Women in South Africa" (April 6, 2018) now identify her role in influencing South African women, from aesthetic style and self-presentation to political advances, pushing against the boundaries meant to contain women's advancement:

> Winnie Madikizela-Mandela's fight was the fight of every woman raised in a sexist society . . . In a society that seems to demand that women play a subservient role in all aspects of life, Winnie Madikizela-Mandela refused to be a passive bystander, patiently waiting for her husband's release from prison. Instead of sinking into the shadows, she held the spotlight and became a living, breathing, visible symbol of the struggle for justice. We are everything we are because she was not afraid to be all that she was.[26]

We have already seen that creating negative media coverage about Winnie Mandela was a fundamental strategy of the South African government's STRATHCOM, which maintained her as a critical person against whom they needed to build bad press, besides banning, exile, detention, incarceration, and a whole host of other destabilizing tactics. For this reason, I view as suspicious all media coverage that paint/ed her in a negative light.

One such assessment is "We Are What We Pretend to Be: The Cautionary Tale of Reading Winnie Mandela as a Rhetorical Widow" examines what happened when the press constructed Winnie Mandela's identity as Nelson Mandela's "widow" by studying her portrayal in the US media, using the frame of the "rhetorical widow" or the wife who is able to speak on behalf of the husband who is not present (70). Interestingly this study found that throughout the 1980's she was represented in US popular journals and magazines in both African American media and the general public instruments as "mother of the nation" and as a "rhetorical widow" even to the point of being named in a poll of 250 international newspaper editors as fourth in popularity in 1987, ahead of Queen Elizabeth II (75). This would change, however when in 1989 she was implicated in the murder of Stompie Seipei by her security team, the Mandela Football Club.[27] This would be seen as a fall from grace and accompanied by a series of negative constructions. As indicated earlier much of the publicity about her and around this issue was constructed by STRATHCOM, which had at its disposal the over forty journalists who were willing to place negative stories about her and engage in a negative publicity campaign to damage her reputation. This activity would be heightened when Nelson was released once the decision was made to exclude her from the first lady status.

In my view, US and international media constructions from dominant culture are less valuable in getting the full representation, particularly from someone who the majority Black population of South Africa and the African Diaspora still revered for having served them for twenty-seven years during the incarceration of Nelson Mandela. It is significant still then to carefully examine accounts like Sheila Meintjes which created in its titling the contradictory questions: "Winnie Madikizela Mandela: Tragic Figure? Populist Tribune? Township Tough?" in *Southern Africa Report* (August 1998), eight years after Nelson's release, the end of their marriage, and her re-immersion into South African political life. Meintjes begins by claiming from the outset that: "Not even her divorce from Mandela affected her popularity and support. Although she did not win nomination to the Deputy Presidency of the ANC in December, 1997, she remain[ed] President of the ANC Women's League, a member of the ANC National Executive Committee and the ANC Member of Parliament" (14). The question which drives her article then was "How are we to understand her unique power and position?" (14). Perhaps we can consider this helpful question which charts how she "became a very skilled political actor, this taking her well beyond the subsidiary role normally accorded women within the nationalist framework. Her political independence and leadership developed gradually in different contexts" (14).

Putting Winnie Madikizela-Mandela within the context of studying Black women and political leadership in the African decolonization and pre-independence period, this becomes a central and important framing, also applicable in other contexts particularly men who exercised leadership in a similar timeframe.[28] Clearly Winnie Nomzano Midikizela-Mandela advanced a much more militant position than the conservative ANC and garnered a reputation as one who would mobilize, represent and defend her community after the Soweto Uprisings in 1976, developing a support for and rapport with the younger generation of South Africans and their aspirations for freedom, more aligned with Black Consciousness politics of Steve Biko and left politics of Chris Hani, both of whom were murdered by agents of the state.

Shireen Hassim's "A Life of Refusal. Winnie Madikizela-Mandela and Violence in South Africa" focused on the fact that Winnie actually had become a soldier in the fight against apartheid. As early as the late 1960's "she developed an underground network, acting as a satellite cell of Umkhonto we Sizwe (MK) in Soweto" which was the armed resistance arm of the ANC during the period of its male leadership's long incarceration. So, on the one hand we have the state and global construction of her as "mother of the nation" and her actual practice of a kind of "radical motherhood" in defending the youth of South Africa. Hassim is at pains to understand this identity as a soldier in a liberation movement that was Winnie with her "mother of the nation" framing (73) creating therefore a false opposition between these two identities as though it were not possible to be both. Still, she finds that question of leadership relevant as in reality she admits to a particular failing in the male dominated ANC itself:

the centrality of her identity as a leader of MK and her sense of the margin-alization of women from powerful decision-making structures of the political movement. Accorded a secondary role as the wife of Nelson, her agency as a committed cadre was always called into question. She had no status within the leadership collective until her husband was released from prison and under his direction, she was given positions in both the African National Congress and the new government. (75)

Brenna Munro's "Nelson, Winnie and the Politics of Gender" analyzes their relationship within the context of the national "family" drama but reads Winnie as a "tragic figure: the mother" of the struggle who fell from grace (92) but significantly reads them as enacting a "compassionate heterosexual marriage that signified as both respectable and modern" (94). Munro sees her though as becoming a leader in her own right after being her hus-band's spokesperson.

Franz Fanon in "On Violence" in *The Wretched of the Earth* describes South African apartheid as an extreme form of colonization and offers that "decolonization is always a violent event" (1) and goes on to provide descrip-tions of the nature of state violence and an understanding of the particular positioning of those struggling against this extreme form of violence, which, in his view, "governed the ordering of the colonial world" (5). In a state that was the most violent in its period, the ones who defended themselves from this violence cannot ever have an equivalent status in terms of any actions that fought back against the state's destruction. In every discussion of this issue, Winnie Madikizela-Mandela has been judged retroactively, particularly by white journalists and biographers, by a standard of morality that was not in place at any level during apartheid, when she was in reality operating by the standards of self-defense during war, which was the anti-apartheid struggle against state violence.

New assessments by South African writers of another generation provide different understandings. Sisonke Msimang, *The Resurrection of Winnie Mandela* (2018) offers an assessment more typical of younger South African women. She argues in an essay titled "Winnie Mandela and the Archive: Reflections on Feminist Biography"[29] that "[B]ecause sexism is so central to how the world is interpreted, the 'facts' about Winnie Mandela's life and times were often misrepresented or weaponized against her. I saw myself as part of a movement of people who wanted to ensure that Winnie Mandela could be understood on feminist terms."

In the process of writing her study of Winnie Mandela, Msimang focuses on the deep love and desire they had for each other, which in the end was destroyed by the machinations of what they went through under apartheid. In her words, as Nelson Mandela was rising after his release and calculating his role as a man of state, Winnie Mandela was exploding, and refusing to compromise the values for which she had fought throughout his incarceration. Msimang describes Winnie as combative in a way that inspired the larger South African population during Mandela's absence, which she describes as ironically in a protected bubble as the state was clear that it did not want to make him a martyr. By contrast, Winnie experienced the full onslaught of the state's torture machine. Msimang works well the contradictions in her reception and assessment in the context of freedom fighters use of violence to fight back against the South African state. All the language that Winnie had expressed in terms of South African radicalism was also indicated as part of the popular language of resistance. Yet, Winnie gets judged more harshly in Msimang's eyes largely because of who she was, the wife who is supposed to *behave* even in a context in which the state denied that same ability to be the wife of their leading freedom fighter; "the way the world wants to understand women's actions vs. men's actions."[30] For her, the redemption of Winnie must include the entire breadth of her life, being consistent about how we view activists of all genders. Additionally, her assessment insists that we continually do self-questioning about how we often do not see and respect Black pain and Black humanity. Thus, for these reasons, she tells the story as a feminist biographer in two voices—the straight authoritative biographer's voice and the conversational voice—as she engages Winnie Mandela's personal story.

At the time of her passing, a review by Lucille Davie titled "Winnie's Pain and Torture in Prison," which described what became the book *491 Days* (April 8, 2018), details that "from the moment of her marriage to Mandela in 1958, Madikizela-Mandela was doomed to decades of harassment, imprisonment and torture at the hands of the apartheid security police. It started in 1958, when she was detained for her participation in a women's anti-pass campaign" (3).

We learn in *491 Days* that at one point she even contemplated suicide after days of torture and illness from the ills of both solitary confinement, awful food, and extended days of brutal torture. The text ends with her statement: "Solitary confinement was designed to kill you so slowly that you were long dead before you died. By the time you died, you were nobody. You had no soul anymore and a body without a soul is a corpse anyway. It is unbelievable that you survived all of that" (234). And Winnie's assessment of the contrast that the government created is telling:

When I was in detention for all those months, my two children nearly died. When I came out, they were so lean; they had had such a hard time. They were covered with sores, malnutrition sores. And they wonder why I am like I am. And they have the nerve to say: "Oh Madiba is such a peaceful person, you know. We wonder how he had such a wife who is so violent." The leadership on

Robben Island was never touched; the leadership on Robben Island had no idea what it was like to engage the enemy physically. The leadership was removed and cushioned behind prison walls . . . We were the foot soldiers. We were their cannon fodder and it was us who were used as their political barometer each time the wanted to find out how the country was going to react . . . Tata could not comprehend how I had become so violent in the eyes of the police. They knew I was involved with the military wing of the ANC and they knew I was a leader of the struggle underground. (234–235)

THE ALTERNATIVE IM/POSSIBLE PRESIDENCY

This chapter deliberately reads Winnie Nomzamo Madikizela-Mandela as an alternative president, a role she never acquired as a formal political office but one which she absolutely held in the larger Black population's eyes. My argument is that for the twenty-seven years of Nelson's incarceration, Winnie actually held the leadership role in what was described as a "government in exile" in Black South Africa. Upon Nelson's release as a white-haired old man who "stood for a negotiated peace, for forgiveness and reconciliation" in Brenna Munro's terms not usually coded as masculine (98), one can assume from this reading that it is Winnie who gets coded as masculine and the enemy of the state and therefore the one against whom continuing actions would be waged. This is in keeping with the ways that Black women historically in other racial contexts are gendered male, as in the United States examples of Sojourner Truth, who is denied the given values of womanhood, a position captured well in Hortense Spillers's (1987) "Mama's Baby, Papa's Maybe: An American Grammar Book." Desiree Lewis concurs in seeing her as a "symbol of contradiction, of subversion, of disrespect, of impatience, an anarchic symbol, a symbol that appeals to those who have nothing at stake in the available status quo" (2003). The im/possible presidency Winnie Madikizela-Mandela presents still offers an alternative view of the possibility of a more equitable South Africa for Black people and definitely for Black women. For African feminist Patricia McFadden, the assessment of Winnie Mandela should never align itself with demeaning the beauty and strength of this woman.[31] I absolutely concur, seeing this stance of demeaning her contribution as doing the continued work of the former apartheid machinery.

My reading of Nomzamo Madikizela-Mandela as an "alternative president" offers an imaginative view of a different South Africa under a woman's leadership that would have affected the care of the nation in ways that so far have not happened. In the end, by not accepting or acquiring "first lady status" Winnie in many ways was removed from the intent of such a role, that of the "tamed" (with all its animal connotations) and supportive wife.[32]

Instead, Nomzamo Madikizela-Mandela continues to occupy a more distinct alternative and independent leadership position in the history of South Africa.

NOTES

1. This chapter identifies her full name but will use her preferred original name including her first name Nomzamo most of the time.

2. See my "Finding Some Space: South African Women Writers." *A Current Bibliography of African Affairs* 19:1 (1986–1987), 31–45. [Rpt. in *Ufahamu: Journal of the African Activists Association* 14:2 (1986): 121–136.] I met Kuzwayo at one of the African Literature Conferences when she was a resident in the University of Iowa International Writers program which hosted a number of writers from the continent every year. Gloria Joseph has written about SISA in an unpublished essay in this writer's possession titled "Race, Class, Gender and Revolution."

3. "Race, Class, Gender and Revolution" (unpublished paper shared by author).

4. https://www.brandsouthafrica.com/governance/developmentnews/south-africa-s-women-in-politics Accessed 6/25/2020.

5. https://www.sahistory.org.za/article/womens-charter which in its preamble says: "We, the women of South Africa, wives and mothers, working women and housewives, African, Indians, European and Coloured, hereby declare our aim of striving for the removal of all laws, regulations, conventions and customs that discriminate against us as women, and that deprive us in any way of our inherent right to the advantages, responsibilities and opportunities that society offers to any one section of the population." Accessed 6/25/2020

6. Antonio Gramsci, *Selections from the Prison Notebooks* (New York: International Publishers, 1971), p. 10 which describes the organic intellectual leader.

7. See Carole Boyce Davies, "Private Lives and Public Spaces: Autobiography and the African Woman Writer," *Crisscrossing Boundaries* by Ngate, Harrow and Zimra (Three Continents Press, Washington, D.C., 1990): 109–127.

8. https://youtu.be/fCXgmS7ofVk has a discussion with the filmmaker, indicating details about the state-sanctioned propaganda program by STRATHCOM by PW Botha in which the tarnishing of her reputation became the focus.

9. These are the same tactics used against Black activists in the United States, such as in the creation of COINTELPRO. Many details are now available via the FOIPA release of FBI files on activists throughout US history. Many major state intelligence units operate similarly.

10. https://www.sahistory.org.za/article/freedom-charter

11. See Sisonke Msimang's The Resurrection of Winnie Mandela, 2018.

12. https://www.theguardian.com/world/2021/nov/29/xiomara-castro-declares-victory-in-honduras-presidential-election. Since this is unfolding in the present (November, 29, 2021, the outcomes will be revealed after this work is published. Manuel Zelaya the husband was removed in a US-backed coup which sent him into exile and Honduras into turmoil as is usual.

13. https://originalpeople.org/charlene-mitchell-first-black-woman-to-run-for-president-of-the-united-states/

14. http://woman.ng/2018/04/chimamanda-ngozi-adichie-asks-hillary-clinton-why-the-first-word-that-describes-her-on-twitter-is-

15. https:///www.huffpost.com/entry/michelle-obama-

16. See entire volume of *Feminist Africa* on the theme of Panafricanism and Feminism Issue 19 (2014).

17. See her "A Living Archive for Amy Ashwood Garvey [2010–2020]" on https://www.nydiaswaby.com

18. *Boston Review*, March 13, 2019.

19. Hugh Masekela - Bring Him Back Home (Nelson Mandela) from Paul Simon's "Graceland - The African Concert" (Zimbabwe, 1987).

20. The name "Winnie," she indicates, is a constant reminder of our oppression (50).

21. Act cited in *Part of My Soul Went With Him*, 37

22. See Carole Boyce Davies, *Left of Karl Marx* (2008), for discussion.

23. Chapter 1 of *De/Colonizing the Subject* (1992).

24. https://www.pbs.org/independentlens/videos/winnie-losing-identity-mandelas-wife-clip/ see full film on https://www.pbs.org/independentlens/videos/winnie/

25. *Al-Jazeera*, April 14, 2018, "South Africa's Winnie Madikizela-mandela laid to rest" describes her in these terms: "Winnie Madikizela-mandela, who died in Johannesburg on April 2 after a long illness, has been celebrated for helping keep Nelson Mandela's dream of a non-racial South Africa alive while he was behind bars for 27 years."

26. https://www.africanimpact.com/winnie-mandela-blog/

27. The facts are that Jerry Richardson, who was the person who killed Stompie, was a South African agent who infiltrated the Mandela Football Club and confessed that he killed Stompie to protect this information from coming out. Attempts to implicate Winnie Mandela in the Stompie execution were all part of a larger South African state construction aimed also at destroying her in the public eye. Winnie knew this and so would not admit to any of that participation in wrongdoing. Desmond Tutu wanted to impose a particular Christian morality in a time of Apartheid's consistent attack on her, which he would have known about.

28. See for example the advanced role of women in the independence of Guinea and Guinea Bissau in "The Liberation Stories of Guinea Bissau" by Ricci Shryock in Africa is a Country blog, https://africasacountry.com/2021/02/the-untold-liberation-stories-of-guinea-bissau?fbclid=IwAR10Sl-WsnT0hfLoAeXmRltL1CViWgheD-J2d3vrNtrmnAbZLZKdHSVHHX14 (Accessed 2/8/2021)

29. In Desiree Lewis and Gabeba Baderoon, eds. *Surfacing. On Being Black and Feminist in South Africa*. Johannesburg: Wits University Press, 2021: 15–27.

30. https://video.search.yahoo.com/yhs/search?fr=yhs-iba-syn&hsimp=yhs-syn&hspart=iba&p=The+REsurrection+of+Winnie+Mandela#id=1&vid=175620022dc8a05d01aeb5175b95f692&action=click

31. "The Memory And Unmemory Of Women In Liberation Struggles." The Centre For Women and Gender Studies (CWGS), Nelson Mandela University, South Africa. Webinar October 23, 2020.

32. In 1998, Nelson Mandela married Graça Machel, the widow of Samora Machel of Mozambique, a woman already prepared to assume the "first lady experience."

Chapter 4

"Yes. We Want the Power!"

Writing African Women's Political Leadership with Ellen Johnson Sirleaf and Wangari Maathai

"Woman's Place in African Culture" is the outline of a study of the Black Woman historically, proposed by Amy Ashwood Garvey, the first wife of Marcus Garvey and co-founder of the Universal Negro Improvement Association.[1] It is significant that Amy Ashwood Garvey visited physically and spent time in Africa, and had traced her family to Juaben, Ghana. The extent of the proposed project revealed that Amy Ashwood saw an important gap in the knowledge of the Black Woman that necessitated substantial scholarly attention. Written as a product of Amy Ashwood Garvey's many visits to Liberia, the project was informed by her assumptions and available knowledge at the time about African women, as seen by a woman of African descent from the African Diaspora who viewed this topic from a Pan-African lens. Relevant as well is that it included "The African woman" within a larger construct of "The Black Woman" as title of the document suggesting that it meant to engage additional aspects of the Black woman's experience globally, starting with Africa.

As it relates to this work's consideration of African women in leadership historically, many of the knowledge gaps Amy Ashwood identified then have already been filled by ongoing research on women in African history. However, what was operative during the time of her African experience in the years leading up to the formal ending of European colonialism met the classic "neglect" thesis of Claudia Jones. Contemporary scholarship includes gendered re-readings of African women's history which reconstitute the historical place of African women in leadership.

Amy Ashwood Garvey, who identified herself as a feminist, was conscious of the role of Black women's leadership witnessing, in the 1930's to 1950's, the colonially driven subordinations of women in the waning moments of British colonialism and a new African male supremacy in its ascendance. Thus, several of her themes include terms such as "self-realization" and "free choice." Significantly Amy Ashwood Garvey[2] is known as voicing in 1944 "Women of the World Must Unite"[3] which can be seen as a feminist slogan that made it into the present as "Women of the World Unite." Additionally she is identified as speaking in 1953 during her Caribbean lecture tour to a group of Pan-African women in San Juan, Trinidad, on the topic "Women as Leaders of World Thought." I include a portion of Amy Ashwood Garvey's proposed research plan at the start of this discussion as several identified topics continue to be addressed in current scholarship and activism of African women. The section that pertains to leadership is relevantly cited here:

THE BLACK WOMAN[4]

I. WOMAN'S PLACE IN AFRICAN CULTURE
   A. What are some of the present needs of the African woman?
      1. Leaders to relieve them from the prevailing male domination
      2. Need for a new concept of herself as a human being equal to man
      3. Right to make a free choice of mate
      4. Right to be the only wife of one husband
      5. Right to live in a unit family without dictation from elders
      6. Political rights equal to those of men

There is a certain timelessness of key items in this outline on issues such as leadership, education, political rights, marriage, self-realization, business, sexuality and initiation rites. Many have become rights and principles encoded in the Protocol on the Rights of African of Women in Africa, 2003.[5] For example, Article 9 of the Protocol, the "Right to Participation in the Political and Decision-Making Process" says:

1. States Parties shall take specific positive action to promote participative governance and the equal participation of women in the political life of their countries through affirmative action, enabling national legislation and other measures to ensure that:
   a. women participate without any discrimination in all elections;
   b. women are represented equally at all levels with men in all electoral processes;
   c. women are equal partners with men at all levels of development and implementation of State policies and development programmes.

2. States Parties shall ensure increased and effective representation and participation of women at all levels of decision-making.

We note relatedly that Article 9:1(b) the need for national legislation to ensure that—"women are represented equally at all levels with men in all electoral processes"—is at the core of all discussions of women's rights to political leadership and central to African feminist activism. Amy Ashwood Garvey, who died in 1969, would have drafted and written her outline during the 1950's when she traveled and spent time in Liberia. Two other items are about leadership: B (3) indicates "Lack of feminine leaders to define problem and establish goals" is indicated as one of the barriers to full liberation, and D (1) is about challenging male assumptions about leadership: "Leaders to relieve them from the prevailing male domination."

AFRICAN WOMEN AS LEADERS HISTORICALLY

Considering her proposal within the context of contemporary research, we observe several limitations in Ashwood's knowledge of African women. Contemporary African historians continue to provide us with clearer details of the actuality of women's power. As several African feminists have noted, under colonialism, women lost the political power they had had in the pre-colonial period.[6] There is enough research information now for a documented history of African women in political leadership in pre-colonial time. We can begin with historian and scientist Cheikh Anta Diop,[7] whose research revealed that women were key in the decision-making process of kingdoms. African civilizations were often matriarchal and had queens or at times "female rulers," such as Iyoba Isegie, Aline Sitoé Diatta, and Anna Nzinga. Other women articulated politics from which their chosen sons would rule. In some instances, Queen Mothers played key roles in the governance of the kingdom. One of these Queen Idia N'Iyesigie was also for years identified as a man, as "king of Benin, Nigeria" because of her powerful artistically rendered presentation mis-read by colonial anthropologists who assumed leadership was always male.[8]

At the onset of the colonial period, Yaa Asantewa of Ghana took leadership in struggles against colonial domination. In 1900 she led a war against the British to retain the golden stool, the symbol of Ashanti sovereignty, which the British were trying to usurp.[9] Many women were also inspirational spiritual leaders in their societies. Exemplars in this pattern of leadership are women, such as Queen Amina of Zaria, who challenged the normal codes of what was defined as female behavior and who practiced an assertive militarism that was also brutal in its execution.[10]

Several of these documentations are being moved from oral to written history. Veronique Tadjo's *Queen Poku* (2009) rewrites the legend of Abraha Poku, Queen of the Baoule people, and offers an interesting model of converting an oral narrative into written form. This model includes creating several narrative versions, almost replicating what happens each time a listener hears one of these stories, depending on the narrator. My own reading of this indicates a central point about women and leadership and the navigation between the personal and the public; being a mother and being a leader involves making choices that favor self, family, people's survival, or transcendence. For the translator, Amy Baram Reid, "the work's multiple retellings of the story of Abraha Poku open avenues for discussion about the past and the challenges of the present . . . Tadjo asks her readers both to identify with Poku as a woman—a sister, a mother, a lover, a leader . . . " (63). Relevant to this discussion as well is Kofi Anyidoho's introduction which identifies several other legends that show women in leadership: "There is that of the Mossi, the 12th century Legend of Yennenga, in which a princess from the Dagomba royal house leads an exodus disguised as a male warrior riding on an old stallion, eventually founding a new Mossi Queendom in what is now known as Burkina Faso" (xx).

Similarly Elizabeth Ofosueah Johnson reports Queen Ndate Yalla Mbodj, queen of the Waalo, now Wolof, kingdom, who died in 1860 and is identified as leading several military battles to defend her people from Moorish, Arab, and French incursions, leading to the creation of Senegambia.[11] Hilary Jones, in "Originaire Women and Political Life in Senegal's Four Communes," provides a section titled "Women and Political Power before French Rule," which details some of this history of women's leadership in political life, using the example of the *linger* (queen or princess), including Ndate Yalla, whom she described as becoming "de facto rulers in the place of weakened kings."[12]

A dual-leadership narrative appears in Kenya within the framework of "Daughters of Mumbi,"[13] which identifies Gikuyu and Mumbi being the founders of the Kikuyu. This narrative of empowered women has been advanced by some male creative writers, as in this case Ngugi wa Thiong'o, as described by Charles Nama in his early essay "Daughters of Moombi" (1986). Nama describes Ngugi's advancing of the Kikuyu creation myth in *The River Between* (1965) and in giving women less stereotypical roles in his novels. This particular creation myth presents a leadership role for both women and men: "This land I hand over to you. O man and woman, its yours to rule . . ." (141).

As Michael Gomez's history of that period indicates, "The history of the early and medieval Savannah and Sahel was of a piece with kings and queens and rulers of the earth consolidating lands and resources. Empires expanded and contracted in response to the vagaries of location, in tandem with combinations of creed and greed" (2).[14] Before Gomez, Walter Rodney in his "African History and Culture" chapter of *The Groundings with My Brothers* (1969/2019) had said simply based on the historical evidence available in the time of his research that: "Women played an important part in the political structure of Kush, and this is something found in most parts of Black Africa. There were many queens of Kush, and it is felt that Candace mentioned in the Bible as queen of Ethiopia, may really have been a queen of Kush" (41). Fuller documentation by African historians continues, studying oral history archives, rebuilding from fragments of stories, beyond the highly stylized artistic commercial calendars, or comic book representations which have been available. Nevertheless, in the kingdom of Meroe and Kush, we learn that:

> Queens called by the title *Kandake,* known in Latin as "Candace" played a vital role in Meroitic political life. The most famous of them was Amanirenas, a warrior-queen who ruled Kush from roughly 40 B.C. to 10 B.C. Described by the Greek geographer Strabo, who mistook her title for her name, as "a masculine sort of woman, and blind in one eye," she led an army to fight off the Romans to the north and returned with a bronze statue head of Emperor Augustus, which she then buried in Meroe beneath the steps to a temple dedicated to victory. In the town of Naga, . . . another *kandake*, Amanitore, who ruled from about 1 B.C., to A.D. 25, is portrayed beside her coregent, King Natakamani, on the entrance-gate wall of a temple dedicated to the indigenous lion god Apedemak; they are depicted slaying their enemies –Amanitore with a long sword, Natakamni with a battle-ax—while lions rest symbolically at their feet. Many scholars believe that Amanitore's successor, Amantitere, is the Kushite queen referred to as "Candace, queen of the Ethiopians" in the New Testament, whose treasurer converted to Christianity and traveled to Jerusalem to worship.[15]

Providing more detail on the position of women in ancient Kush, Solange Ashby in "Priestess, Queen, Goddess. The Divine Feminine in the Kingdom of Kush" indicates that the study of the leadership of women in that period tends to be limited to the queens of Egypt and even so in a way that undermines "the fact of their power while it also completely ignored the culturally aligned and geographically proximate rule of the queens of Kush" (24). Ashby provides the details of the queens of Nubia indicating the Kerman Queens (2700–1500 BCE and the Napatan queens (800–300 BCE), The Meroitic Queens (300 BCE–300 CE) (25–28). In the case of the latter she indicates that "while the level of power attained by Napatan queens was highly unusual in the ancient world, Meroitic queens consolidated even greater power, resulting in in a series of sole-ruling queens during the first century BCE and the first century CE" (28). An interesting connecting bit of information is that the ruling queens of Meroe were depicted as powerful feminine presences: "Meriotic queens are often depicted with their breasts bare on temple walls and in their funerary chapels. Displaying evidence of their fecundity queens alluded to their reproductive abilities and allied their power with that of the goddesses who bestowed divinity on the king by suckling him" (31). The alleged display of her breasts by Sojourner Truth as she claimed her rights as a woman has a precedent in this representation.

Studies by African women historians on women's political leadership in ancient Africa have been enhanced by the work of Nwando Achebe in *The Female King of Colonial Nigeria. Ahebi Ugbabe* (2011) and *Female Monarchs and Merchant Queens in Africa* (2020), and Lynda Day, in *Gender and Power in Sierra Leone. Women Chiefs of the Last Two Centuries* (2012). Nwando Achebe's timely and accessible *Female Monarchs and Merchant Queens in Africa* provides a corrective which she describes in her methodology:

> From Amma to *Inkosazana, Sobejnefer* to *Nzingha, Nehanda* to *Ahebi Ugbaba*, the *kandakes* of Meroe to *Omu Okwei*, and the daughters of *umuada* of Igboland, *Female Monarchs and Merchant Queens in Africa* documents the worlds and life histories of elite African females, female principles, and (wo) men of privilege. It centers the diverse forms and systems of leadership, as well as complexities of female power at the highest level, in a multiplicity of distinct African societies. (23)

Thus, discussing women in historical leadership roles in Africa entails understanding the hierarchies embedded in royalty, monarchies, and their complex class implications. As in our contemporary society, elite status often accompanies the assumptions of oppressive practices,[16] in order to secure and maintain authority, even as the leader purports to represent the entire group.

Noted historian Linda M. Heywood has documented Nzinga of Angola, a 17th century ruler of the then Kingdom of Ndongo, who fought against colonialism and Portuguese occupation.[17] Heywood's research offers another important contribution to the history of African women leaders, noting that leadership was linked to assumption of military postures, donning masculine military clothing and/or creating or pushing men, often their sons, toward more assertive leadership roles. For Heywood, Nzinga's story "reveals larger themes of gender, power, religion, leadership, colonialism and resistance" (3). Heywood balances the historical record, which in its early versions distorted Nzinga's image (as has often been done to Black women in history) and describes the ways that Nzinga has been recuperated from historical bias in poetry, in oral narratives that survived in Brazil given their historical Portuguese linguistic connections. For the government of Angola, following their long-fought independence struggle, Nzinga is a founding mother, represented in the forefront of the military museum in their capital Luanda. Nzinga is also well known anecdotally in African Diaspora popular culture; several young girls named for her during the Black Power and Black Feminist Movements of the 1970's and 1980's, respectively. She also appears frequently in the Americas, in a variety of Afrocentric calendars featuring kings and queens of Africa, in museum spaces such as the Art Museum of Colonial Williamsburg, Virginia.

The contemporary African modern "post-colonial" period, therefore has at its disposal the historical examples of women in leadership in ancient societies that can be recuperated. These offer possibilities for accepting women in leadership. This becomes evident since African countries have already had women as presidents before a world leading power like the United States. Thus, according to Nwando Achebe in her "African Women Today" chapter:

> The postcolonial era has seen the emergence of select African women occupying office at the highest levels of national government. They have governed as heads of state—the highest executive legal authority of their nations—either as presidents or as prime ministers. They have been world leaders. Some have been appointed on an interim or acting basis; others have been elected. Still others have served their countries as vice presidents, members of parliament and ministers. (152)

Nwando Achebe presents a detailed listing of various women who have occupied positions of leadership across the African continent, often not well known and not recognized in Western media. Examples include Rwanda, with its over 60% parliamentary representation and Malawi with Joyce Banda (2012), and Aminata Touré in Senegal as prime minister (2013–2014). Women have also occupied leadership positions in Mali, Gabon, and most recently Ethiopia, where Sale-Work Zewde became president in 2018 and most recently Tanzania's Samia Suluhu Hassan in March, 2021, having served as Vice President from 2015.[18]

Still, the difference between being appointed to ceremonial leadership as president and political leadership acquired via election contestation reveals different types of abilities to effect change in countries still recovering from colonially inherited structures of leadership. Zewde, as president of Ethiopia (2018–present) and Michaëlle Jean in Canada (2005–2010), who became governor general of Canada, and Paula Weekes, who became president of Trinidad (2018–present), occupy largely ceremonial positions of power, although embedded with the power of the state and limited constitutionally.

WANGARI MAATHAI ON CREATING
"REVOLUTIONARY CITIZEN-LEADERS"

The post-independence period, often referred to now as the rise of the "post-colonial" state, transferred political leadership to African males, or assumed male leadership as the norm. Women who aspired to political leadership or were active in other fronts ended up in the role of supporters. Kwame Nkrumah, prime minister of Ghana, the first country in Africa to gain independence in 1957, presented a speech titled "To Ghana Women and Women of African Descent," July 18, 1960, at a conference organized by Ghana Women's Movement, which, for its time, comes across as one that recognized the power of women. This is clearly the larger source or context of a popular quotable saying assigned to Nkrumah (sometimes to Chairman Mao) that the position of women in a society is a gauge of how advanced that society is in practice. Here he offers a charge to women to be involved in the struggle for entire continental, and therefore full, African liberation. These are his words in 1960:

> What is woman's part in the great struggle for African liberation? You have to provide an answer to that question. But I can say something of the role adopted by Ghanaian womanhood in the past. The women of Ghana have played a most glorious part in our struggle for independence. They were solidly behind the Ghana revolution. Guided by the Convention People's Party, thousands of our women flocked to the nationalist banners and, side by side with the men, fought heroically until freedom was achieved for Ghana (110) . . . Your role in this direction is of great importance. Not only can you carry back this message to the men of your respective countries, but, if you are convinced that unity is the right answer, you can also bring your feminine influence to bear in persuading your brothers, husbands and friends of the importance of African unity as the only salvation for Africa. For my part, I stand resolutely and inexorably by this conviction and will work with unrelenting determination for its attainment. (112)[19]

Even in what was ostensibly an advanced position then, there was also embedded the logic that women were to assume a supportive, subordinate role, largely helping men to assume leadership. And yet, he provides evidence that women "side by side with the men fought heroically" for the acquisition of independence. Clearly it was a heady time, in which pushing back the "ruinous penetration of colonialism and imperialism in Africa" (113) was important. Nkrumah asserts still that women have to answer these questions based on their history on the continent but also in the context of the present.[20] Nonetheless, in that particular independence time frame, the role identified as women's role in African revolution, even "combatant troops," was not as leaders but as using their "feminine" influence and skills to advance these goals. Indeed all of the nationalist independence leaders came to power with large scale support of women's activism which was often not rewarded but met with fear by some men of women's "leadership bristling with dynamic women intellectuals and revolutionaries . . ." and therefore "the position could well arise, where Ghana would be ruled by a woman President and an all-women cabinet . . ."[21] The result has been an African continent with male leadership for the last fifty years and only recent movement of women into leadership roles.

It is significant then that in the contemporary period, the daughter of Kwame Nkrumah, Samiah Nkruamh, who has also run for office in Ghana, talks about the need to bring back his vision of Pan-Africanism but is also conscious of women's rights to leadership.[22] An interview with her is available in the appendix to this work in which her responses to our questions offer additional details about the particular pathway she has chosen as a young woman, a daughter of an iconic Pan-African leader who is sometimes tagged as "Keeping Nkrumah's Dream Alive."[23] In her words: "Having a fatherhood larger than life in the African political term and worldwide, it has always made me very keenly interested in politics and I have always followed developments everywhere not only in Ghana and Africa but in the whole world" (7). For her as well, the gender implications, though she is a wife and mother, are circumscribed within the political: "We know as true Nkrumaists we have to sacrifice; one of the pillars, and we just don't sacrifice our personal or family life but we also have to be selfless because that is how the man was. We are trying to emulate the man, this was how he was and we are trying to imbibe with his spirit . . ." (8). Yet, the implications of being the daughter of the famous political father are both a liability and an advantage; an instinctive familial loyalty, sometimes without full analysis and simultaneously a political benefit but often a loss as well depending on which political party is in ascendancy and/or therefore in political leadership of the nation.

The support of women and women's groups in the move to independence was indispensable to that generation of male leaders' being able to galvanize mass support. But women were also at times active freedom fighters in revolutionary struggles. However, access to decision-making and political power has been generally reserved to male leaders. For example, both Sekou Toure of Guinea and Kwame Nkrumah of Ghana became presidents of their respective countries through mass mobilization of and support of women's groups. However, once they acquired leadership, women were not given equivalent leadership portfolios in their governments. Thomas Sankara (1949–1987) in his famous March 8, 1987, speech on International Women's Day on the emancipation of women indicated that there can be "no revolution without the emancipation of women"[24] and also included a rejection of forced marriages as he proposed the outlawing of female genital mutilation, creating as well a Ministry of Women. Sadly, Sankara's assassination that same year halted the kind of progressive leadership that would have created a decided shift in African political futures and instead, we have the maintenance of status quo African male leadership.

Women like Wangari Maathai were therefore unwilling to accept subordination and poor leadership. By then herself defined globally as an African woman leader, Wangari Maathai makes this important point about not *just* leadership but *good* leadership. In her chapter on leadership in her book *The Challenge for Africa* (2009), she says:

> The exercise of good leadership would end government violations of human rights and restrictions on freedoms such as the right to move, assemble, access information and organize. Good leadership could decide for instance, not to sell off Africa's natural resources for such low prices, and then to invest the additional revenue to accelerate human and economic development. Good leadership could curtail corruption, one of the most corrosive aspects of poor leadership that has been rife in post-independence Africa. Good leadership would provide the milieu in which citizens can be creative, productive, and build wealth and opportunity. (113)

The rest of her chapter engages some of the failures of a largely male leadership profile,[25] which has led the continent since independence, even if some of the more dynamic leaders were stymied or even killed in the process. In several assessments, as much as half of some budgets are spent on militarization and "almost 60 percent of foreign exchange generated leaves the region in debt repayment"[26] often for projects that never transform the lives of the majority of the population. Thus, for Wangari, the assumption of undue deference to leaders, the interests of those surrounding the leader to remain in power, lack of vision, and definitely corruption have created a leadership deficit. She looked forward, nonetheless, to "a new form of leadership, one that will put the African people first" (128) as the future. The extent to which women who have been largely kept out of leadership in Africa can become part of that new leadership is the concern of this chapter.

This "Crisis of Leadership" is examined in more detail in Besi Brillian Muhonja's *Radical Utu* (2020), in which the author presents the Maathai model for "*utu* citizenship and revolutionary ethical leadership construct appropriately functioning communities and democratic spaces . . ." (81) with the idea of engendering "revolutionary citizen-leaders." According to Muhonja, *Utu* (actually a version of *ubuntu*, meaning "I am because you are") refers to "what it means to be human." "This orients radical living as both a philosophy and an active process—individuals and communities (re)imagining themselves as engaged in relations and encounters with other humans rooted in ethics and values of equity and honor for the humanity of others and for their environments" (x).

In her autobiography, *Unbowed* (2007), Wangari Maathai linguistically evokes Shirley Chisholm's *Unbought and Unbossed* (1978) in the language of not circumscribing oneself as a woman to male domination. Hers is a journey from her earliest memories, through her difficult marriage and harassment by the state, and finally global recognition in 2004 as the first African woman to win the Nobel Peace Prize. But before that, we note her rise to becoming a member of parliament in Kenya in 2002, in her words, "working on the issues that matter in people's lives, like health care, education, food security, HIV/AIDS, income generation, and of course environmental restoration" (302). Wangari Maathai, in the process, became an environmental feminist icon, but one who remained grounded in setting the terms for an environmental movement—The Green Belt Movement—which has become a model for many similar movements around the world.

Significant in the life of Wangari Maathai are her multiple arrests by the state, along with charges of sexual infidelity and looseness, coming both from her former husband and from the government. On several occasions the charges against Wangari were for suspicions of sexual wrongdoing, entertaining men in her house, and infidelity, based on attending meetings at night or in mixed company.

"Jail, again. Another night in a dirty, cramped police holding cell" (282) [and] "That was the last time I was held in a jail or a police holding cell in Kenya. I can only hope that those days are over. Even though the country truly changed after the 2002 elections, to this day I cannot say for sure that I will never be arrested again or spend another night in police custody. You can never tell. Things can change overnight." (284)

The policing of the sexual lives of activist women describes the precariousness of activist women's lives in Africa as elsewhere. As we saw in our discussion of Winnie Nomzamo Madikezela-Mandela in the prior chapter, a clear pattern appears in the way that the policing of women often has to do with control of their bodies and unfounded charges related to their sexuality.

Unbowed allows the reader to journey with Wangari following a chronological pattern in the first chapter titled "Beginnings," about her origins in a mountain range near Nyeri, within sight of Mount Kenya. As discussed before, in "Private Lives and Public Spaces," Jomo Kenyatta's *Facing Mount Kenya* following the male autobiographical model, functioned as the autobiography of the self-constructed with the birth of the state, the human self being contemporary with the merging nation. Women's autobiography, in the same time frame, often dealt with the self-in-process, the individual woman coming to voice, to activism, and to a political self-realization along the way. Thus, with Wangari, we see an advance of this model, the private is also the public for Wangari, as she details difficulties in raising children, jealousies in her marriage that lead to a public divorce, and her reclaiming and extending her public name by adding an additional "a" as in Maathai, making it subtly different from her husband's name. Her becoming an environmentalist was also grounded in her childhood, in which she experienced the wonders of nature, such as fresh-water streams:

> In my mind's eye, I can envision that stream now: the crystal-clear water wash-ing over the pebbles and grains of soil underneath, silky and slow moving. I can see the life in that water and the shrubs, reeds, and ferns along the banks, sway-ing as the current of the water sidles around them. When my mother would send me to fetch water, I would get lost in this fascinating world of nature . . . (46)

She links independence to her own coming of age, in a chapter titled "Independence—Kenya's and My Own" (98–118). During her "Difficult Years," we see a woman ready to challenge the limitations of the post-colonial state, sacrificing her individual personal and professional happiness for a larger realization. Throughout *Unbowed*, Maathai presents a fair balance between the personal and the political: for example, her mother's death is linked by date to International Woman's Day, as is the burial afterward, and her sister's as well, a few years later. Her chapter "Opening the Gates of Politics" (274–276) also includes her internationally recognized environmen-tal activism within the Green Belt Movement on behalf of the Karura Forest.

Another relevant study, *Wangari Maathai's Registers of Freedom* by Grace Musila documents her life, beginning with her birth in 1940 and ending with her passing in 2011 after battling ovarian cancer. For Musila, "a major ele-ment of Maathai's legacy [includes] her lifelong confrontations with Kenyan patriarchy, both in her personal life and in politics" (306). Maathai epitomizes those women indicated in Nkrumah's declaration, who instead of working to advance the nationalist path in support of male leadership, critique these male leadership limitations and advance different leadership paradigms. In her case it is an eco-feminism which even manifested her teachings in her passing as local women created a woven environmentally friendly casket to carry her remains. Rob Nixon describes an "intersectional environmentalism, gender and conservation" in his "Slow Violence, Gender and the Environmentalism of the Poor" (246–271), which describes what Wangari Maathai struggled against as she simultaneously created another leadership paradigm that advanced women's rights in the African context.

In 2007 Maathai entered formal politics, opting to run with the Party of National Unity (PNU). Like Shirley Chisholm, though she did not win, her loss was not a failure but an inspiration to countless other women, including Stella Nyanzi in Uganda, who suffered some of the same state punishments.[27] This is also the sentiment of Njala Nyabola's "Wangari Maathai was Not a Good Woman," which highlights Maathai's resistance to Kenya's "political misogyny": "She did more to give Kenyan women space to simply be themselves in the context of this casual misogyny and political schizophrenia than any woman of her generation merely by refusing to be a 'good girl'" (304).

In her optimism for new leadership by women on the horizon, Wangari Maathai saw the presidency of Ellen Johnson Sirleaf as part of that promise of "embodying a new form of leadership" and thereby elevating "the standard of leadership" (*The Challenge of Africa,* 127).

BEING MADAME PRESIDENT

Ellen Johnson Sirleaf made history by becoming "Africa's First Woman President" in 2006, but the 24th president of Liberia. Her pathway to this important historical achievement is documented well in her memoir, *This Child Will Be Great* (2009). One can see from this titling that the self-construction for leadership is a central component of the narrative. For her, "to be a great leader means to get to a place where personal considerations and needs become secondary to the achievement of your goal. That is the great sacrifice you can make, but that is precisely what leadership demands" (309). And here it is as well, supported by a family narrative in which an elder, on seeing the baby she was, had made the pronouncement: "This child shall be great. This child is going to lead" (7). In many ways the inclusion of this prophetic statement represents a retrospective justification for leadership, as it also offers the preliminary permission to pursue leadership as identified by family and community. It is significant that this is her mother's story, which as Alice Walker in "In Search of Our Mother's Gardens" (1983) indicates, was one of the ways that the prior generation of women prepared their daughters for success. They legitimized through their language and their narratives of future success the assumption of "greatness" and leadership for women, even in times when it seemed impossible, while still preparing the next generation for the opportunity when it is presented. For Johnson Sirleaf, even when she had personal challenges and doubts: "Where's all this greatness that was predicted?" (7), this memory remained a constant in her mental architecture. We note relatedly that this particular narrative is recalled operationally at the start of her autobiography and gives the work its title. For certainly this early construction of eventual greatness became for this woman who became Africa's first woman president, a realizable and ultimate goal, as she moved through the various difficulties of life.

Those life's difficulties which included domestic violence from an abusive husband were part of the negative conditions that she had to transcend but were also magnified in the state violence which men in her country also practiced. In my view these traumas provided her with the lived experience that she was able to confront and were expressed in at least two of the questions I raised in conversation with her and that inform this work in general: Were there issues you were able to address better as a woman? And, how does sexuality inform the construction of women in political leadership and in your case? (See Conversation Summary in appendix.) In her autobiographical narrative, she is quite explicit about how her own experience of domestic violence provides the awareness of what other women continue to face:

> Domestic violence knows no geographical boundaries. It exists in every nation, every society, every corner of the world, and neither Africa in general, nor Liberia in particular is immune to this particular disease. Right from the start of my administration, even in my inaugural address, I pledged to bring the full weight of the government against those who would continue this terrible abuse: "Those who violate our women and girls now know they will bear the force of the law," I said. We have begun to do just that. (39)

In the "Childhood Ends," chapter of her autobiography, she narrates the nature of the abuse cycle, an early marriage, the decline of her father's health, and the increasing jealousy from a husband that translated into verbal and physical abuse. Besides the personal/psychological nature of an abusive husband is the fact that many larger male-dominated societies permit domestic violence against women. Thus the ending of a disastrous marriage for her creates the conditions for her final transcendence via a life of professional successes and attempts to challenge the troublesome, very masculinized forms of violence that were also coming from the government, which she herself does not fully escape.

As in the experience of Wangari Maathai and Winnie Mandela, incarceration and detention were also part of the actions of masculinized state control. Here she summarizes that experience while under house arrest:

> Sometimes I think about how frightening the events of my life must have been to my mother. But she never broke down, never crumbled, never told me to stop doing what I had to do. She was a very strong woman, and she believed with all her heart in the power of prayer. She prayed for me unceasingly. I believe I got my strength from her. (126)

As time passed, I began to sneak out messages to my supporters throughout Monrovia and the world. One day one of these messages was intercepted. I had written, "To the people: Stand firm! Don't give in! Our course is right and we will win." Such sentiments did not go over very well with [former Liberian president Samuel] Doe. He ordered me moved from house arrest and taken to the infamous Post Stockade at the Barclay Training Center—the military prison—where nine students from the university were already being held. It was the first time in my life I was locked away in a jail cell, imprisoned against my will. It would not be the last—or, by any means, the worst. (126–127)

Many Black women leaders have faced the experience of incarceration, only to triumph afterward, from Angela Davis to Claudia Jones on the Black left in the United States of America, to Winnie Mandela, Nawal el Saadawi, Wangari Maathai, Stella Nyanzi, and others in continental Africa. This attempt to publicly contain women reveals a sad example of how the state deals with claims for equitable relationships. For Ellen Johnson Sirleaf, this treatment occurred with a realization that the men leading the country were indeed "idiots," (122–123) a statement she made which became one of the reasons for her incarceration by Samuel Doe who was then president of Liberia.

According to Helene Cooper in her biography, *Madame President,* however, "Ellen had begun to see herself as presidential material. It was still a zygote of a thought, not fully formed or explored. But she was already sure she could do a better job than the men who had governed Liberia into the ground" (57). Thus when Johnson Sirleaf was finally released from prison after national and international protests, "All she saw was the sea of people cheering and crying with her—people, she determined to herself, whom she would one day lead" (93).[28] This in many ways describes her leadership story and her responses to me initially that a leader must be "inspirational, courageous, determined and compromising but also definitive in decision making."[29]

Her pathway to becoming president included numerous setbacks. Ultimately, she undertook extensive campaigning in every part of the country and the harnessing of support from women, in a "vote for women" campaign, producing a victory not just for herself but for Liberian women. As reported by Cooper, "I want to talk to the women," Madame said. "The women of Liberia, the women of Africa, and the women of the world" (174).

Two key issues are relevant: (1) the role of women in advancing women to political leadership and (2) what happens when that woman becomes a leader. These two inter-related issues apply to the presidency of Ellen Johnson Sirleaf. Beyond her own aggressive campaigning all across Liberia, Johnson Sirleaf identifies the "market women's role" as critical support for her to attain the presidency. Helene Cooper describes them as "an army of market women" (154). For Johnson Sirleaf, in advancing her possibilities to be president, the essential actors were, "my staff and large group of supporters, including the amazing market women who mobilized on my behalf, could campaign even in my absence. They went from village to village, meeting

place to meeting place, handing out stickers and posters and raising my profile" (255). Additionally, in the process of her second and successful attempt
at the presidency ". . . we re-mobilized our secret weapon—the women of
Liberia—and sent them out campaigning. These indomitable women were the
real force behind this election . . . More than anything, it was the women of
Liberia who turned this election, for me and for themselves" (264).

Unlike the leaders of African nationalist movements who got to leadership with the assumption of women's support, when she became president,
Johnson Sirleaf publicly recognized Liberian women as essential to her success and therefore her primary political base. Her co-winner of the Nobel
Peace Prize, Leymah Gbowee, who did much to advance grassroot organizing to end the violence and war in Liberia, documented this role of women
as well in her autobiography, *Mighty Be Our Powers* (2013). In other words,
without the groundwork of Leymah Gbowee, the presidency of Ellen Johnson
Sirleaf would not have been possible; the uncontrollable violence of men who
had been in leadership was precisely what had propelled Liberia into such a
dire situation: "Men have failed us," people said over and over again. "Men
are too violent, too prone to make war" (250). That kind of awareness came
from the activist work of Gbowee. This activism allowed Johnson Sirleaf
to assert:

> Women, my strong constituency, told me they wanted the same chances that
> men have. They wanted to be literate. They wanted their work recognized. They
> wanted protection against rape. They wanted clean water that would not sicken
> and kill their children. These women had not only supported me consistently in
> my climb to the presidency but, far more important, they had worked tirelessly
> during the war to bring the various factions to the negotiating table. The women
> of Liberia were and remain the country's core, and I have made it a priority to
> include them in its reconstruction. (277)

For Johnson Sirleaf, this determination to lead was generated by women, and
in turn it demanded her reciprocation, and a determination that "she would
one day lead" (Cooper, 93). Thus, as Johnson Sirleaf took office, she spoke
directly to women, saying in her inauguration speech:

> My administration shall thus endeavor to give Liberian women prominence in
> all affairs of our country. My administration shall empower Liberian women in
> all areas of our national life. We will support and increase the writ of laws that
> restore their dignities and deal drastically with crimes that dehumanize them.
> We will enforce without fear or favor the law against rape recently passed by
> the National Transitional Legislature. We shall encourage families to educate
> all children, particularly the girl child. We shall also try to provide economic

programs that enable Liberian women to assume their proper place in our economic revitalization process. (333–334)

Still, we must consider the extent to which these aims were realized. One of our generating questions remains: How do we subject Black women in leadership positions to a critique that is fair and necessary? So let us examine the Johnson Sirleaf presidency from this particular angle of the platform of education for girls and young women.

In *This Child Will Be Great*, she indicates that schooling was primary with an "emphasis on the girls, because traditionally girls have been neglected—not only in Liberia but in all of Africa. . . . We also passed new regulations making it a punishable fine for children to be on the street doing petty trading during school hours" (292). Educating girls then is a laudable goal for a woman president to claim, especially when girls are often denied education in several African contexts. Still, the results are mixed in terms of realization at the adult level. For example, Dr. Ophelia Weeks was named the 14th president of the University of Liberia, becoming the second woman to hold this post and with a promise of advancing a number of related educational projects. But it was a short-lived tenure, lasting only from 2017 through 2019.[30] Nevertheless, according to UNICEF on the issue of women in education:

> Since the end of the conflict, significant progress has taken place in the education sector. In 2015, close to 1.4 million children were registered in pre-primary, primary and high school. In addition, the Ministry of Education, UNICEF and other partners teamed up and continue to repair or build new classrooms, train teachers, revise curricula and develop policies and plans for the education sector.
>
> Yet, Liberia is significantly behind most other African countries in nearly all education statistics. It has one of the world's highest levels of out-school children, with an estimated 15 to 20 percent of 6–14 year-olds who are not in class. Just over a third of pre-schoolers have access to early childhood learning programmes and only 54 per cent of children complete primary education.[31]

The Liberian Educational sector analysis of 2016, published by the Ministry of Education, however, shows a significant increase from 2006 to 2015, corresponding to the time that President Johnson Sirleaf was in office. Primary education rates doubled, although there were some lags in rural communities and a problem of overage gaps in various grades, which often means less of a chance of success. Higher rates of enrollment in tertiary education is also indicated, although Liberian universities are indicated as having inadequately trained faculty.

An assessment of the legacy of President Johnson Sirleaf by Elizabeth Donnelly credits her with maintaining peace after the end of the civil war and taking "positive steps to improve the livelihoods and particularly the protection of women in Liberia." Although Liberia ranked near the bottom of the Human Development Index,[32] at 176 out of 189, it is still ahead of countries like Mali.

Still, many felt that because of the economic experience Johnson Sirleaf acquired from her prior affiliations with the World Bank and her business connections with transnational corporations, the level of socio-economic transformation expected should have been more realizable and much higher than what was achieved. A counter response is that the need to stabilize Liberia after a major civil war demanded the president's full attention. As a result, fewer gains were made economically than would have been possible if Madame President were inheriting a country without a history of such conflict. The African Reality assessment provides a balanced view of achievements and losses. Gains included debt forgiveness, investment in training government officials, growth in the economy at a rate of 8%, the championing of women's rights issues, and improvements in freedom of speech.[33] Among the losses, the worst claim is a continuance of corrupt practices, nepotism, and above all the perception of Johnson Sirleaf's not supporting the succeeding candidate of her party, leading to her being expelled from the Unity Party. An analysis of the concluding report "Liberia's Truth Commission Report: ESCR in Transitional Justice"[34] offers substantial concerns about fuller evaluation of what they call "missing gender dimensions."

GENDERED MEDIA ASSESSMENTS AND WOMEN'S RIGHTS

Winning the 2017 Mo Ibrahim Prize for Achievement in African Leadership was one of Johnson Sirleaf's significant accomplishments. In her second term, beginning in 2011, when she was in her early seventies, she was referred to critically as an "Old Ma." But clearly this disparaging terminology remains a biased, gendered assessment, applied only to women, because many of the male African leaders were of similar age or older, without receiving the comparable designation of "Old Pa" to demean their capabilities. In the same time frame, Robert Mugabe of Zimbabwe was ninety-three years old before finally being made to step down from the presidency. Additionally, the ascription of the "Iron Lady," which Johnson Sirleaf also received, a moniker assigned initially to Margaret Thatcher,[35] is often assigned to women who become the first leader after a largely male-dominated political field and who have often taken hard positions in order to be acceptable to their patriarchal colleagues. According to Helene Cooper, though, Johnson Sirleaf "knew when to adopt her Old Ma persona and when to cast it off." In this context, she could offer a combined maternal approach with political savviness where necessary, that is, to see Liberia as a sick child that she had to make whole again; simultaneously, a country in crisis that she had to repair. "The country was in dire straits and needed immediate leadership" (260).

But according to Leymah Gbowee, the women's agenda was never fully delivered and while Johnson Sirleaf rejected an identification with feminism, calling it extremist, Gbowee indicated she was proud to be an extremist in this case. Still, in an assessment of her legacy as it relates to women's rights, we learn that:

> Under President's Sirleaf's tenure a new tougher rape law came into force but was then amended reducing the tough sentences and making it a bailable offence. During her final week in office, President Sirleaf signed an executive order on domestic violence, protecting women and children against "physical, sexual, economical, emotional and psychological abuses." Johnson Sirleaf is however disappointed that a key part of her proposal, the abolition of genital mutilation (FGM) against young girls under the age of 18, was removed. [36]

Access to political leadership, and even the idea of parity, which some countries like Senegal made official in 2010, did not happen under President Johnson Sirleaf. Additionally, according to Tamasin Ford's report, her presence did not mean that more women got to political office. We are mindful, nonetheless, of the Walter Rodney thesis in *How Europe Underdeveloped Africa* (1972),[37] that repercussions following European interventions linger in its history as after-effects of the transatlantic slavery of African peoples from the continent to the Americas, extractive economic and political colonialism, and the reality of the ongoing recovery of neo-colonial states. Still, we are left with having to recognize and account for the limited place of women in contemporary national leadership structures. While Liberia had the success and distinction of electing the first African woman president of a continental African country, changes in women's experience remain gradual and limited. In *This Child Will Be Great*, Johnson Sirleaf identifies that her intent was to support women because in her words: "The women of Liberia were and remain the country's core, and I have made it a priority to include them in its reconstruction. At the time of this writing women head the ministries of Commerce, Foreign Affairs, Finance, Youth and Sports, and Gender and Development. Five out of the country superintendents are women, out of fifteen" (277–278). However, in the 2019 United Nations' "Women and Politics" report, Liberia was 152 of 191 states in terms of representation of women, with 12.3% of members of parliament being women, and 10% in the Senate. Although the position of women in Liberia is higher than that in a country like Nigeria, which ranks 181st with 5.6% of women represented, the fact that Liberia had a woman as president has not substantially lifted representation of women to the level of parity.

The appointment of Nigeria's former Minister of Finance Ngozi Okonjo-Iweala to be the first African and woman to head the World Trade Organization indicates external and more global leadership possibilities if not inside the nation-state.[38] Her autobiography *Fighting Corruption is Dangerous: The Story Behind the Headlines*,[39] describes some of the projects she undertook to clean up the legendary Nigerian corruption, which resulted in her mother being kidnapped but which are described as long-lasting. Though her positions on the national scene were short lived, her appointment on the international level still bodes well for a future in Nigerian leadership. Her position that "women tend to be more honest, more straightforward more focused on the job and bring less ego" is worth testing as more women come into leadership. Still for her, the fight against corruption aligns well with Wangari Maathai's concern about male leadership on the continent which has allowed certain negative excesses to take hold.

So, the gains in Liberia have been specific to education, and they contribute significantly to a discourse of women in leadership internationally, according to Belinda A. Stillion Southard's "Crafting Cosmopolitan Nationalism: Ellen Johnson Sirleaf's Rhetorical Leadership." Thus, "Sirleaf's nation-building rhetoric needed to reimagine Liberia as a participatory democracy, especially for women and girls, whose political, and economic lives had always been dominated by men" (396). Southard attributes much of Johnson Sirleaf's credibility to the fact that she was a "survivor of imprisonment, as an activist who spoke truth to power throughout her career, and as a woman deeply familiar with the cost of genocidal warfare positioned her[self] as a leader with the strength to lead the new democracy" (398). Southard studied many speeches, made in numerous international forums, and concluded that the gains happened at the rhetorical, not actual, level. Yet it is clear that during Johnson Sirleaf's tenure, programs were launched to benefit market women, develop entrepreneurial training, educate girls, and produce anti-rape laws. These, in the end, can help to create a "cosmopolitan citizenship" in which women have equal investment in their society's advancements. Thereby a conclusion: "While it will take years to gauge the social, political, and economic effectiveness of Sirleaf's cosmopolitan rhetoric and policies, it is clear that the process of undoing the patriarchal mores of a post-conflict culture is much more arduous than undoing patriarchal policies" (408).

Finally, a visible contradiction was noted in the fact that Johnson Sirleaf endorsed the party of George Weah, which ran a campaign with a woman for vice president, in spite of the fact that the woman, Jewell Howard Taylor, was the former wife of the warlord Charles Taylor, who led Liberia into its deadly conflict. While her own party expelled her for not supporting its candidate, the fact of the candidacy of Jewell Howard Taylor as vice president, perhaps for Sirleaf (i.e., seeing another woman advance was more significant than endorsing the man who was aspiring to leadership in her own party). According to reports:

> [Jewell] Howard Taylor divorced Charles Taylor in 2006, after he fled to exile in Nigeria. Despite her ex-husband's reputation as a ruthless warlord, Howard Taylor went on to build her own political base in a central region north of Monrovia. In 2005, she was elected senator of the Bong County, the nation's third most populous, for the National Patriotic Party (NPP). She then chaired the Senate Health and Social Welfare Committee on Gender, Women and Children. Howard Taylor is a devout Christian who is said to begin every morning with a prayer. In 2012, she tried to push through legislation that allows homosexuality to be punished with the death penalty.[40]

In many ways, Jewell Taylor's pathway to leadership is a version of the "first lady to president" model. The extent to which her ability to operate as a leader is actualized is still in process. To those looking in from the outside on the one hand, it often seems an unfair practice to blame a wife for all her husband's misdeeds, with an accompanying lingering doubt about how the woman creates her own leadership profile outside of her husband's narrative as we saw with the Hillary Clinton case. Questions remain as with the Kamala Harris US Vice Presidency (2021) about whether the move from vice president to president is a possibility that history will accommodate. Still the reality is that Jewell Howard Taylor holds over twenty years of political experience, and she served in the Senate under Johnson Sirleaf's leadership as Chair of the Senate Health and Social Welfare Committee on Gender, Women and Children.[41] She indicates that she helped President Johnson Sirleaf achieve her agenda in this regard. Thus, many expected her to run for the presidency herself and saw her participation on George Weah's team as what guaranteed his success.[42]

Joseph Foray's "Liberia: Ellen Johnson Sirleaf to George Weah" offers an assessment of the gains and losses. Foray wonders how, with all her financial experience, she did not achieve more. But just stabilizing post-war Liberia, and effecting a transition to another government, both of which Johnson Sirleaf achieved, still must be seen as significant contributions. Interviews with Johnson Sirleaf indicate her misgivings about the future of Liberia and a recognition that the government is still male dominated. Women, including herself, are kept out of the significant discussions by the way meetings are called and in which women do not participate and consensus is built. She indicates on this score: "At times I feel disrespected and ignored."[43]

Perhaps a more positive assessment of success in rebuilding Liberia comes from Helene Cooper, who in her *Madame President*, includes chapters on the many unheralded successes of Ellen Johnson Sirleaf. Charges of corruption pale in comparison to the standard corrupt nepotistic practices of African male leaders. But of course, women are held to a higher standard. Rebuilding roads, getting debt forgiven, restoring Liberia back into the graces of international organizations, moving it from a failed war-torn state to a normally functioning country, beating back an Ebola epidemic, advancing women with knowledge of business interests, and above all, representing women in political leadership in global contexts are all the positive contributions made by Ellen Johnson Sirleaf.

STILL ADVANCING WHILE RECOGNIZING THE *KANDAKES* AND THE MEANINGS OF POWER

Today, there is perhaps more excitement about African women taking leadership than exists anywhere else in the world. However, there has been steady progress of African women in leadership. A 1970's publication suggested a post-independence groundswell of women in a variety of locations but no accessing of political power for a few more decades. Several of these women have somehow been erased in the larger national framing. For example, Lucy Lameck (1934–1993) is identified as Tanzania's first woman to hold a ministerial portfolio, once serving as Deputy Minister of Health and Social Development, after being active in independence movement. While she is recognized in her home region of Kilimanjaro and a street has been named after her in Germany, she is not someone who readily comes to attention in assessments of African women's contributions to African countries advancement.[44] Often the documentation exists in disparate locations like period magazines. For example, an issue of *Africa Woman*[45] in my possession describes a range of women of various positions including an interview with Aduke of Alakija the then president of the International Federation of Women Lawyers (8–11), a special report "Women Militants in the PAIGC" (12–13) and an interview with Micere Mugo then a senior lecturer in the Department of English, University of Nairobi in which she offers a still relevant assessment which uses a systems of oppression approach:

> We cannot only speak of women's oppression by men. In capitalist systems, women tend to be exploited by the very nature of the society, particularly the working and peasant women, just as the men are exploited. The difference is that women are hit particularly hard. Their most obvious hardship is being educationally disadvantaged. Then you have forms of abuse that cut across class lines:

sexual abuse, wife-beating and the fact that men take advantage of the woman's role as child-bearer. But I won't give the impression that I foster any illusions. Sexual abuse, rape, etc. do take place in socialist societies, but I believe statistics will bear me out that the degree of such abuses is less than in capitalist societies, whose conditions of maldistribution and ownership tend to breed many social problems. (14–15)

Paul Tiyambe Zeleza's "The Significance of Johnson-Sirleaf's Victory"[46] begins his candid assessment with the statement that "The global record of women's political representation among heads of state and government is dismal" (1). He identifies the then forty-six women worldwide who had served in the twentieth century, indicating though that several of the ones in Africa served short periods sometimes for less than a year and that the progress was uneven.[47] He lists Elizabeth Domitien (1975–1976) of the Central African Republic, Sylvie Kinigi of Burundi and Agathe Uwilingiyimana of Rwanda, Prime ministers in 1993–1994, the latter killed in the genocide of 1994 (1). His conclusion though is that the "needs and interests of women will remain peripheral until there is a critical mass of women in leadership positions and decision-making processes" (4). He sees Johnson Sirleaf's presidency as also a beneficiary of the ongoing assertions of women's movements which "helped to establish a new global normative and discursive architecture for women's rights and human rights" (5). Still to his credit, he laments the "only one" phenomenon and sees her achievement as laudatory but "not a cause for great celebration" (7).

According to Aminata Dramane Traoré, who served as Minister of Culture and Tourism in Mali from 1997 to 2000 and was the Directrice des Etudes et des Programmes au Ministère de la Condition Féminine de Côte d'Ivoire (1979–1988), one can blame women and men equally:

I have had the unfortunate idea of denouncing this system from within as a minister for a portfolio to which I was nominated only to be silenced. I have learned how and why a strong African civil society is slow to emerge. The fact of being a woman changes nothing in this fact. I was ferociously fought against by men as well as by other women who swear to the opening of Mali to foreign investors.[48]

In my interview with Aminata Dramane Traoré, included in the appendix to this work, she stressed that she was less impressed with women coming to leadership, although there is a clear necessity for balance, and a need for progressive politicians, not women who are jockeying for power and ready to do anything to achieve power. Her critiques have more to do with the ways that Africa is still subject to European-driven narratives and economic projects, including those projects suggested by Western feminists.

In many ways, Aminata Dramane Traoré's position coheres with "The Status of Women's Leadership in West Africa" report based on a study commissioned by West Africa Civil Society Institute (WASCSI, 2008) which concludes particularly on the issue of food insecurity that a gender rather than women-focused approach particularly on the issue of "gender mainstreaming" would mean that "gender analyses will enable partners to take account of roles, responsibilities and gender relations—thereby strengthening the efficacy of their collaboration." A study of "Women Leaders in Senegal" by Halima Diallo which was based on field surveys with women found that social background often "lead them to engage in these masculinized professions which are not thought to be as inaccessible as I imagined." Also, she found that women leaders use strategies that aim to minimize their visibility including at times clothing selection, working harder to achieve their goals and not automatically counting on the solidarity among women. "Women leaders cannot always use manly methods, those that work for men because it is often to their detriment and unsuccessful. Their colleagues and subordinates would expect them to be as firm as men but also to be more attentive to others, more humane."[49]

In a younger generation of leaders, for N'diaye Ramatoulaye Diallo, former Minister of Culture of Mali, who I interviewed in 2019[50] politics was a pathway that she followed reluctantly, after seeing her mother incarcerated with a group of politicians after a coup in Mali. A career in marketing led to a successful election of then president Ibrahim Boubacar Keita (1945–2020), since removed by military coup and deceased, who recognized her talents and appointed her to the Ministry of Culture. Mme. Ramatoulaye Diallo who received university training in the United States, indicates the influence on her of European women's groups, which have supported women coming to leadership. Delightfully, she repeated the phrase "Yes, Women Can" at several significant occasions in the presence of Ibrahim Keita, then the president of Mali, during an audience we had with him in January 2018. Although their government was deposed in August 2020, Mme. Diallo still has her public relations skills that can be used in other professional contexts. In her interview with me in Dakar, Senegal,[51] she indicated that initially she had no interest in politics, given her mother's experience and that when she was in high school she had to negotiate with the prison officials for permission to visit her mother in prison daily after classes. Thus, she saw politics from that lens, as a dangerous pathway. Her path to being Minister of Culture came from creating a public relations campaign to ensure that more people, particularly women, were involved in the electoral process. The success of this campaign, as did Stacey Abrams's campaigns in the United States, brought her to the attention of the person who became president.

Generally, then, much excitement exists about African women moving into political leadership, no doubt buoyed by the example of Rwanda, which in 2020 had the world's highest representation of women in parliament, at 61%. And while the Rwanda high level of representation has several interpretations from the 1994 genocide to the role of its president Kagame, Nzegwu[52] credits Aloisea Inyumba (1964–2012) then a young Senator in the Rwandan parliament as the true "Mother of New Rwanda" as she was the one who used her office to develop and advance women's access to power, using strategies of mothering and caring, creating as well a network of mothers to rebuild a traumatized and damaged nation. She saw the Rwandan women as critical in this process as she believed that "the key to reconstruction and peace was to involve women in community development at the grass roots levels in society. She created a national women's movement based on the former administrative structure with local groups run by women in every neighbourhood." For Nzegwu, she "inserted a feminist framework" to re-order "the bifurcated, masculinized structures of power" that led to the violence Rwanda experienced.

Many other countries are indicated in the 40–50 percentile. These include Namibia with 46%, South Africa with 42%, and Senegal with 41%. Senegal is interesting because it has a gender parity law,[53] advanced by women's rights activists over the years, which requires that all political parties "introduce absolute gender parity in electoral lists for all elected representation, national or local." This law has certainly increased women's participation in politics, at 41%, much higher than that in many other countries including the United States. However, in northern Senegal, it is virtually impossible to have active gender parity, given the Islamic dominance that relegates women to the private sphere. Professor Aminata Diaw (1959–2017) who was honored at the 2018 CODESRIA 15th Assembly in a session titled: "Gender, Liberation and Political Struggles: Celebration of Professor Aminata Diaw,"[54] was identified as one of the leading advocates of the Senegal Parity Law through her tireless work on gender and citizenship.

The recent rise of Samia Suluhu Hassan to the presidency of Tanzania after serving as the vice president to a well-liked president who died in office indicates one of the unpredictable advances of African women once they are in the leadership stream. Still there is an internal critique such as mounted by left and grassroots women's organizations like Christina Mfanga, a lawyer and self-described grassroot social justice militant, General Secretary–Tanzania Socialist Forum and Board chair of Manzese Working Women Cooperative. While images of President Suluhu graced the streets in much the same way as male presidents' images dominate, Christina Mfanga's "To the Red Carpet Feminists: Congratulations for Breaking a Glass Ceiling" indicates that "nobody says that we shouldn't have a female president because of those poor women, my only concern is how that presidency reflects in those women's daily struggles." For her "a ceiling is just part of a bigger structure, whether hardly or simply broken it doesn't entail the structure's complete dismantling."[55] In my conversations with the author in Dar es Salaam, January, 2022, Tina Mfanga demonstrated the basic pride that women feel in witnessing this accomplishment, but expressed a serious concern that we do not miss the fact that the late president Magufuli had worked on instituting some progressive policies that benefited the working poor by simply applauding a women's accession to leadership without examining her policies as well. To date, she saw no major advances in this presidency.

Contemporary statistics for the rest of the continent hover around 23%, cumulatively revealing a wide fluctuation, with Mozambique, Ethiopia, Tunisia, Uganda, Zimbabwe, and Angola in the 30%–40% range; several countries in the 10%–15% range, including Liberia, Sierra Leone, Chad, Egypt, Gambia, Democratic Republic of the Congo, Cote d'Ivoire, Burkina Faso, and Guinee Bissau, and Nigeria, at 5.6%.[56] Political gains are often related to particular historical periods and specific to the leadership in particular countries, such as in contemporary Ghana, under the leadership of President Akufo-Addo (2017–present), where several women have been appointed to positions by the head of state. Examples include female chief justices like Georgina Wood (2007–2017) or Sophia Abena Boafo Akuffo, the second female chief justice of Ghana (2017–2019); many chairpersons of electoral commission like Jean Adukwei Mensa (2018–present), and Speaker of the Parliament Joyce Adeline Bamford-Addo (2009–2013).[57] Female government ministers in 2018 are identified as 13%. And, as it relates to political transformation, women in Sudan were seen as leading the movements for social change in 2019. In fact, according to Solange Ashby, "the Kushite history of powerful women (*kandakes*) served as a potent symbol in the protests that toppled the Arabized dictator al-Bashir is stunning and testifies to the enduring centrality of women in this culture."[58]

In Ethiopia women are presidents of both chambers and also the identified appointed Head of State. In 2019 women constituted 38.8% of the Ethiopian parliament. However the disruptions of warmongering male leadership threatens to derail the gains that women had been steadily making. Cameroun has a version of parity expressed in a new electoral code in 2012, whereby gender became a legal prerequisite in the compilation of all candidate lists for elections [Section 15, paragraph (3)]: "Each list shall take into consideration the various sociological components of the constituency concerned. It shall also take into consideration gender aspects." The result is 31% women in the National Assembly in 2020. In Angola, The Charter of Political Parties includes gender representation of not less than 30% in their governing bodies at all levels (Article 20 of law 22/10 on Political Parties). Today women are

30% of the National Assembly. After Rwanda, South Africa is indicated as a positive example, when in 2006 the African National Congress adopted a 50% gender quota in local elections and extended this to national elections in 2009, with the result that women represent 46% of the National Assembly. Several other countries, including Namibia, have indicated at least at the party level a 50% representation in political bodies and structures. Although the average is still around 23%, the gains have been substantial in a relatively short time as compared with the United States and even the United Kingdom.

The Protocol on the Rights of African Women provides a guidepost for the advancement of African women in the political sphere in the future.[59] The Protocol lists several rights for women's participation in society, and guide manuals such as "A Guide for the Usage of Organizations for the Promotion of Equality between the Sexes and the Participation of Women" (UN Women, March 2016) offer practical steps for increasing the participation of women in elections and women's accession to leadership roles. Yet for African women and political leaders like Siga Jagne Jallow, Commissioner of Social Affairs and Gender at the Economic Community of West African States (ECOWAS), leadership at the local level is perhaps even more relevant to social change, for the local level is where the impact of state policies can be executed and actualized.[60] In this regard, she concurs with Halima Diallo's[61] findings that women in the informal sector are the ones often involved in politics. "Many of them support intellectual feminists who are fighting for the enforcement of the gender parity (flouted by men)" and "express an interest in sitting in the National Assembly because it is the place where one decided on the use of resources of the nation and it is the place where one votes the laws which will govern the lives of women and men."[62]

The intricacies of the contexts in which Black women within global capitalism assume and exercise national leadership must be part of the understanding and critical analysis. Work on post-colonial societies by scholars such as Sylvia Tamale, focusing on Uganda (1999), Amina Mama on Nigeria at the time of the military dictatorships (1999), Patricia McFadden in her exploration of the southern African region (2001), and South Africa (Amanda Gouws, 1996, and Shireen Hassim, 2003), indicate that many women in post-colonial states become deeply enmeshed in patriarchal, neo-liberal, and neo-colonial imperatives—both in the authoritarian styles that they adopt and in the policies and principles to which they adhere.

Such conclusions are sobering insights into the hegemonic institutional cultures and class dynamics that shape contemporary politics, especially those in the global South. Here, extremely high premiums are placed on entry into political office, and accessing political power, which often allows individual women to secure social and economic power in ways that compromise even the most basic commitment to national woman-centered and anti-imperialist ethics. What remains dominant includes capitalist economic systems as these intersect with patriarchal institutional political cultures. Still, within a world abounding in particular constructions of Black women's sexuality and social roles, as well as hegemonic patriarchal and racialized constructions of leadership, national leadership must be subjected to scrutiny. Patricia McFadden (2001) makes this point in "South Africa, African Feminism and the Challenges of Solidarity," as does Desiree Lewis (2009) in "Baleke Mbete: On Queens Who Would be Kings," the latter suggesting that "the national machinery has offered extremely limited scope for transformation." Mc Fadden's position is that while African women enter social transformation in many ways, as "trade unionists, political leaders, wives and mothers," often in the more traditional ways that women have entered politics, unless conscious "many women position themselves conservatively in response to the state's new ruling function . . . To as great a degree as men, women within the state bureaucracy act in accordance with class logic. They become ruthless defenders of the status quo and operate in ways that protect their power and authority." For this reason, for her, "The African Women's movement . . . has to move to a new place, where we recognize that we are a political force . . . the only movement which can give leadership to a new African political agenda for the future."[63]

Black women have been historically, and continue to be, significant and visible contributors to the formation, establishment, and advancement of African societies on the continent and throughout the world. Beyond contemporary limited representations, the evidence reveals that African women on the continent are the projected leaders of the future. "Half the world" representations have even more meaning in the African context.

NOTES

1. Included in Tony Martin's *Amy Ashwood Garvey: Pan-Africanist, Feminist and Mrs. Marcus Garvey No. 1 or a Tale of Two Amies* (Wellesley, MA: The Majority Press, 2007).

2. Nydia Swaby's "Amy Ashwood Garvey and Black Diaspora / International Feminism" (forthcoming essay made available to author) from her dissertation on Amy Ashwood Garvey and forthcoming monograph *Amy Ashwood Garvey and the Future of Black Feminist Archives* (2022). https://www.nydiaswaby.com/amy-ashwood-garvey-and-the-future-of-black-feminist-archives (accessed 3/8/2022)

3. Revising the classic Marxist assertion "Workers of the World Unite" (*The Communist Manifesto*, 1848).

4. This is identified as a fragment of a book outline in the Amy Ashwood Papers at the National Library of Jamaica and reproduced in Tony Martin's *Amy Ashwood Garvey* (2007): 377–378. A relevant portion is included here for two reasons: one the

need to take forward what was obviously the first part of a major study of the Black woman in global context beginning with Africa, and second, because many of the points raised then are still relevant now.

5. https://www.un.org/shestandsforpeace/content/protocol-african-charter-human-and-peoples-rights-rights-women-africa

6. See Nkiru Nzegwu's discussion of this point in her "Mother of a Nation" section of a her longer essay titled "Aloisea Inyumba: Mother of New Rwanda," *JENDA: A Journal of Culture and African Women Studies*, 10(2007): 10–46.

7. Amadiume, Ifi. "Cheikh Anta Diop's Theory of Matriarchal Values as the Basis for African Cultural Unity." Introduction. *The Cultural Unity of Black Africa: The Domains of Matriarchy and Patriarchy in Classical Antiquity* (London: Karnak House, 1989).

8. See my essay "Respecting African Cultures: Advancing Our Knowledge" in *Benin A Kingdom in Bronze* (2005, 74).

9. A. Adu Boahen, *Yaa Asantewaa and the Asante-British War of 1900–1* (2003).

10. Amina Mama sees her as also exacting violent suppression of surrounding ethnicities as well (personal phone conversation, November, 2020).

11. *Face to Face Africa,* April 5, 2019.

12. Jones cites noted Senegalese historian Boubacar Barry's *The Kingdom of Waalo. Senegal before the Conquest* (New York: Diasporic Africa Press, 2012) as a source.

13. https://www.standardmedia.co.ke/entertainment/local-news/2001355403/how-the-daughters-of-mumbi-are-reclaiming-central-from-male-control., Writer Charity Waciuma published an autobiographical work, *Daughter of Mumbi* (East African Publishing House, 1969). There are websites with this naming now. See also https://mukuyu.wordpress.com/2011/07/21/wamuyu-the-single-mom.

14. *African Dominion: A New History of Empire in Early and Medieval West Africa*, 2019.

15. Isma'il Kushkush, "In the Land of Kush." *Smithsonian Magazine* (September 2020). www.smithsonianmagazine.com

16. Phone conversation with Amina Mama, November, 2020. But see also her important essay, "'We Will Not Be Pacified': From Freedom Fighters to Feminists," *European Journal of Women's Studies* (2020).

17. *Nzinga of Angola. Africa's Warrior Queen* (2017).

18. https://www.aa.com.tr/en/africa/tanzania-swears-in-first-female-president/2181464

19. In *Selected Speeches - Kwame Nkrumah,* Volume 1, Compiled by Samuel Obeng (Afram Publications, Ghana, Ltd., 1979).

20. Amina Mama. Inaugural lecture as the Fourth Kwame Nkrumah Chair in African Studies at the University of Ghana, Legon presented "Nkrumah's Legacy, Feminism and the Next Generation" on February 15, 2022.

21. Tawia Adamafio, *Autobiography* (1982). Cited in Amina Mama lecture. Ibid.

22. *Glitz and Glamour* (2009).

23. Ibid.

24. "The emancipation of women, and the liberation struggle of Africa: on the Liberation of women" Trans. Babacar Mbow.

25. Maathai develops this issue well in her chapter 2, "A Legacy of Woes" in *The Challenge for Africa.*

26. Pat McFadden, "The Challenges and Prospects for the African Women's Movement in the 21st Century" (1997).

27. See her collection of poetry *No Roses from My Mouth, Poems from Prison* (Ubuntu Reading Group, 2020).

28. She had been sentenced to ten years of hard labor (129) but ended up serving two weeks (131).

29. Personal interview. November 9, 2018.

30. https://www.liberianobserver.com/news/dr-ophelia-weeks-named-14th-ul -president; https://www.liberianobserver.com/news/pres-weah-dismisses-ul-president -weeks

31. https://www.unicef.org/liberia/basic-education

32. Indicators including expectancy, per capita income, and education. Nations that rank higher on this index have a higher level of education, a higher lifespan, and a higher gross national income per capita than do nations with lower scores.

33. Joseph Foray, "Liberia: Ellen Johnson Sirleaf to George Weah. Achievements, Challenges, the Way Forward. Lessons for Governance in Africa." *African Reality* (October 3, 2019).

34. *Praxis: The Fletcher Journal of Human Security* xxiv (2009).

35. Tamasin Ford, "Ellen Johnson Sirleaf: The Legacy of Africa's First Elected Female President" *BBC News* (January 22, 2018).

36. Ibid. The Government of Liberia enacted legislation to amend the new Penal Code of June 1976 Chapter 14, Sections 14.70 and 14.71 (the Rape Law). This Act states that a person who has sexual intercourse with another person (male or female) without his/her consent has committed rape that is punishable by ten (10) years or lifetime imprisonment depending on the degree of the rape (rape of a minor, rape resulting in serious bodily harm, rape using a weapon, gang rape). The new rape law came into force in January 2006. The Act also requires on-camera hearings for all rape cases.

37. London, Bogle L'Ouverture, 1972.

38. See Kunle Falayi, "Ngozi Okonjo-Iweala set to Make History at WTO," *BBC News* (February 2, 2021).

39. MIT Press, 2020. See also *Women and Leadership: Real Lives Real Lessons* by Julia Gillard and Ngozi Okonjo-Iweala (MIT Press, 2021) which includes a series of conversations with women in political leadership like Hillary Clinton, Theresa May and Joyce Banda.

40. https://www.france24.com/en/20180105-first-lady-vice-president-liberia-jewel -howard-charles-taylor-sierra-leone

41. Howard Taylor attempted to introduce a hard Anti-Gay Bill in 2007, which was rejected by Johnson Sirleaf.

42. https://www.thecable.ng/jewel-howard-taylor-meet-woman-behind-epic -victory-george-weah

43. See FPA interviews: https://www.youtube.com/watch?v=KBxIhGqVl6E

44. The Arusha Declaration National Museum in Tanzania, which I visited in January, 2022, includes a photograph of her and a description of her contributions. That was the first time that I learned about her critical presence in the independence period.

45. *Africa Woman* 6 (September/October, 1976): 14–15.

46. *JENDA* (9:2006): 1–7.

47. See also Nkiru Nzegwu's Editorial: "Women and Political Leadership," *JENDA* 9(2006): 1–5 which provides some of these details as well including a focus on Luisa Dias Diogo, who was Prime Minister of Mozambique 2004–2010.

48. Translation of Traoré, Aminata Dramane. *Le viol de l'imaginaire.* Libraire Arthene Fayard: Editions Actes Sud, 2010 provided by Babacar Mbow. I interviewed Mme Traoré at her residence in Bamako Mali in January 2018 and her positions are consistent on this issue.

49. Summary of conclusions and conversation on the findings of her MA thesis research provided by Halima Diallo at the Museum of Black Civilizations, Dakar, Senegal, June 2018.

50. The government of Ibrahim Boubacar Keita was deposed in August 2020 by a military coup which still controls Mali. At present former ministers like Mme Diallo have stayed out of the public eye.

51. King Fahd Hotel, July 1919. Text of unpublished interview in my possession supplied by Mme. Diallo.

52. "Aloisea Inyumba: Mother of New Rwanda," *JENDA* 10(2007): 10–46. See also: Pari Farmani, "Aloisea Inyumba: Politician Who Played a Key Role in the Rebuilding of Rwanda." April 16, 2013. https://www.inclusivesecurity.org/2013/04/16/aloisea-inyumba-politician-who-played-a-key-role-in-the-rebuilding-of-rwanda/

53. (June 7, 2010) The Senegalese Parliament recently adopted a new law requiring all political parties to introduce absolute gender parity in electoral lists for all elected representation, national or local. Lists that do not comply with the law will be void. (*Le Sénat adopte la loi sur la parité*), AGENCE DE PRESSE SÉNÉGALAISE (May 19, 2010), available at http://www.aps.sn/aps.php?page=articles&id_article=68583.

Women represent 52% of the total population of Senegal but are only 23% of the representatives in the National Assembly, approximately 10% of the government officials, 13% of regional council members, 20% of municipal council members, and 27% of rural council members. (Abdoulie John, *Women's Advocacy Group Salutes Senegalese MPs for Absolute Parity Law,* JOLLOFNEWS (May 19, 2010), *available at* http://www.jollofnews.com/womens-advocacy-group-salutes-senegalese-mps-for-absolute-parity-law.html.) See: https://www.loc.gov/law/foreign-news/article/senegal-adoption-of-gender-parity-law/

54. https://codesria.org/generalassembly15/wp-content/uploads/2018/12/CODESRIA-15th-GA_15eme-AG_Draft-Programme.pdf

55. *Sauti Ya Ujamaa*, 22 July, 2021.

56. Source: *Femmes et Politique: 2019. Situation au 1er janvier 2019. ONU Femmes, Entite des Nations Unies pour l'egalite des sexes et l'autonomisation des femmes.*

57. Research provided by personal assistant to Samia Nkrumah.

58. Solange Ashby, p. 31.

59. Source: Museum of Black Civilizations, Dakar, Senegal. Exhibition and Conference on African Women and Political Leadership (Co-Sponsored by UN Women), March 2020.

60. Presentation on contemporary currents in leadership of African Women on the continent to my Black Women and Political Leadership class, Cornell University, October 15, 2020.

61. Personal communication at the Museum of Black Civilizations, Dakar with author Halima Diallo from her recently completed M.A. Thesis, "Women Leaders in Senegal," 2018.

62. Ibid. General Conclusion of thesis, notes provided by author.

63. Pat McFadden, "The Challenges and Prospects for African Women's Movement in the 21st century." Women in Action. Issue 1 (1997), http://www.hartford-hwp.com/archives/30/152.html. Accessed 2/8/2021.

Chapter 5

Black Women Lead the Desire for a Transformed United States

The Pivotal Role of Shirley Chisholm

In many ways, the current rise of women to political leadership in the United States reflects decades of feminist, decolonial, Civil Rights and Black Power activism that challenged the logic that leadership is always and only white and/or male. Although there were Black male U.S. senators in the immediate post-emancipation period, it was not until after the Civil Rights movement that Black male and then Black female leaders rose to political positions, and even then, not without contestation. Unsurprisingly, the election and accomplishments of a first Black president in the United States (President Barack Obama, 2008–2016), seen as the culmination of at least a century of activist work, has been met with mixed responses, ranging from extreme racism at one end, disappointments, or satisfactions in the middle, and, for some, amazed joy in the final revelation of a dream that many held from the period of enslavement to the contemporary.[1]

Black women's leadership encompasses their contributions to a range of fields, often advancing the creation and maintenance of basic human needs for food, clothing, and shelter but also offering transcendence over imposed restrictions. These are revealed in their contributions to developing agricultural techniques and food production, and by extension the culinary arts; textile production and fashion; modes of child rearing and family organization; herbal medicine and natural cures; and architecture and home management. Many of these have enhanced or led to further scientific inventions which have aided human wellbeing. In the early 21st century, Black women continue to demonstrate political and intellectual leadership, to assert personal, social, and cultural autonomy, and to challenge inequities and patriarchal oppression as they propel more advanced and equitable versions of the societies in which they live.

Harriet Araminta Tubman and Sojourner Truth provide the symbolic and historic resonances that show how Black women, from the start, confronted and negotiated the systems of oppression in which we are still positioned in the United States. Harriet's unwillingness to accept enslavement as she liberated others[2] and Sojourner Truth's purposeful walk out of her New York plantation with a continuance to speak the truth provide early models of Black women leaders who challenged the boundaries of containment and then led others to more liberated mental and physical places. The fact that Black women have continuously exercised leadership, in many different ways, is revealed in the constellation of Black women in the United States at the turn of the 20th century who were also central in advancing the rights of Black people. Although Frederick Douglass and his cohorts were advancing the larger Black community as nationalists and Pan-Africanists, even as they were representing Black men, few included Black women's rights in their assessments.[3] Maria Stewart (1803–1879) is identified as giving the first public lecture on the subject of women's leadership, in which she spoke specifically about rights for Black women, whom she referred to as "Daughters of Africa."[4] These are Stewart's words: "O ye daughters of Africa! Arise! Awake! What have you done to immortalize your names beyond the grave?" Maria Stewart would also use a similar phrasing when she referred to "Africa's daughters"[5] in her speech in Boston in 1832, when chattel slavery in the United States was still being practiced. She forecast the future:

> I am of a strong opinion that the day on which we unite heart and soul and turn our attention to knowledge and improvement, that day the hissing and reproach among the nations of the earth against us will cease. And even those who now point at us with the finger of scorn, will aid and befriend us. It is no use for us to sit with our hands folded hanging our heads like bulrushes, lamenting our wretched condition; but let us make a mighty effort, and arise, and if no one will promote our respect us, let us promote and respect ourselves. (28)[6]

Her challenge to Black women was to extricate themselves from being consigned to service work. She criticized the assumptions and practices of Black women being relegated to domestic work, having to "bury their minds and talents beneath a load of iron pots and kettles" (29).

Targeting women's political power directly though is Frances Watkins Harper (1825–1911) who addressed issues of voting: "what we need to-day is not simply more voters, but better voters" (41) and women's leadership, she says ". . . and it is the women of a country who help to mold its character; and to influence if not determine its destiny, and in the political future of our nation woman will not have done what she could if she does not endeavor to have our republic stand foremost among the nations of the earth" (41). Harper's words are still relevant today and guides this chapter in several ways.

Another star in this particular constellation of early Black women leaders in the United States is Anna Julia Cooper (1859–1964), who is recorded as having attended the first Pan-African conference in London in 1900. Her presence there re-confirms that women have been foundational from the very start of Pan-Africanism. This is significant because often so far, it is only the male delegates whose contributions are recognized. Nevertheless, her attendance was documented in reports:

> Delegates, "all eminent in their sphere" represented the United States, Canada, Ethiopia, Haiti, Liberia, Sierra Leone, the then Gold Coast, most of the islands of the then British West Indies . . . In the powerful American Delegation were: W.E.B. Dubois, Miss Anna Jones (Kansas), and Mrs. Annie Cooper (i.e., Anna Julia Cooper, Washington, D.C.) (First Pan African Conference, 1900)[7]

In her classic assertion of what today would be called intersectionality, Anna Julia Cooper provides an early understanding of the positionality of Black women: "The colored woman of today occupies, one may say, a unique position in this country. In a period, itself transitional and unsettled, her status seems one of the least ascertainable and definitive of all the forces which make for our civilization. She is confronted by both a woman question and a race problem and is as yet an unknown or an unacknowledged factor in both" (45).[8]

Given the ways that histories have been written to privilege white/male power, leadership by Black women has tended to be subject to historical erasure, until the institutionalizing of Black Women's Studies in the early 1980's.[9] Until the work of Black women historians and literary critics, who found and studied the body of material that defines Black women's intellectual and creative contributions, many of these presences remained under-recognized and unacknowledged For example, although Marcus Garvey has become synonymous with the leadership of the Universal Negro Improvement Association (UNIA) having been ceremonially mythologized from photography to the lyrics and iconography of Rastafari, both Garvey's wives and a range of other women such as Henrietta Vinton Davis assisted in creating and advancing this organization in the United States and especially throughout the Americas. The international organizational work and sustenance of the Pan-Africanist project of the UNIA can be studied as well through co-founder Amy Ashwood Garvey who travelled to "forty-two states of the U.S.A.; all the islands of the Caribbean, South and Central America; Europe as far north as Turkey and the British Isles, and now in the West of Africa, she has made a detailed tour of Sierra Leone, Liberia, Nigeria, the

Gold Coast (now Ghana) French West Africa, French Equatorial Africa, British and French Cameroons, Spanish Guinea and the Belgian Congo."[10] Thus, Amy Ashwood Garvey became the visible representation in Europe and Africa of some of the intentions of their political movement. Moreover, during Marcus Garvey's struggles against concocted mail fraud charges against him and his subsequent incarceration, Amy Jacques Garvey assumed leadership of the UNIA-ACL and became the face of the movement. Ultimately, she too left the "Great Man" and returned to Jamaica with her two sons. And, because she lived some thirty years afterward, she documented and affected much of what the movement sought to achieve.

After the relationship between Marcus and Amy Ashwood Garvey ended, Caribbean-born, New York-based Hubert Harrison, socialist activist-intellectual who Garvey emulated at the start of his Harlem, New York period, described how significant Amy Ashwood was to the advancement of that political movement in these words: "But this little West Indian is a well-spring of ambition and inspiration. No wonder Garvey called her his 'Star of destiny!' She veritably was . . . I wish it were possible for me to get her as my helpmeet. I think I should rise to giddy heights of achievement" (629).[11]

Hubert Harrison is credited with being the radical intellectual who created the "race-first" argument which Garvey would apply more deliberately in his conceptual political framing. He also was the first to define the "New Negro Movement," one of the descriptors of the Harlem Renaissance Movement.[12] Though evidently "a lady's man" and a reputed lover of Amy Ashwood Garvey, he is on record as also advocating the advancement of women's rights. In one photograph from the time, in New Jersey during the 1913 Paterson silk strike, Harrison is seated on the lecture platform with communist feminist activist Elizabeth Gurley Flynn.[13] Still, because women's contributions in that period were often taken for granted, many of these advancements, such as Grace Campbell as one of the leaders of the African Blood Brotherhood, were omitted from history.[14]

This tendency to discount Black women's leadership—when they are, in reality, the most "super-exploited" and yet also the most engaged in various leadership roles—has been noted by Black left theorist Claudia Jones. In her 1949 essay, "An End to the Neglect of the Negro Woman," she describes the contribution of Black women's leadership in the immediate post World War II period in "all aspects of the struggle for peace, civil rights and economic security . . . having profound meaning, both for the Negro liberation movement and for the emerging anti-fascist, anti-imperialist coalition" (74). She saw the avoidance of Black women's leadership as an ongoing concern that needed to be corrected:

To understand the militancy correctly, to deepen and extend the role of Negro women in the struggle for peace and for all interests of the working class and the Negro people, means primarily to overcome the gross neglect of the special problems of Negro women. This neglect has too long permeated the ranks of the labor movement generally, of Left-progressives and also of the Communist Party. (7)

This framing of activism and dedicated contribution in the face of neglect becomes the paradox in which Black women continue to be located. It is precisely that "neglect" that Shirley Chisholm similarly challenged in her own narrative of a political life and which she sought to contest deliberately and consistently in framing a role for herself in New York and national politics, explicitly questioning why there should only be white males in leadership. For this reason, Shirley Chisholm's central role in Black women's electoral politics in the United States and the influence of her example on subsequent generations of Black women activists who entered the formal political system, has to be repeatedly articulated to be seriously considered if heard at all.

UNBOUGHT AND UNBOSSED/GOOD FIGHT POLITICS

Shirley Chisholm is central to any assessment of Black women in politics in the United States and indeed the world. She is also central to this book's structure. Her life and political struggles provide benchmarks and guides for subsequent and future women's advances to political leadership at the highest levels. Often neglected, in the sense in which Claudia Jones intends it, this study is deliberate about employing the "ending neglect" position. Additionally, this chapter deliberately locates Shirley Chisholm within a larger African Diasporic pattern of Black women who challenged imposed limitations. First, Chisholm repeatedly indicated that she had the right to run for political office, and second, that failing to achieve that goal as she did in her early run for the presidency, was not really losing. Her affirmative statement on this right typifies her politics: "The mere fact that a Black woman dared to run for President, *seriously*, not expecting to win, but sincerely trying to, is what it was all about. 'It can be done'; that was what I was trying to say, by doing it."[15]

For Shirley Chisholm, from her position as a Black woman outside of the frameworks of political power, it was better to compete for a higher office and lose than not to run at all. Thus, by these means she provided the example for Black political women after her, such as Stacey Abrams who, competed for office, and then channeled the energy of that anger against the injustice which resulted in her loss of the governorship of Georgia into a "Fair Fight" campaign, using similar language as did Chisholm. The deliberate play on "fair fight" in my view also recalls Chisholm's "good fight" conceptual language. As a result, Abrams's strategic work towards a "Fair Fight" made Georgia a key Democratic Party win in 2020, thus positively affecting the outcome of the national election, after years of that state being identified as a Republican stronghold.[16] Succeeding generations of women who similarly embark on attaining leadership in high political office should be informed by Chisholm's and Abrams's resistance to erasure.

Shirley Chisholm represented New York's 12th Congressional District for seven terms from 1969 to 1983. In 1968, she became the first Black woman elected to Congress. In 1972, she again made history by being the first African-American and the first woman to run for the US presidency, as a Democrat. But she remained forgotten by or unknown to subsequent generations.[17] A recent text by Daina Ramey and Kali Nicole Gross, *A Black Women's History of the United States* (2021) attempts a revision that replaces women in several political junctures and positions Shirley Chisholm within Black Power and Black Feminist Politics as their chapter is titled: "Shirley's Run, Black Power, Politics and Black Feminism 1970–2000" (185–207). Another stark example of a similar neglect and erasure is observable in the fact that Charlene Mitchell, in 1968 had also run for the presidency as a Communist Party candidate. Given the negative framing of socialism and communism by dominant media and political culture in the United States, Mitchell's historic run tends to be seen as irrelevant or even non-existent in subsequent assessments of women who have historically challenged the highest echelons of power. It is important that Charlene Mitchell cites the influence of Claudia Jones on her political formation.[18]

Another Black woman of political power, missing from assessment, in the same time period as Shirley Chisholm is Congresswoman Barbara Jordan, a Texas senator from 1966 to 1972. Jordan entered the US House of Representatives in 1972, the same year that Chisholm ran for president. Barbara Jordan became a powerful and popular political figure, especially during the 1974 Watergate Hearings and at her zenith was even mentioned as a possible running mate to Jimmy Carter (James Earl Carter, Jr.) who became president in 1977. At the Democratic National Convention that year, she was the first African-American woman to deliver the keynote speech. Many people today in contemporary student populations, are unaware of Barbara Jordan's illustrious career, though statues of her grace the Austin airport and the University of Texas at Austin, campus. In a similar way, this current generation had to be apprised of the major investigative journalism and activism for race and gender rights of Ida B. Wells Barnett,[19] a major activist and journalist in the decades before the Civil Rights movement, through her posthumous winning of the Pulitzer Prize in 2020.

By the end of the 20th century, with the rise of Black feminist assessments, many recognized in hindsight that it was Black women's particular combination of race and gender that kept Barbara Jordan and Shirley Chisholm from becoming US presidents; certainly, it was not a lack of ability, competence, preparation, or political skill. Since then, several women have served as local, state, or national representatives in the United States. There is an interesting chartable leadership movement of Black women in United States politics through Carol Mosley Braun the first Black woman as US senator (1993–1999), before Condoleezza Rice was appointed as Secretary of State, from 2005 to 2008, by President George W. Bush Jr. Another significant state representative is Barbara Lee of California (1998–present) the only congresswoman to vote against the War on Iraq, who sponsored the bill making June Caribbean-American Heritage Month. Lee, a Democrat, credits Shirley Chisholm and her challenge to Lee as a then young student as having inspired her to pursue political leadership.[20]

Scholarship on Shirley Chisholm is still limited to her two autobiographical books, a few published articles and book chapters and one study.[21] In content, these available works are biographical, emphasizing her presidential run against all odds in 1972. Sporadic media coverage follow major events, such as her initial campaign, her being the first Black congresswoman and a candidate for the presidency, and her death in 2005. John Nichols's "Shirley Chisholm's Legacy" (*The Nation,* January 4, 2005) is a retrospective essay on her gains and influences. Natasha Lavender's "The Incredible Real-Life Story of Shirley Chisholm," published after Kamala Harris's nomination in 2020, documents how Chisholm was patronized by the media, including the legendary Walter Cronkite. According to Lavender, "[P]lenty of white people openly refused to vote for a Black candidate while Chisholm felt that her gender was used against her more than her race." In 1982, Chisholm told an Associated Press reporter: "When I ran for the Congress, when I ran for president, I met more discrimination as a woman than for being Black." That discrimination clearly extended to some Black men too, from whom she received vilification in the days before *misogynoir*[22] was defined. According to the *LA Times,* Chisholm once said, "Not many Black people can really believe that a Black person, who also happens to be a woman, can become president of this country."[23]

Quite a bit more information is available now, with the rise of online sources and social media and two Shirley Chisholm Foundations and Institutes at Brooklyn College and the Empire College of the State University of New York. There are also several children's books on Shirley Chisholm such as *She Was the First. The Trailblazing Life of Shirley Chisholm*[24] and Veronica Chambers, *Shirley Chisholm is a Verb*[25] and *Shirley Chisholm Dared. The Story of the First Black Woman in Congress*[26] by Alicia D. Williams and April

Harrison. However, full academic studies are still limited. Ellen Fitzgerald's *Women's Quest for the American Presidency*[27] includes a long chapter titled "Shirley Chisholm 'Shake It Up, Make It Change,'" which puts Chisholm in an American historical context. It begins with the journalistic coverage, details Chisholm's background, and assesses that her "entire political career had been an exercise in overcoming wild probabilities" (147). Fitzgerald's chapter addresses the issues that Chisholm advanced, including aid for the poor, racism, and women's rights. Her position on busing was that it was an "artificial solution" to the racially based problem of segregated schools, particularly when Black children were historically "bussed" to poorly maintained schools outside of their communities. Additionally, one of her important challenges on the unequal treatment of the Black community was directed to city officials on the absence of consistent trash collection in Black neighborhoods, the absence of police protection and the lack of maintenance of housing codes (Fitzgerald, 166). She saw these as all designed to maintain Black communities in an unequal and subordinate position to white ones with direct impact on personal and economic well-being.

An issue unique at the time to Chisholm, however, was her identification as a product of the Caribbean Diaspora in Brooklyn. Her explicit Caribbean connection was indicated further in that she spent her early and formative years in Barbados, living with her extended family and particularly under the influence of a grandmother whom she would identify subsequently as a role model. The writer Paule Marshall, whose writing time-frame covers the same period as Chisholm's active political life, offers the best creative elaboration of this specifically Barbadian experience between Brooklyn and Barbados. In *Triangular Road: A Memoir* (2009), Marshall charts a familiar pattern of Caribbean migration for employment, from Barbados to Panama to New York. Many of Marshall's writings, based in Brooklyn, capture some of the same experiences that Chisholm describes briefly in the early chapters of her autobiography. For example, a version of Chisholm's grandmother in Barbados comes alive in Marshall's short story "To Da-Duh in Memoriam."[28] According to scholar Anastasia Curwood, "Chisholm's Barbadian grandmother Emmeline Chase Seale, she [Chisholm] recalled, was her most influential childhood mentor. Emmeline's bold self-carriage and modeling of fearlessness were 'where I got my nerve . . .'" (207). Marshall's classic *Brown Girl Brownstones* (1959) presents a protagonist, Selina, who can be read as a version of the young woman that Chisholm was in her Brooklyn College experience. With Chisholm's autobiographical narrative, though. we get a specific experience of the pathway she would take in student organizations and movements, leading her to become an active politician representing her Brooklyn community. A leading scholar of African-American literature, Mary Helen Washington, working on a biography of Paule Marshall, documents that Marshall's son Evan describes going to a Shirley Chisholm rally with his mother.[29] Marshall's novel closes with Selina Boyce going to Barbados; Shirley St. Hill, who becomes Shirley Chisholm, had already made that journey in her childhood, and was ready and armored by the time she gets to adulthood, unlike Selina, with the confidence of that early upbringing to tell people either to help her or get out of her way. Based on my knowledge of the discourse of the Caribbean woman they both describe, Chisholm may have heard her grandmother say exactly that to anyone attempting to deter her from accomplishing some goal.

Significantly, one accomplishment that allowed Shirley Chisholm to become the representative politician she became was her fluency in Spanish. According to Fitzgerald: "Chisholm graduated from college in 1946 with honors and with a fluency in Spanish that would later become a great asset to her" (163). Chisholm recalled using her skill in several Spanish-speaking communities during her various campaigns which contrasts still with rudimentary greetings in Spanish which are more normative for American politicians.

Her woman's rights activism also placed her in an earlier recognition than that of contemporary political analysis, of the "women's vote" and specifically the "Black woman's vote" as a decisive voting bloc which would be fully realized in the Obama period. Very early in her process, Shirley Chisholm had delineated the structure of the Brooklyn community as having a large number of female-headed households, which became a usable demographic during campaigning. Additionally, her support staff was comprised predominantly of women, many of whom volunteered because of the historic nature of her campaign. Chisholm additionally became a champion of New York State's unemployment insurance for household workers, thus providing domestic workers with a way of accessing some security for their labor: "She focused her energies on the issues most central to her constituents—labor, education, housing, health care, and the scourge of racial discrimination. The needs of working women also fully engaged her" (Fitzgerald, 183).

These issues that concerned domestic workers which Chisholm's legislation advanced had been raised in activist contexts by Marvel Cook,[30] Ella Baker, Claudia Jones, and others who exposed the exploitation of Black women, many immigrants or recently migrated from the US south, in what they described as "The Bronx Slave Market" (1935 and 1950). Claudia Jones had in 1949 already presented the "super-exploitation of the Black woman" thesis and in my view, these publicly discussed positions would be automatically part of Chisholm's basic political consciousness particularly since she also supported and advanced the Equal Rights Amendment and spoke in Congress on its behalf (Fitzgerald, 197) informed by the race and gender implications of women's rights positions. The link with Paule Marshall is again relevant here as the writer of "From the Poets of the Kitchen"[31] evokes a scene familiar to Chisholm, in which the women meet on weekends and talk about the many forms of oppression they experience in domestic work in white women's households. In Paule Marshall's creative description of these now-legendary Caribbean domestic workers:

> Several mornings a week these unknown bards would put an apron and a pair of old house shoes in a shopping bag and take the train or streetcar from our section of Brooklyn out to Flatbush. There, those who didn't have steady jobs would wait on certain designated corners for the white housewives in the neighborhood to come along and bargain with them over pay for a day's work cleaning their houses. This was the ritual even in the winter.
>
> The basement kitchen of the brownstone house where my family lived was the usual gathering place. Once inside the warm safety of its walls the women threw off the drab coats and hats, seated themselves at the large center table, drank their cups of tea or cocoa, and talked . . . (*NYT*, January 9, 1983)

These are the women that Chisholm came from and also represented, and they also made her acutely aware of the race/gender/class conjunction, experiencing the negative aspects of being a Black woman, even in her own professional life as a politician and most definitely in her campaign for president.

Clearly, Chisholm espoused a version of Black feminism, even challenging white feminists like Bella Abzug and Gloria Steinem for not fully supporting her or offering her partial support. Chisholm who supported the Equal Rights Amendment, wholeheartedly as indicated, articulated a very pro-feminist position, spoke to the National Organization for Women, supported a woman's right to choose, and supported or led several feminist organizations. Citing Chisholm's activism, Anastasia Curwood in "Black Feminism on Capitol Hill: Shirley Chisholm and Movement Politics, 1968–1984"[32] indicates that Chisholm's Black Feminism represented an early "an intersectional approach to wielding political power. Chisholm's own feminist analyses reflected her interlocking concerns with the effects of poverty, sexism and racism in the United States" (205). Characteristically, and particularly for Black women of her generation, Chisholm did not have to claim feminism as an identity even as she advanced women's rights positions. But clearly, Chisholm advocated feminist politics over claiming a particular identity position that "led her to support feminism alongside the Black freedom struggle" (213). Perhaps more to our focus, according to Curwood: "Chisholm supported the growing Black feminist movement by delivering a speech at the inaugural conference for the National Black Feminist Organization [NBFO] in New York City in November, 1973" (216).

One available monograph, *Shirley Chisholm Catalyst for Change, 1926–2005,* by Barbara Winslow, uses a chronological narrative and includes numerous primary documents, some of which were published as chapters in Chisholm's *Unbought and Unbossed*, and some of Chisholm's speeches during her time in Congress. Among them, her 1982 speech on US policy toward Black refugees is still timely, wherein she linked racism and immigration policies, asserting that "the color question overlays the politics of our refugee politics" (172). Chisholm cited several examples, including the still current preferential treatment of Cubans over Haitians and of Eastern Europeans over Africans. She also evoked the "brain drain" from Africa at the start of the large migration of continental Africans to the United States and closed with the injunction that African-Americans should be involved in the shaping of refugee policy.

Winslow's "catalyst for change" titling and description comes from Chisholm's own words: in 2004, a year before her passing, Chisholm stated what she wanted her contribution to be.[33] Geared toward students, Winslow provides "Study Questions" at the end of the book, with one of them including the assertion that "Shirley Chisholm was a Feminist" (176). In the chapter titled "The Unquiet Congresswoman" Winslow details "the formative, influential role she played in the women's movement" (83) such as reintroducing the Equal Rights Amendment on August 10, 1970. Even today, the United States is one of only a few countries that have never passed an Equal Rights Amendment or ratified CEDAW, the Convention on the Elimination of All Forms of Discrimination Against Women.[34] Relevantly, Chisholm's support for Fannie Lou Hamer and her work with the National Women's Political Caucus also stem from her position that women's organizations needed to advance poor and working women of color. According to Winslow, "Chisholm understood that setting a minimum wage for domestics and unionizing them would reduce their dependence on their employers (usually white women). She maintained that a minimum wage for domestics could alleviate the burden of poverty on Black families, 50 percent of which were headed by a woman" (84). This was precisely the position that Claudia Jones advanced also in her support for the unionization of domestic workers in "An End to the Neglect of the Problems of the Negro Woman" (1949) where she makes a similar case, including the rights to organization of domestic workers, which Chisholm also supported.

Noteworthy as well in any assessment of Congresswoman Shirley Chisholm is the introduction to *Want to Start a Revolution,* which puts her also squarely in the Black radical tradition which asserts that Black women's self-emancipation makes them critical to fully understanding post-war radical Black politics. The chapter by Joshua Guild titled "Shirley Chisholm's Radical Politics of Possibility" also locates her within Black feminist radical politics. It follows the usual biographical trajectory of most writing on Chisholm, particularly highlighting the James Farmer/Shirley Chisholm campaign for

New York's 17th congressional district, which ended up being symbolically a Black nationalist vs. Black feminist competition that Chisholm won handily. For Guild, "Chisholm's emergent radicalism derived from her resistance to a kind of Black militant rhetoric—and to a formulation of Black politics more generally—that privileged male leadership, while ignoring the specific concerns of women." Still, Chisholm had the support and endorsement of the Black Panther Party (264), which she never disavowed. Chisholm is on record as well as supporting Angela Davis, who was then incarcerated on gun charges after being on the FBI's Most Wanted List. Many of Chisholm's male colleagues thought such a position to be political suicide.

Controversially, though she rejected an appearance at the National Black Political Convention in Gary, Indiana, perhaps following the same trajectory of her defeat of Farmer as not accepting Black male sexism and building an independent Black woman's profile. Guild sees her actions then as demonstrating a form of Black women's independent radicalism, rejecting Black masculinist tendencies in leadership. In my assessment, it may have been, as well, her unwillingness to be "pigeonholed" into any camp, which she demonstrated as a political stance even as she worked to build coalitions with feminist groups, cofounding the National Women's Political Caucus (263), and being a member of the National Organization for Women (NOW).

The impact on subsequent Black women in the political spectrum but also the examples she set would spur women such as Congresswoman Barbara Lee in California (1998–present) and Councilwoman Una Clarke in Brooklyn (1992–2001). Una Clarke would occupy the same seat as Chisholm in the 17th district; her daughter, Congresswoman Yvette Clarke, represented New York's 11th district from 2007 to 2013, now its 9th district. Several other contemporary political women claim Chisholm as their guiding model as we see with Vice President Kamala Harris acceptance speech in 2020.

SHIRLEY CHISHOLM'S SELF-DEFINED RADICAL CHALLENGE

Unbought and Unbossed (1972) and *The Good Fight* (1973) remain classic assessments of a Black woman's entry into the formal American political landscape. In the first, Chisholm creates the idea of Black candidates writing their own political autobiographies, a practice emulated by Barack Obama, Stacey Abrams, and Kamala Harris as essential tools in creating a presidential level political trajectory. As a result, *Unbought and Unbossed* remains the authorized source for essays, books, and films on the Congresswoman, capturing a political posture that refused shady political business, monopolistic interests, white male dominance and other controls that mark contemporary politics.

Unbought and Unbossed opens with a section titled "Growing Up," which deals with her early schooling and family experience in Barbados and then her move back to Brooklyn and her start in politics. The epigraph that begins this section summarizes her already keen insight into an inequity that many had accepted as a norm. What stands out for this writer in that early section is her first meeting with her grandmother: "When the bus stopped, there was Grandmother—Mrs. Emily Seale, a tall, gaunt, erect, Indian-looking woman with her hair knotted on her neck. I did not know it yet, but this stately woman with a stentorian voice was going to be one of the few persons whose authority I would never dare to defy, or even question" (18–19).

She also describes seeing the Caribbean "provision grounds" or "Creole gardens" as a natural part of the Caribbean landscape: "each had a garden in front to grow yams, sweet potatoes, pumpkins, cassava, and breadfruit—mainstays of the Caribbean diet" (19). Barbadian life in the 1930's, including the nature of schooling, still in the colonial context of honoring British royalty was also discussed, this having an important preparatory effect on the girl that she was then. An interesting historical view of Brooklyn in the 1930's and the various Caribbean communities, which she calls "colonies," and the hard-working life of Caribbean immigrants, navigating the cold of New York in those days without central heating is subsequently presented. Problems in placing children of migrating families in the appropriate classes in schools, and surrounding political and economic struggles, are also shown. Indeed, these early chapters provide important documentation of Caribbean peoples' lives in New York, informed by Marcus Garvey's positions on Black advancement still strongly evident in family discussions and positions in the 1930's. As a result, the then Shirley St Hill's college years usher in a political life that constitutes the rest of the text, from her Brooklyn College experiences to her running for office in New York and navigating the larger state and national political spectrum.

Subsequent chapters appear under the title "Getting There" include "Teaching, Marriage and The Political Era," "Running for Congress," and "Breaking the Rules." Often in political autobiographies, the personal is subordinated or not included, but for Chisholm the personal begins the narrative and her political self-assertions and successes. After a chapter on marriage, the rest of the text deals with her political pathways, initiatives, struggles, and speeches. Later chapters include her assessments of Congress, positions she took, and her analyses of the classic speeches she made on the key issues during her time in office: abortion rights, the war in Vietnam, racism, and women's liberation. Chisholm felt that the only saving grace for the United States would be the various people of color: "They, if any, will become the conscience that the country has lacked. They will try to force it to practice what it has preached" (188). Her comment though seems to foreshadow current Democratic representation in which the first Black, Latino, and gay members of congress become her projected vision of the nature of a new generation of political representatives, referred to as the "left" even though they are not leftists politically: "Such leaders must be found. But they will not be found as much as they will be created, by an electorate that has become ready to demand that it control its own destiny. There must be a new coalition of all Americans –Black, white, red, yellow and brown, rich and poor—who are no longer willing to allow their rights as human beings to be infringed upon by anyone else for any reason" (190–191).

The Good Fight (1973) is Shirley Chisholm's personal documentation of her presidential run. Its title resonates subsequently in former congressman John Lewis's "Good Trouble," his mantra for describing his interventions for social change. A significant aspect of this "good fight" political campaign biography is her acknowledgment that her run was without the kind of financial support of which white men are assured. Her campaign was a patchwork quilt of different supporting interests. Yet we see that it became a strategic framework when later used by Barack Obama, particularly with the advancements in technology and the possibilities of on-line donations. Additionally, her consistent articulation which Obama would emulate was that she was not running singly as a Black candidate, but as representing several other American interests which expanded her constituencies.

One of the most critical aspects of *The Good Fight* is her documentation of sexism, as received from Black male patriarchy. Historically, Black male sexism has been less addressed than white male sexism. This is often more visible when the experiences of African women are discussed. Still, the logic of Black feminist organizing in the United States comes directly from the assumptions of Black women's subordination, built into the American gendered/racialized hierarchy. This was brought to formal institutional recognition in the landmark anthology *All the Blacks are Men, All the Women are White, But Some of Us Are Brave* (1982). For this reason, in many ways, Chisholm is one of the best persons through whom one can understand and articulate the effects of these combined experiences. In her chapter on "Black Politics," she details both the Black male activist and politically entrenched assumption that the first Black presidential candidate had to be a Black man. Therefore, it followed that a Black man would be the de facto representative leader of the African-American community in the United States. A by-product of this assumption was the idea that her presence in the political leadership landscape, by itself, was taking away the rights of Black men to this leadership. Chisholm gives several examples of how this was voiced in 1971 at the Northlake meeting in Chicago where these decisions were made by Black male leadership and summed up in a *Washington Post* report: "In this first serious effort of Blacks for high political office, it would be better if it were a man" (31). This led Chisholm to conclude that she had received more discrimination as a woman than as a Black person (32). Her articulation of the particular location of Black women in politics in this time period is important: ". . . Black women are not here to compete or fight with you. If we have hang-ups about being male or female, we're going to waste the talents that should be put to use to liberate our people. Black women must be able to give what they have in the struggle" (34) was a critical aspect of her response. This was based on her observation that:

> Women are a majority of the population, but they are treated like a minority group. The prejudice against them is so widespread that, paradoxically most persons do not yet realize it exists. Indeed, most women do not realize it. They even accept being paid less for doing the same work as a man. They are as quick as any male to condemn a woman who ventures outside the limits of the role men have assigned to females: that of toy or drudge.[35]

Shirley Chisholm consistently indicated that her decision to run came from listening to young people who supported her positions and who inspired her decisions, because they wanted the kind of change that she represented. Relevantly and specific to student activism at Cornell University which led to the formation of Africana Studies as a field, Chisholm cited the Willard Straight Hall takeover as epitomizing the legitimate reasons for Black student activism, and the media distortions that followed (17–19), concluding that "student rebellions are seldom, if ever, the irrational and anarchistic behavior that older people believe they are. Each one is comprehensible, and many are praiseworthy" (19).

In the end, Shirley Chisholm's decision to enter the presidential campaign was based on the idea of being a "catalyst for change" (33), the same logic of change that Barack Obama actualized in his "Change" platform in his 2008 bid for the presidency. In my assessment then, her influence is not primarily on the women candidates who followed her (Hillary Clinton, Elizabeth Warren, Amy Klobuchar, Kamala Harris), but also on providing the example of Obama, a framing that extended beyond racial politics: "I am not the candidate of Black America, although I am Black and proud. I am not the candidate of the women's movement of this country, although I am a woman, and I am equally proud of that. I am not the candidate of any political bosses or special interests . . . I am the candidate of the people" (71). Additionally, Shirley Chisholm's campaign was also based on mobilizing a young generation of eligible voters who were often overlooked in political organizing but who had spurred her on to entering the campaign for the presidency.

The issue of radicalism in the context of Shirley Chisholm's daring in her challenge to democratic status quo politics is worthy of targeted consideration. The idea of what is "radical" in social transformation became a lever of support or rejection at the political level, and it did so in her bid for the presidency. She indicates this in her statement that: "To a lot of Black people I am a real radical, and they never could support me. Imagine how they feel about all-out Black radicals of the kind most prominent in national politics."[36] For her, a certain radicalism can be indicated in her daring to run for the presidency of the United States as a Black woman. In *The Good Fight,* Chisholm addresses this issue directly and provides here the classic definition of the word "radical" as in going to the root of a problem. She counterpoints this seeming radicalism with the prescient conclusion that American democracy is mostly conservative, that "the United States is moving to the right, and that the main force behind the movement is a resurgence, in a new form, of racial prejudice" (149). Here Chisholm anatomizes what became more blatantly visible, advanced in the United States under Trumpism between 2016 and 2020 and culminated in the white supremacist insurrection and the now infamous taking over of The Capitol on January 6, 2021.

Clarifying the specifics of left radicalism further, in an earlier context, Claudia Jones—also defined as radical because of her active membership in the Communist Party, USA—confronted this position on radicalism directly in her assessment of United States history. Asserting rhetorically the right to radicalism, Jones said: "Do not an oppressed people have a right to have radicals?" Her response is very specific to the history of what Black radicalism has been and continues to be: "The very core of all Negro history is radicalism against conformity to chattel slavery, radicalism against the betrayal of the demands of Reconstruction, radicalism in relation to non-acceptance of the status quo!"[37] In the United States, the struggle for full citizenship rights remains the overarching claim, consistent in all movements, the right to the economic and social benefits that the state assumes for its dominant population. Any challenge by Black people to an entrenched hierarchy that presumes white supremacist domination is deemed radical.

For Shirley Chisholm, entering electoral politics as a Black woman was itself a radical move. For Claudia Jones, entering Communist Party activist politics was also seen as radical. For Black women, just living, loving oneself and being happy and free and self-assertive is seen as being radical in white supremacist thinking. What Shirley Chisholm and Claudia Jones share in this context is that they were both Black women, who by being Black and women were above all, unwilling to accept subordination within a system oppressive to both of these identities. Additionally they were challenging the status quo and for this therefore deemed radical.

In my view, Shirley Chisholm is the central figure in any understanding of Black women navigating the political landscapes of race, gender, class, sexuality, and the US political system. Subsequent Black women politicians have continued to create coalitions out of these otherwise disparate positions, the ones that Black women live often separately but more often in combination. In the Shola Lynch film Unbought and Unbossed, Congresswoman Barbara Lee of California credits Shirley Chisholm with influencing her entry into political consciousness and eventually her own participation as a congresswoman. But the influences extend in directions often not visible. The golden thread of Chisholm's politics runs through the entire tapestry of Black women's political activism inside the United States but also internationally. The spirit, style, and energy of "The Squad"—Congresswomen Alexandria Ocasio-Cortez, Ayanna Pressley, Ilhan Omar, and Rashida Tlaib—representing their communities in 2018 with Cori Bush added in 2020, all with a distinctly assertive presence, reflect similar experiences that in her time were expressed and lived by Congresswoman Shirley Chisholm. In particular, the combined racism and sexism she experienced from Congressional colleagues when she entered the United States House of Representatives has contemporary versions but are also observable in the ways that she and they fight back against these oppressive tactics.

GWENDOLYN SAWYER CHERRY'S BLACK FEMINIST ASSERTION AND THE NEW YORK/FLORIDA CONNECTION

Repeatedly, the Florida/New York conjunction looms large in politics, not so much as related geographies but of a certain political nexus operating culturally and politically between these locations. Here, Florida can be seen as presenting another set of variations on Black women in state leadership as described by Nadia Brown's *Sisters in the Statehouse. Black Women and Legislative Decision Making* (2014). The connection I want to make here rests with Gwendolyn Sawyer Cherry's role as identified by Shirley Chisholm as one of the motivators for her beginning her campaign in Florida. Gwen Cherry (as she was popularly called) herself seems to have fallen out of recognition as the first Black woman in the Florida House of Representatives but played a major role in national and state politics in the 1970's. As Chisholm described this Florida conjunction:

> There were a lot of people in Florida who wanted me to come in, and that was the reason I had to go. One of the first was Gwen Cherry of Miami, the lawyer already mentioned, whom I had met while were both active in organizing

the National Women's Political Caucus early in 1971. She telephoned me in Washington and said she was talking with other Black leaders and with women in the women's movement, and that Chisholm for President organizations were ready to swing into action in several parts of the state if I would say the word. (55)

Gwen Cherry was the first Black woman to serve in the Florida state legislature, serving from 1970 to 1979. Her presence though has a direct, though not explicit, influence on the current proportion of women in the Florida legislature (33%, which is higher than the national average of 26.9% in the House).[38] Sadly, Gwen Cherry gets only a brief mention in *Black Miami in the Twentieth Century,* a photograph (199) with a note that she was the daughter of the first landmark Black medical doctor in Miami, Dr. W.B. Sawyer who founded Christian Hospital to care for Black patients who were then often denied treatment in Florida hospitals. An essay by Dorothy Jenkins Fields, "Black in Time: Gwen Cherry's Enduring Legacy Creates Opportunities"[39] provides a bit more detail of this amazing woman who was an educator, Florida's first Black woman attorney and first Black congresswoman, remembered now largely for a park named after her in Miami and a Department of Education Child Development Center in Tallahassee at Florida A&M University.

As an educator, Cherry was clearly conscious of the history of Black women. She co-authored *Portraits in Color: The Lives of Colorful Negro Women* (1962), a book which according to Dorothy Jenkins Fields public historian, archivist, and founder and past director of The Black Archives in Miami, is perhaps the first book of its kind.[40] Since this text is not readily available, its time-based use of the word "Negro" notwithstanding, it is worth a bit more recognition here as it was a forerunner of contemporary anthologies and critical collections on Black Women such as the volumes titled *Black Women in America: An Historical Encyclopedia.*[41] In its preface, the editors indicate that it was clearly not a complete survey including some eighteen portraits of Black women in fields of literature, music, theatre, art, education, meant to "enlighten young people of the achievements of Negroes, especially Negro women in our American life." The editors recognized that they were "charting a new course" as they "could find no truly comprehensive book that had been done on women of color since the beginning of America" (preface). The editors were conscious also of the issue of erasure, particularly of scholars "often overlooked when history is being recorded."

My intent here is to place Gwendolyn Sawyer Cherry back into full consideration in Black feminist politics. Here was a Black woman who led in many important areas: law, politics, literary creativity, and Black feminist organizing during its early expressions. As did Shirley Chisholm, Gwen Cherry set the terms of what Black women in congressional positions at state and national levels were able to achieve. Congresswoman Carrie Meeks (1993–2003) who replaced Gwen Cherry in the Florida State legislature after Cherry's untimely passing, and current Congresswoman Frederica Wilson[42] (2011–present) both became Florida State congresswomen following Cherry's influence. Both were educators first, before entering politics, and both were clearly guided or influenced by Gwen Cherry. Having introduced both the Equal Rights Amendment and the Martin Luther King Jr. holiday in the Florida House of Representatives, Cherry made several other contributions to African-American and women's experiences at the state level and nationally.

According to Jenkins-Fields article, one of the succeeding authors of *Portraits in Color,* indicated to her that in a book which highlighted Harriet Tubman and Mary McLeod Bethune, they "wanted to expose our students to women of color who felt deeply and were concerned with America's basic principles—freedom and liberty. We sought Black women who were not afraid to speak their convictions and were relentless in their efforts to succeed."[43] Chisholm would certainly have qualified for consideration then as a Black woman of similar leadership with the potential to contribute and to provide a legacy for subsequent generations and explains why Gwen Cherry would reach out to her and encourage her to come to Florida to begin her campaign.

Extensive coverage of Gwendolyn Sawyer Cherry's life is the subject of Roderick Dion Waters' 1994 dissertation titled "Sister Sawyer. The Life and Times of Gwendolyn Sawyer Cherry." This work includes background on the Black community in Miami, particularly about the Sawyer family, her father being the first Black medical doctor to practice in what was then "Colored Town," now called Overtown.[44] Waters cites Mary McLeod Bethune as a family friend and Gwen's godmother who encouraged Gwen to attend Howard University, which she did for a year before completing her education at Florida A&M College. Gwen Cherry was both a feminist and a nationalist, understanding well the now-defined "intersecting" nature of both political positions. She was the one who challenged the Congressional Black Caucus (CBC) for leaving Chisholm out of national discussions that had to do with Black futures. State Representative Cherry of Miami, one of Chisholm's earliest supporters, we learn, stood up in the state House to ask how it was that Chisholm had been left out. Because Cherry resented the blatant sexism in the way that Chisholm was treated, she deliberately invited Chisholm to Miami to begin her campaign. According to Waters, Cherry believed that sexism was the prime reason for the lack of support for her friend.

One of the better-known examples of Cherry's political generosity occurred in 1972 when she assisted Shirley Chisholm in her bid to become the first African American and the first woman president of the United States. Cherry and

Chisholm had much in common. They both completed their secondary education in New York City, obtained advanced degrees at a New York university, both became involved in politics, and both were active in the women's movement. Cherry urged Chisholm to run for president and pledged her support. When Chisholm decided to run, Cherry became her campaign coordinator in Florida. (17) Indeed, Representative Cherry had been one of Chisholm's first and most loyal supporters. (78)

In her "Florida" chapter of *The Good Fight,* Chisholm describes her uneven reception, at times enthusiastic at times disorganized, as she made her way around the state, campaigning for the presidency in which at times she would often lead Mayor John Lindsay in garnering attention and support. Photographs of a motorcade through Miami reveal children witnessing her presidential run. In Chisholm's assessment, however, campaigning in Florida had the same issues still present as those of today: the conservative Cuban community who, unlike the Puerto Rican supporters she had in Brooklyn, seemed uninterested in supporting a Black woman politician, regardless of what she had to say; the Deep South politics of Pensacola and locations north; a Black population still struggling for full recognition and battling racism; and new immigrant displacement of the traditional Black communities, in a state that is difficult to harmonize because of these disparate tendencies. Florida also figured as the site of the Democratic Convention of 1972, where Chisholm formally attempted to activate the coalitions needed to gain enough delegates to lobby for Black political and economic interests (125), attempts that Chisholm defined as "pragmatic politics" (127).

Explicitly identifying Cherry as an African-American feminist, Roderick Waters develops, in a chapter so named, Gwen Cherry's ability to do that balance that now seems commonplace for Black feminists between their interaction with racial and gender politics. As many Black feminists still do today, Gwen Cherry fought "racism and sexism simultaneously." She served as a legal counsel to the Miami office of the National Organization for Women. On November 17, 1970, Cherry was sworn in as the first African-American woman ever to serve in the Florida legislature. She joined the National Women's Political Caucus (NWPC), chairing their Houston meeting in 1973 with Fannie Lou Hamer, Shirley Chisholm, and others. Together they had to create a Black women's caucus, because the NWPC did not include issues that were specific to Black and other Minority women. And after the Congressional Black Caucus's treatment of Chisholm, Cherry helped found the National Black Women's Political Leadership Caucus in 1971. Waters's assessment is that Gwen Cherry was explicit about her feminist identification, claiming: "When elected to the legislature, Cherry claimed that she was 'the first feminist elected to a state legislature'. . . . her legislative record unquestionably indicated that she was strongly committed to feminist issues. Fifty-two of the one hundred sixty-seven bills she prime-sponsored pertained to women's or children's issues" (106). At the same time, she fought for African-American positions and contracts, for example, when the Democratic National Convention was slated to be held in Miami in 1972.

Clearly, Gwendolyn Sawyer Cherry is one of those Black feminist leaders who as usual escape full identification in the spectrum of Black and women's political frameworks. Her presence was a major influence on Congresswoman Frederica Wilson, as it was on Dorothy Jenkins Fields, who reports that they both were in high school when Cherry was teaching math at Miami Northwestern Senior High, the school Frederica Wilson graduated from in 1960: "At that time there were no women lawyers in Miami and certainly no Black women in the Florida Legislature. Then, I thought women could only be teachers or nurses" (personal communication 1/10/2021).[45]

KAMALA HARRIS—LEGACIES OF STRUGGLES AND A PROMISE

Any assessment of Kamala Harris now is only provisional, as we witness the unfolding of this new dimension of Black women's leadership and in becoming the first Black woman vice president in the United States. Once she was nominated as the vice-presidential candidate in 2020, it seemed to me more a promise which was yet to be fulfilled. Thus, in "The Promise of Kamala Harris," I asserted that:

> In the end, it was this boldness to challenge Biden that made Harris more recognizable as the strong candidate that she is and that those who know her prosecutorial history already recognized. These contrasting histories come together now to offer us the promise of her leadership. It is the boldness of the contemporary Black woman in 2020 that we are witnessing. This same audacity that propelled Harris to this position has been done throughout history, where Black women from Harriet Tubman to Shirley Chisholm were able to see ahead, with clear vision, and lead.[46]

We are still very early in what we can project is a long trajectory of leadership. Having initially been one of the democratic candidates for the presidency and then withdrawing delicately, Kamala Harris ended up adding to the electability of the Biden-Harris leadership team.

Several overviews of her family history, such as "How Kamala Harris's Immigrant Parents Found a Home, and Each Other, in a Black Study Group" document Kamala as the child of an Indian mother and Jamaican father.[47]

As a result, she was able to claim a multi-dimensional ethnic position, even beyond Chisholm's (Afro-Caribbean) by also claiming support from Asian communities, but with the same intent, in her acceptance speech. As it was for Barack Obama, she identifies her success as the result, or product, of legacies of struggle in which her mother is always frontally indicated:

> So, I'm thinking about her (Shyamala Gopalan Harris) and about the generations of women—Black women. Asian, White, Latina, and Native American women throughout our nation's history who have paved the way for this moment tonight. Women who fought and sacrificed so much for equality, liberty, and justice for all, including the Black women, who are too often overlooked, but so often prove that they are the backbone of our democracy. All the women who worked to secure and protect the right to vote for over a century: 100 years ago, with the 19th Amendment, 55 years ago with the Voting Rights Act, and now, in 2020, with a new generation of women in our country who cast their ballots and continued the fight for their fundamental right to vote and be heard. Tonight, I reflect on their struggle, their determination and the strength of their vision—to see what can be unburdened by what has been—I stand on their shoulders.[48]

In reviewing media coverage of her nomination, I noted that in *The Hindustan Times* her acceptance speech provided the range of Black women who cleared the way and necessarily gave her Indian mother the credit, often elided or minimized in US national coverage though her South Asian identity is often one of her defining markers:

> In her nomination acceptance speech in August 2020, Kamala Harris had invoked several civil rights and political leaders like Mary Church Terrell, Mary McCleod Bethune, Fannie Lou Hamer, Diane Nash, Constance Baker Motley and Shirley Chisholm. "We're not often taught their stories. But as Americans, we all stand on their shoulders. There's another woman, whose name isn't known, whose story isn't shared. Another woman whose shoulders I stand on. And that's my mother—Shyamala Gopalan Harris."[49]

Harris thus acknowledges the pivotal role of Shirley Chisholm's running for president in 1972. Still, again, we recognize here, as well other unspoken/ unrecognized precedents, as Charlotta Bass (1874–1969) was nominated to the Vice President slot on the Progressive Party ticket in 1952, and Rosa Clemente on the Green Party ticket in 2008. By putting her in these contexts, we can see how the "legacies of struggle" narrative is already embedded in Kamala Devi Harris's very presence and in her ability to claim a political identity as a Black woman in the United States, or anywhere.

Her first political autobiography available so far also contributes to that identity: "My daily challenge to myself is to be part of the solution, to be a joyful warrior in the battle to come" (Kamala Harris, 281). *The Truths We Hold. An American Journey* (2019) evokes the language of the US Declaration of Independence, which completes the sentence with "that all men are created equal." The need for us in this discussion to linger on the use of "men" is also self-evident; at the country's founding the "men" were exclusively white men, some slave-holding, definitely not women. This framing of white men consistently claiming for themselves the equivalence with the "over-representation as the human" has already been unpacked by feminists of various identities including Audre Lorde in her identification of "the mythical norm" and significantly by theorist Sylvia Wynter, recognized for asserting this point theoretically.[50]

Clearly published with an eye toward leadership, as was Barack Obama's political autobiographies,[51] *The Truths We Hold: An American Journey* (2019), presents a carefully selected series of events and images depicting her trajectory toward becoming the attorney general of California, and then that state's senator and the only Black woman in the Senate at the time. Sadly, once she became vice president, there was again no other Black woman Senator in the United States Senate in 2021 as after the departure of Carol Elizabeth Moseley Braun in 1999, though the Vice President has a more elevated Senate tie-breaking vote. Her chapter "For the People" begins by boldly asserting what "these truths" are. They are those societal ills remaining to be defeated if the "American Dream" is to be experienced by all:

We need to speak truth: that racism, sexism, homophobia, trans-phobia, and anti-Semitism are real in this country, and we need to confront these forces. We need to speak truth: that with the exception of Native Americans, we all descend from people who weren't born on our shores—whether our ancestors came to America willingly, with hopes for a prosperous future, or forcibly, on a slave ship, or desperately, to escape a harrowing past. (xv–xvi)

From the start, Harris presents an alternative vision of American "truths," one that clearly recognizes the dark side of American exceptionalism, one that is not the narrative that America sells to its citizens and would-be citizens and others witnessing the American experiment on popular media. But Harris goes in further:

We must speak truth about our mass incarceration crisis—that we put more people in prison than any country on earth, for no good reason. We must speak truth about police brutality, about racial bias, about the killing of unarmed Black men. We must speak truth about pharmaceutical companies that pushed addic-tive opioids on unsuspecting communities, and payday lenders and for-profit colleges that have leeched on to vulnerable Americans and overloaded them with debt. We must speak truth about greedy predatory corporations that have turned deregulation, financial speculation, and climate denialism into creed. And I intend to do just that. (xvi)

Her intention to "do just that"—speak the truths about what the underbelly of America is—means, however, that it is necessary to challenge the glossy media-friendly version of America that the public wants to consume. We recognize that a Black woman running for political office and then occupying that office sees and experiences a different version of these truths (e.g., that "all men are created equal"), which the American founders asserted, than the actuality of experience for Black people and women.

Experiencing both of these subordinations, then, we are in a good position to study how these built-in structural inequities will be experienced, since this is the highest leadership position a Black woman has ever attained in the United States of America, and therefore in world politics. So how does one navigate these two different sets of truths: the favored American exceptionalism narrative and the one of an America that remains unequal, with a legacy of imperialism and subordination of several communities, including its indigenous population. That negotiation between these two realities will mark the Harris vice-presidency, for good or ill. And there will be more assessments by Kamala Harris herself, and others, however this experience is lived.

Still, *The Truths We Hold* is an introduction to Harris's political life. In it, Harris describes her family of origin, her mother Shyamala from India and her father, Donald Harris, then a student and subsequently a political economist from Jamaica, and how they met. Harris describes her grandparents in India and her father's family and her parents' study group, which included Cedric Robinson, later an acclaimed political scientist, identified in chapter 1 of this book for his discussions about leadership. The artwork in her childhood home included Trinidadian master artist, LeRoy Clarke (1938–2021). California-born and raised in Black community, Kamala Harris attended the leading Historically Black College and University (HBCU) Howard University, affectionately called "The Mecca" by its students. She also described being shaped by Rainbow Sign, a Black cultural community center founded by Black women that she, her sister Maya, and her mother frequented. There, an engagement with Black excellence in the creative and political spheres included a momentous knowledge encounter: "In 1971, Congresswoman Shirley Chisholm paid a visit while she was exploring a run for president. Talk about strength! 'Unbought and Unbossed,' just as her campaign slogan promised" (18). All of these experiences lead to Kamala Harris's creating her own professional profile in her words: "through the lens of my own experience and perspectives from wisdom gained at my mother's knee, in Rainbow Sign's Hall and on the Howard Yard" (26).

One of the harshest critiques of Kamala Harris to date is that even though as a prosecuting lawyer she recognized mass incarceration as a problem, her office in California led in incarcerating many people. In her version, she described her courtroom work as putting rapists behind bars, while working for criminal justice reform, creating programs that intervened in juvenile offenders to get them "back on track," and changing the bail system so that people are not kept incarcerated in exchange for financial payments they often do not have but becomes a bail system based on the crime and flight-risk. Police brutality on Blacks, as the most visible and heightened practice of systemic racism, is also clearly an area that Harris recognizes as needing correction (70). Resolving this dire issue is one by which Harris will be assessed, as she moves through the process of being vice-president. How are issues that pertain to and negatively affect Black people in the United States going to be addressed? Are Black people the ones who will always bear the burden of America's major gaps in equality? At the beginning of this new phase, questions must be posed and will be answered only with time and process. For Kamala Harris, change happens once social and political movement outside of the corridors of power creates the environment that allows politicians to move forward with policy (73).

It may be useful to study her definitions of leadership expressed in the context of her "What I've Learned" chapter which no doubt will become one lever of assessing her when her term ends:

> Good leadership requires vision and aspiration. It requires the articulation of bold ideas that move people to action. But it is often the mastery of the seemingly unimportant details, the careful execution of tedious tasks, and the dedicated work done outside of the public eye that make the changes we seek possible (262). It's our job to stand up for those who are not at the table where life-altering decisions are made. Not just those people who look like us. Not just those who need what we need. Not just those who have gained an audience with us. Our duty is to improve the human condition in every way we can, for everyone who needs it. (267–268)

As was Obama's (2005–2008), Senator Harris's time in the senate was short (2017–2019) before she began her presidential campaign later in 2019. During her time in the Senate, her prosecutorial skills were on display (269–276) in her hard questioning during the confirmation hearing for Supreme Court Justice Brent Kavanaugh. Many people were gratified when current president Joseph Biden (2021 to present) selected Harris as his running mate for vice president, and together they fought hard, winning their campaign in 2020. A vice president, however, takes a secondary role, being able to influence, though not provide, the leadership that defines how their team views the world, to create and affect policies but still not lead their execution. And so far, the public presentations by Harris have been less than desired by the Black, Brown, and progressive portions of the population[52] who see her missing in action from major and relevant issues, particularly as these have to do with migration, the treatment of refugees, and other issues related to the lives of the constituencies she is supposed to represent. Her speech to Guatemalans on June 7, 2021, that they should not come to the United States ("Do not come! Do not come!") voicing a basic US sentiment to migrants was perceived as insensitive to the histories of why people take on such precarious journeys from someone whose presence in the United States was generated by two sets of migrations.

STACEY ABRAMS AS A "SISTER OUTSIDER"

The "sister outsider" framework, defined by Audre Lorde in her book titled the same, *Sister Outsider* (1984),[53] provides another analytical paradigm as it refers to a particular placement outside the mainstream heterosexual, feminist, American nationalist milieu, a location nevertheless from which one can harness and leverage one's power. "Outsiderness" has an additional meaning for those who have an immigrant identity outside of a nation-state and are labeled "aliens" or "outsiders." But it also refers to the fact that US African Americans, defined outside of the original intent of US citizenship, were historically constructed as "sojourners" in the country of their birth and origin (Hanchard, 1990). The logic of racial exclusion was central to the framing of Western democracies and remains a struggle that most new nations still have to overcome (Hanchard, 2020). But, beyond racial exclusion, for Black women, as the Audre Lorde example indicates, the combination of race and gender with constructions of heterosexual privilege have rendered them even further outside of mainstream institutional structures. Yet, this marginality also presents a location from which Black women have been able to do the kind of work that challenges the boundaries of those very structures.

It was not surprising then that Stacey Abrams decided to occupy this "outsider" position and even claim it titularly in her first political autobiography *Lead from the Outside* (2018). There she signaled that this "outsider" position would actually be her leadership vantage point, in or out of political office. Theoretical leadership became praxis, as she led the hard work that significantly affected the outcome of the 2020 US national presidential election. In this example, Abrams made the state of Georgia an exemplar of political organizing, which revealed the full popular dynamics of the state, not just the traditional, official racial narratives of the nature of the electorate. After running for the governorship of the state against the state's Secretary of State who was in charge of the elections and losing to him by very narrow margin, in what many saw as an unfair electoral process, Abrams defined her "Fair Fight" campaign, which became a national movement that in the end positively impacted the 2020 election.

Lead from the Outside is a leadership manual, perhaps a self-help book for would-be leaders. She begins with an assurance of what her campaign for governor meant:

> In May 2017, I became the first Black woman to receive the gubernatorial nomination of a major party in American history. On November 6, 2018, I received more votes than any Democrat in Georgia history, outpacing President Barack Obama and Secretary of State Hillary Clinton. I learned later that our campaign tripled the turnout of Latinos and Asian Americans, more than doubled the youth participation rate. I received more votes from African Americans than the subtotal of Democratic voters in 2014. My candidacy created a path to win a congressional seat and flip sixteen legislative seats. I received the highest percentage of the white vote recorded in a generation. And I was within 1.4 percent of the man who had run the election and run against me—serving as both contestant and referee. (xiii)

Stacey Abrams offers perhaps the best contemporary example of Shirley Chisholm's logic of running and losing as "not failing." As she defined it, "leadership is a constant search for the distinction between when compromise is an act of power and when concession masks submission—or when the fight is on" (xv). For Stacey, the fight was on and even named as such: "The Fair Fight" (xvi). In this case, it was a fight to retain some of the basics of the claimed American democracy.

Replete with definitions about leadership such as: "Leadership requires the ability to engage and to create empathy for communities with disparate needs and ideas, and that's why as outsiders, we can make the best and most effective leaders" (xvii–xviii), Abrams's book takes the reader through her own formation and limitations, identifying the many ways that she as a Black woman has confronted racism, sexism, ageism, and other phobias and biases. Abrams provides a "reminder that leadership is not divined by pedigree or demography and that origin stories are simply the beginning" (xxvii). Thus, in her understanding, "leadership stands at the crux of how we get to power, and it demands the willingness to go first, to take responsibility as well as hold authority, to help others get where they need to go" (xxvii).

Abrams recounts her failings in personal relationships, which became triggers to her ability to define what she wanted to do and be, out of a host of other possibilities. Each chapter ends with a series of steps and exercises that define action and ambition, as opposed to waiting to be invited to participate. She speaks of fear and rejection, struggling with financial obligations, and determining if one needs mentors and what their role should be. Further, about leadership, Abrams cautions that although the prospect is alluring, "you should not accept a position unless you can effectively meet the obligations that come along with it" (163).

Stacey Abrams remains another and distinct example of leadership recognized by other Black women who were world leaders as did former President of Liberia, Ellen Johnson Sirleaf.[54] In many ways, Abrams brings together the kind of dynamism of Fannie Lou Hamer (1917–1977), who in her fight for the seating of the Mississippi Freedom Democratic Party at the Democratic National Convention in 1964, combined activism with political interventions, particularly on issues of voting rights and the combination of racial and gendered representation.[55] Fannie Lou Hamer's was fundamentally a model of a fight for full representation but also for women's rights, in her co-founding the National Women's Political Caucus and also in her campaigns for the senates of both Mississippi and the United States. In many ways, Stacey Abrams manifests the dreams, aspirations, strategies, and presence of Fannie Lou Hamer. And not surprisingly there is another creative side to Abrams that recently became evident in that she has published eight romance novels under the pen name Selena Montgomery.[56]

CARIBBEAN AMERICAN WOMEN FROM NEW YORK AND FLORIDA: HAZELLE ROGERS AND UNA CLARKE

Contributions from Caribbean American women to political culture in the United States are identified here as another important aspect of studying Black political leadership. Given that Miami was the site of the historic 1972 Democratic Convention, which featured an address by the first Black and Woman candidate for the presidency, there were some related reverberations. Chisholm's campaign autobiography, *The Good Fight*, which includes photographs of her in a variety of Florida locations which cannot be understated for its visual impact on the politics of the possible. Similar imagery of engaging the "grassroots" would circulate in her New York campaigns. She also describes that, in her speeches at times, from her view from the stage, she could see a tear-filled room at several locations when she spoke.

According to Una Clarke, Assemblywoman from Brooklyn, New York (1992–2001, representing the 40th district) and the mother of current Congresswoman's Yvette Clarke (2006 to present), she herself was influenced by Shirley Chisholm's political participation, knowing Chisholm's husband as a family friend. For Clarke,[57] the formation of the National Association of Caribbean Elected Officials and Leaders enhanced the status of Caribbean nations and their residents as it was open to all political parties, religious persuasions and included members from across the United States. With branches in several states, especially those with large Caribbean communities, the National Association of Caribbean Elected Officials and Leaders, above all, had a pivotal role in launching and supporting the campaigns of several Caribbean-American political leaders.

Una Clarke describes her leadership process as beginning when she was part of a campaign, during a New York redistricting process. Her group was getting Caribbean residents in Brooklyn to see themselves as the large voting block that they were and encouraging them, after their many years as residents, to regulate their immigration status and register to vote instead of remaining as "temporary immigrants." Prior to this, most Caribbean residents in Brooklyn lived as visitors, even with resident credentials, while having lived in the United States for many years, raising and schooling children, and owning property, but always with a dream of returning home at some time in the future. In her interview with me, she indicated her leadership pathway as stepping up to the plate; since the men with whom she worked did not want to run, she did. This decision would become pivotal as Una Clarke became instrumental in the career of Florida's Hazelle Rogers and, of course, that of her daughter, current Congresswoman Yvette Clarke.

In Florida, the current (2021) Mayor Hazelle P. Rogers of a working-class Caribbean community, Lauderdale Lakes was the Democratic Member of Florida House of Representatives, Districts 94 and 95 sequentially from 2008 to 2016, became involved in politics largely by participating in community organizations and realizing that she was doing much of the work and that she was just as capable as, or more capable than, some of the men with whom she worked. Having first lived in New York as a young woman, before moving to Florida, she said:

> Seeing Shirley Chisholm run for office became a reference point for me when I moved to Florida . . . only a teenager, from the Caribbean, observing, seeing how people were treated differently. When I realized her roots: I said: "You can come to America and do this?" It made me proud of her heritage . . . the same way I felt about Kamala putting herself out there to run as a democratic nominee for the presidency. She would not be in the position she is today (Vice-President Elect) if she had not made that initial run. (see appendix)

In terms of self-presentation, we learn from Nadia Brown's research that hair and skin tone often greatly affect peoples' perceptions of Black political women (Brown, 2014). The choice of clothing and style also becomes an issue in women's public reception. I posed this question to Dianne Abbott in October 2020, when she visited my class, and to Una Clarke and Hazelle Rogers (February 2021), as I worked on this chapter. What they responded in common was a knowledge, which Chisholm demonstrated, that Caribbean women elders in their families dressed in their best available clothing ("dressed-up") in their opportunities for public presentation (church, weddings, and other social and public events). All indicated that they were not worried so much about what others think but are concerned with looking their best for each occasion, and that this was quite important in how they, as political leaders, presented themselves publicly to their audiences. A distinction that is perhaps worth noting is that this counts particularly when their audiences are predominantly Black working-class communities, as opposed to facing members of a variety of ethnic communities. Hazelle Rogers' position is that:

> I believe Black people know how to dress up . . . the clothes you wear in church and the year and the occasion. I went through every hairstyle . . . Geri curl, big Afro, everything and have pictures with African outfits, tie dye tops. You are who you are and not afraid to wear your African outfits, or Jamaican colors. So I have lived in America all my life, I have learned a lot and know that we have been through the same class and color prejudices among ourselves that we also experience from others; brown skin gets more opportunities. I did not wear makeup until 1974 when I got married. I always felt I was beautiful enough.

We can note relatedly that African women political leaders also dress in fashionable styles relevant to their communities, worn in their cultural contexts: embroidered caftans and shawls, matching headwraps and dresses in popular African patterned wax fabrics, and *kente* cloth outfits.[58]

According to Una Clarke, in response to the question: Do you feel that women in positions of power are scrutinized more heavily on issues such as competence? She said, "It depends on what office and how one carries herself. You should have a presence and command respect of people around you, so people know who you are. During my time in office, I wore an Afro, cut off all my hair."[59]

Instead, particular issues on which they campaigned were more relevant as these came from the assumption that one was running to represent one's community and their issues. For Clarke, since her theme was a "voice of the voiceless and a face of the faceless," issues that happened in her community that gave her a national profile, such as the Abner Louima case in 1997 or Patrick Dorismon (2000) both from the Haitian community, abused and the latter killed by New York Police had to be confronted headlong. Thus, she indicated, police brutality was clearly an issue she had to address directly, before the current popularity of the "Defund the Police" campaign. Therefore, in her view, women who lose children through police violence end up with the empathy to address larger concerns of Black Lives Matter politics.

In her Florida political landscape, Hazelle Rogers said, "When I went to Tallahassee, I knew they were funding programs locally . . . so I wanted to fight for libraries, which was one of her loves from Broward County. Roadways were always challenging and I wanted my city to get attention. Monies for roads and bridges, educational programs, urban league and social programs and economic development, small business, minority business. You had to speak that language for Black communities . . . definitely support HBCU Black Colleges and universities. That was the focus, to continue to fund those institutions, as these educated most Black Americans. These institutions were always my focus."[60]

As did Shirley Chisholm, Rogers indicates that having a supportive male partner who filled in the spaces of their absences and managed households without question made a big difference in women politician's ability to do the people's work. In Hazelle Rogers's words: "You have to know who you are and why you run for office and why you seek public office and because for your entire family, you carry them with you and all wounds are reopened. Speak to the issue and share the wounds and scars and everyone becomes you . . . God gave me an awesome husband . . . Nieces are around . . . my niece is a State Rep, Anika Omphroy, State Representative (to the Florida House of Representatives for District 95). Families pass on the connections."

Finally, both Clarke and Rogers, like Shirley Chisholm, felt that women have a better grasp of bread-and-butter issues, such as income and budget. "Men think they are entitled period. Women don't think we are entitled. We collaborate. We work hard. We believe in partnership. We are more inclusive . . . Women have grown up into knowing that they can do it. We are always in the room thinking and working but now they realize we can go forward. We do everything."[61] She felt as well that women need to put themselves forward as Kamala Harris did and that willingness to jump into the ring as a presidential candidate is what made her visible as a choice for the Vice Presidency.

"THE SQUAD" AS CHISHOLM'S *GOOD FIGHT* GENERATION MANIFESTED

Now a new generation enters, with a sobriquet that has lingered, "The Squad," young and dynamic congresswomen entered the US political landscape in 2018 and began as a four-member group of women of color, instantly perceived as contentious for their willingness to challenge the entrenched patterns of the US government that facilitated continued oppression of women and people of color. Consisting of Rep. Alexandria Ocasio-Cortez (D-New York), Rep. Ilhan Omar (D-Minnesota), Rep. Ayanna Pressley

(D-Massachusetts), and Rep. Rashida Tlaib (D-Michigan), "The Squad" soon became the victims of political the same, with open racialized and gendered attacks, even death threats, about their competence or unwillingness to learn how the US Congress works. But these are the women who Chisholm predicted were on the horizon when she said: "Such leaders must be found. But they will not be found as much as they will be created, by an electorate that has become ready to demand that it control its own destiny. There must be a new coalition of all Americans—Black, white, red, yellow and brown, rich and poor—who are no longer willing to allow their rights as human beings to be infringed upon by anyone else, for any reason" (190–191).

Similar racist and sexist conditions surrounded the entry to Congress of former Congresswoman Shirley Chisholm who received the same vitriol if not as publicly obscene response to her presence in Congress. Still, Chisholm described the benefits and losses of being the only Black woman, as a member of nine Black congresspeople. She indicates that she often sat alone in the Congressional dining room, sometimes asked to move from where she was sitting and was racially insulted or confronted by colleagues as a matter of course. In her chapter "How I View Congress," Chisholm offered a scathing critique of both the openly racist and sexist hostility she experienced and also the flawed ways in which government is practiced in the United States: "Our representative democracy is not working because the Congress that is supposed to represent the voters does not respond to their needs. I believe the chief reason is that it is ruled by a small group of old men" (117). She continued to describe the ridiculousness of congressional hearings held to "impress the public" rather than achieve its goals (118). In that context of open racism and sexism, she felt the need for a voting bloc, which the Congressional Black Caucus became, which would at least mitigate some of these issues and be able to represent Black interests more deliberately. But more relevantly, like the Squad's intention, her position was, "I did not come to Congress to behave myself and stay away from explosive issues so I can keep coming back" (125).

In many ways, Chisholm had the ability to forecast and encourage that succeeding generation: "We must turn away from the old-line, tired politicians to open our society to the energies and abilities of countless new groups of Americans—women, Blacks, browns, Indians, Orientals and youth—so that they can develop their own full potential, and thereby participate equally and enthusiastically in building a strong and just society, rich in its diversity and noble in its quality of life."[62] This is the fighting spirit of "The Squad" the generation that Chisholm viewed on the horizon. When Congresswoman Alexandria Ocasio-Cortez was insulted by a vulgar racial and sexual epithet from a colleague, Rep. Yoho of Florida, in 2020, she took the floor to expose what he had done and to denounce him publicly for his verbal sexual abuse.

She had the support of thirteen other congresswomen, including Speaker Nancy Pelosi, all of whom went on record as reporting that they too have been on the receiving end of openly sexist hostilities.[63] And, following the now infamous storming of The Capitol by white supremacists on January 6, 2021, they all spoke openly and publicly about that experience and their racial and gendered visibility which rendered them targets but simultaneously about the need to pass budget relief that would aid the poor of their communities and the nation.

Because they are deliberate about representing their constituencies, Ocasio-Cortez and the other three members—Ilhan Omar, Ayana Pressley, and Rashida Tlaib—retained their seats, even while strongly opposing the entrenched while male dominance and conservative positions of most of the men in Congress and added new members in 2021. Among them, Rep. Ocasio-Cortez has been particularly vilified by conservatives but celebrated by progressives for her presentation of the Green New Deal, a forward-thinking project that links environmental sustainability to economic advances and Medicare for all. Her position supports political principles already advanced by fellow democratic socialist Congressman Bernie Sanders, a popular Democratic candidate in 2015 and 2019 and one of her political mentors. Lingering redbaiting in the United States, consistently positions "The Squad" and Senator Sanders as communists in a US political tradition which has little space for alternative political positions.

Unsurprisingly, current Gallup polling indicates that most young people see a socialist platform as being closer to their worldview.[64] A headline, "Socialism as Popular as Capitalism Among Young Adults in U.S.," reveals a gradual challenge to policies that subordinate the general welfare of most people in favor of a market economy based on heightened neo-liberal assumptions. In this context, responses to former President Obama's *The Promised Land* (2020) have been mixed, and not as celebratory among young people, as was captured in Malik Pitchford's widely circulated essay indicating his disappointment with Obama's centrism as being more suitable to older generations.[65]

So, it is significant that in 2020, Cori Anika Bush, a Black woman activist who represents a district that includes Ferguson, Missouri, entered formal political participation after community activism within the Black Lives Matter movement. The killing of Michael Brown by a policeman in her home community was one of the most visible examples of continued extra-judicial killings by white supremacist policemen and vigilantes. Later captured most graphically in the suffocation of George Floyd in May 2020, this actual and symbolic example of state destruction of its Black citizens fueled mass international protests and movements. Congresswoman Cori Bush, running as a progressive Democrat, defeated a well-known and well-financed Democratic rival, to be elected to Congress. Her immediate appointment to the House Judiciary Committee in her first year as a state representative allows us to reprise the importance of relevant House Committee appointments which was a key issue that Shirley Chisholm launched a legendary fight to change: (i.e., the tendency to assign new members of Congress to remote and relatively unimportant committees that are less critical to their primary interests and constituencies). As a new member of "The Squad," Cori Bush[66] ran on a platform that included challenging the US justice system to be more equitable. She indicated that her role on the House Judiciary Committee would be to "affirm the dignity and humanity of Black and brown communities," to work "to legislate in defense of Black lives."[67]

Across the United States, Black women not only lead the desire for a transformed United States but also make political moves at various levels to achieve this change. For example, Barbara Smith, one of the writers of the Combahee River Collective Statement, named in honor of Harriet Tubman's liberation of some seven hundred enslaved Africans in South Carolina, also wrote the Hamer-Baker plan against white supremacy that is named after Fannie Lou Hamer and Ella Baker, women who were active in combatting white supremacy and for creating progressive futures for successive generations of Black people.[68] India Walton ran for the position of Mayor of Buffalo, New York, and winning at the primary level, after organizing a working class campaign and running on "socialist principles and progressive polices."[69] Like Shirley Chisholm she sees her first losses as also wins in knowledge of strategies to take forward subsequent campaigns.

Claudia Jones, in her essay "We Seek Full Equality" (1949) cited the famous dictum that once Black women move, the rest of the society also moves: ". . . the triply oppressed status of Negro women is a barometer of the status of all women, and that the fight for the full, economic, political and social equality of the Negro woman is in the vital self-interest of white workers, in the vital interest of the fight to realize equality for all women."[70] In the formal, organized political leadership realm, Black women are trending upward in their acquisition of positions in many local and state assemblies and even in nominations to the United States Supreme Court as is Judge Ketanji Brown Jackson in 2022. In Puerto Rico, in the 2020 elections, Ana Irma Rivera Lassen became the first lesbian and Black woman elected to the Puerto Rican Senate.[71] The stories of these moves and their challenges "in their own words" are being documented in my Black Women Lead project at Cornell University.[72]

At the national level, some gains are followed by losses of representation of Black women. In the California Senate, the move of Kamala Harris to the Vice Presidency meant the appointment of a Latino male, to fill her seat.[73]

While this became a gain for the Latino community, within the logic of scarcity and not the idea of equal representation, again, there will be no Black women in the United States Senate in 2021 and 2022. Political scientists will chart these moves in the future, but for now, a steady movement is occurring in state assemblies, an increase that is in keeping with global percentages but still way behind in national averages. Yet one statistic that is worth identifying is that with 43.3% of Black women in Congress[74] in relation to Black men, the Black community in the United States is close to parity in political representation.

NOTES

1. See my "Black Voting Rights, Kwame Toure, Barack Obama and the Im/Possibility of a Black President." *Pluriel Magazine* (June-July, 2008): 42–43.

2. Edda Fields Black is working on the history of Harriet Tubman liberating over 750 Africans at the Combahee River Raid using Pension records and a range of sources for a forthcoming manuscript tentatively titled *Harriet Tubman, the Combahee River Raid, and Black Freedom during the Civil War* (Oxford University Press, forthcoming). Conversation 1/3/2021.

3. See Ta Nehisi Coates, "Frederick Douglass: 'A Women's Rights Man,'" *The Atlantic,* September 30, 2011. https://www.theatlantic.com/personal/archive/2011/09/frederick-douglass-a-womens-rights-man/245977/. In the Douglass case the advocacy for Blackwomen has to be assumed in his support for women's rights and DuBois published *Dark Princess* in 1928.

4. Title of Margaret Busby's 1992 collection of Black women's writings and her updated *New Daughters of Africa* (2019).

5. "Religion and the Pure Principles of Morality, the Sure Foundation on Which we Must Build" (Pamphlet, 1831). It is significant that she publishes this in pamphlet form first and then delivers this as a lecture some thirty years before the ending of enslavement of African Americans in the United States.

6. Cited in Beverly Guy-Sheftall, *Words of Fire*, 28.

7. Cited in Carole Boyce Davies, "Pan-Africanism, Transnational Black Feminism and the Limits of Culturalist Analyses in African Gender Discourses" in *Feminist Africa* (2014).

8. "The Status of Women in America" in *Words of Fire*, 44–49.

9. Hull, Scott, and Smith, *But Some of Us are Brave* (Feminist Press, 1982) is credited with providing the major text for this institutionalization.

10. Nadji Hillal H (1949) "A Garvey comes home to Africa," *Chicago Defender Magazine,* August 6, 230.

11. Hubert Harrison, *The Struggle for Equality, 1918–1927,* 629. Amy Ashwood Garvey and Hubert Harrison are documented as having an affair in the context of her breakup with Marcus Garvey.

12. See also Part 3, "The 'New Negro Movement'" of Jeffrey B. Perry's *Hubert Harrison. The Voice of Harlem Radicalism, 1883–1918* (New York: Columbia University Press, 2009), and specifically p. 282. *The Struggle for Equality* has a photograph of the front cover of his *New Negro* magazine.

13. Hubert Harrison, *The Voice of Harlem Radicalism,* p. 204. Which also provides a description of her activism as well as his. See *Left of Karl Marx,* chapter 3, for discussion of Elizabeth Gurley Flynn and related references to her contributions which led to her being sentenced for Communist ideas in the same trial as Claudia Jones.

14. One of the few available discussions of Grace Campbell is Lydia Lindsey's "Black Lives Matter: Grace P. Campbell and Claudia Jones"—An analysis of the Negro Question, Self-Determination, Black Belt Thesis. *Journal of Pan African Studies* 12:9 (March, 2019): 110–143.

15. Shirley Chisholm, *The Good Fight,* 161.

16. Stacey Abrams contested the governor's seat in the state of Georgia in 2018 but was unfairly positioned as she was in contestation with Brian Porter Kemp, the man who was actually the Secretary of State and also in charge of elections, and now is that state's governor, hardly an example of the United States touted democratic fairness in elections. One can also read late Congressman John Lewis's "Good Trouble" also through Chisholm's assertion of the "Good Fight."

17. Teaching her autobiography *Unbought and Unbossed* (1972) to this current generation of students often elicits incredulity that she existed before Obama and that they did not have a clue about her presence until that discussion.

18. Personal conversation at Radical Black Women Conference, CUNY, 2010.

19. The work of Paula Giddings on Ida Wells Barnett. Her "Missing in Action: Ida B. Wells, the NAACP, and the Historical Record," *Meridians* 1:2 (Spring, 2001), pp. 1–17 and her biography *Ida: A Sword Among Lions: Ida B. Wells and the Campaign Against Lynching* (Illinois, 2009) indicate that Wells was a co-founder of the NAACP and was also the instrumental force for the first national Black women's movement in the United States.

20. We will not list all of the Congresswomen here but see the Center for American Women and Politics at Rutgers which provides a graph indicating a steady rise of Black women from 1961 to the present indicates 26 Black women serving in the 117th Congress, 4.9% of all members of Congress, 18.1% of all women in Congress and 43.3% of Black members (i.e., close to parity in Black representation). Cawo.rutgers.edu

21. Though two books are in process, one by Anastasia Curwood and a collection by LaTasha Brown.

22. A concept defined by Moya Bailey to identify the specific way that Black women experience misogyny.

23.   https://www.grunge.com/285238/the-incredible-real-life-story-of-shirley-chisholm/

24. Katheryn Russell-Brown (Lee & Low Books Inc., 2020 and *You Should Meet Shirley Chisholm* by Laurie Calkhoven (Ready to Read, Simon Spotlight, 2020).

25. Dial Books for Young Readers, 2020.

26. Anne Schwartz Books (Random House Children's Books), 2021.

27. London and Cambridge, Harvard University Press, 2016.

28. See *Reena and Other Stories* (1993).

29. Personal e-communication, 12/12/2020

30. https://viewpointmag.com/2015/10/31/the-bronx-slave-market-1950/

31. https://www.nytimes.com/1983/01/09/books/from-the-poets-in-the-kitchen.html

32. *Meridians* 13:1 (2015): 204–232.

33. One notes relatedly that Barack Obama's campaign also used the language of "Change" in its framing.

34. https://www.un.org/womenwatch/daw/cedaw/states.htm

35. Shirley Chisholm Introduction *Unbought and Unbossed*, 12.

36. *The Good Fight*, 155.

37. "A Right to be Radical: A Genealogy of Black Left Feminist Claims." University of Texas, Austin, February 23–24, 2020.

38. Diane Rado, "Despite inroads for women, Congress and the FL Legislature remain male bastions—and it's an embarrassment" November 16, 2020, indicates that while it is higher than the national average it is still low since women are 51% of the state's population. https://www.floridaphoenix.com/2020/11/16/despite-inroads-for-women-congress-and-the-fl-legislature-remain-male-bastions-and-its-an-embarrassment/ (Accessed 1/4/2021)

Following the 2020 elections, lawmakers in both the Florida House and Senate will be lopsided, with far more men than women. The state House will have 80 men and just 40 women, or 33% of the chamber, based on Florida division of election results and the Florida House of Representatives. That means women will make up only a third of the House chamber. That 33% appears to be higher than the percentage for the US House. Even so, I'm not clapping and cheering because it's embarrassing that the Florida House has so few women lawmakers.

As to the Florida Senate, there will be 25 men and 15 women senators, with women representing 37.5% of the chamber. That figure is higher than the percentage of women senators in the US Senate and higher than the state House numbers. But I'm not clapping and cheering because 37.5% isn't good enough.

39. Dorothy Jenkins Fields, "Black in Time: Gwen Cherry's enduring legacy creates opportunities," *Miami Herald*, September 24, 2015, https://www.miamiherald.com/news/local/community/miami-dade/community-voices/article36478458.html (Accessed 1/3/2021).

40. Conversation 1/3/2021. Jenkins-Fields was the moving force behind the renovation of the historic Lyric theater in Overtown, Miami, Florida.

41. Edited by Darlene Clark Hine et al. (1994) and Oxford University Press, 2005.

42. Carole Boyce Davies, "Abuser-in-Chief Strikes Again," *Trinidad Express,* January 13, 2018. http://www.trinidadexpress.com/20180113/editorial/abuser-in-chief-strikes-again describes the president and his administration's attack on Congresswoman Frederica Wilson.

43. Fields, 2015.

44. See also *Back to Black, No On/Off Ramps.* Art Africa, 2017 catalog curated and with an introduction by Babacar Mbow describes some of the historical legacies of Overtown.

45. Several attempts were made to interview Frederica Wilson, but the many demands on her time during the difficult year of 2020 with elections, the pandemic, and the 2021 Trump insurrection resulted in communications from her staff, who were unable to schedule an interview.

46. Boyce Davies, August 2020.

47. Ellen Barry, *New York Times*, September 13, 2020.

48. https://www.msn.com/en-us/news/world/read-kamala-harris-s-full-acceptance-speech-as-vice-president-elect/ar-BB1aOfxC Accessed 12/16/2020

49. https://www.hindustantimes.com/world-news/us-vice-president-elect-kamala-harris-remembers-mother-shyamala-gopalan-harris-on-her-birthday/story-znjfiYJx6i0pyNgVUcswLP.html Accessed 12/16/2020

50. See for example her "Beyond Miranda's Meanings" afterword to *Out of the Kumbla* (1990) and my discussion in *American Quarterly* (2018) but also McKittrick, ed. *Sylvia Wynter: On Being Human as Praxis* (Duke University Press, 2015). Greg Thomas and Sylvia Wynter, "Yours in the Intellectual Struggle." *The Caribbean Woman Writer as Scholar.* Ed. Keshia Abraham (Coconut Grove: Caribbean Studies Press, 2009), 31–69.

51. *Dreams from My Father* (2004) and *The Audacity of Hope: Thoughts on Reclaiming the American Dream* (2007).

52. See discussion in Matthew Brown, "Progressives Saw Kamala Harris As a Unique Champion. Lately, They're Disappointed," *USA Today,* November 5, 2021. https://www.yahoo.com/news/activists-disappointed-kamala-harris-isnt-090134600.html

53. Audre Lorde, *Sister Outsider: Essays and Speeches* (Freedom, CA: Crossing, 1984).

54. In my 2018 interview with Ellen Johnson Sirleaf, she presciently identified Stacey Abrams as positioned to have tremendous impact on the American and world political landscape at a time when Abrams was still recovering from being denied the governorship.

55. See Keisha Blain's *"Until I am Free": Fannie Lou Hamer's Enduring Message to America* (2021) on the many struggles of Fannie Lou Hamer.

56. McKenzie Jean-Philippe, "Stacey Abrams Has Written 8 Romance Novels Under the Name 'Selena Montgomery'" *Oprah Magazine,* November 6, 2020.

57. Interview December 18, 2020.

58. This ability to wear national clothing, though criticized by Pat McFadden as providing sometimes exotic flavor, was gratifying to witness at the UN and ECOWAS African Women and Political Leadership Conference at the Museum of Black Civilizations, Dakar, March, 2020, with women leaders from several different African countries wearing elegant boubous and gelees and other more contemporary African fashion styles.

59. Personal interview, February 2021.

60. Personal interview, February 2021.

61. Hazelle Rogers, interview 1/13/21 available in appendix.

62. *The Good Fight,* 73.

63. https://www.nytimes.com/2020/07/23/us/alexandria-ocasio-cortez-sexism -congress.html

64. https://news.gallup.com/poll/268766/socialism-popular-capitalism-among -young-adults.aspx

65. https://granthshala.com/im-young-Black-and-not-all-that-impressed-with -barack-obama-opinion/

66. https://www.newsweek.com/latest-squad-member-cori-bush-nominated-house -judiciary-committee-1556115

67. Televised Public interviews after election.

68. "How to Dismantle White Supremacy," *The Nation,* September 21/28, 2020.

69. Shamira Ibrahim, "India Walton Isn't Slowing Down" *Essence Magazine,* January/February, 2022, 60.

70. *Beyond Containment,* 87.

71. Announcement of candidate to constituency.

72. See also Barbara Ransby's "The White Left Needs to Embrace Black Leadership." *The Nation,* July 2, 2020.

73. "Newsom Picks Alex Padilla to Fill Kamala Harris' Senate Seat." CNN Politics, December 22, 2020, 399.

74. "By the Numbers: Black Women in the 117th Congress" in CAWP, the Center for American Women and Politics, Rutgers University. (Accessed 2/9/2021).

Chapter 6

Advancing Global Leadership Paradigms from the Caribbean

"When will leaders lead? Our people are watching, and our people are taking note," is one of the many striking lines delivered by current prime minister of Barbados, the Honorable Mia Amor Mottley (2018–present) as she addressed the Glasgow COP 21 Conference.[1] Clearly conscious that this was a call to leadership in times of crisis, she addressed the predominantly white and male fellow world leaders with an assumption of her equal footing as a leader and brought forward a progressive planetary consciousness that challenged them to action on behalf of the two-thirds of the world living a global inequality that threatens humanity's survival. "Leaders must not fail those who elect them to lead," she added and thereby entered herself and the Caribbean on the world stage with a dynamic level of leadership not seen since the days of the decolonial struggles leading to political independence in the 1960's. Mia Amor Mottley in 2021 as she operated with confidence on a world stage, became an internationally recognized leader.

Two years earlier when she addressed the United Nations Climate Summit and the United Nations General Assembly on September 27, 2019, she had asserted that Caribbean islands will not survive climate change,[2] and there had deliberately challenged the assumptions of the dominant continental countries in the north that create practices detrimental to the Caribbean region. In the latter, Prime Minister Mottley offered, in both international contexts, one of the most affirmative of the various responses to the latest and impending environmental catastrophes but also linked the issue of climate change to ongoing issues of migration and political instability that Caribbean residents face, often from their powerful northern neighbor, the United States. Additionally, as the then current head of the Caribbean Economic Community (CARICOM), she offered a relational and historical analysis of the continuous war threats from the United States to Venezuela. Soon her words, circulated on social media and were replayed on numerous sites. Her challenge that "Our Caribbean Sea must remain a zone of peace, and for that we shall fight" rang with the eloquence and political clarity which identify her as the leading member of a new generation of women providing a new paradigm of world political leadership.[3]

The Caribbean is often seen as a series of archipelagoes of islands, therefore separated by water from each other as well as from larger continental locations in North and South America. But new definitions of the Caribbean, such as those explored in *Caribbean Spaces* (2013) and a variety of studies by Caribbean scholars, consistently describe the entire circum-Caribbean as central to an understanding of this geography. Islands in the Caribbean, especially those in the direct pathway of global currents, like Ayiti, take direct blows from trade winds from Africa to the Americas. Each year Caribbean residents of islands and pathway continental locations await a metaphoric roll of the hurricane dice, unsure which island or coastline will be hit next. The same trade winds that brought Columbus to the "New World" and enslaved Africans to the Americas are the same pathways that hurricanes follow, now with a ferocity never seen before, their force credited to extreme climate change. Assertions that these mega-hurricanes result from the intense new climate patterns caused by global warming are no longer relegated to obscure science journals; this analysis now appears in newspaper articles, in magazines, on television and the world wide web. Mimi Sheller's "Caribbean Futures in the Offshore Anthropocene: Debt, Disaster, and Duration"[4] offers a good assessment of the conjunctions of climate disaster and the unresolved histories of exploitation of Caribbean land- and seascapes.

An even uglier historical truth which linked African enslavement to negative climate conditions and the current residents of the Caribbean was discovered after Hurricane Irma in 2017, when the island of Barbuda was literally depopulated. A famous headline, "Hurricane Irma: For First Time in 300 Years, There Is No One Living on the Island of Barbuda,"[5] unwittingly revealed that some smaller islands were populated only following transatlantic slavery when Africans were placed there singularly for creating wealth on sugarcane plantations for Europe.[6] Deducting 300 years from 2017 produces 1717, a year at the height of transatlantic and plantation-bound chattel slavery. Before the arrival of Africans from the 16th to the 19th centuries, indigenous Caribs, Tainos, and Kalinagos lived on larger islands or mainland locations in South or North America; and often moved, as is done in contemporary Cuba, out of pathways of impending storms.[7]

PAN-CARIBBEAN

Nobel Laureate Derek Walcott said it best in "The Sea is History" framed as a poetic answer to an oft-posed question: "Where are your monuments, your battles, martyrs? Where is your tribal memory?" Caribbean people today are nationals of various island nation-states: ". . . and then each rock broke into its own nation"[8] the poem had continued, with people now proud of their island origins as they celebrate each island's particularities (Spice Island, Home of Carnival etc.). While flag independence signaled a formal political separation from colonial powers, nevertheless the islands and their related continental locations are still imperiled equally when set upon by the ferocious actions of nature or from the external politics of Euro-American economic imperialism. After disastrous storms or earthquakes, as happened to Haiti (2010, 2021) and Puerto Rico (2017) it is possible to become climate refugees, ending up on other islands or in the United States or South America. One sees a similar pattern in the continental United States as following Hurricane Katrina, many people were displaced and never returned to their original residences in New Orleans. Similar displacements have happened after volcanic eruptions in Haiti, St. Vincent, Montserrat, St. Lucia, Martinique and now La Palma in the Canary Islands. Still, most people have historically "indigenized"[9] and bonded with their places of birth, their land, sea and river scapes, the places where they buried their children's placentas, remembering childhoods in places they called home. Yet, with looming precarity and instability, no one can rest assured that wherever we are in the world are permanent residences. Were Caribbeans not brought originally to live on these islands for someone else's economic benefit? And, are they still making homes in locations defined as transient, perennially living in places identified as escapes for tourists looking for short-term happiness? Black Power activist Stokely Carmichael describes his family as "Pan-Caribbean":[10]

> Although I was born in Trinidad, in a real sense it would be inaccurate—actually *incomplete* would be a better word—to call me Trinidadian. Ultimately our roots are in Africa, but in a more immediate and recent sense they are truly Pan-Caribbean. Consider.
>
> My mother's mother was born in Montserrat to an Irish planter and his wife, an African woman, said to have been his former slave. But my mother was born in the US Canal Zone in Panama, from whence as a child she returned to the care of maternal relations in "the Emerald Isle," as Montserrat is known, while her parents and older sibling left for New York. (14)

The logic of Pan-Caribbean identity is one which perhaps offers the most optimistic model of seeing the Caribbean not as disparate fragmented island spaces, but as a site of continuing circulations of people, families, often in the search for better economic options and for social and professional relationships; sometimes because of crises, but always within the larger framing of a hoped-for possible political unity. Still, Mia Mottley's 2019 warning that "there will be mass migration by climate refugees that will destabilize the countries of the world that are not on the front line of this climate crisis" is worth considering seriously when dominant nations have developed policies against immigrants. Particularly relevant is the fact that these countries themselves live with a cavalier inability to control their use of energy, and thereby they create policies that lead to the same immigrations they fear. Mottley's conclusion: "We refuse to be relegated to the footnotes of history and to be collateral damage for the greed of others, for we have contributed less than 1% of greenhouse gas emissions" (UN Climate Summit, 2019).

But what should Caribbean governments be doing? The Cuban strategy of moving people out of danger is one model. But residents of smaller islands, lacking that ability to move, may want to decide for themselves what is feasible in particular locations. People living in poverty have to work wherever they can and sometimes in urban areas find or create shelter in flimsy housing that cannot withstand any category of hurricane. Still, rather than being victims of what feels like hurricane roulette, island residents need, as Mottley suggests, to make assertive plans that can be supported, challenged, and improved, thinking ahead rather than awaiting the next disaster. But is this the responsibility of those formerly-colonized alone now, the individuals liberated from slavery without any compensation across the Americas still finding ways to find opportunities for transcendence?

An international reparations agenda is still active, even as countries like Britain and the United States seem mired in their self-imposed political dramas. Creating usable future plans for the survival of people who were brought to the Caribbean, often by force, and now still live in precarious locations is a major international challenge. So, how do new paradigms of leadership instrumentalize Caribbean futures? This chapter argues that progressive women's leadership in the Caribbean can offer alternatives that more fully meet the needs of their communities and provide the world with usable examples. Indeed, according to UN Women, "based on the research, Caribbean society is broadly supportive of women in political leadership on the basis of fairness and equity, and [we]perceive that woman will focus on the core social development priorities that they themselves prioritize" (UN Women, 2019).

FAULT LINES: DAME IS STILL A COLONIAL TITLE[11]

The rise of women to political leadership positions in the Caribbean has followed an interesting arc. The first woman leader in the immediate independence period was the prime minister of Dominica, Mary Eugenia Charles (1919–2005), who became Dame Eugenia Charles. As indicated above, "Dame" is still a colonial title, the female equivalent of a formal "Sir," signifying full belonging in the class hierarchy of British imperialism, at least at the level of receiving honorific titles which assure one a certain rank and respect within British imperialist contexts. Eugenia Charles, is described as "an ideologically conservative, right of centre politician who was unafraid to publicize (or benefit from) her conservative views in an era when it was more fashionable, even if unprofitable, to articulate a progressive political philosophy" (Barriteau, 2006: 12). Her leadership included being the first Caribbean woman to head a political party, and then leading that party to victory in three consecutive elections, while serving simultaneously as Prime Minister, Minister of Finance and Economic Affairs, and Minister of Foreign Affairs and Defence (12). In her aptly titled chapter on Eugenia Charles, "Enjoying Power, Challenging Gender," Eudine Barriteau sees Charles as a paradox, particularly given her "Ambivalence about Feminism and Gender" (17–25) which serves as one of the section sub-titles of her introduction:

> I do not think we have unpacked the paradox that was Eugenia Charles. However, I believe the research team has made a significant contribution to documenting, analysing and disseminating knowledge about a Caribbean woman who enjoyed political power and defied traditional categories of gender. Her refusal to fit into pre-existing definitions forces a rethinking of the existing classifications of women's political behaviour and leadership along conventional, linear readings of gender. (25)

The paradox Barriteau indicates is that while Eugenia Charles enjoyed exercising power and made space for other women to serve, she demurred when there were attempts to place her actions into the then contemporary analyses of women's location in politics. In this refusal Charles was apace with other women in similar positions at that historical period; few or none of those first generation women leaders would say that they were feminists or that they supported its positions publicly. This lack of self-conscious political awareness has an impact as, significantly, her leadership in Dominica did not lead to more empowerment for women in a similar position in the political sphere. Still, Dominica occupies the 25% percentile in terms of women being represented in parliament, higher than several countries but lower, according to UN Women's 2019 charts, than Trinidad and Tobago, Cuba, and Guyana.

The chapters in *Enjoying Power. Eugenia Charles and Political Leadership in the Commonwealth Caribbean*, one of the first texts to study women and leadership in the Caribbean, present several different angles for studying and understanding the mid twentieth century. Commendably, the former prime minister provided access and support for all the researchers from the University of West Indies, led by Eudine Barriteau, as they pursued this project. She was cited as commenting on the nature of women's leadership as follows: "When persons ask me 'how do you feel about being the first woman Prime Minister of the Caribbean?' I say, 'I just wonder why it took so long to be the first, because in fact our women have always stood out strong'" (Eugenia Charles, in Barriteau and Cobley, 19). The research model for studying political leadership, created by the Barriteau team is worth emulating. Examining the contributions and shortcomings after women (and men) who become prime ministers or presidents in Africa and the African Diaspora, leave office will create a kind of political knowledge leadership archive. We can only benefit from their experience; assess their accomplishments or failures; learn from their mistakes.[12]

Cynthia Barrow Giles, in "Straight Roads or Bumpy Rides? Eugenia Charles's Path to Power," provides background on the nature of the quest for parity in Caribbean politics, specifically on the various levels Charles surmounted in order to become prime minister. However, for the purposes of this chapter, issues discussed in "Stereotyping Women's Political Leadership" by Carmen Hutchinson Miller offer some interesting connections. For example, the "Old Woman" stereotype is almost identical to the "Old Ma" disparagement levied at Ellen Johnson Sirleaf in Liberia at the height of her campaign for office. Notably, these were not old women when compared to the men who ran for office. Eugenia Charles "became prime minister of Dominica at age sixty-one" (255), but she was the contemporary of most of the other Caribbean male leaders (including Herbert Blaize, Forbes Burnham, and Errol Barrow). All were of comparable age, most of the men becoming prime minister at younger ages. Hutchinson Miller concludes rhetorically: "It would be very interesting to do a comparative analysis towards discovering whether the issue of the age of these male leaders was as important to their publics as it seemed to be in the case of Eugenia Charles" (255).

For Eugenia Charles, as well, the "Iron Lady" stereotype also remained. It may have been concretized because she became the first Caribbean leader to support then president Reagan's invasion of Grenada in 1983; other regional prime ministers refused such a violation of Caribbean space from the northern super power.[13] For this action, Eugenia Charles entered history as a kind of Thatcher-like Caribbean counterpart, as "The Iron Lady of the Caribbean."[14] She is, therefore, one of that first generation of women leaders who, like

Margaret Thatcher or Golda Meir, felt that to be equal to the men or to run a government in which men tended to exercise masculine prerogatives, they had to be even harder than the men in power. According to Hutchinson Miller, the moniker "Iron Lady" was applied because "Charles demonstrated that she was not afraid to be strong and to use the power she had as a leader, even if it meant that others would be against the decisions she made" (252).

As indicated, the Eugenia Charles leadership trajectory included co-founding a winning political party and with that election victory being appointed to the legislature in 1970. In 1975 winning a seat to the House of Assembly, she became leader of the opposition, fighting for independence from Britain, and becoming prime minister in 1980, when her party won that year's election. Joan Cuffie's "Eugenia Charles and the Psychology of Leadership" provides a useful conclusion that clarifies this issue at the level of context, gender, and practice:

> Eugenia Charles entered politics at a time when males dominated the political sphere and she was therefore exposed to a masculine, autocratic model of leadership that she emulated. It could be stated that some of her personality characteristics predisposed her to adopt this leadership style, but the situational factors promoted her continued use of the autocratic leadership style. (147)

The question of gender remains significant, as one of the guiding questions for this project remains: Is there a difference between women's leadership and men's use of political power? Do you think anything changes, or will change, when more women get to political power? And as raised in my study of Condoleezza Rice,[15] is it simply enough to have a woman in political office if she pursues politics antithetical to the larger community, such as going into unnecessary wars or providing access that would destroy a particular country's operations for ideological reasons? A parallel can be drawn therefore in terms of Dr. Rice's complicit role in the US invasion and destruction of Iraq and Eugenia Charles's role in facilitating the US invasion of Grenada.[16]

Eugenia Charles is referred to as "The Reluctant Feminist" by Alicia Mondesire (259–281), but for feminists like Peggy Antrobus: "She operated as a man, without compassion" (267). The more nuanced position of Barriteau and Reddock is that "concepts of masculinity and femininity recognized the dynamism and fluidity of both masculine and feminine behaviours" (266, 269). Thus, the conclusion is important that "gains for women under her leadership might be expressed more in terms of improvements in women's morale and confidence, and less in material terms" (279). Although for some women there were "increases in women's participation in government and politics," most women in the Caribbean did not benefit appreciably from having Eugenia Charles, a woman, as prime minister.

FAULT LINE: POWER GAPS

An early power gap for women can be seen in their absence from Carribbean leadership, beginning with Haitain independence. Though legendary women have been identified in the launching of the Haitian Revolution, including Marie-Jeanne Lamartiniére, Suzanne Béliar, Cécile Fatiman, Marie Sainte Dédée Bazile, Catherine Flon,[17] in its long history of independence since 1804, few women have had leadership. This absence of women from the leadership of Ayiti following its revolution could be one analysis of the Haitian leadership debacle which continues to the contemporary. Questions about leadership and succession and the state in general were clearly not worked out in a democratic way. Still, those women identified who have been in the leadership role presented more possibilities than occurred in the United States: Ertha Pascal-Trouillot (1943 to present) served as provisional president of Haiti from 1990 to 1991. Mirlande Manigat was a constitutional lawyer and former first lady as the wife of Leslie Manigat who served as a senator during his brief term as president (February to June 1988) when he was overthrown by a coup; but she bravely contested the presidential election in 2010. Indicated in the 28th percentile in terms of women in leadership, two women have served at the highest levels: Claudette Werleigh was the first woman appointed prime minister of Haiti from 1995 to 1996, appointed by President Aristide, and Michèle Duvivier Pierre-Louis, the second woman prime minister, served from 2008 to 2009. Today the latter is the president of FOKAL, an urban educational center of excellence who in her term as prime minister is identified as developing women's rights agenda. She served as the local Chair of the Caribbean Studies Association conference in Haiti in June 2016 and maintains a positive presence in Haiti's lived realities, particularly as it pertains to educating the youth.

A "Let Haiti Live Women's Rights Delegation" is described in "Rewinding History. The Rights of Haitian Women"[18] as investigating women's rights in Haiti and finding a climate of violence against women pervasive in Port au Prince, making women susceptible to armed bandits, rape, physical and economic violence. Still, in this regard, it is important to identify Le Ministère à la Condition Féminine et aux Droits des Femmes (MCFDF) (Ministry of the Women's Condition and the Rights of Women) founded in 1994 precisely to engage the issues of equality as it pertains to women and to advance their political rights.

In the former British Caribbean commonwealth, another important power gap exists between the elected office of the prime minister and the appointed ceremonial one of the president, the latter being a status akin to the former governor general in the colonial period. When I began the process of trying to interview Paula-Mae Weekes, who became president of Trinidad and Tobago in 2018, her official response was that it was important for me to note that "Under our Constitutional arrangements the President of the Republic of Trinidad and Tobago is only a 'political' figure in the widest sense and her authority and powers are circumscribed by law and convention" (8/23/2018). "My reply was, 'I do understand this and would like to still understand the nature of this relationship further as I still see President Weekes as significant for accessing this role after so many years of male leadership.'"[19] President Weekes filled out my questionnaire (see appendix), although two critical questions remained unanswered. Her responses tended to be generic, perhaps because we were unable to do an in-person interview. Weekes was, however, affirmative about male and female leadership in answering the question:

> *Do you think anything changes, or will change, when more women get to political power?*
>
> I have no doubt. Today, our President of the Senate and Speaker of the House are women, as are roughly 30% of our Parliamentarians. Women are also rising to the top of many national organisations which, while not "political" have effect on political decisions being made. The overall effect has been a subtle change in the method of communication, greater willingness to be collaborative and more sensitivity to the circumstances of women, children and other vulnerable groups in the society.
>
> I believe that these changes will be magnified as more and more women access political power. (Full text available in appendix to this work.)

FAULT LINE: IS AN INDIAN WOMAN IN TRINIDAD A BLACK WOMAN? SEX AND RACE IN CARIBBEAN POLITICAL LEADERSHIP

Still, Trinidad and Tobago is one of the few Caribbean countries to have already had a woman prime minister. Its complications, nonetheless, this precedent allows us to move beyond the situation of simply having a woman leader, as with Eugenia Charles, to actually analyzing what was achieved and what the limitations were in exercising leadership. Kamla Persad Bissessar was the subject of my essay titled "'She Wants the Black Man's Post.' Sexuality and Race in the Construction of Women's Leadership in Diaspora" (2011), a title generated by a calypsonian's song on her wanting the prime minister's post, loaded with all the sexual double entendre of calypso.

The calypsonian's lyrics about Persad-Bissessar's vocal contestation of government policies in parliament summarized a masculinist interpretation of women's leadership being rooted in the desire for the phallus: "She wants

Manning post / She wants Manning post / She talking the most / Because . . . / She want the Black man post." As described earlier, "Post" in that essay, was a synecdoche for a high-level office or position. The lyrics, in the characteristic double entendre of the genre, also evoke "post" as an allusion to the male sexual organ. Yet "post" in postmodernist discourse also refers to "afterness." What is produced then is a kind of "triple entendre." Within the logic of the lyrics is also a consistent sexualizing of Trinidadian women, particularly Indian women, who, ironically, are often seen as the primary conveyors of "douglarisation" the term given to the product of miscegenation between Africans and Indians.[20] Scholars like Patricia Mohammed who have studied this racializing of Indian women in Trinidad indicate that "douglarisation" is often explained by claims about the sexual laxity of Indian women in relation to Black men.[21] Mohammed discusses some of these related issues in her section on Indo-Caribbean Feminist Intersections (162–330).

The political aspirations of women are thus reduced to their desire for neo-colonial/imperial leadership, historically given to Black men and which continued into the post-colonial state. But in the second connotation, women's leadership aspirations are reduced to raw sexual desire for power. Several related metaphors spiral outward from the initial assertion. The former prime minister, a Black man, had the biggest "post" and therefore had then the most political power in the country. In Trinidad, the rhetorical question became: can a woman take over that post or access that power? Kamla Persad-Bissessar, described as the first woman of Indian/South Asian descent to become prime minister outside of India, precedes similarly named Kamala Harris, the first United States Vice President of South Asian and Caribbean descent in this national profile. Persad-Bissessar became prime minister in Trinidad, winning by a landslide in 2010 but losing subsequent elections, unable to rekindle the energy and advance gender as a winning strategy in her campaigns in 2015 and 2020.

Still, issues of women accessing power were central on the day Kamla Persad-Bissessar became Leader of the Opposition, which would position her to be the next Prime Minister. The only publicly visible activist woman in the public gallery (where I was also present, viewing this momentous occasion) was Hazel Brown, Coordinator of the Network of non-governmental organizations (NGOs) of Trinidad and Tobago for the Advancement of Women.[22] Hazel Brown had actively worked with Emily's List in organizing women for political office.[23] When we talked over coffee at the Hyatt Hotel afterward, Hazel Brown was reflective about what these new developments meant for women and about the "Put a Woman Campaign,"[24] a project to prepare women for political service. Having spent years as an NGO organizer of women's political rights, she provided a valuable insight into what was unfolding. She described women across the Caribbean as poised to assume the highest leadership in Jamaica, Barbados, Dominica, and Trinidad and Tobago, and spoke about legislation for the protection of women from rape and incest. Stating that these developments were not fully supported by male leadership, she expressed gratitude that Persad-Bissessar, in whose campaign for the Prime Ministership she served as an advisor, had made a historic leap. Overall, a sense of profound fatigue with the past, coupled with high expectations for the future, best summarized her stance on that historic day.

Although the "Put a Woman" project aimed to prepare women for leadership at many levels, Brown saw the next step as determining how to manipulate the system for full access. Implying that getting to leadership is only half the task,[25] she raised the question that, once there, how does a woman leader create networks for advancing projects without losing principle or responsibility to communities? Hazel Brown argued that activists such as herself needed to be "out there in the trenches," because in politics one is often forced to make many compromises.

Relatedly, when in 2014 I asked then candidate Keith Rowley at a pre-election diasporic circulation event at Florida Memorial University about why the PNM (Peoples National Movement) did not have a woman also run in the election, since the opposition had run Persad-Bissessar, he responded to me quite adamantly: "That woman question. I don't respond to that woman question" in a way that offended even some men in the audience who expressed this afterwards. My sense is that Rowley would have had to change that adamance along the way. Still the PNM advanced somewhat on the gender front as women occupied major positions in subsequent campaigns, though from all accounts, not enough.

In that 2010 timeframe, the number of women sitting in Parliament worldwide was still small, averaging 17%, with Trinidad and Tobago slightly higher than the world's average in the 20th percentile range.[26] By 2019, however, Trinidad and Tobago had moved to the 30 to 35th percentile, still ranked 44 of 192 countries, and behind other Caribbean countries Cuba, Costa Rica, Grenada. and Guyana (UN Women, 2019). The work of a party which sought to break through the racial divide, the Congress of the People (COP), a middle-class, professional, Indo-African[27] party was notable for its deployment of a majority of women to contest seats. Although unsuccessful at the first showing, they strategically pushed the envelope of the possibility of more women in leadership. Paula Morgan,[28] a then university professor, had herself been active in COP's founding and had written an unpublished piece on "Women in Politics" that was excerpted in COP pamphlets. After this, the Peoples National Movement removed several of its older, more experienced women, and brought in a slew of younger women, who were among the group put forward in the 2010 elections. Yet, for the 2020 elections, ten years later, there was no measurable increase in women getting to leadership. Ultimately the People's National Movement did not field as many candidates as they could have. A timely assessment from Gabrielle Hosein, then head of the Institute for Gender and Development Studies at the University of the West Indies, St. Augustine, was that "Thirty Percent is Not Enough." There she sounded a pessimistic note on the possibilities of moving beyond 30% representation in this cycle and documented her disappointment with Persad-Bissessar:

> My deep disappointments about Kamla Persad-Bissessar were, among others, that she failed to end legal child marriage, approve a national gender policy, and create a Children's Act that wasn't discriminatory, all to keep patriarchal religious leadership on side the UNC. Will this election bring any change? What do voter trends and predictions regarding "marginal" constituencies mean for women's leadership and gender equality? The PNM is fielding 14 women candidate . . . Indeed, one can argue that women candidates were primarily placed in losing seats. This is typical globally, and is also one of the reasons for women's lower levels of public office.[29]

In the end, the Peoples National Movement,[30] led by Keith Rowley, won the election in 2020, defeating Kamla Persad-Bissessar's UNC as they did in 2015. But this time, sadly, his campaign was the recipient of a heavy anti-Black racism, which still surprises many who grew up with the logic of more collaborative relationships between Indians and Africans in Trinidad.

Still, in a Trinidadian context, the way that Persad-Bissessar was racialized and ethnicized was significant. In other global readings, Kamla would be identified as a "Black woman," and many Indians in other locations refer to themselves as "Black people" as did some Indo-Trinidadians in the past. The history of South Indians who ended up in the Caribbean islands via indentureship indicate that this particular form of racialization renders them Black in the political definition of that term remains. The answer to my rhetorical question: Is an Indian Woman in Trinidad a Black Woman? seems to change based on location and time and politics. For scholar/activists like Walter Rodney (Guyana) or Claudia Jones (*West Indian Gazette and Afro-Asian Caribbean News*) or the Organisation of Women of African and Asian Descent (OWAAD) in the United Kingdom, the answer would be: "Yes," particularly given the subordination of both communities in terms of African enslavement and Indian indentureship in the Caribbean and their continuing treatment in relationship to whiteness in the UK and the parallel political definition of Blackness. The entire history of colonial and post-colonial discrimination that both communities suffered, not to mention actual physiognomy and skin color of many South Asians, also indicate a "Yes." Moving away from political and other forms of definitional Blackness remains a feature of anti-Blackness, which many ethnic communities feel is needed for their advancement. This is also happening in Trinidad and Tobago.

That Persad-Bissessar resoundingly defeated the male-led PNM under Patrick Manning's leadership in 2008 challenged many assumptions about leadership in the Caribbean. Earlier women prime ministers such as Eugenia Charles (Dominica, 1980–1995) seemed to operate at the behest of US imperialism: Reagan's desires as signified by Eugenia Charles's allowing her country to be used for the Grenada invasion of 1983 as the prime example. A univocal racial or ethnic reading yields an inadequate analysis, and much fuller insight can be gained by tracking intersections of ethnicity and gender, acknowledging the specific local and global contexts in which leadership occurs, and carefully disentangling the landscape shaped by popular culture, public discourses, and individual gender performances. Kamla, alert to social theory, was conscious of her position within the context of her country's complex configurations of race, ethnicity, class, and neo-imperialism, offered a commentary on the then miniscule percentage of women in leadership globally:

> My dear sisters, as I conclude I wish to stress that as one of the small percentage of current female world leaders, indeed there are only 9% of world leaders who are at this point in time female. And there are only three in the Commonwealth, 3 out of the 54 Nations. Australia, Bangladesh and of course Trinidad and Tobago, we hope to change that in coming years, to have more numbers. And so rest assured I will continue to use my position both here and abroad to effect changes which will resound to the benefit of all women. (Persad-Bissessar, 2011)

Nonetheless, mistakes accumulated during her term in office, particularly her promise of alternative, anti-patriarchal leadership. Rumors and skits persisted about the prime minister's alleged alcoholism and of her being subject to the manipulations of men in government, in business, and in her personal life. Persad-Bissessar's governance (2010–2015), which seemed gradually to benefit the East Indian male leadership and marked by a series of corrupt practices, contributed to the return of the Peoples National Movement in 2015. An assessment of Kamla Persad-Bissessar on her policies and track record as the first woman prime minister of Trinidad and Tobago, and, indeed of Black women entering politics today, reveals some significant failures. The Kamla Persad-Bissessar prime-ministership represented, in discursive, ideological, and practical ways, some notable advances. These include redefinitions of leadership, and re-imaginings of Black women as globally influential actors in the public sphere. Her limitations had to do with entering leadership on the same terms as the men who preceded her, rather than pursuing transformative leadership. For, although not the same as Eugenia Charles's explicitly pro-US/UK imperial policies and practices, Kamla Persad-Bissessar's leadership fell short in terms of meeting the needs of the general population and the needs of women.

Unable to be in Trinidad myself, in 2020 elections held during the COVID-19 pandemic and related travel closures, I sought out an on-the-ground assessment from Yvonne Bobb-Smith, who had previously worked with the "Put A Woman" campaign. Our e-conversations revealed that she saw some regressions taking place. On July 31, 2020, I asked her:

> What in your assessment happened to her (Kamla's) vision as the first woman PM of T& T that she has lost so much respect? My sense is that she is being manipulated by a variety of overlapping masculinities. Is there a recent assessment that can guide thinking on this? What are her prospects for the next election? They don't seem good from here.

Yvonne Bobb Smith's response:

> Yes, I agree most of her utterances do not match the level of experience she should have gained as a former Prime Minister. It seems as though she is engaging her weaknesses rather than embracing her strengths. She has emitted so far nothing which is fresh and invigorating, she sticks to making ground, hopefully, backbiting Rowley and the PNM. I will keep my ear to the ground for voices this week on TV or Radio of the political analysts. (August 1, 2020)

And a few days later:

> Kamla seems to be less original, and more in the realm of "throwing words," not mindful that they may seem to reflect the thinking of the much hated President of the USA. I am disappointed that there is no upliftment, for me, coming from the campaigns. I suppose I grew up when philosophical thought was applauded as providing means of self-fulfillment, with or without flagging dollars. (August 5, 2020)[31]

PORTIA SIMPSON-MILLER: A STANDING OVATION

The first time I saw Portia Simpson-Miller it was in a large public conference center in 2006 at an African Diaspora Conference in Salvador-Bahia, Brazil. Recently elected Prime Minister of Jamaica, her presence was riveting. In her speech, she invoked names of many Caribbean leaders from Nanny of the Maroons to Marcus Garvey who preceded her, to great applause and a standing ovation. But it was the dynamism of seeing a Black woman as a head of state, the only Black woman political leader many had ever seen, that brought the crowd of a capacity 1,000 people to their feet. A few years later, I attended her second inauguration in Jamaica in 2012 and listened to popular reggae singer Shaggy sing "Strength of a Woman."[32]

Portia Simpson-Miller held the Jamaican presidency after P. J. Patterson passed the party leadership baton to her. She failed to win the subsequent election, being caught up in what has been referred to by Jamaican men in public media campaigns as "panty politics" and by several Jamaican women as "lack of preparedness" but was elected in her own right in 2012.

The following official biographical statement was shared by her assistants following an attempt to get texts of speeches, and an interview with the former prime minister who was described to me as in ill health:

> The Most Honorable Portia Lucretia Simpson Miller made history on March 30, 2006 when she became Jamaica's seventh and first female prime minister, and only the third female head of state in the Caribbean. She served as Jamaica's prime minister from March 2006 to September 2007, and again from January 2012 to March 2016. She retired from public life in June 2017, after serving as the Leader of Opposition. Throughout her four decades of public service, Simpson-Miller has been hailed as "a metaphor of hope in the face of adversity" and as a champion of the poor, oppressed, and marginalized in our society. Her ascension to Jamaica's highest political office came after she served for 17 years as a cabinet minister with portfolio responsibility for Labor, Social Security and Sport; Tourism, Entertainment and Sport; and Local Government, Community Development and Sport; in addition to Women's Affairs. Mrs. Simpson-Miller has a distinguished record of service at the regional and international levels. She served as a member of the Council of Women World Leaders, which is an international network of current and former women presidents and prime ministers whose mission is to mobilize on women's issues. (official biographical statement)

According to UN Women for 2019, Jamaica still remains in the 15–20th percentile in terms of representation of women in parliament. The issue about whether women as leaders are able to advance the general representation of women in subsequent iterations of government seems to indicate no major correlation so far. But Simpson-Miller was the leading architect of Jamaica's Master Plan for Sustainable Tourism Development, and she was tireless in promoting and strengthening urban renewal and community development, leading to fundamental reforms in local government.

But defining Prime Minister Portia Simpson-Miller in her home context was challenging and for some limiting. Carolyn Cooper's "Deporting Portia: Creole Language Politics in the Jamaica Labour Party's Advertising Campaign for the 2011 General Election in Jamaica," a paper presented at the Caribbean Studies Association Conference in Guadeloupe, described an "advertising campaign launched by the Jamaica Labour Party's youth arm, G2K, for the 2011 national election in Jamaica . . . designed to contest Portia Simpson Miller's capacity to function as prime minister." Demeaning ads portrayed the then Leader of the Opposition as one who did not have the intellectual ability or the "class" to represent Jamaica on the world stage. In Carolyn Cooper's reading, Simpson-Miller's use of Jamaican linguistic registers was misrepresented by the Jamaican bourgeoisie as evidence of her "natural" exclusion from the ranks of those entitled to rule while the urban and rural working class and peasantry understood and supported her candidacy.

> . . . in effect, the language of mass citizenship in Jamaica became the shibboleth that engendered Portia Simpson Miller's deportation from the inner circle of preferred political leadership for the elite. Conversely, the masses of the Jamaican people, rejecting the G2K's caricature, endorsed Portia Simpson's candidacy for prime minister, thus affirming the authority of populist definitions of national identity and citizenship.[33]

An adept scholar of Jamaican popular culture and the larger African Diaspora literature and culture, Carolyn Cooper publishes a column in Jamaican language in the local newspaper, *The Gleaner.* Often using that column to challenge class-based linguistic biases, she defended Sister P (as she is affectionately called) from the attempts to demean her use of the language of the people in her communication style. Her "Drawing Sister P's Tongue," *The Gleaner*, December 25, 2011, is representative of these articles. And of relevance to this chapter, particularly as it pertains to the need for Simpson Miller to write her own history, Cooper's advice was for Portia Simpson-Miller not to run for another election term, but to secure her legacy: "Sister P doesn't have to be concerned about her legacy. It's safe. The first woman to become prime minister of Jamaica! That could never have been easy. . . . If Sister P gives up the job as prime minister, there are lots of other things she can do. I think her first project should be writing her autobiography."

Her essay "Supporting Sister P: Feminist Alliances in Class-Prejudiced Jamaica"[34] develops these positions further, demonstrating how Sister P's working-class origins were often used against her in a context in which political leadership was seen as a "natural inheritance" for Jamaica's elite club of politicians. Cooper to her benefit, was able to make the link to women's political leadership in African diasporic and therefore global context: "We know that women have long been warriors on that continent providing military and political leadership in the struggles of their people to resist domination and create humane societies. Our own Nanny of the Maroons is not a mythical creature. She is a historical figure of noble lineage"; (9) she indicates in a section titled "Women for Sister P" which also includes a list of great women leaders of Africa but also those in Jamaica who are identified as pioneering politicians: Mary Morris Knibb, Iris Collins, Rose Leon, Mavis Gilmour (9–10). Several other Jamaican women who exercised leadership such as Catherine Mc Kenzie, Amy Ashwood Garvey, Amy Jacques Garvey have already been identified in this work.

The idea of writing one's autobiography after service as we have already indicated, and as Carolyn Cooper suggested, is one of the significant avenues to documenting women leaders' contributions and remains a norm in the arsenal of male leadership. Providing access to having a full study done of one's accomplishments as in the Eugenia Charles case remains still an additional model to be pursued. A full biography of Portia Simpson-Miller[35] will no doubt capture some of these hidden nuances. Meanwhile, a children's book by writer Opal Palmer Adisa, *Portia Dreams* (2021), describes her childhood background in rural Jamaica, her coming of age as well as her developing consciousness of the role of service and a meeting with then Chief Minister Norman Manley, which inspired her about possibilities for leadership and includes a "One Big Dream" statement on its back cover identifying her achievement and signed "Auntie Portia." Included in its paratext is a chronology of her accomplishments and a section which allows children to write their own dream for the future.

Simpson Miller has received several local and international awards and accolades, including the Bureau of Women's Affairs Award for outstanding contribution to the advancement of women's affairs in Jamaica. In March 2007, she was awarded the International Olympic Committee's World Women and Sport Trophy for outstanding dedication to women in Jamaican Sports—both athletes and administrators. One can perhaps credit the prominence of Jamaican women in sports at the international level to Portia Simpson Miller who even by her own example as an athlete provided that model of success. More international accolades included her induction into the International Women's Forum (IWF) Hall of Fame in recognition of the "incredible impact that women of courage, creativity, and passion have made towards improving society, inspiring others, and building better leadership in the world." In 2012, *Time* named her among its "100 Most Influential Persons in the World."[36]

A lecture on Caribbean integration titled "A New Vision for a New World Reality: Prospects for the Anglophone Caribbean" for the 11th Eric Williams Memorial Lecture at Florida International University (November 6, 2009) was a masterclass on the topic, taking the audience through the history of Caribbean's contributions to world politics, and emphasizing that the people themselves are the Caribbean's greatest asset.[37] For Simpson Miller, regional integration had to resolve some centrally unfinished issues opened by the creation of the Caribbean Economic Community (CARICOM) under Trinidad and Tobago's first prime minister, Eric E. Williams's leadership. Further work through a Regional Governance System she argued would include more advanced communication and transportation systems, collaboration in promoting tourism to reduce competition among locations but shared arrangements; health advancement; financial sector integration; energy policies; food security; environmental protection as in managing hurricane damage and related climate-change issues, and above all, creating a new reality whereby the brain power of the Caribbean is used more directly across the Caribbean region and the diaspora.

Gender imbalances, whether they disadvantage men or women, must be addressed, Simpson-Miller stated, and multi-linguality is a necessity for building a "borderless work space." Any development paradigm would reveal that, should some of these forward-thinking prescriptions be executed, the Caribbean would be far ahead of other regions in its ability to build sustainable and advanced communities. Still, while Jamaica remains in the 15–20th percentile in terms of representation of women in parliament, its stunning visibility of women in athletics and in other forms of popular culture and the arts indicates, at the performative level, a definite set of fully realized possibilities.

While no full biography is available yet for Jamaica's first woman prime minister, Beverley Anderson Manley's autobiography, boldly titled *The Manley Memoirs* (2008),[38] challenges that logic of erasure or her story being constructed by others. Here one observes the self-creation of a leadership pathway from her own angle of vision. Beverley Manley is indicated here because before Portia Simpson-Miller who became prime minister twice (2006–2007 and 2012–2016), another Black woman was at the center of political power, in the classic first lady position though consistently seen throughout her career as making an explicit commitment to women's rights. In 2002, at the fourth Eric Williams Memorial Lecture, a forum on "Women, Politics and the Caribbean," notwithstanding never having served in political office, Beverley Anderson Manley came across as the most convincing and experienced speaker. She cited her own life as example, having filled over fifteen roles while being married to a politician. She charted the gains over the years from relative absence of women (when there was a struggle in the 1970's even to get women into the armed forces) to the limited presence. For her, one had to understand gender issues relationally, in terms of their "webs of complexity." She traced the movement from the first conference on women in Mexico in 1975, which examined where we place value in society as it related to women and the need for a changed environment so that choices for women are enlarged. She described the importance of better childcare and equally shared responsibilities in the larger society for women to have access to leadership. Her compelling statement was that women's questions are society's questions. Beverley Manley is on record as well for supporting and defending Simpson Miller in various media fora, asserting for example the class distinctions in Jamaican society that worked often to her disadvantage.

FINALLY, COMPETENCE OVER SEXUALITY

In September, 2002, "Women and Politics in the Caribbean" was the theme of The Fourth Annual Eric E. Williams Memorial Lecture at Florida International University, co-organized by this writer with Erica Williams Connell. It brought together three distinguished Caribbean women politicians on the same platform: Honorable Cynthia Pratt, Deputy Prime Minister and Minister of National Security of The Bahamas; Honorable Mia Mottley, Attorney General of Barbados; Ms. Beverly Anderson Manley, Former First Lady of Jamaica, wife of the deceased and beloved Jamaican Prime Minister, Michael Manley.[39] In that group of speakers, Mia Mottley was the young and inexperienced member of the panel, who drew audience applause because when she was called to speak, she was quick to challenge the moderator Professor Colin Palmer for usurping of the time with a lengthy fifteen-minute introduction while limiting panelists to three minutes each in response to his first question. Mia Mottley was then the youngest of the group yet the most assertive, capturing the hearts of the audience with her demonstration of her obvious ability to compete head-to-head with her male colleagues. Cynthia Pratt's presentation was an exercise of the politics of the possible, with her opening remarks, that with her athletic background and statuesque size, she was built for the podium and thereby had all the necessary preparation for her position. Beverly Anderson-Manley, a former journalist combined her own research and study of the condition of women to the larger question of how to navigate all the various issues that women face with assurance.

In that same time frame, the then recently published essay by Dessima Williams, who had served in the Grenada New Jewel revolutionary government, "Bringing More Women Into Leadership" (March 8, 2000), defined "global gendered apartheid," the fact that women who make up 50% of the world's population hold only 6% of seats in national cabinets, 13% of seats in world parliaments was relevantly cited as framing the event and had direct importance to a discussion of Caribbean women and leadership. Removing "gendered global apartheid" necessitated then, in Dessima's view, the advancement of women's leadership as this often has a direct effect on policies related to our youth, education and the planet's well-being. In this context it was important to note that 165 countries, and the entire Caribbean region, have ratified the U.N. 1980 Convention on the Elimination of All Forms of Discrimination Against Women.

A similar situation of a limited number of women in leadership exists in all relatively new Caribbean nations, where independence movements and efforts toward neo-colonial leadership also repeated the embedded logics of the European nation-state. In each case, leaders utilized the governmental structures already in place, generally without any major changes in these structures, under the guise of maintaining order. Deviations from that model as we see with Cuba lead directly to the wrath of the United States. In an earlier (2003) essay on this topic Monica Jardine and I described this conjunction of the Caribbean navigating between a dying colonialism and rising US Hegemony. This is a point made more directly in Claudia Jones essay "American Imperialism and the British West Indies" (1958) which argued that via the Anglo-American Commission, the Caribbean was being mortgaged to US interests in a handover between the British to the American sphere of interest. Una Marson of Jamaica would make a similar argument as it relates to communication industries in a letter to the then Prime Minister of Jamaica.[40]

But how to challenge those structures and create new paradigms? We recall here Caribbean feminist leadership activist Peggy Antrobus, cited in chapter 1 for providing an approach to two principles— transformational leadership and feminist leadership—which indicate that "women's leadership is a different concept from transformational feminist leadership" (55). There she makes a distinction between transformational leadership and transformational feminist leadership, the latter pertaining to economic, political, and social transformation and a "commitment to an agenda for social change" (55). In transformational feminist leadership, remedying gender inequities is paramount. And it also empowers all women. I want to suggest that this is one of the models that Mia Mottley uses in her so far successful tenure as the prime minister of Barbados.

A look at some of her contemporary decolonial and simultaneously innovative actions are relevant. In 2019, Barbados signed agreements with Ghana, West Africa, establishing more African diasporic relationships[41] with the expressed purpose of opening up more direct transportation and communication between the continent and the diaspora. According to the report, "The agreement will help to facilitate the expansion of trade between the two countries, in terms of trade transiting through Barbados from Ghana and onward to other Caribbean and Latin America destination ports." The creative political leadership of Barbadian-American, Paule Marshall as also fellow Barbadian Kamau Brathwaite were thereby also revealed.

Kamau Brathwaite had experienced and written poetically about the various journeys of displacement and return, but also sojourns between the Caribbean and Africa in his *The Arrivants: A New World Trilogy* (1973). Novelist Paule Marshall, in *The Chosen Place, The Timeless People* (1984) had described a more direct and possible geographic spatial/aerial relationship to the continent, creating a different return pathway that does not always assume the presence of Europe or North America aviation routings in the journey. She describes Merle's decision to go to Africa to reconnect with her daughter:

> And she was not taking the usual route to Africa, first flying north to London via New York and then down. Instead, she was going south to Trinidad, then on to Recife in Brazil, and from Recife, that city where the great arm of the hemisphere reaches out toward the massive shoulder of Africa as though yearning to be joined to it as is had surely been in the beginning, she would fly across to Dakar, and from there, begin the cross-continent journey to Kampala. (471)

The Mia Mottley Prime Ministership of Barbados, historically described as one of the most traditionally conservative Caribbean countries, is still being written as this chapter is developed. This therefore assumes that much of what is discussed here are largely entry points to a career that will be much longer and will make considerably more contributions than it has so far. In the Mia Mottley case, some interviewers have tried to pull in sexuality in discussing her innovative agendas, raising questions about LGBTQ rights without any direct implication of the Prime Minister but often with a worth-emulating rebuttal of the interest in her sexuality or even the question itself.

In the Mia Mottley case as she contested the Prime Ministership of Barbados, the whispered issues of her sexuality lingered even if not discussed publicly. Newspaper items such as "Barbados Elects pro-LGBT female prime minister" from a pro LGBT Newspaper—*The Bay Area Reporter*, indicates that "Mottley won despite a homophobic smear campaign in which the ruling Democratic Labour Party questioned her sexual orientation. Homosexuality is illegal in Barbados. Individuals charged with homosexuality face life in prison. LGBT people face extreme levels of discrimination and violence. The BLP's (Barbados Labour Party) platform calls for a referendum on LGBT laws, but party members suggested otherwise following the election."[42] Interestingly for the *Jamaican Gleaner* the caption is indicated as: "Barbados Vote 2018 | Mia's Sexuality Nobody's Business—Catholic Priest"

> Questioning how speaking about her sexuality would help the country, he said that political campaigns, which serve to bring down women, are disgraceful and inhumane. "All of us are at the mercy of society and the mercy of God, so I don't see the reason why she should be asked. If she is asked, then every woman and every man in society should be asked to do likewise, because all of us are public beings."[43]

More recently an initiative to have remote workers come to work from Barbados to help revitalize the hotel industry during the COVID pandemic in 2020 was met with some critique about the heterosexist wording of the request. The need to create a new model in which business-level tourists were encouraged to work from Barbados and enjoy the warmth of the Caribbean with full access to media was also deployed to counter the absence of much needed visitors. At the same time, LGBTQ activists saw this move as still not fully liberating as old-fashioned sodomy laws are still current in Barbados as in many other post-colonial societies.[44]

Prime Minister Mottley though took to the floor of the Barbados parliament on Tuesday July 21, 2020, to offer a response that was strategic in responding formally by suggesting that there was going to be a bill put forward that "there shall be no discrimination on any grounds in the workplace" but more significantly:

> Well, I want to say, as long as I am Prime Minister of this nation, we welcome all. Everyone. And that this country has been forged regrettably in the bowels of discrimination cannot now want to discriminate against anybody for any reason. All must breathe. All must breathe in this world. All must breathe in this country. And to that extent Mr. Speaker . . . I am not going to be part of any communication that suggests that Barbados is trying to be half of who or what it is and that we are sponsoring discrimination or phobias of any type.[45]

A Black feminist reading indicates that it is significant that the language did not include the traditional "husband and wife" that is still replayed even by queer couples, but used the language: "applicant, spouse, partner and dependants" also seeming to leave room for elders who can be dependents which is very much the case today.

Perhaps a more balanced view of Mottley's trajectory is offered by Roberta Clarke[46] in her essay "Social Justice in the Time of Austerity: The Promise(s) of Mia Mottley" which cites instead her experience as Minister of Economic Affairs and Attorney General in the past as recognized by Barbadians over her sexuality and the need to bring Barbados into a more advanced economic posture. Thus, "[W]ith a 60% voter turnout, a full 80% of voters rejected homophobia and misogyny as a basis for making electoral decisions. Instead, they responded to the BLP promises (under Mottley's leadership) to stabilize the currency, reduce indebtedness, fix the horror of a broken sewage system and secure social provisioning and protection." Yet, according to Carmen Hutchinson Miller, in "Stereotyping Women's Political Leadership," Mia Mottley had, in 2003, already suggested that Barbados should introduce legislation to decriminalize homosexuality (249).

So far, Mottley has operated with competence as the Head of Caricom, 2018–2020, representing the Caribbean Economic Community at the United Nations and her country during the time of COVID-19 in impressive ways. In the meantime, she talks affirmatively to interviewers as in one of the best discussions of these problems generated by, but pre-existing COVID-19, are the vulnerable locations of the Caribbean. She describes to interviewer Christiane Amanpour[47] (4/29/2020), the need for a new "vulnerability index" which the Commonwealth Secretariat had developed thirty years before and suggests the need for a new approach to contemporary needs.

Significantly there has been some research indicating that women leaders have done better in handling COVID-19.[48] Mia Mottley is one of those who similarly excelled using both the family model and the country model with the phrase deployed in response to Amanpour's related questions: "We care!" She restated as well the need for "moral leadership" to meet contemporary challenges. The need for the debt to be forgiven as a fundamental principle of reparative justice as well carries forward to negotiations with the United States as reported in her last address to CARICOM.

Further advancing a new decolonial paradigm though was the recent decision by Barbados under Prime Minister Mottley's leadership to take Barbados into Republican status. This is a related action which clarified that even with popular discourses of postcoloniality, many countries in the Caribbean, including Jamaica, never completed the formal separation from the British or French political dominance. Caribbean media such as the *Jamaican Gleaner* applauded the move in its bold caption "Time to Leave the Queen . . . Barbados to Become Republic in 2021"[49] indicating as well that the Queen is still head of state of several CARICOM countries: The Queen is Head of State for nine CARICOM member states: Antigua and Barbuda, The Bahamas, Barbados, Belize, Grenada, Jamaica, St Lucia, St Kitts and Nevis, St Vincent and the Grenadines. And there are other countries like The Turks and Caicos Islands and several smaller island units in the Caribbean which still maintain a more explicit older British colonial tie with photographs of the queen one of the first things that one sees prominently displayed in its airport as one enters the country.

Announcing the decision of Prime Minister Mottley, Governor-General Dame Sandra Mason indicated: "the administration of Prime Minister Mia Mottley, will take the 'next logical step' to make Barbados into a republic in time for the country's 55th anniversary of independence in November 2021." For the London *Guardian,* the caption and the story also located this move within the larger "Commonwealth" framework and an older history of this desire: "Barbados revives plan to remove Queen as head of state and become a republic."[50] Effectively reading Ms Mottley's speech, the governor-general of Barbados, the Governor General Mason, announced: "The time has come to fully leave our colonial past behind. Barbadians want a Barbadian head of state."[51]

This decolonial move was even more dramatically symbolized in the removal of the statue of Lord Horatio Nelson from its prominence in front of Barbados Parliament building on November 17, 2020, in celebratory yet funeral-like procession to a museum quarters. According to *Huffington Post,* coming in the wake of a series of similar moves around the world, "It joins a number of other statues across the globe, including slave traders in Britain to Confederate generals in the United States, to have been hauled down as the Black Lives Matter campaign gathered momentum."[52]

The early articulations of writers in providing this creative leadership have to be cited here. Sylvia Wynter in *The Hills of Hebron* (1962) had created a character, Gatha Randall Burton, who has an opportunity to lead the community after her husband's demise. But while Gatha possessed good leadership skills and was clearly a competent leader, she was limited in an older framework of holding on to leadership so that it would empower her son. In the end he proves not worthy of any kind of leadership and of course also absconds with community's resources. In her play "Maskarade" which I discuss in "From Masquerade to Maskarade. Caribbean Cultural Resistance and the Re-humanizing Project,"[53] she also has Miss Gatha who Wynter describes as a version of Amy Ashwood Garvey, who creates a play-within-the-play, an alternative narrative, which re-writes the wrong done by the erstwhile leader of the *jonkonnu* (maskarade) band which was displacing her for a younger woman. In both representations, the full acceptance of the power leadership of a people still in the colonial context, is yet to be realized by women.

Offering a direct critique of the residual colonial appropriative situation, Jamaica Kincaid in *A Small Place* (1988) had noted the following:

> In the Antigua that I knew, we lived on a street named after an English maritime criminal, Horatio Nelson, and all the other streets around us were named after some other English maritime criminals. There was Rodney Street, there was Hood Street, there was Hawkins Street, and there as Drake Street (24). . . . In the middle of High Street was the Barclays Bank. The Barclay brothers, who started Barclays Bank, were slave-traders. That is how they made their money. When the English outlawed the slave trade, the Barclay brothers went into banking. (25–26)

This allows us to put into relief the decisions of Barbadian Prime Minister Mottley, who quoted the Caribbean Island nation's first premier, Errol Barrow, who warned against "loitering on colonial premises" and as such instituted a series of overt decolonial moves. With an eye to the still left unresolved issues of colonially created economic gaps in the Caribbean at the start of the postcolonial state, Prime Minister Mia Mottley's participation in the Reparations forum on July 6, 2020, and as Chair of CARICOM represented well the interests of the Caribbean community as it relate to the economic recuperations implied in reparations debates. There she emphasized that there was no "development compact" after emancipation, which left the Caribbean depleted and without economic resources after "flag independence" (i.e., with political independence but lacking resources to rise to the stability after hundreds of years of European extractive colonialism). Relatedly, the transfer of Barbados to republican status happened in November 2021 with all the necessary pageantry indicating another success of the Mia Mottley tenure followed by a sweeping unprecedented unanimous victory at the polls. Major tasks of transformative leadership are being advanced by Mia Mottley giving us new paradigms of leadership worth emulating on the global level.

DIASPORA POLITICS OF AFRO-CARIBBEAN WOMEN LEADERS IN EUROPE: DIANE ABBOTT AND CHRISTIANE TAUBIRA

Migrations from the Caribbean to major metropolitan countries—the United States, Europe, and Canada—have produced a population that is identified as "Caribbean diaspora."[54] The rise of Caribbean women to political office in European and North American countries is also noteworthy, whether they were born of Afro-Caribbean parents in those locations as was United States Vice President Kamala Harris or were part of the larger diaspora which developed in the United Kingdom. For a long time, Diane Abbott was perhaps the most significant representative of Britain's Caribbean diaspora, serving as a Labour Party Member of Parliament for Hackney North and Stoke Newington since 1987; she is now the longest serving Black MP in the House of Commons. Her personal essay in *The Guardian,* "I Fought Racism and Misogyny to become an MP. The Fight is Getting Harder" documents that history[55] and summarizes some of the battles she has faced, and the continuing primitive racism and sexism that she continues to experience. From her account, like Shirley Chisholm, and like "The Squad" in the United States as discussed earlier, she has received the most explicit misogynistic threats and verbal assaults of any parliamentary leader:

> I receive racist and sexist abuse online on a daily basis. I have had rape threats, death threats, and am referred to routinely as a bitch and/or nigger, and am sent horrible images on Twitter . . . I have written about all this before. I am well aware that there are people who will deny it happens, others who seem to think that sexist abuse is the price women pay for being in public life.[56]

Sociologist Lisa Amanda Palmer offers an important reading of the treatment of Honorable Diane Abbott within a long history of imperialistic projects in which the Black woman carried the brunt of negative representations, from Saartjie Baartman to the present. She uses the framework of the "Sable-Saffron" iconography within the larger conceptualizing of "misogynoir," or misogyny directed specifically at Black women, to situate the ongoing racialized and gendered representations of Diane Abbott. Significant for her are the practices of Black British feminism, which also carried the anti-colonial challenges that provide a counter discourse to these representations: "The sexualized gendered racism faced by Abbott focuses our attention on the ongoing colonial racialized, sexualized and gendered inheritances which straddle the multiple ways in which Black women in Britain have historically been faced with resisting erasure" (520).

A recent biographical study by Robin Bunce and Samara Linton, *Diane Abbott. The Authorised Biography,*[57] provides extensive detail. Abbott, the daughter of Caribbean immigrants to the United Kingdom, is conscious of these connections and describes returning to Jamaica to spend time with family members as normal.[58] In her words, colleagues were surprised when she would say she was off to spend Christmas with relatives in the Caribbean as casually as they talked of going to theirs in England. But it is from this family connection and her relationship with Black communities that she developed and maintained her political sensibilities, even after and perhaps because of attending Cambridge University as one of the first Black students to do so because there she developed a socialist consciousness (57). Her understandings based on experiencing racism directly is indicated as coming from assignment to the Home Office, "the epitome of structural racism" (63), leading to her joining the Labour Party and working as a Race Relations Officer in 1979. While organizing conferences on race there, she developed a heightened awareness of the experience of Black people in Britain. Abbott describes working with the Organisation of Women of African and Asian Descent (OWAAD) in Brixton as pivotal:

> OWAAD was an umbrella organization which aimed to unite Black and Asian women and Black and Asian women's organizations. Formed in 1979 by radicals including Olive Morris and Stella Dadzie, OWAAD emerged from a decades-long tradition of Black resistance which included the work of radicals such as Una Marson and Claudia Jones. (76)

The biography describes her arrival in Brixton, being lost and encountering Alrick "Ricky" Cambridge, one of the founders of Black Unity and Freedom Party, and their collaboration on several projects over the years (76–77). It is here that the definition of "political Blackness" as identified in the prior discussion on Kamla Persad-Bissessar has meaning: "Political Blackness was based on the notion that whatever your cultural identity, you had a unified experience of British colonialism" (77). For OWAAD the definition was very specific:

> We will use the term "Black" to refer to the two major ethnic groups of Black people in this country, namely: those people who came originally from the Indian subcontinent . . . those people who have their origins in Africa. These two groups were united by common persecution by the police, by white racists, by immigration laws and were disadvantaged by the legacy of colonialism." (77–78)

Although this definition has morphed into the larger BME (Black and Minority Ethnic) in England, attempting a more inclusive reference as is BIPOC (Black and Indigenous People of Color) in the United States, the grounding of the politics of this definition still remains residually present in several ways.

The rest of the biography recounts Abbott's various political campaigns and leadership roles in Labour's ascension and its losses. Through it all, Abbott remains constant in her support of Black communities, her availability, and her willingness to support and advance related projects. The "In the Belly of the Beast" chapter describes some of the political struggles related and affiliations with the Congressional Black Caucus (CBC) in the United States (211) and Britain's formation of a Parliamentary Black Caucus (PBC), following the US model, and Abbott's visiting the CBC as a special guest in 1989. Abbott ultimately feels confident that her contributions have been successful in terms of her life's goals and her community's recognition:

> The constant bureaucratic micro-aggressions and slights from her colleagues did not deter her nor did the fact that "as a Black woman MP you face two things: you face sexism—men not wanting to take you seriously, and people generally taking men more seriously than you. You face racism—people feel you can't be as good, you can't be as competent." (219)

Comparisons are easily drawn between Shirley Chisholm, the first Black women elected to the US Congress, and Diane Abbott to Parliament in the UK (478).[59] The difference in structures notwithstanding, Diane Abbott has maintained a solid representation of herself and community, winning election again in 2020, sadly witnessing again the upheavals created by continuing racism and the responses that Black Lives Matter movements globally ushered in to advance the world beyond these lingering oppressive structures. Diane Abbott, when she entered public service, encountered from the start the same issues of racial police brutality, and the SUS (Suspected Person Stop and Search) laws in the UK practiced similarly with related "Vagrancy Laws" or subsequent Stop and Frisk practice in New York State and elsewhere which was one of the prime vehicles for the United States becoming the leading country with over two million people incarcerated, the majority of them being people of color.[60]

In another iteration of Caribbean women in global politics, the life of Christiane Taubira, in France, confirms Lisa Palmer's discussion about how sexism and racism affects Black women political leaders. Originally from Guyane (French Guyana), also the birthplace of one of the founders of the Négritude literary/political movement, Léon-Gontran Damas, Taubira moved from founding a political party in Guyana to becoming an elected member of the National Assembly of France for French Guyana, eventually becoming an elected member of the European Parliament. In June 2012, she was appointed Justice Minister in the François Hollande government. Later in 2002 she ran for the French presidency as a Left candidate and won 2.3% of votes.[61] Christiane Taubira has also been the recipient of a variety of racial slurs.

Because of issues of language separations that define Caribbean colonial structures, few essays are available in English about Christiane Taubira. Feliz Germain and Silyane Larcher's *French Women and the Struggle for Equality, 1848–2016* discusses a range of related issues pertaining to women in former French-speaking colonial gender relations. The book includes a chapter on "Christiane Taubira, a Black Woman in Politics in French Guiana and in France"[62] which concludes that since "white men are still the norm in positions of leadership."

> First in French Guiana and later in the national political space, Taubira embodied a renewal of politics, a condition that allowed her to gain national recognition. She was a political outsider from multiple angles: not only is she Black, but she is also a woman who gravitated to the margin of the party and its traditional political networks. In the last decade, the politics of minority representation and issue of diversity lessened and perhaps transformed these "handicaps" into "assets." Nevertheless, the racist attacks demonstrate how a Black woman's access to the highest governmental functions disrupts the nation. (33)

Important too in assessing Taubira is her diasporic politics and influences from the earlier creative/political activists of Négritude, including Aimé Césaire (1913–2008) and Léon-Gontran Damas (1912–1978) but also African American activists like Malcolm X (1925–1965). In this regard the recent work identifying women who were leaders in the creative movements is still advancing. Chapters on Suzanne Cesaire and Paulette Nardal open the work *Reimagining Liberation. How Black Women Transformed Citizenship in the French Empire.*[63]

THE FUTURE OF LEADERSHIP FOR WOMEN IN
THE CARIBBEAN AND A RETROSPECTIVE

According to UN Women, representation of Caribbean women is still led by Cuba, identified as having surpassed parity with 53.41%. And in terms of ministerial posts, it is Grenada, with 46.7%, both countries having had political and social revolutions. Most other countries, including Trinidad and Tobago, operate at the 30–35% percentile, and the rest remain at or below 25%. Haiti has 27.8% of women in ministerial posts. Surprisingly (or not surprisingly) St. Vincent and the Grenadines have 0.0% representation of women in ministerial posts, but they have 13%, or 3 of 23 members of parliament. Barbados, with a female prime minister, still is at 20%. Jamaica, which had a woman prime minister in its history, was indicated at 17%. Trinidad and Tobago has had a woman as Prime Minister, and current ceremonial governor as president of Parliament.[64] The correlations between women in leadership and the representation of women in the larger populations will have to be made by future scholars.

Current and available material on women in Caribbean leadership tends to go directly to the business sector which is a pattern observable in mainstream United States and European contexts. An available essay by Lisandra Rickards, CEO of the Branson Center of Entrepreneurship—Caribbean, writing on "The Rise of Female Leaders in the Caribbean" does similar work. In a way this is consistent with the United States proportionately, as most publications in the United States on leadership come from the business world. In business, the foremost issue is the need to have "a critical mass of female managers who are poised for promotion to the highest levels of leadership in the region" (3).[65] Still, earlier works on women in Caribbean history, by Verene Shepherd, for example[66] or by Hilary Beckles[67] on resistance by women during the period of enslavement, are critical to understanding Caribbean women's legendary courageousness in the face of longstanding repression.

In general, as we have seen, countries that have had socialist revolutions seem to have higher representations of women in government, as seen in Cuba with 53.41%, ranked second in the world after Rwanda, at 61%. Grenada, which had a brief revolutionary government in which women had substantial leadership, still maintains some leadership in this area, ranked sixth in the world at 46.7%. Guyana, which had a socialist government under Cheddi Jagan and then under his wife Janet Jagan, ranked 40th with 35.71%. Janet Rosenberg Jagan (1920–2009), born in Chicago, who with her husband co-founded the People's Progressive Party, is in reality the first woman prime minister of Guyana and if we work with an expanded geography, the first

American woman president in the Americas, serving from 1998 to 1999. More scholarship is needed on Janet Jagan in the context of women and leadership with a book on the subject in process by sociologist Patricia Mohammed.

Documenting women in the Grenada Revolution, *Comrade Sister: Caribbean Feminist Revisions of the Grenada Revolution* (2020) begins with a provocative opening sentence; What would it mean to reimagine the Grenada Revolution with women at its center? For author Laurie Lambert, Caribbean literary and political iconography centers men as leaders: "Caribbean writers have been fascinated by this history of revolution, resistance, and male leaders. As such, the masculine iconography of revolution, sovereignty, and political independence has also informed the development of the region's literatures" (4). Here, Lambert makes an important link between the canonization of male writers and politicians. The rise of Caribbean women's literature may perhaps have significance then in terms of writing women into political leadership, as we saw in African literature. Dessima Williams, who was also part of the Grenada Revolution, issued the call for more women in political leadership at the turn of the century which is the primary thread that runs through this work. Phyllis Coard, one of the founders of Grenada's NWO, subsequently wrote *Unchained: A Caribbean Woman's Journey Through Invasion, Incarceration and Liberation* (2019), the horrible unfolding of the destruction of the Grenada Revolution and her husband's role in this. Her book begins with the invasion, that is the period after the execution-style killing of Maurice Bishop, which precipitated the invasion by US forces in 1983. The rest of the narrative is a detailing of capture and incarceration, illness, and acquiring freedom and a life afterward in Jamaica. An appendix titled "Phyllis Coard—Address from the National Organising Committee for International Women's Day Rally, 8 March 1980" provides a kind of *in medias res* understanding of the language and concepts that guided women in that particular Grenadian context. Still the absence of women in actually leading the movement is a factor in the masculinist violence which unfolded to its demise.

A document, "About the National Women's Organization of Grenada," indicates that the group was founded in 1977 as the Women's Arm of the New Jewel Movement. The group was open to "all women who want to see our country move forward, and our women achieve full equality as part of the process of development." By May 1981, NWO included forty-nine groups island-wide. Their credo closed with the logic of parity:

> We believe that our country can only develop, our Revolution can only go forward, if women *who are more than half of* our adult population take full part in this process. (my emphasis)

And:

> By Building The N.W.O. We Build The Revolution; By Building The N.W.O.
> We Build The Equality Of Women[68]

But while it created the template for the advances Grenada made at the time, the unraveling still presents challenges. Much of the activation of the Grenada revolution depended on the activism of women in Grenada and across the Caribbean, and it spurred the creativity and activism of a range of women, such as writers Dionne Brand and Merle Collins and activists like Beverly Bain.

By contrast, the life and work of Andaiye, now documented in *The Point is to Change the World* (2020), provides one of the best examples of a woman who was committed to a transformed and equitable Caribbean society in this contemporary period. Her editor Alissa Trotz defines her as "one of the Caribbean's leading radical political figures, social and political thinkers and public intellectuals" (frontispiece). The collected essays describe her engagement with a range of causes, including classic women's rights issues like the struggle against domestic violence, as worked into her own frameworks of radical politics, and taking forward legacies created by Caribbean transformative figures like Maurice Bishop and Walter Rodney, both of whom were assassinated in the interest of nation state's attempts to maintain a certain order. Her conclusion is that Caribbean radical movements "were created out of courage and vision and leadership to confront the root causes of oppression and exploitation in the region as they manifested themselves during those decades" (242).[69] However, as a founding member, she is clear that mistakes were made in the Guyana Working Party Alliance (WPA) context indicating that "we saw our leadership of the struggle as temporary and didn't relate to ourselves as a government in waiting" (51). There was also insufficient consideration of what the next steps in leadership would be and instead they had faith that leaders would be created in the "process of struggle" (52).[70] The title of this book, "The Point is to Change the World," taken directly from Karl Marx which appears as the concluding sentence as a political activist mandate puts her in conversation with Claudia Jones, who similarly practiced this logic of positive and practical social transformation along equitable lines.[71]

Although this chapter has focused more on the Anglophone Caribbean, other geo-political language versions of a project like this one is deserving further attention in subsequent studies. In the mean time, Augustin Lao-Montes, *Diasporic Counterpoints* includes a chapter titled "Afro-Latin American Feminisms Birthing New Political and Epistemic Currents" identifying a series of movements and signaling a body of scholarship that will go further. He concludes that:

The intellectual and political culture of contemporary Afro-feminism in Latin America and the Caribbean is a rich and diverse stage in which women belonging to rural and urban social movements share and debate ideas and strategies with students and professors in the emerging program of Gender and Black Studies. The intellectual and political culture of contemporary Afrofeminism in Colombia is a rich assemblage where women from rural and urban social movements share and debate ideas and strategies with students and professors in the emerging programs for Gender and Afro-American Studies. Afro Latin American intellectual-activists leading the Colombian intellectual and political scene, such as Betty Ruth Lozano, Mara Viveros, Ochy Curiel, Katherine Arboleda, Maria Campo, Natalia Santiesteban, and Aurora Vergara Figueroa, play multiple roles as militants, professors, theorists, and translators between diverse strands of liberation theories and politics. (Ch. 6, 180)

While the Cuban model remains, wounded and contested and embargoed, it still provides a totally different pathway to leadership and service to community. Cuba's strategy of moving people during impending hurricanes out of danger is symbolic of the state, as is its medical care system. Cuba is identified as having a leading percentage of representation of women in political leadership in the world, 53.41%, but how many of these are Black women needs to be identified even though Cuban women have attained representational parity according to 2019 UN statistics. Black women in Columbia such as Sofia Garzon Valencia of Proceso de Comunidades Negras Colombia and Aurora Vegara-Figueroa, Director of the Centro de Estudios Afrodiasporicos, Universidad Icesi described their work with young women to create community and competences in a range of fields. The rise of Black women to national political leadership in Latin America is slow but presents a range of activisms at the grassroots or local level.[72] Mia Mottley had asserted that "We have brought our plans as small nations. We are implementing them, and we have fully embraced our responsibility to act" (Speech to UN 2019). Her words resonate here because perhaps more can be achieved sometimes in small political units, smaller states or countries, and local communities, such as Cuba, than in large, troubled democracies such as the United States.

It is useful to look retrospectively at the framing of the already discussed "Women and Politics in the Caribbean," forum at Florida International University in 2002, created as one of the earliest considerations of this topic, the timeliness of which allows us the opportunity to assess the gains within a twenty year time span. One of the by-products, we hoped, would be to encourage young and mature women to make similar political contributions in their communities. To amplify this goal, we also invited a range of South Miami Black and women politicians to take part in the evening's discussion. In the end, among local leaders, Commissioner of Lauderdale Lakes Hazelle Rogers attended, and other invited guests sent greetings, including

Congresswoman Carrie Meeks, former Democratic representative in the US House, from Florida's 17th district in Miami from 1993 to 2003.

Removing "gendered global apartheid" in Dessima Williams, "Bringing More Women Into Leadership," that call at the turn of the century necessitated promoting women's leadership because women's participation in politics often has a direct effect on policies related to young people, education, and the planet's well-being. Twenty years later, we concur with Dessima Williams that women's leadership, in accordance with most assessments, has a direct relationship to the world's continued well-being. More than 70% of the world's people living in poverty are female. Women work longer hours than men in most countries but are paid less. These are some of issues that necessitate progressive women's leadership. In other words, we can no longer simply use "Put a woman!" as a standard; now we must scrutinize, analyze, and foster transformative feminist Black women's political leadership.[73]

NOTES

1. The 2021 United Nations Climate Change Conference, more commonly referred to as COP26, was the 26th United Nations Climate Change conference, held at Glasgow, Scotland, October 31 to November 12, 2021. Prime Minister Mottley spoke on November 1, 2021, and her address was so powerful that it circulated worldwide and captured the strength of challenge along with the determination to enter history in a way that is ethical, politically wise and unafraid with decolonial fervor. Her speech was replayed on multiple social media platforms and carried in newspapers worldwide. See https://www.theguardian.com/environment/2021/nov/01/digging-our-own-graves-world-leaders-speak-cop26 [accessed 11/28/2021]

2. *Huffington Post*, September 23, 2019.

3. Most regional news media such as *Caribbean Today* in South Florida indicate that she demonstrates the most leadership of Caribbean heads of state.

4. *Society and Space*, 36(6) 2018: 971–986.

5. *The Independent* (September 15, 2017)

6. Hilary Beckles, *How Britain Underdeveloped the Caribbean* (University of the West Indies Press, 2022) provides economic and historical details which develop this position as does his former work, *Britain's Black Debt* (2013).

7. See for example Ignacio Olazagasti, "The Material Culture of the Taino Indians," *in* Samuel Wilson, *Indigenous Peoples of the Caribbean* and Scott Fitzpatrick, "The Pre-Columbian Caribbean: Colonization, Population Dispersal, and Island Adaptations" *PaleoAmerica* 1:4(2015): 305+.

8. Derek Walcott, "The Sea is History" from *Selected Poems* (Farrar, Strauss, Giroux, 2007).

9. See discussion of this theme in "From Masquerade to Maskarade. Caribbean Cultural Resistance and the Re-humanizing Project." Katherine McKittrick ed. *Sylvia Wynter. On Being Human as Praxis* (Duke University Press, 2015), 203–225.

10. Carmichael, Stokely, with Ekwueme Michael Thelwell, *Ready for Revolution* (New York: Scribner, 2003).

11. "Dame, properly a name of respect or a title equivalent to lady, surviving in English as the legal designation for the wife or widow of a baronet or knight or for a dame of the Most Excellent Order of the British Empire; it is prefixed to the given name and surname." *Brittanica.com.* Another Caribbean Dame Nita Barrow (1916–1995) who became governor general of Barbados (1990–1995) though with a title defined as largely ceremonial also exercised world leadership in crises such as the ending of apartheid, visiting Nelson Mandela before his release from incarceration.

12. For example, using this model, it would be instructive to do something similar with former president Barack Obama, who became the first Black president of the United States, rather than to rely singly on his own assessment from his point of view. Imagine if Kwame Nkrumah had had that opportunity to have his leadership assessed from multiple points of view.

13. See her obituary from September 8, 2005, at https://www.independent.co.uk/news/obituaries/dame-eugenia-charles-311011.html.

14. Hutchinson Miller sees the book by Janet Higbie, *Eugenia Charles: The Caribbean's Iron Lady*, as enshrining this, with the term used "as a curse or as a compliment depending on who used it" (252–253).

15. "Con-di-fi-cation: Black Women, Leadership and Political Power," *Feminist Africa*, March, 2007. This essay was popularly received in some feminist circles and was reprinted as "Diaspora, Transnationalism and the Limits of Domestic Racial and Feminist Discourses," in *Jenda e-journal* (2007). Reprinted as "Con-di-fi-cation": Black Women, Leadership, and Political Power. In *Still Brave. The Evolution of Black Women's Studies.* Ed. Stanlie James, Frances Smith Foster and Beverly Guy-Sheftall (New York: Feminist Press, 2009), 392–414.

16. See Audre Lorde's "Grenada Revisited" in *Sister Outsider* (Crossing Press, 1982) for example.

17. https://restavekfreedom.org/2019/08/06/5-notable-women-from-haitian-history

18. Peacewomen.org website

19. Email communication 8/28/2018.

20. Attending the African Diaspora in India conference in 2006, I learned that there is a prior identity for Indo-Africans or Afro-Indians in India that supersedes the category "dougla" and that many of the Trinidad and Tobago Indians may have indeed come from an already prior racial mixture. Africans had been in India since the days of Malik Amber and before, and possibly as early as the 5th century. A significant advance, at the level of representation at least, is Afro-Indian Droupadi Murmu, from one of India's indigenous tribal groups, who became the 15th president of India on July 15, 2022. See *Encylopedia of the African Diaspora* (2008) for more information on the African diaspora in Asia.

21. Patricia Mohammed, *Writing Gender into the Caribbean: Selected Essays 1988 to 2020* (Hansib, Maracas, 2021). See also R. Reddock, "Douglarization and the Politics of Gender Relations in Trinidad and Tobago" in Barrow and Reddock (2001).

22. Appointed by the prime minister as special envoy on Women's and Children's Issues to the Caribbean Commonwealth on March 8, 2011.

23. Examples in the twentieth century are Indira Gandhi (1966–1977 and 1980–1984) of India and Benazir Bhutto of Pakistan (1988–1990 and 1993–1996).

24. I interviewed Yvonne Bobb at her residence on this subject (March 2008, Port of Spain, Trinidad and Tobago). Bobb had been a workshop leader for some of these projects that prepared women for political leadership at local, regional, and national levels.

25. Patricia McFadden (2001) makes a similar point in "South Africa, African Feminism and the Challenges of Solidarity," and Desiree Lewis (2009) in "Baleke Mbete: On Queens Who Would be Kings," the latter suggesting that "the national machinery has offered extremely limited scope for transformation." McFadden's position is that: "many women position themselves conservatively in response to the state's new ruling function . . . To as great a degree as men, women within the state bureaucracy act in accordance with class logic. They become ruthless defenders of the status quo and operate in ways that protect their power and authority" (McFadden, 2001).

26. See *The World's Women*, 2010. In that period there was also an increase of women in parliament.

27. See the work of Rhoda Reddock (2001) and Shalini Puri (2004) and others on this. "Dougla" is a racially pejorative word in a variety of cultures, from Persia to India; it refers to bastardization, being stained, dirty, and polluted; like the word "nigger" it has been reappropriated by some.

28. Interviewed March 2010, at the University of the West Indies, St. Augustine, Trinidad and Tobago.

29. *Newsday,* August 5, 2020.

30. See Laura Dowrich-Phillips, "Party Promises: UNC and PNM manifestos for the creative sector," August 5, 2020. http://www.looptt.com/content/party-promises -unc-and-pnm-manifestos-creative-sector

31. Personal email conversation, 8/5/2020. Thank you to Yvonne Bobb Smith for her assistance in this portion of the research.

32. In the reception afterwards, she embraced me closely when I reminded her of meeting her at Florida International University. "FIU!" she exclaimed as she gave me a memorable hug of recognition in an otherwise dignified formal greeting.

33. Abstract of paper presented at Caribbean Studies Association Conference.

34. *JENDA Journal: Women Political Leaders:* Part 1 (Issue 9) January 2008. Has two issues on women as political leaders.

35. Scheduled to be written by UWI historian Verene Shepherd.

36. See also 2006 video "Over 40 Years of Selfless Dedicated Service" (available on You Tube) which documents in her words some of her achievements and testimonies from colleagues and communities she represented.

37. Video available from Eric Williams Memorial Collection, University of the West Indies.

38. See my review essay "Beverley Manley—History on Her Terms" *Abeng News Magazine*, June 29, 2008. See also a four-part video documentary of her life story by Joelle Simone Powe, "Beverly Manley Uncensored: An Intimate Portrait of a Jamaican Icon," Adtelligent TV, August, 2022.

39. The prior lectures in the series were the Inaugural lecture with Professor John Hope Franklin, followed by the former president of the Zambia, Kenneth Kaunda and Prof. Hilary Beckles, then Pro vice Chancellor of the University of the West Indies, now Principal of the Cave Hill Campus, University of the West Indies, Barbados.

40. See Ph.D. thesis of Kesewa John, University of Chichester. "People Papers: The Pan-African Communities and Afro-Caribbean Radicals between Paulette Naardal and George Padmore 1918–1948" (2021).

41. https://www.abcnewsgh.com/ghana-barbados-sign-agreement-to-establish-sis ter-port-relationship-between-tema-bridgetown/

42. Heather Cassell, "Barbados Elects Pro-LGBT Female Prime Minister," March 30, 2018 https://www.ebar.com/news/news//260630

43. http://jamaica-gleaner.com/article/news/20180524/barbados-vote-2018-mias -sexuality-nobodys-business-catholic-priest

44. https://barbadostoday.bb/2020/07/23/lgbt-leaders-unimpressed-by-pms-equal ity-pledge/

45. https://www.livingoutloud20.com/post/exclusive-barbados-prime-minister-res ponds-to-report-of-lgbtq-exclusion-changes-visa-requirements. Full text:

> There's an issue as to who Barbados will welcome and who it will not welcome. Well, I want to say, as long as I am Prime Minister of this nation, we welcome all. Everyone. And that this country, that has been forged regrettably in the bowels of discrimination cannot now want to discriminate against anybody for any reason.
>
> All must breathe. All must breathe in this world. All must breathe in this country.
>
> And to that extent Mr. Speaker . . . the incident in which . . . and we get it, there's difficult discussions we must have as a nation and now is not the time to have those discussions. But what I do know, is that the member for St. Peter has a bill before this honorable chamber that says that there shall be no discrimination on any grounds in the workplace. And that debate will probably start later today.
>
> No discrimination on the grounds of race, no discrimination on the grounds of age, no discrimination on the grounds of color, no discrimination on the grounds of gender, no discrimination on the grounds of sexual orientation.
>
> And the people that want to put us in a box that will allow people to be discriminated against for any reason, Mr. Speaker, that is not who we are. We are not that person. We are not that person. And we've never been. You know the irony is that this country has welcomed people for decades and centuries without being that person. This country has made people feel comfortable.
>
> I am not going to be part of any communication that suggests that Barbados is trying to be half of who or what it is, and that we are sponsoring discrimination or phobias of any type.

46. https://sxpolitics.org/social-justice-in-the-time-of-austerity-the-promises-of -mia-mottley/18748

47. https://www.cnn.com/videos/tv/2020/04/29/amanpour-barbados-mia-mottley -coronavirus.cnn

48. A story carried by *Forbes Magazine* by Cami Anderson https://www.forbes .com/sites/camianderson1/2020/04/19/why-do-women-make-such-good-leaders -during-covid-19/#46a1ddb142fc

49. http://jamaica-gleaner.com/article/caribbean/20200915/time-leave-queen -barbados-become-republic-2021

50. https://www.theguardian.com/world/2020/sep/16/barbados-revives-plan-to -remove-queen-as-head-of-state-and-become-a-republic

51. https://www.independent.co.uk/news/world/americas/barbados-republic-queen -elizabeth-head-state-b450871.html

52. https://www.huffpost.com/entry/barbados-removes-nelson-statue-break -colonial-past_n_5fb3e4e9c5b6aad41f735c16

53. In Katherine McKittrick ed. *Sylvia Wynter. On Being Human as Praxis* (Duke University Press, 2015), 203–225.

54. See my *Caribbean Spaces* (2012) for further discussion.

55. https://www.theguardian.com/commentisfree/2017/feb/14/racism-misogyny -politics-online-abuse-minorities

56. Ibid.

57. London: Biteback Publishing, 2020.

58. Zoom visit to Black Women and Political Leadership class, October 2020.

59. Diane Abbott indicated never meeting Shirley Chisholm but definitely being influenced by her daring political challenges to the status quo of electoral politics. October, 2020 visit to Black Women and Political Leadership class.

60. See the work of Angela Davis on prison abolition on this issue such as her *Freedom is a Constant Struggle* (2016) *and Are Prisons Obsolete* (2003).

61. Source of information is Christiane Taubira biography at the Center for Latin American and Caribbean Studies, University of Wisconsin, Milwaukee. https://uwm .edu/clacs/chrstiane-taubira-bio

62. University of Nebraska Press: 19–36.

63. University of Illinois Press, 2020: 29–81. See also Myriam Moise on Antillean Women and Black Internationalism on the erased leaders of Negritude" *Black Scholar*, 51:2 (2021).

64. United Nations, Women in Politics, and Interparlimentary Union 2021, ipu. org/parliament.

65. See https://www.virgin.com/virgin-unite/rise-female-leaders-Caribbean. Acc essed 7/25/2020

66. *Engendering History: Caribbean Women in Historical Perspective* (edited with Bridget Brereton and Barbara Bailey Palgrave MacMillan, 1995) and *Women in Caribbean History: The British-Colonised Territories*, (1999); *Women in Caribbean History* (2012).

67. *Natural Rebels: A Social History of Enslaved Women in Barbados* (1989) and *Centering Woman: Gender Discourses in Caribbean Slave Society* (1998).

68. About the National Women's Organization (Statement in the archives of the Teresa Lozano Long Institute of Latin American Studies, The University of Texas at Austin, GR18Pg/25). Retrieved February 20, 2020.

69. Emblazoned on Marx's bust in Highgate Cemetery, London, this phrase appears as a frontispiece to the book. Robin D.G. Kelley indicates as well in an introductory foreword to the book titled "Between Home and Street: Andaiye's Revolutionary Vision": xxii-xvii, that "the title comes from Karl Marx's eleventh and final thesis on Feuerbach (1845)" (xxii).

70. Alrick Cambridge in "C.L.R. James' Socialist Future and Human Happiness" in *Decolonizing the Academy. African Diaspora Studies* (61–91) and "When Socialist Values Harmonize with Human Desire for Liberation: Assessing Claudia Jones' Politics," the Afterword to *Claudia Jones. Beyond Containment*, 207–220 asserts that there are several aspects of what would happen after a socialist government was in power that were not worked out in these various social movements, resulting in problems such as what occurred in Grenada. The Cuban model with all its issues most generated by continuous US embargoes is still the closest to this post-revolution realization.

71. See my review in *SX Salon* 38/39 (2022).

72. Keisha Khan Perry has an essay which is in conversation with Walter Rodney's essay with a similar title and is called "The Groundings With My Sisters" in which she sketches some of the issues that pertain to women and activism in Latin America.

73. Prior lectures in the series were the inaugural lecture with Professor John Hope Franklin, followed by the former president of the Zambia, Kenneth Kaunda and Prof. Hilary Beckles, then Pro vice Chancellor of the University of the West Indies, now Principal of the Cave Hill Campus, University of the West Indies, Barbados.

Chapter 7

Marielle Franco and Black Left Feminist Leadership in Brazil

MARIELLE PRESENTE!

One of the most visible contemporary representations and articulations of Black left feminist leadership existed in the person of Marielle Francisco da Silva, popularly known as Marielle Franco. This Afro-Brazilian political activist was assassinated on March 14, 2018, clearly for the advanced political positions she took on the need for full human rights for historically disadvantaged communities in Brazil: Black women, the poor urban dwellers, largely combinations of African-descended and indigenous people, the LGBTQ and trans communities. As usual, the assassination had the opposite effect for while it eliminated her physical presence, it instead advanced, enshrined and extended the particular recognition of her contributions and her iconic presence in Brazilian history has been made permanent. In all news reports, essays and visual analyses, her assassination turned her into a formidable icon. *"Marielle Presente!"* or *"Marielle Vive!"* became the cry at several commemorative events in Brazil and around the world after her passing. Indeed, the meaning of Marielle's life and death has become a tangible presence in a range of projects across the country of Brazil itself and worldwide, from large murals to the naming of institutions and projects, a statue erected in her honor in 2022, and above all the influence. Several online platforms, such as Instituto Marielle and Agenda Marielle, also provide details of the projects emanating from her still visible presence.

In Afro-Brazilian cosmology, the elevation of the deceased who has lived a life of service to ancestorhood (*ancestralidade*) is a critical component of transition, which allows the spiritual presence to continue to do its work at a higher level, no longer being impeded by the constraints of the physical body. These transitional rites, called the *axexê* rituals in Yoruba cosmology[1] as practiced in Candomblé, one of which I witnessed for Mae Menina de Gantois, in Salvador da Bahia, are meant to liberate the spirit for spiritual ceremonial access. In *axexê* rituals, deceased *mães-do-santo* receive several other spiritual and religio-social-hierarchical functions, privy only to the initiated. But in the context of Marielle's passing, an activist/materialist reading reveals a similar usage in the present in that assigning of her a powerful spiritual and political function via the conceptual *"Presente!"* which also calls the power of that person's political meaning into active presence and asserts that the actions of a dominant state cannot ever quench that energy of liberation.[2] Thus, *"Marielle Presente!"* became the equivalent, of not only the transitional process ushering her into a spiritual/political plane but also as the invocation of her political bravery and ideological positions, usable now in other contexts. *"Marielle Presente!"* then provided the energy which led to the creation of tangible institutions to make her work and contributions permanent and visible and to inform the rising generation of political activists after her state-sanctioned assassination.

The power of Marielle's transitional experience is documented in analyses such as "The Resurgent Far Right and the Black Feminist Struggle for Social Democracy in Brazil"[3] by Keisha-Khan Perry, who described in her closing section titled "The Future Struggle," an intervention at a conference on Brazil at Harvard University's Afro-Latin American Research Institute, where Marielle Franco had been scheduled to speak. There, Erica Malunguinho at the moment of Marielle's scheduled speech, according to Keisha-Khan Perry's description, "looked into the camera transmitting a livestream to the world with mostly Brazilians watching and announced her candidacy for political office in the same party as Marielle" (161). Erica Malunguinho was elected in 2020, becoming the first Black transwoman councilor in Brazil and also on the way to becoming a political icon.[4]

Several other events provide a life-after-life for Marielle, from a series of presentations where women embodied her in "I am Marielle" representations in clothing, political presentation, art installations and murals, photography and commemorative videos, to Carnival representations, where a float depicted her silencing.[5] Carnival lyrics dedicated to Marielle were described by one of the composers, Deivid Domenico, who co-wrote Mangueira's samba anthem for the 2019 Carnival in the following terms: "Marielle was a woman, a fighter, from the *favela*, who overcame inequality, went to university, was elected councilwoman, fought for minorities, denounced and investigated public power."[6]

At Smith College in Massachusetts, a *"Marielle, Presente!"* event organized by Brazilian student Marcela Rodrigues Guimaraes, in collaboration with several faculty members, on March 21, 2018, was documented in an article with the same title.[7] In King's College, London, "A Sunflower in Her Hair: Poems and Testimonies for Marielle Franco"[8] presentation included poetry, testimony, and live communications and updates on the cause of justice for her. In every event, Marielle was described as one who "fought for the rights of minorities in Rio de Janeiro, and at the time of her death she was emerging as a strong political voice with great promise for the years to come" (Ibid.).

Numerous media articles have since documented and condemned her assassination and its aftermath. And sites like RioOnWatch[9] include the "Words of Marielle Franco." For Nicole Froio, "Marielle, Presente!: A Movement Remembers," it is the roll call of making her present that maintained her presence in vigils and in social media, where activists began using #MarielleFrancoPresente, which can be translated as "Marielle Franco is Here" or "Marielle Lives!," to raise awareness about the murder. The word *"presente*," meaning "present," which we know as the standard student response to a roll call, has a different intent when used by activists across Latin America and Brazil. In this case it is to recall and remember and therefore re-present victims of violence, to combat the practice of political assassinations.[10]

BLACK WOMEN CREATIVITY AND POWER: THE HISTORICAL CONTEXT OF BLACK WOMEN'S ACTIVISM

This chapter opens with the Marielle effect to capture her explicit Black left feminism, but it also argues that she belongs to a larger Afro-Brazilian and Black women's leadership trajectory. Although no collection of writings by Marielle exists yet, scholarship on Afro-Brazilian women is growing, as advanced by feminist organizations like *Geledes*, based in São Paulo under the leadership of Sueli Carneiro and a variety of online sources and live organizations like the Instituto Marielle Franco, created by her life partner to ensure that her meaning survives and is taken forward to succeeding generations.

In 1993, following a first visit to Brazil in 1992,[11] I started a project on "Women, Creativity and Power" in Brazil, which pursued women's writing as linked to political power. This in many ways is the genesis of this particular book. In Salvador da Bahia, my study of an all-women's *afoxe* (a Carnival group that becomes a mobile representation of Afro-Brazilian cosmology) examined how the issues of politics, representation, women, and power came together. "Re-/Presenting Black Female Identity in Brazil: Filhas de Oxum in Bahia Carnival"[12] was one of the first tangible products of this project. In that same time frame, my study revealed the work of women writers such as Conceição Evaristo, Miriam Alves, Lia Viera, contributors to *Cadernos Negros*, whose work was included in English for the first time in *Moving Beyond Boundaries. International Dimensions of Black Women's Writing* (1994). Maria da Conceição Evaristo de Brito, known popularly as Conceição Evaristo, now recognized and honored as one of Brazil's most prominent writers, contributed a poem "Eu-Mulher" ("I-Woman") which expresses the theme of that project and to a certain extent the central theme of this chapter. In the following excerpt, she places women at the center of creation and thereby continuance of life and above all of the source of continuous power that keeps the world in motion:

Eu forca-motriz . . . / Moto-continuo / Do mundo[13]

[I the moving force . . . / Prime mover / of the world]

Embarking on a full study of "Women, Creativity and Power in Brazil," in 1993, I was able to trace a direct link between *mães do santos* (translated in English as "mothers of saints") and writers, some being both Umbanda and Candomblé adherents.[14] In my first interview with Miriam Alves in São Paulo who expresses both identities, as Candomblé devotee and writer, in response to the question about the specific struggles of Black women, she identified Benedita da Silva, who emerged out of a movement in the *favelas* (the name for Brazilian urban residence for the impoverished) to become a federal deputy, in the political context of writing the new constitution of Brazil. For Miriam, "she [Benedita da Silva] was always fighting to include something in favor of the woman, for us." In that interview, Miriam discussed at length the exoticizing of the Black woman in Carnival and the developing consciousness around the issue of Black women in Brazil, which she and writers in the *Quilhomboje* project helped advance. In that period, as documented in *Mulher Negra Resistencia e Soberania de Uma Raça*,[15] Black women were 80% of domestic workers in Brazil, and only 1% of Black women finished elementary school and went on to secondary school. Much work from organizations like *Geledes* in São Paulo has produced information on Black women and worked collaboratively with groups in Rio de Janeiro and Salvador to challenge and correct the inequalities in Black women's experience in Brazil, achieving relatively more advancement and recognition in the contemporary period.

One of my most memorable interviews was with Iyá Mãe Beata De Iemanjá, a beloved practitioner of the *Candomblé* Afro-Brazilian spiritual/cultural belief system, who had written a book titled *Caroço de Dendê*.

A Sabertoda dos Terreiros (1997), as well as short stories and poems. Accompanied by poet-activist, Lia Viera, I visited her own *terreiro* (spiritual, environmental space of *Candomblé*), *Ile Axé Omiojuaro* in Miguel Couto, Nova Iguaçu, which functioned as a site for community development and youth well-being and sustainability. Mãe Beata in many ways embodied precisely that conjunction of creativity and power as the visit included her reading from her creative work.

In studying that political conjunction and power in 1993, an informal meeting with Jurema Batista, then a young ascending politician, facilitated by poet Lia Viera, informed my "Women, Creativity and Power in Brazil"[16] project and provided political context. After a visit to the site of The Candelária massacre, where eight homeless young boys were killed by police near the historic church, Lia walked me to see Jurema Batista, whose work then consistently advanced activist politics on behalf of Black communities.[17] Jurema Batista, elected three times as a councilor in the Workers Party (PT), which she co-founded in Rio de Janeiro, was one of the first generation of Black women elected to office, worked then on making the commemoration of the *quilhombo* of *Zumbi* of *Palmares* more visible. Above all she communicated in her being and presence the forthcoming rise of Black women in political activities and the necessity for activism on behalf of one's community, in which so many needs remain unmet.

This link between politics and activism, as still indicated by Jurema allows us to recognize the activist trajectory which Marielle Franco would subsequently follow, both women being created in and coming forward to represent *favelas,* deprived also of basic facilities. Jurema's leadership story, she indicated, began as a teacher of literature in her community when a Black worker was killed mistakenly by the police. As a result, she and others created the Morro do Andarai Residents Association, of which she became president.[18] But in her view, even as Black women are educated, they are still often the recipients of violence: ". . . because this independence of the Black women that occurs in the area of education also ends up having repercussions on their sex-affective relationships. These are very complicated, because putting up with an intellectual Black woman is hard, right?"[19]

When a journalist identified as Tatiana posed to her a question on this subject as follows:

Boa tarde Jurema. Eu queria saber como é que você vê o futuro das novas gerações de mulheres negras, que hoje frequentam a universidade. Porque antes só diziam ser necessário educação. Então como é que você vê o futuro das novas gerações?

[Good afternoon Jurema. I would like to know how you see the future of the new generation of Black women who today attend universities. Because before we were oriented with the idea that it was a necessity to get an education. Then how do you envision the future of the new generations? (my translation)]

Her response was:

Eu vejo que daqui pra frente é inevitável. Meu sonho é isso, né? "I have a dream": que as próximas gerações continuarão falando, lutando e mudando o quadro deste país.

[I see an inevitability in our process. What is my dream, right? "I have a dream" that the next generations will continue to speak, to struggle and move forward the framework of this country. (my translation)][20]

While much of the recognition of Black women in Brazilian political leadership focuses on Benedita da Silva for several reasons, notably because she was the first Black woman who attained the highest political levels in Brazil, it is important also to put her rise into historical context. Also born and raised in a Rio de Janeiro *favela*, she became the first Black woman senator in Brazil, also having been elected a councilwoman and federal deputy in 1987, 2010, 2014, and 2018. Political credentials amassed as she was also elected vice governor of Rio de Janeiro in 1998. She assumed the governor's seat briefly in 2002, and she ran for Mayor of Rio de Janeiro in 2020.[21]

Titled *Benedita da Silva: An Afro-Brazilian Woman's Story of Politics and Love* (1997), her political autobiography made her more visible to an international audience. Indeed, it became one of the most known books, after the wide recognition of the famous novel, written in journal form, of the experiences of a Black woman living and working out of a *favela,* translated into English as *Child of the Dark* by Carolina Maria DeJesus (1967). The first political autobiography of an Afro-Brazilian woman, Benedita recounts her life struggles as a girl coming of age in a Rio *favela,* her love life, her struggles with poverty, sexual assault, marriages, and her candid assessments of mistakes she made in her personal and professional life. Significantly she describes how she came to consciousness about her situation and her resolve to be politically active in order to effect a transformation of the bases of the existence of Black people in Brazil. Chapters including "Feminism with Passion" and "Exploding the Myth of Racial Harmony" delve into the historical context of the Black woman's experience in Brazil and combat the national narrative and myth of "racial democracy" that have long fueled Brazil's exclusion of Black people from full political participation.

Recent critical texts by African American scholars making visible the experiences of Afro-Brazilian women to a larger African Diaspora community include Christen Smith's *Afro-Paradise. Blackness, Violence and Performance in Brazil* (2016) and Keisha-Khan Perry's *Black Women against the Land Grab. The Fight for Racial Justice in Brazil* (2013). In a preceding generation, Michael Hanchard's *Orpheus and Power* (1994) on the Movimento Negro in Brazil and his *Racial Politics in Contemporary Brazil* (1999) and before him Anani Dzidzienyo's, *The Position of Blacks in Brazilian Society* (1971) contributed to the scholarly demythologizing of the Brazilian racial narrative of "racial democracy" from African diasporic scholars who problematized this issue through the ideological context of Afro-Brazilian activists. These works advanced the untiring political activism begun by the most well-known Brazilian Pan-Africanist, Abdias do Nascimento (1914–2011), particularly his *Brazil, Mixture or Massacre. Essays in the Genocide of Black People* (1979). But there was also a less-identified Pan-Africanist feminism coming from Afro-Brazilian women like Lélia Gonzalez, one of the co-founders of the Movimento Negro Unificado, central to these articulations.

AMERFRICAN CONNECTIONS: THE BLACK FEMINIST LEADERSHIP OF LÉLIA GONZALEZ

Re-connecting the dots in Black feminist leadership among Afro-Brazilians of necessity re-locates Lélia Gonzalez's importance at a critical juncture (particularly the 1960's and 1980's) in Brazil's history but also as a major contributor to Black feminist thought in its international dimensions. As perhaps the lone major Black feminist intellectual of her generation, a comrade of US activist intellectual, Angela Y. Davis, among her cohort of Black intellectual activists, Lélia Gonzalez was cited by sociologist Flavia Rios as being an advisor to Benedita da Silva in her first legislative term in Rio de Janeiro but consistently activated as a Black feminist political activist:

> Given Brazil's diminutive Black and female political representation, Gonzalez and her generation also had a stake in the formation of participatory councils, serving on the national women's council which was fundamental to the questioning of gender in the interaction between state and civil society. It was therefore part of the search for representation and participation on the political playing field of the state public sphere in the democratization of the country. (76)

Sueli Carneiro's *Lélia Gonzalez, O Feminismo negro no palco da historia* (2014) offers a full-length study of Gonzalez's intellectual and political trajectory. Significant to the Lélia Gonzalez process has been what Keisha-Khan Perry and Edilza Sotero describe as a Black Diaspora Feminism,

or alternatively a Black left feminism, in their essay "*Amerfricanidade:*
The Black Diaspora Feminism of Lélia Gonzalez," they argue that her
advancement of this formulation of *Amerfricanity* places her among African
diaspora theorists, situating her "as a critical thinker in the Black radical
and feminist traditions" centering her as well as a producer of knowledge.
"*Amerfricanidade*" describes the experiences of Africans in the Americas,
a specific terminology that addresses the continuity of Black experience
across the Americas: "A historic process of intense cultural dynamic (resistance, accommodation, reinterpretation, creation of new forms) referenced
in African models that shape the construction of an ethnic identity."[22] More
recently Sueli Carneiro's "Black Women's Intellectual Contributions to the
Americas: Perspectivas from the Global South" asserts the importance of
Lélia Gonzalez describing Angela Davis's indication of the importance of
feminists in the United States having access to the writings, ideas and practices of Black Brazilian feminists more than the other way around. Angela
Davis had described Lélia Gonzalez as one of the women from whom she had
learned a great deal and from whom succeeding generations of Afro Brazilian
feminists needed to learn even more. Carneiro outlined the various moments
of Black feminist platforms that have been launched by Afro-Brazilian feminists over the years since then.[23]

Ana Martins in "Running Away with Language: Inventing Wor(l)ds in
the Work of Lélia Gonzalez in 1980s Brazil"[24] focuses similarly on Lélia's
politics of inventing the language to describe the experience as one in which:

> Gonzalez deliberately translates "amefricanity" for a Black and indigenous,
> female and feminist Spanish-speaking audience. If the Black unity symbol-
> ised by the term "amefrican" in the earlier essay depends on the merging of
> two terms (African + American), the translation of that specific unity into
> regionally-resonating feminist discourses and politics in the later one involves
> an expansion rather than a merging, so as to better address the rather compli-
> cated political relationships between all the women involved. The expansion is
> signalled via the use of the expression "*feminismo afrolatinoamericano*," which
> refers to the specific unity of an excluded Black and indigenous, female major-
> ity in the continent: amefricans and Amerindians. (257)

Further in her pursuance of language inventiveness, Gonzalez had defined
Pretoguês (Black Portuguese)[25] to indicate the ways that Afro-Brazilians have
redefined the Portuguese language to meet their realities:

> [. . .] what I call "*pretoguês*" and which is nothing more than the mark of
> Africanization of Portuguese spoken in Brazil . . . is easily found especially
> in Spanish in the Caribbean region. The tonal and rhythmic character of the
> African languages brought to the *Novo Mundo* (New World), as well as the

absence of certain consonants (such as the l or the r, for example) point to a little explored aspect of Black influence in the historical and cultural formation of the continent as a whole (and not to mention the "Creole" dialects of the Caribbean). (Gonzalez, 1988)[26]

Relatedly, Gonzalez was also the co-founder of one of the first groups of Black women in Rio de Janeiro, challenging, as well, male domination in Brazilian politics, according to Martins she had formed "a historic Black women's organisation entirely separate from the MNU, called *Nzinga—Coletivo de Mulheres Negras do Rio de Janeiro* [Nzinga—Collective of Black Women of Rio de Janeiro] on 16 June 1983. Whilst the choice of the name Nzinga was meant as homage to Nzinga Mbandi Ngola, Queen of Matamba and Angola (1587–1663) who defied the Portuguese empire, its emblem—a purple bird—brought together the bird as a symbol of female ancestry in the Nago tradition, and the colour purple as a mark of the international women's movement" (257).

If we follow Sylvia Wynter's argument for the relocation of the conceptual prominence of Afroindigenization over creolization,[27] we can argue for a pattern in which Gonzalez's *Amefricanidade* becomes critical. According to Perry and Soltero, it was Lélia's travel across the Americas and Africa that gave her the language and ideas to create the conceptual paradigms that define her work as her travels intensified her notions of Blackness and feminism. Thus many credit her with the diasporization of Black feminist activism in Brazil . . . As Bairros (1999, 355) wrote, Gonzalez articulated "other ways of thinking the African diaspora synthesized in the category '*amefricanidade,*' to define the common experience of Black people in the Americas" (63).

Placing Gonzalez in a trajectory noted by other scholars like Luiza de Bairros and Sueli Carneiro, Kia Caldwell indicates that it was Gonzalez who, in her essay "*O Lugar da Mulher*" ("The Place of the Woman," 1982), argued that Afro-Brazilian women experienced triple oppression from gender, racial, and class domination. Carneiro and Santos's book, *Mulher Negra* (*Black Woman*, 1985), provides documentation for these arguments. Significant to this project is the fact that Gonzalez was one of the earliest Black women intellectuals, an anthropologist working in Brazil while also advancing political collaborations with community and with Black women's organizations across Africa and the African Diaspora. For example, Gonzalez was one of two Black women who attended Pan-African conferences in Africa, the other being Eulalia Bernard of Costa Rica.[28]

Renewed awareness and knowledge of Lélia Gonzalez is beginning to increase via a variety of online portals and intellectual projects. For example, the blog "Learning with Lélia Gonzalez In Defense of Afro-Latin Feminism,"[29] links the position of Black and Indigenous women and cites

Gonzalez as providing an analysis of racism in Latin America "sophisticated enough to keep Blacks and Indians in the subordinate condition within the most exploited class, because of its most effective form of ideology, the ideology of whitening, so well analyzed by Brazilian scientists. Transmitted by means of communication and the traditional ideological systems, it reproduces and perpetuates the belief that the rating and values of white Western culture are the only true and universal."[30] An allied position articulated in the same vein though much later was expressed by Maria Lugones (2010) in "Toward a Decolonial Feminism," which begins with the beautiful formulation "Contemporary women of color and third-world women's critique of feminist universalism centers the claim that the intersection of race, class, sexuality, and gender exceeds the categories of modernity. If woman and Black are terms for homogeneous, atomic, separable categories, then their intersection shows us the absence of Black women rather than their presence" (742).

The mutually engaged translation work of African American and Afro-Brazilian activists into Portuguese and English and the reverse appropriately has been fundamental in bringing back for consideration the work of Lélia Gonzalez. As indicated in the Rios, Perry, and Soltero essays in the Latin American Studies Association Forum indicated above, this was begun particularly so that translations go in both directions. These mutually engaged and bi-directed translations contribute to re-connecting the linkages and learning sometimes striking similarities in these articulations coming from women of color in disparate locations. The translation of Lélia's 1979 classic, "The Black Woman: A Portrait," by Tais de Sant'Anna and Keisha-Khan Y. Perry is therefore a significant contribution. Their introduction locates Gonzalez within a gallery of Black left feminist activists and their ideas.[31] For example, Lélia Gonzalez captured creatively, with a certain self-reflexivity, a simultaneously auto-ethnographic and anthropological analysis of the experience of a Black woman living in a Rio *favela*. It is a stark portrayal of life in a contradictorily beautiful location, which overlooks the city with a view of the ocean but which is also the site of poverty, police brutality, and desperation:

> They went to live in a *favela* that people said had once been a *quilombo*. The view from up there is beautiful. You can see the ocean, the statue of the Christ, the luxurious homes of the madams down there and also when the police van comes to carry out a police raid on the *morro*.[32]

In these juxtaposing images Gonzalez presents the contradictory construction of the Rio *favela*, still the residential site of the workers of the city, but also simultaneously the objects of the state's policing, and locally the predatory sexual exploitation of young women. In her creative-political sketch she also captures a desire for advancement of succeeding generations via knowledge, beyond being adept in the performative aspects of samba:

> We who are poor people have to study to see if we can improve our lives. We see it through the children of our employers. Everyone studies and becomes a doctor. Why then would we not want our children to study? At least elementary education, right? Then you can get a better job, earn a salary, have a formal employment and even go to high school later. There are many people who study at night and work during the day. Right here on the *morro* there are a lot of people who do this. I'm too old to learn these school things: I'm going to be twenty-seven years old. Children are the ones who have a fresh mind for this.[33]

Lélia Gonzalez is adept here in her ideological orientation, theorizing a symmetrical relationship between *Amerafricans* as parallel with *Amerindians*. Thus, we see how Sylvia Wynter's call for the prominence of Afro-indigeneity provides the space in which Lélia Gonzalez concept can fully reside. To illustrate, in Gonzalez's essay, "For an Afro-Latin Feminism," she describes her project as analyzing "the internal contradictions of Latin American feminism—a modest contribution from a Black feminist to the advancement of the feminist movement." As indicated, this essay precedes, but has affinity with, Maria Lugones' "Towards a Decolonial Feminism." Still, it simultaneously offers a critique of the avoidance of racial positioning in Latin American feminism as advanced by women who would be considered of European origin in Latin America and thus would fit the category of "white or mainstream feminism."[34] Gonzalez therefore offers another locational examination of the intersection of feminism with racism which carries a certain "forgetfulness about the racial question," using Lacanian and Fanonian analysis of the subjectivity to analyze this erasure of the Black female and indigenous subject. This allows her to assert the call "for an Afro-latinamerican feminism" that embraces both Amerindians and Amerafricans, in which racial discrimination and class exploitation are analytically present.

Like Claudia Jones's 1949 essay, "An End to the Neglect of the Problems of Negro Women" which insists, similarly, that the racial question precedes the gender and class question, Gonzalez's argument is that race is often the first line of oppression for all Black and indigenous subjects. She concludes nonetheless that in spite of various challenges, new networks are created that "give priority to the struggle against racism and patriarchy from an anti-imperialist perspective."

Online sources that identify the important work in this regard includes the organization *Geledes* in São Paulo included in Jaimee Swift's "Afro-Brazilian Feminists and the Fight for Racial and Gender Inclusion"[35] *Portal Geledes*, https://www.geledes.org.br/, for example, provides ongoing details on the

Black experience globally while it also focuses on Black women in Brazil and still keeps open the question: "Who Killed Marielle?" The blog also documents the gains and products that have come after her death. The work of Sueli Carneiro the founder and leader of *Geledes* is significant in this context. For example she identified Afro-Brazilian feminism as always and already "Left of Karl Marx."[36] We concur with Sueli Carneiro that Lélia Gonzalez has to be instated as one of the founders of a now definable Black feminism across the Americas but specifically for a Brazilian Black feminism.

After the assassination of Marielle Franco, Black feminist anthropologists who work on Brazil issued "On the Imperative of Transnational Solidarity. A Statement on the Assassination of Marielle Franco."[37] In the process, they located Marielle in a history of intellectual activism that also included Lélia Gonzalez. What was also significant was the relationship between Black feminist scholars in the United States with the Afro-Brazilian realities, particularly as it pertains to the resistance of Black women to all forms of violence. The translation of the text "The Black Woman: A Portrait" by Lélia Gonzalez was preceded by an introduction that indicated that, on the night she was killed, Marielle Franco had attended an empowerment event at the Black women's organization, *Casa das Pretas,* expressing there a knowledge of Audre Lorde's "The Uses of Anger: Women Responding to Racism" (1984).

Thus, a distinct connecting line can be drawn between Lélia Gonzalez's Black women's version of *Ameriafricanidade* to a Black feminist internationalism of Audre Lorde who in her life articulated similar positions. In the preface to *Moving Beyond Boundaries. International Dimensions Black Women's Writing* (1995), we cited Lorde's description of this as a network that needed to be created: "I think that an international network is absolutely essential, and I think it is in the process of being born . . . This is what Black feminism is all about; articulating ourselves, our needs and our resistances as women, and as women within our particular environments . . . Our Black women's vision has no horizon."[38]

In this context, Angela Figueiredo's "Letter to Judith Butler from an ex-Mulatto Woman" (*"Carta a Judith Butler de una mujer ex mulata"*) describes the comparative nature and collaborative analysis of race in Brazil and the United States. Angela Figueiredo's "letter" marks the distinction in the nature of Black identity that in Brazil had to be fought for but that in the United States is part of a given racial reality. For her the rejection of "mulatto" identity is expressed in her "ex-mulatto" formation as a rejection of that Brazilian racial hierarchy that created a particular sexualized identity for Black women of a certain desired youthful gendered biracial representation.[39] Figueiredo cites Lélia Gonzalez's discussion of racism as a neurosis of Brazilian society generated from the sublimated desire of white men for Black women, which, in Lacanian psychoanalysis, arises from the fact that

Black women are the ones who nurtured and breastfed white men who end up having a subordinated "desire for Black women from a very tender age. However racist structures prevent this dream from coming true, creating violence and racial hatred" (139). Still, for Angela Figueiredo it remains impossible to assume the identical appearance of United States racial formations in the Brazilian context, the latter offering its own particularities arising from its historical contexts:

> In the Brazilian case, it was only through the sense of identity and politics awarded to the Black category, in opposition to the mixtures and fluidity of the numerous racial categories (some 300) which structured racism in Brazil, that achievements were accomplished. (143)

For Angela Figueiredo, the process of becoming Black, that is, rejecting the "mulatto/mulatta," operated as the diametrical opposite of the protagonist's decision in James Weldon Johnson's classic, *The Autobiography of an Ex-Colored Man* (1912), who decided to pass for white. This has allowed her to break from the cycle of these racial categorizations, which she indicates is the only way in which Black people in Brazil have been able to access political and educational gains.

MARIELLE FRANCO'S BLACK LEFT FEMINIST LEADERSHIP

Providing affirmative action quotas to formerly barred Black Brazilians[40] a policy crafted under the leadership of President Lula and instituted during the presidency of Dilma Rousseff in 2012 enabled Marielle to acquire a master's degree in public policy. Thus, acquiring a university education as Lélia Gonzalez predicted in her "The Black Woman: A Portrait," as described above, was central to Marielle Franco's ability to acquire the ideological language to articulate a particular set of political positions. In her academic work she had analyzed state violence as meted out by police as agents of the state. As described in the joint statement "On the Imperative of Transnational Solidarity: A U.S. Back Feminist Statement on the Assassination of Marielle Franco":[41] "Her master's thesis in sociology explored this brutality at length, particularly tying it to the militarization of the Brazilian police forces and the occupation of the majority Black, majority poor favelas of her city, Rio de Janeiro" (3). Ironically and sadly, her assassination was linked to those same "global practices of anti-Black genocide," which also take place in the United States. The critique of these state practices which have genocidal implications as the "We Charge Genocide" international complaint coming from the Civil Rights Congress in the United States established in 1951, has been at the center of subsequent movements like Black Lives Matter, initiated by three Black women in the United States: Patrisse Cullors, Alicia Garza, and Opal Tometi following the acquittal of George Zimmerman for the killing of Trayvon Martin in 2013.

It is important to locate Marielle Franco nonetheless within a longer genealogy of Black left feminist women.[42] Marielle's explicit left identification, first of all, includes the fact that she was officially a member of Brazil's political party, Party for Socialism and Liberty (PSOL) through which she ran for office. From this political position, she was able to articulate explicit left feminist positions, with a LGBTQ orientation as well. Meeting the emotional needs of her larger community, her political campaign drew as well on the African *Ubuntu* philosophy of "I am Because We Are." Applying this philosophical position to Black women, this phrasing was extended to mean: "My life is at risk when the life another *favelada* is also at risk. My experience as a Black woman is stigmatized because so are all other Black girls."[43]

In her essay "After the Take Over. Mobilizing the Political Creativity of Brazil's Favelas"[44] Franco begins by expressing her concern for the coup that displaced the president Dilma Rousseff, who was a member of the Workers Party (PT) and led on that basis. Like Lélia Gonzalez, Marielle analyzed the particular conditions of Black women living in Rio *favelas* as still facing "inequalities that distinguish them from women of other social strata—the middle class, and those who don't work for a living." For her it was important to underscore the ways that structural racism and institutional *machismo* come together to impact Black *faveladas.* Yet, for her, these women "remain a powerful force for creativity and inventiveness, with the capacity to overcome their circumstances through their daily struggles and forms of local organizing." Thus, for Marielle, it was poor Black women who had the capacity to mobilize for social transformation. Thereby, her conclusion is that it is "the task of the left in the twenty-first century is to expand this potential, creating narratives that foreground the freedom, participation and emancipatory activism of Black *favelada* women."[45]

> The task of the left in the twenty-first century is to expand this potential, creating narratives that foreground the freedom, participation and emancipatory activism of Black favelada women . . . Building structures that help empower poor, Black women to take on the role of active citizenship, aimed at winning a city of rights, is fundamental for the revolution the contemporary world requires. (Marielle Franco, "After the Takeover," 2017)

This is the same analytical framework that Claudia Jones proposed in her essays "An End to the Neglect of the Problems of Negro Women" and "We

Seek Full Equality," both published in 1949,[46] which identified the ways that various white and male structures combine to subordinate Black women. For Claudia Jones as for Marielle Franco, Black women still were actually the ones who held the power of social transformation in their hands by the very nature of their subject positions in society. For Claudia Jones, in "We Seek Full Equality" (1949):

> . . . the triply-oppressed status of Negro women is a barometer of the status of all women and that the fight for the full, economic, political and social equality of the Negro woman is in the vital self-interest of white workers, in the vital interest of the fight to realize equality for all women. (87)

Marielle Franco similarly concluded that

> . . . building structures that help empower poor, Black women to take on the role of active citizenship, aimed at winning a city of rights, is fundamental for the revolution the contemporary world requires.[47]

A speech that Marielle Franco was scheduled to deliver was eventually read after her death by sister-Councilor Tarcísio Motta. In that speech, she described violence against women in Brazil, the "structural misogyny and racism on our bodies," which was also captured in the gross inequality in salaries. For her in this context, gender equality was about the ability to live life itself: " . . . it is indispensable that we speak of gender equality!" Ironically, her speech also aimed to challenge the removal of the word "gender" from the Municipal Education Plan and concluded with the statement:

> That we speak about sexuality, respect, secularity, racism, of LGBT phobia, of misogyny. To speak of these themes is to dedicate oneself to life in its multiple manifestations. It is to dedicate oneself to combating violence and inequality! It is beyond urgent that this House does not remain silent about the lives that are interrupted every day in this municipality. To speak of gender equality is to defend life![48]

Essays on Marielle Franco are emerging which highlight her various left positionalities. Such an essay is Gabriela Loureiro's "To be Black, Queer and Radical: Centring the Epistemology of Marielle Franco."[49] Here, Loureiro places Marielle in a line of Black feminists who articulated the subjectivity of Black *faveladas* including Lélia Gonzalez, Sueli Carneiro, and Benedita da Silva. As the first Black woman to become a member of the Rio de Janeiro city council, a congresswoman, a senator, and a vice-governor of Rio de Janeiro state in the 1990s, Benedita da Silva had also used the political slogan: "woman, Black and favelada"; her candidacy had been built around her symbolism as someone who was "three times a minority" (da Silva et al., 1997). Loureiro concluded that "Marielle paid a tribute to her political predecessor, Benedita da Silva in the last event she attended before being executed." Loureiro also reports that Marielle, who became one of the most voted-for candidates for city council in Rio de Janeiro, ran on three pillars: gender, race and the city, and was going to "lead the debate about race and gender in this exclusionary city as a woman who is Black and *favelada*, using these three points as a vehicle to give voice" to those experiences (Franco, 2016, quoted in Loureiro, 2020)

In the available published interviews with Marielle, a clear sense of political strategies, confident leadership and progressive self-presentation emerges. Like African women who identify the need for physical presentation, she was conscious of this in her statement that the turbans she happily wore portrayed the royalty and elegance of Black women: "*Então, é uma pedreira, mas a gente ocupa e eu fico feliz hoje, por exemplo hoje, estou com turbante e essa é uma das formas de turbante que coloco, e vários deles elogiaram, e eu falo: 'pois é, um turbante que traz a realeza da mulher negra'*" (5).[50] (You know, we are put in an extremely difficult and hard location, but we embrace the challenge fully. I am happy today, for example today because I am wearing a headwrap which is one of the various styles of turbans that I wear. Many have recognized them. So for me, I say that: "Indeed! a turban (or *gélé*) always brings out the dignity of the Black woman") [my translation].

When this interview was conducted in 2017, women in Brazil occupied 13% of the elected offices and were 121st in world ranking of the world's political representation. According to UN Women, at the end of 2019, Brazil was still in the 15th percentile, with 15% of women in the lower chamber and 14.8% in senate and tied at 133rd place with Paraguay and Bahrain among the 191 countries listed. Marielle, like the Black women before her, Benedita and Lélia, mentioning only two that we have considered here, entered the political field with a platform that in her words combined gender, *favela* and Blackness (*Entramos nesse campo nesse lugar e nesse debate com o fundamento do gênero, da favela e da negritude*), the three primary aspects of her identity. Although she did not include sexuality in this triple identification, her position as a Black queer woman was also publicly expressed against homophobia, as it pertains to her personal life and the ways the society treats all its citizens:

> que as pessoas possam ocupar de favelado, ocupar de negros e negras, ocupar de mulheres trans, ocupar com tudo que se tem direito. E assim essas pautas, essas temáticas estejam presentes também na Comissão de Defesa da Mulher, que é o que estamos presidindo. É fechar bem este mandato, estar aí no debate da política, cumprindo um papel importante. (interview, 2017)

[people have to take care of the needs of those in the *favelas*, take care of Black men and Black women, take care of transwomen, take care of all who are entitled to their rights. These are the guidelines and themes that are also present in the Commission for the Defense of Women, which is what we are leading. We accept this mandate, to engage a political debate, in which we will play an important role. (my translation)]

Consistently foregounding the issue of her non-conforming sexuality, S. Tay Glover and Flavia Meireles, (2020) "Towards a Transnational Black Feminist Theory of the Political Life of Marielle Franco," argue for a theoretical example which Marielle's fully inclusive model is present, especially since "the reported motive for her execution was her Black lesbian feminist political success and exposure and her denouncement of neo-colonial necropower . . . as it manifested in militaristic police occupation, brutality and corruption in favelas like her own" (64). The link with the theoretics of Audre Lorde, who articulated similarly, return here, all the more because this was one of the last references that Marielle made before her physical life was lost to state violence.

Marielle Franco described her leadership orientation as coming precisely from being a Black person, a Black woman, and a *favelada* (from the cluster of sixteen *favelas* called Maré) in Rio de Janeiro. She suffered the same challenges, as described by Lélia Gonzalez, of poverty, teen pregnancy, and a difficult life. Like Lélia Gonzalez, Franco was able to follow a different political trajectory because of the political changes that created more educational pathways for Black youth, fought for and realized by the generation that created the Movimento Negro Unificado. Her leadership story included working with State Representative Marcelo Freixo and managing the Human Rights Commission of the legislative assembly of Rio de Janeiro, and her continuing involvement when there was need for the articulation of women's perspectives. Those experiences led to her being elected as a councilwoman and subsequently being in charge of the Women's Commission. She describes the fact that as Black women she and her other Black woman political colleagues represented the minority within the minority of women represented, but that her approach was to transform that status to a position of power:

Nós, mulheres negras, somos uma minoria em termos de representatividade, somos sub-representadas, e isso é muito ruim porque nós mulheres a maioria da população, então é uma contradição que pegamos o tempo todo para ver como alterar, avançar nessa relação e nesse processo. Das seis vereadoras hoje na Câmara, tem eu e outra vereadora, que é a Tânia Bastos do PRB, que é da base do governo, que é mulher negra, que presidiu também a comissão da mulher, mas que certamente dependendo das pautas irá discordar, como pautas em relação a violência contra a mulher, certamente temos posições dialogáveis e próximas. Mas pautas como no debate que fiz hoje na tribuna, no pequeno expediente, para falar sobre um caso de homofobia, dos milhares que ocorrem todos os dias, nós duas não vamos ter tanto acordo assim, porque ela é da base do governo, o debate dela ainda será sobre a família tradicional, contra o aborto, de cura da homossexualidade.[51]

[We, Black women, we are the minority in terms of representation, underrepresented, and this is very unfortunate as women for we are the majority of the population, a contradiction we come to, time and again, for how to alter, advance out from under these relations, this process. Of the six councilwomen in the city legislature, there is only one other, Tania Bastos (PRB), who is aligned with the government, who as a Black woman presided over the Committee on Women, but with whom I would certainly not be in agreement depending on the issue, finding some common ground on the issue of violence against women. Still when it comes to debates like the one I spoke at today during my recognized time (*pequeno expediente*) at the rostrum (*tribuna*), where I addressed a case, of the thousands that occur every day, of homophobia, we wouldn't find much by way of agreement, as she's part of the ruling government coalition, taking as yet the position for the traditional family structure, against abortion rights, and for a cure to homosexuality.[52]]

POLITICAL PRESENCE OF WOMEN IN BRAZIL BEFORE AND AFTER MARIELLE

Although Marielle's assassination robbed us of her physical presence, it unwittingly made her permanently into a global icon in the Black Movement in Brazil and Black feminist movement in international context. In spite of her loss, and, sadly, because of her loss, Black women have advanced the process of self-recognition and activism and are making deliberate strides in political leadership in Brazil. But there is a history that precedes Marielle which comes to light as well once we put her in context. One of the first Black women identified in Brazilian elected politics, Antonieta de Barros, was a teacher and journalist in the state of Santa Catarina, committed to advancing literacy and women's rights simultaneously through founding her own newspapers and educational projects. Once women got the right to vote, she joined the Partido Liberal Catarinense (Liberal Party of Santa Catarina) and was elected as a state representative (1934–1937), running again in 1947 and serving until 1951.[53]

In São Paulo, a similar early advancement of women in political life is noted in the career of Theodosina Rosário Ribeiro also a teacher and the first Black woman to be elected city councilor in the city of São Paulo, with an advanced articulation of the much-needed role of women in politics.[54] The advancement of Black people in Brazilian life remained on pause during the various military dictatorships, with Black rights and human rights in general having to be reconstituted after 1985 when the last dictatorship ended. For this reason, many women in Brazil, including Theodosina Rosário Ribeiro still applaud the work of Dilma Rousseff who was the first woman president in Brazil (2011–2016) for continuing the advancements of her predecessor Lula da Silva and are saddened that she was removed by what is still seen as a kind of military coup.[55] Historian Vanicléia Silva Santos indicates that even in Brazilian historical circles, Laelia Alcantara often does not get appropriate inclusion. Her full name, Laelia Contreiras Agra de Alcantara seved as a senator in 1981 and from 1982–1983 as indicated in the *Centro de Pesquisa e Documentacao de Historia Contemporanea do Brasil.* In the section on "Women and Political Parties," of this work, listed under the November 1982 Elections is the following: "Women alternates occupied seats for a short period in São Paulo (Dulces Salles Cunha Braga and Laelia Alcantara, a Black physician), in 1981."[56] A number of other women representatives at the state level included singer Leci Brandao, and Marina Osmarina da Silva Vaz de Lima (Marina Silva) who actually ran for president in 2010 with an environmental rights platform and Janete Pieta in 2006 who is identified as one of the founders of the Workers Party in 1980.

In Salvador da Bahia, the state with the largest explicitly identified African population, one would expect a larger number of Black women in representative politics. Black women of power tend to be in the African spirituality sphere as was Mae Stella de Oxóssi (1925–2018) of Ilê Axé Opô Afonjá one of the largest compounds of Afro Brazilian *candomblé* who after her passing has public representation on the landscape of the city. Though I met Black women who were running for office in Salvador, we are still limited to lone though popular political figures like Olivia Santana who was elected councilwoman in Salvador in 2004 and 2008 and was a candidate for vice-mayor in 2012. In 2015, she was appointed by the Governor of Bahia, Rui Costa, to head the Secretariat for Policies for Women, and in 2018 Santana was elected the first Black woman state deputy in Bahia.[57] Olivia frequently appears in community events like the various *lavagems* and the *Irmandade da boa morte* festivities, in several places where I have encountered her over the years. Beginning her activism as a student in the Union for Blacks for Equality (UNEGRO), she also became the National Director of the PCDOB (Communist Party of Brazil) and President of the Reparations Commission of the city of Salvador's City Council.

While the gains have been largely in city and state politics, as in the United States,[58] in Rio de Janeiro, after Marielle's passing, the representation of women in politics has increased substantially, causing international recognition of the significance of four victories for women in the last elections, including Marielle's partner Monica Benicio. Described as an architect, feminist, and human rights defender, Benicio has also won a council seat and vowed to fight for justice.[59] Yet these have to be put into perspective as *America's Quarterly* reports still that Black women make up almost 30% of the population, but occupy just 2% of Congress, however, the March assassination of Marielle sparked a genuine movement. More than 1,000 Black women all over Brazil ran for office in October's elections for Congress and state assemblies, a 60% increase over the 2014 election cycle (1). Among them, Renata Souza, who was Marielle's co-worker, "was elected in October, 2019, with even more votes than Franco once received." She indicates that: "In 2006 they campaigned together in their native Maré to elect human rights activist Marcelo Freixo, a white, middle-class male, to the state assembly. Once elected, Freixo hired both as his advisors. The two women worked side by side at the state assembly for 10 years supporting Freixo as he headed the human rights commission. But fellow community activists started to pressure them to come out from the shadows and run for office themselves."[60]

This group of activists also include Taliria Petrone Soares, a Black feminist and history teacher, who also faced the threat of violence but was elected to represent the Niteroi municipality. Her affirmative position in response to threats of violence is captured in an interview in which she expressed concern about:

> The level of political violence that the bodies of women, especially Black women, experience when they occupy politics is very high. For example, I am criticized for the way I dress and speak. I've heard that politics is not for me. In addition, I am offended on social media and by colleagues in the legislature. I've been called crazy . . . these are ways of imprinting the negation of those spaces on the bodies of Black women. These are offenses that can get worse and lead to death, as it was with Marielle.[61]

A notable progressive pattern emerges in the representation of Black women in Brazilian politics. Most of the Black women candidates identify themselves with Black feminist political positions, and many indicate friendship with or influence by Marielle. Several of these now political representatives indicate that being Black women means that they have to articulate those positions for the constituencies they represent, which includes Black women who are often unrepresented. For example, Macae Evaristo, who I met during a UNESCO *General History of Africa* meeting in Belo Horizonte in 2018 is now a councilwoman elected on a Workers' Party ticket. At present she holds online discussions with constituencies, continuously updates and describes her work for a Commission of Women in the *Camara de Vereadores*, and had a very strong response and demonstrable political engagement during the COVID-19 pandemic in Brazil when working class Brazilians bore the brunt of the casualties, holding hearings via virtual platforms as well. She indicates that she supports workers, students and professors' economic rights. She and Aurea Carolina de Freitas Silva also identify as Black feminists. For example, de Freitas Silva is on record as fighting against sexism, racism, LBGT phobia, and various forms of violence, and she serves on the Commission on Domestic Violence Against Women. Her website indicates a statement "For Women's Life and Rights," which raises awareness about rape, femicide, and partner assault. Additionally, Andreia de Jesus Silva was also elected in Minas Gerais, Brazil, also indicating that she continues to defend public policies, especially for Black women.

The Campaign of Women [https://campanhademulher.org/] presents an array of women running for office in 2018 and 2020, with increasingly favorable results. Describing themselves as coordinating people, collectives, circles, movements linked to human rights, culture, communication, education, and well-being, these women fight for democratic rights and an end to inequality. They claim to have facilitated the electing of twenty-nine women to political office in 2018, and in 2020 they advanced that number even further.

FINALLY, US/*EMFIM NOS*[62]

The numbers of Black women elected to political office in Brazil at the city and state level, with platforms that advance women's and Black people's rights, have advanced substantially.[63] However, the NACLA report, "Marielle Franco's Seeds: Black Women and the 2020 Brazilian Election," provides several cautionary details. For one, the historical underrepresentation of the Black population and therefore of Black women continues, even though 2020 provided some advancements. The reality is that although Black people are the majority of the population, they do not hold any kind of proportional representation a point that Marielle is on record as making. Data on racial identification indicate an increase from 20% identification to 24%, which attests to more Black people claiming that particular racial identification as Angela Figueiredo's "Letter to Judith Butler" discussed above indicates. In 2018, thirteen women were elected, including the first Black transgender woman, Erica Malunguinho, who we indicated above declared her candidacy deliberately after the passing of Marielle.

Among Marielle's protegees in Rio de Janeiro, Monica Francisco describes the significance of being mentored by Marielle, and she is now a state representative in Rio de Janeiro. Daniella Monteiro da Silva, also elected in

2018, describes herself as a youth representative with a mandate to advance feminism, public security, Blackness culture and art, and also education and employment. In other locations, particularly the North East, where there are larger Black and indigenous populations, cities like Recife and Porto Alegre have elected Black women. In the interesting Pernambuco case, five women identified as Las Juntas (Maria Joselita Pereira Cavalcanti, Robeyonce Lima, Carol Vergolino Joelma Carla, and Katia Cunha) were elected to occupy one seat. Consistently, these Black women identify as Black and feminist, some even as Black left feminists. We note as well that the decision to have 30% racially diverse representation in politics advanced by Benedita da Silva created the space for women to compete.

Despite these gains, the situation remains difficult for the majority of Black women identified as the most marginalized sector of the working class, disproportionately employed in the least protected and lowest compensated sectors: service and care work. According to a 2019 study, "Black women today are 64 percent of domestic workers (a drop by 16% from 1994)—the profession with the least labor rights in all Brazilian legislation, only winning the same level of rights as other workers, including the rights to unionize, in 2013."[64]

Advancing Marielle Franco's presence at grassroots levels are developments and movements like the Marielle Franco Occupation in the North Zone of São Paulo . . . "named explicitly in their words in honor of the Black socialist city councillor of the Socialism and Liberty Party assassinated for her work with communities and families affected by the genocide of the populations of the peripheries. The name given to the encampment was important not only to keep Marielle Franco's story alive, but also to not let the investigations into her execution be suppressed or forgotten" (Ibid.).

The NACLA report indicates that "Congresswoman Benedita da Silva from Rio de Janeiro presented a proposal at the Supreme Electoral Court to require proportional distribution of party resources among Black and white candidates." Additionally, she too is definite that in representing women she is representing at least half the nation: "When I defend the rights of women, I am defending *52 percent of the population*" (7). Vilma Reis, who ran for mayor of Salvador in 2020 and who I met in Cachoeira at an event adjacent to the International School of Transnational Decolonial Black Feminism in 2019, indicates that Black women need to occupy all political spaces available. She confirms my assessment that "it was Black women's leadership that shifted political parties' agenda in the 2020 elections."[65]

In that circle of power which indicates less closure but more the power of re-statement and affirmation, each time at another level and with more clarity, a final and relevant concluding statement to this project comes again through the spirituality, creativity and power nexus expressed by Iyá Mãe Beata De Iemanjá. It allows me to end as I began, this time with a certainty about the circularities of power. A shared video of a film about the Black woman founder of Samba in Rio de Janeiro, "Tia Ciata" includes a message from the past to the present by Mae Beata, exactly on the issue of women and leadership:

> Nós precisamos de mais mulheres no poder.
> Nós queremos mais mulheres senadoras.
> Nós queremos mais mulheres governadoras.
> Nós queremos mais mulheres deputadas.
> Em todos os parâmetros. Em todos os lugares.
> Nós queremos empoderar mulheres.
>
> [We need more women in power.
> We want more women as senators.
> We want more women as governors.
> We want more women in congress.
> In all parameters. In all locations everywhere.
> We want to empower women.[66] (my translation)]

NOTES

1. Olupona and Rey, 2008 provides a discussion of this ritual.

2. Conversation with Ithaca anti-drone, anti-imperialism activist Mary Anne Grady Flores on 1/8/2021, who also cited Oscar Romero (1917–1980) of San Salvador, who was assassinated while delivering Mass, and Bertha Caceres (Honduran environmentalist (1974–2018), who indicated that one may kill or imprison the body but the spirit and therefore the movement lives on in the people.

3. *American Anthropologist* 122:157–162.

4. Perry indicates that her four key points that she considered necessary for the democratic transformation of Brazil: (1) the need to recognize Black people, Black women, and transgender people as hypervisible all over Brazilian cities (as domestic workers in apartment and office buildings, and in large numbers as prostitutes in red-light zones); (2) the hate and violence that targets these Black cis- and transgender women is in stark contrast to the demand for their labor, including sexual labor; (3) the right to education and work is key to the LGBTQ fight against antiBlack genocide, as Black transgender people are also killed every day; and (4) the antiracism and antisexism struggle has to be diasporic. For more on Malunguinho, see: Assembleia Legislativa de São Paulo: Deputados—Erica Malunguinho. https://www.a1.sp.gov.br/deputado/?matricula=300625 See also various video interviews such as https://video.search.yahoo.com/yhs/search?fr=yhs-iba-syn&hsimp=yhs-syn&hspart=iba

&p=Erica+Malunguinho#id=5&vid=20f8a1d9bf64d58417ce22a78324f4c4&action
=view

5. Among the allegorical floats of the Carnival, one stood out representing the human rights activist and councilwoman Marielle Franco—killed in a shooting on 14 March 2018—holding a gag, during the first night of the Carnival parade at the Sambódromo in São Paulo, Brazil. https://www.telesurenglish.net/news/brazil-carnival-a -message-of-protest-against-jair-bolsonaro-20200224-0004.html

6. See "Slain Black councilwoman remembered during Brazil Carnival" https: //abcnews.go.com/International/wireStory/headlinein-brazil-carnival-pays-tribute -slain-councilwoman-61461686, March 5, 2019, which also describes some of the myriad ways she was represented in Carnival parades.

7. Flavia Santos de Araujo, "Marielle, Presente!" *Meridians,* 17:1 (September, 2018): 207–211.

8. November 26, 2018, Strand Building, Strand Campus, London. The event indicated that it was organized to introduce the poetry collection entitled Um girassol nos teus cabelos—Poemas para Marielle Franco (Quintal Edições e Mulherio das Letras, 2018). The book brings together selected poems by 50 Brazilian female writers, as a tribute to Rio de Janeiro city councillor and activist Marielle Franco, who was brutally murdered in March. The book was officially launched at the 2018 FLIP - Paraty International Literary Festival, in July. https://www.kcl.ac.uk/events/a-sunflower-in -her-hair-poems-and-testimonies-for-marielle-franco (accessed 1/8/2021).

9. https://www.rioonwatch.org/?p=58297

10. March 14, 2019, https://www.bitchmedia.org/article/dispatch/remembering -marielle-franco (accessed 1/8/2021).

11. A project created as a National Endowment for the Humanities and organized by the University of Maryland took a group of scholars to Brazil with the intent being to open up Brazil for scholarly and cultural inquiry. I was pleased to be a member of this group which included Charles Martin, Clyde Taylor, Robert Stamm, Lourdes Martinez-Eschabal, Michael Hanchard, Charles Rowell and Angela Gilliam among the faculty of color.

12. *Representations of Blackness in the Performance of Identity* Ed. Jean Rahier. (Greenwood Press, 1998), 49–67.

13. *Moving Beyond Boundaries. Volume 1. International Dimensions of Black Women's Writing.* Edited and introduced by Carole Boyce Davies and Molara Ogundipe-Leslie (Pluto Press/NYU Press, 1995), 207.

14. "Afro Brazilian Women, Culture and Literature. An Introduction and Conversation with Miriam Alves." *MaComère. Journal of the Association of Caribbean Women Writers and Scholars* 1:1(1998): 57–74.

15. São Paulo. Editora Vozes, 1990.

16. The result was poetry from Miriam Alves, Lia Viera, Conceição Evaristo, Esmeralda Ribeiro, Sônia Fátima da Conceição, Roseli da Cruz Nascimento, included in the anthology I co-edited with Molara Ogundipe titled *Moving Beyond Boundaries. International Dimensions of Black Women's Writing* (NYU Press, 1995), 116–123; 203–213; an interview with Miriam Alves, "Afro Brazilian Women, Culture and Literature. An Introduction and Conversation with Miriam Alves." *MaComère. Journal*

of the Association of Caribbean Women Writers and Scholars 1:1(1998): 57–74; and an essay on women in carnival in Salvador-Bahia, titled, "Re-/Presenting Black Female Identity in Brazil: Filhas de Oxum in Bahia Carnival," in *Representations of Blackness in the Performance of Identity* Ed. Jean Rahier. (Greenwood Press, 1998), 49–67.

17. Unpublished conversation in her office, June, 1993.

18. See interview with Taliria Petrone and Nilcemar Nogueira in https://apublica .org/2018/08/negras-no-poder/

19. Ibid.

20. Ibid.

21. Maria Aparecida Schumaher, *Dicionario mulheres do Brasil*. De 1500 ate atualidade. 2nd edition Rio de Janeiro; Zahar, 2000 and *Geledes Portal*: 13 mulheres brasileiras de destaque na politica.

22. Gonzalez 1988a, translation of Perry and Sotero.

23. Unpublished paper presented at the Black Women's Intellectual Contributions to the Americas conference at University of Texas, Austin, February 2020.

24. *Gender & History*, 30(1) (March 2018): 255–270.

25. https://Blackbraziltoday.com/in-brazil-we-speak-pretogues/ contains sections from her 1988 essay on this.

26. https://Blackbraziltoday.com/in-brazil-we-speak-pretogues/

27. See "From Masquerade to Maskarade. Caribbean Cultural Resistance and the Re-humanizing Project." Katherine Mc Kittrick, ed. *Sylvia Wynter. On Being Human as Praxis* (Duke University Press, 2015), 203–225.

28. Conversations with Eulalia Bernard at ACWWS Conference, Miami, Florida, 2006. According to Eulalia, she and Lélia challenged the major Pan-African activist intellectuals, many of whom had white wives, that their wives should not be part of official proceedings. They were both seen then as controversially wanting to exclude white women, but in reality they were arguing for a distinction between women who were just accompanying men and those who were intellectual activists and delegates to the conference and therefore had that authority.

29. https://travellingwomanists.wordpress.com/2011/03/03/learning-with-lelia -gonzalez-in-defense-of-the-afro-latin-feminism/https://travellingwomanists .wordpress.com/2011/03/03/learning-with-lelia-gonzalez-in-defense-of-the-afro-latin -feminism/

30. The same translation is carried on the Black Brazil Today website: https:// Blackbraziltoday.com/happy-birthday-lelia-gonzalez-2/

31. According to Keisha-Khan Perry recently republished in *Lélia Gonzalez: Primavera Para As Rosas Negras* (2018).

32. Colloquial for "neighborhood," so more like "hood" in urban African-American expression.

33. Sant'Anna and Perry's translation of "The Black Woman: A Portrait."

34. See the new work of Koa Beck, *White Feminism: From the Suffragettes to Influencers Who They Leave Behind*. Atria Books, 2021.

35. https://www.aaihs.org/afro-brazilian-feminists-and-the-fight-for-racial-and -gender-inclusion/ February 2, 2017.

36. Keynote lecture at conference "Black Women's Intellectual Contributions to the Americas: Perspectives from the (Global) South," The University of Texas at Austin, February 2020; comment in response to my work.

37. Keisha-Khan Perry indicates in the introduction to "Translation of 'The Black Woman: A Portrait'" that the writers included were Kia L. Caldwell, Wendi Muse, Tianna Paschel, Keish-Khan Y. Perry, Christen A. Smith, and Erica L. Williams. *Feminist Anthropology*, 2020 (online journal).

38. Audre Lorde, in interview with Pratibha Parmar and Jackie Kay in *Charting the Journey. Writing by Black and Third World Women* (London: Sheba Feminist Publishers, 1988), 129–181. Cited in preface to *Moving Beyond Boundaries,* v.1. *International Dimensions of Black Women's Writing,* xix.

39. Angela Gilliam and O. Gilliam, "Negociando a subjetividade da mulatta." *Estudos Feministas* 3(2): 479–489. I had the benefit of engaging with and listening to Angela Gilliam as she worked through these issues during our joint participation in the NEH group that visited and studied Brazil in the 1990's. Of particular note was how she saw this identity problematized in her own life and her daughter's, confirming that the mulatta identity is a particular racialized, sexual identity in which Black women are located at a particular portion of their life spectrum.

40. https://www.npr.org/sections/parallels/2016/09/29/495665329/for-affirmative -action-brazil-sets-up-controversial-boards-to-determine-race See also "Brazil approves affirmative action law for universities" *BBC News*, August 8, 2012.

41. Published in *The Black Scholar,* March 23, 2018, and authored by a number of Black scholars who work on Brazilian subjects:

Kia L. Caldwell, African, African American & Diaspora Studies, UNC-Chapel Hill

Wendi Muse, History, New York University

Tianna S. Paschel, African American Studies, UC-Berkeley

Keisha-Khan Y. Perry, Africana Studies, Brown University

Christen A. Smith, African and African Diaspora Studies and Anthropology, University of Texas at Austin

Erica L. Williams, Sociology and Anthropology, Spelman College

42. "Black Left Feminist Claims. Towards a New Genealogy," The University of Texas at Austin, February 2020.

43. See interview by Juliane Gouveia on November 23, 2016, available at https: //www.anf.org.br/entrevista-marielle-franco/

44. *New Left Review* 110 (March-April, 2018).

45. Ibid.

46. Both essays are available in *Claudia Jones. Beyond Containment* (74–89).

47. Articles and presentations of Marielle await assemblage and publication. Meanwhile, what is available are lists of her words and videos of her presentations.

48. According to the statement "As councilwoman and president of the Women's Commission, Franco stood in opposition to amendments 67, 68, 69, 137, and 139, which aimed to remove the words 'gender,' 'sexuality,' and 'generation' from the Municipal Education Plan."

49. *Open Cultural Studies* (University of West London, May 4), 50–58.

50. Entrevistamos Marielle Franco: mulher, negra, periférica e Vereadora do RJ—Mulheres na Política #1 *Revista Sujetiva*, May 16, 2017. https://medium.com /revista-subjetiva/entrevistamos-marielle-franco-mulher-negra-perif%C3%A9rica-e -vereadora-do-rj-mulheres-na-pol%C3%ADtica-7839b7fbfe06

See also: https://www.anf.org.br/entrevista-marielle-franco/ and https://www .espacocoruja.mariellefranco.com.br/

51. Entrevistamos Marielle Franco: mulher, negra, periférica e Vereadora do RJ— Mulheres na Política #1 *Revista Sujetiva*, May 16, 2017.

https://medium.com/revista-subjetiva/entrevistamos-marielle-franco-mulher-negra -perif%C3%A9rica-e-vereadora-do-rj-mulheres-na-pol%C3%ADtica-7839b7fbfe06

52. Translation courtesy of Eudes Lopes, Brazilian anthropologist on 3/7/2022.

53. https://Blackbraziltoday.com/journalist-teacher-and-the-first-Black-woman/

54. https://Blackbraziltoday.com/the-first-Black-woman-elected-to-sao-paulos/

55. Marielle Franco's "After the Takeover" makes this point as well. And this point is advanced by Monica, her partner Monica Benicio in her April 2019 statement to the European Lesbian Conference: "Many women in the 2018 election took to the streets with the motto #EleNão (Not Him) against misogynistic arguments, the project of total militarization of everyday life, and against attacks on the rights of the current president and in defense of democracy." https://europeanlesbianconference.org/ keynote-speech-of-monica-benicio-at-opening-of-elc/

56. Chacel, Julian, ed. *Brazil's Economic and Political Future*. Westview Press, 1988. Personal Communication with Vanicléia Silva Santos.

57. See her Perfil Olivia Santana: http://www/a1.ba.gov.br/deputados/ deputadi-estadual/926908 and Campanha de mulher: Olivia Santana, in https:// campanhademulher.org/olivia-santana

58. Nadia Brown, *Sisters in the Statehouse* (2014).

59. Sydney Bauer, "Interview—Widow of murdered LGBT+ politician in Brazil vows to combat hate with election win," Reuters, November 26, 2020. See also Dalila Fernandes de Negreiros "Marielle Franco's Seeds: Black Women and the 2020 Brazilian Election" https://nacla.org/Black-women-Brazil-2020-elections and Manuela Andreoni, "After Marielle, These Black Women Are Changing the Face of Brazilian Politics" https://www.americasquarterly.org/article/after-marielle-these-Black -women-are-changing-the-face-of-brazilian-politics/ (January 24, 2019).

60. "Renata Souza ocupa ruas neste sábado e lembra aniversário do assassinato de Marielle Franco" *Larissa Ventura*, 13 de novembro de 2020, https://diariodorio .com/renata-souza-ocupa-ruas-neste-sabado-e-lembra-aniversario-do-assassinato-de -marielle-franco/

61. https://www1.folha.uol.com.br/poder/2020/12/ameacada-de-morte-deputada -enfrenta-luto-por-marielle-e-pela-perda-da-propria-liberdade.shtml; "Ameaçada de morte, deputada enfrenta luto por Marielle e pela perda da própria liberdade" Folha de São Paulo, December 21, 2020 and https://www.uol.com.br/universa/noticias /redacao/2020/10/15/taliria-petrone-deputada-do-rio-diz-estar-exausta-e-com-medo -das-ameacas.htm

62. *Enfim Nos/Finally Us* was the title of the first book of poetry edited by Miriam Alves, deliberately applied here given its sentiment on the ways that Black women are

finally included in literary canons as in political leadership principles which they often must assert for themselves. See my "Afro-Brazilian Women Culture and Literature: An Introduction and an Interview with Miriam Alves," *Macomere* 1(1998): 57–74.

63. In the context of the COVID-19 pandemic of 2020, being unable to make the physical journey to Brazil myself, my research on Black Women and Political Leadership in Brazil was carried out by my research assistant. In this process, Maira dos Palmares Santana documented the women who have been leaders in the past, from the first-identified Antonieta de Barros, who was elected deputy in 1934 in Santa Catarina, through to the present. In a project that exceeded all my expectations, this work promises to be a book in its own right for Maira, should she be interested in advancing and a larger research project.

64. "Blackwomen, Mothers, Workers: The Frontline of the MTST," *MR online*, posted by Camila Valle and Tainã Góis, https://mronline.org/2020/12/30/Black -women-mothers-workers-the-frontlines-of-the-mtst/

65. Dalila Fernandes de Negreiros, "Marielle Franco's Seeds: Black Women and the 2020 Brazilian Election": North American Congress on Latin America, p. 6. https: //nacla.org/Black-women-Brazil-2020-elections

66. "Tia Ciata" filme/Doc. 26/2017/RJB. Directed by Mariana Campos and Raquel Beatriz. https://www.youtube.com/watch?v=2-5-_6w8EBQ Shared by Eudes Lopes as I was concluding the revisions of this chapter, because of its timing it seemed a reaffirmation from Mae Beata.

Coda

From Cuba to Colombia: Challenges and Possibilities

A Politics of the Possible: "Vivir Sabroso"

I want to maintain here, even as this work has come to a close, that it is critical to always maintain a politics of the possible. Often what seems to come as a surprise is actually the result of steady activist work of building a momentum until we are suddenly, it seems, able to witness another opening. Conjunctural leaps into the future provide myriad possibilities as new realities appear and status quo is no longer ever the same. *Black Women's Rights: Leadership and the Circularities of Power* has argued consistently that the 21st century will be the century of Black women's assumption of leadership. We are twenty years in now and the portals are revealing themselves. This assertion is matched by the evidence visible once we open the lens regionally, globally and diasporically. This study started as an intellectual project generated out of analytical sense and ongoing contradiction that women were being kept from full political leadership while simultaneously acting in leadership capacities often in unidentified ways. Patriarchal power which erased women's full participation was, I observed, sometimes ineffective and often demonstratively inadequate; sometimes violent and at other times benevolent. This final reflection is for me both personal and political; intellectual and experiential. But above all it rejects closure. Instead, it projects into the future several other studies of individual women which will take this conceptual assertion forward.

The rise of Black women in Latin America to national leadership is indeed the result of years of steady activist and community work at the local level. The most recent example of this qualitative leap is the appearance of Francia Elena Márquez Mina who organized and ran independently for the presidency of the South American country of Colombia in a timeframe which parallels this book's ostensible completion and submission. In March, 2022, she had garnered enough votes to be assured a place on the presidential ticket. By mid May, when I headed to Havana, Cuba to fulfill a research/teaching opportunity, her campaign as part of a historic ticket was in full momentum.[1] I had been aware of her only peripherally when a friend gave me one of those campaign promotional bags[2] which she had acquired during a visit to Cuba with a photograph of a Black woman with her fist clenched in her now characteristic position, revealing a bracelet with an indigenous symbol and another with African cowrie shells, wearing a modern dress made with African fabric. The bag's caption said *"Vivir sabroso no es vivir con plata, vivir sabroso es vivir sin miedos."* I read it as: "To live fully and deliciously is not to just to live with money or wealth; To live fully is to live without being afraid of anything." Listening subsequently to Francia's interview elaborations of *"vivir sabroso"* it included, to live in peace, to live in dignity, without fear, and especially for Black people, to live within their culture without the dominance of the classism that defines our societies, with guaranties of security and of rights. Here is a translation of her definition of *Vivir sabroso* which circulates widely now on social media:

> Marquez Mina: I don't think living a good life has anything to do with having a house. Thank God I have a house of dignity. So, if you're thinking this impoverished woman now gets presidential housing she is living the life, you are misinformed. That is part of the classism of this country if you're looking at it from that angle. And I invite you to reflect about what it means to "live the life" for Black people at the core of our ethnic and cultural base. It has to do with living without fear, it means living with dignity, it means living with guaranteed rights. So, when you situate me with the idea that I am suddenly living lavish because I can stay in a presidential house you definitely have gotten it wrong. Surely living a good life would mean that I could live in my own home with the guarantee of living safely in my home and perhaps without so many armed people. Because that's not living well, that's not living the life. Being surrounded with 30 armed people that's not living the life . . . I didn't get into this political career for personal power . . .[3]

Taken by this seemingly brave and conscious Black woman who lived the African diaspora experience fully and by her presence and activism in confronting one of the most violent political machineries without fear, I viewed a few available videos in which she laid out a series of concerns. Environmental degradation, white male supremacist patriarchy, the violence of poverty, mass incarceration the denial of rights of the Black community led a panoply of issues that accompanied the demand for human rights, racial justice, woman's rights and her vision and activism in response to the combination of oppressions.

In mid-May, I headed off to Havana, Cuba, with the aim of completing some much-needed research on Black women and political leadership, and fulfilling a visiting professorship that I had been invited to do in 2019, before the COVID-19 epidemic intervened and had most of us working from home and unable to travel. Still, during the long days which became months of isolation, this manuscript was completed and submitted to press at the start of this year. Not a scholar of Cuban history or politics, as say Ada Ferrer, author of *Cuba. An American History*,[4] I felt that at least if I knew something about women and leadership in Cuba it would mitigate a knowledge gap that I knew had to be filled on Black women and political representation in Latin America. Arriving in Havana, I spent an intense month teaching, reading, and having conversations with several women in leadership positions, in public and private sectors: activists, scholars, researchers, artists, academic leaders. By the time I returned to the United States in June, Francia Marquez was in the final stages of a run-off election and her ticket with Gustavo Petro, "Pacto Histórico," had a good chance of winning, though mainstream US media still cautiously speculated that it would be difficult for the left to win and instead, the opponent already facing charges of corruption, would consolidate the right and win at the final elections. Still, for me it bode well that "Pacto Histórico" was in the lead with 40% of votes in the first round of elections and had developed a huge following and above all could, with Francia, mobilize the Black and indigenous vote. Francia Márquez, became the first Black woman to be elected to be vice president of Colombia on June 19, 2022.

The title of this coda, "From Cuba to Colombia," is deliberate then as it serves both as a personal and intellectual journey: the first since I have visited various regions of both Colombia and Cuba, and could testify to what I saw in terms of Black representation in both contexts and the second to indicate that outside of US narrative and policy, Cuba serves as a good example of the politics of the possible in Caribbean and Latin American political contexts.

The Black populations of Latin America remained unaccounted for as in other South American countries until scholarship like *No Longer Invisible*[5] provided the actual demographics which has actually led to a field of Afro-Latin American Studies still not fully accounted for in most African American/Africana/Black Studies or Latin American Studies Departments and Programs in the United States where African American is limited to the United States. In actuality, these Black communities often remained impoverished and exploited several preferring the self-management of former *palenques, quilombos* and *cumbes* (maroon communities) with leaders advancing the conceptually-related *el palenquismo* a counterpart to the Afro-Brazilian *o quilhombismo* as defined by Abdias do Nascimento[6] as a conceptual language and framework for cultural work and activism. Still there has been consistent organizing of Black communities, some led by Black women engaged in actions such as long public marches against environmental degradations.

While the absent Black community in Latin America is more fully visible now in the presence of Francia Elena Márquez; she is not a singular figure but the face of a larger community. There are also other examples of Black women's leadership in Latin America that continue to remain unrecognized. Costa Rica has already had a Black woman, Epsy Campbell Barr as that country's first female Vice President, from May 2018 to May 2022.[7] A supporter of Francia, she is, in actuality, the first Black woman to be Vice President of a continental American country, before Kamala Harris, if we widen the lens to take in the entire Americas. Indeed across Costa Rica, particularly in the Afro-Caribbean community of Limón, following the Pan-African literary work of poet Eulalia Bernard (1935–2021),[8] one sees the rise of Black women in leadership as mayors such as Maureen Cecilia Clarke (2003–2009) who served as Ministra de la Condición de la Mujer, Ministra de Justicia y Gracia, Ministra de Gobernación y Policía and has worked as an adviser in the Legislative Assembly. Described as a Black feminist activist, Maureen Cecilia Clarke has coordinated the Central American network of Indigenous and Rural women and has been the Executive President of the National Women's Institute and President of the Inter-American Commission of Women of the OAS. Significantly as well, Clarke has been an advocate of gender equality laws in Costa Rica and has been instrumental to the passing of bills such as one against street harassment of women and against gender discrimination in public sectors. Similarly, Martha Johnson the current governor of Limon is identified as well as connected to the Black feminist movements with a focus on equality and emancipation for Black women in Costa Rica.[9]

PARITY IN PARLIAMENTARY GENDER REPRESENTATION: THE CUBAN MODEL

As quiet as it is kept from the international community, the statistics reveal that Cuba attained parity in gender representation in 2019 with 53.2% women in parliament according to United Nations Women in Politics 2019. The Inter-parliamentary Union records Cuba as having 53.41% as of March 2022.[10] In many ways Cuba serves as example, for the Caribbean and Latin America, both positively in terms of accomplishments and negatively as it pertains to the economic isolation it faced for its political choices, Still, the US blockade and limitations of access to Cuba has worked at times in their favor as it allowed a quiet and deliberate series of movements which now position Black representation beyond the longstanding critique, also by Black activists in the United States, that enough has not been done on racial inequity. While there remains some remnants of the historical racial inequities that still impact the Americas, the story of Black women's representation in Cuba reveals a series of political gains since the victory of its revolution in 1959. Currently holding the second highest statistic for leadership of women at 53%, many of these gains began to be implemented in revolutionary Cuba in which women's rights was always an important component.

Yet the historical representation of masculinity and leadership remains imprinted on the landscape. In Vedado, a sprawling urban neighborhood which blurs into central Havana, the major and historic *Avenida de los Presidentes* borders an extensive presentation of Latin American leaders throughout history which comes across like a parade of sculptures of presidents, all men shown in positions of power: on horseback, in oratorical postures, that dominate and punctuate a lovely walking plaza. And in downtown Havana, near the capitol, another park reveals an additional series of famous Latin American leaders, including a prominent bust of Toussaint l'Ouverture, liberator of Hayti. By contrast, when I visited the burial site of Fidel, in Santiago de Cuba, with a Cornell student group in 2018, his final resting place was a large rock with only his first name, *Fidel,* indicated on a modest plaque in the front. Still public photographic representations of Fidel are ubiquitous across Havana, as are representations of the bust of Jose Marti, Cuba's national hero, on walls, posters, in buildings, on street murals. There is no comparable representation of women as leaders though billboards and posters include women and girls to demonstrate popular accomplishments.

In 2018 in a tour of the Angolan Museum of Military History as part of a UNESCO *General History of Africa* delegation, I was struck by the photographic images of Cuban women soldiers returning home after their major service in the liberation of that country. From all accounts, women's role in actually ensuring the success of the Cuban revolution in its early days accompanied a demand for full participation.[11] Similarly, in museums across Cuba, documentation of women's participation in shaping the country proliferate from literacy programs to military service.

While Fidel is seen as the quintessential charismatic leader,[12] he himself offers good analysis of the theoretics and praxis of leadership. In one of his extended interviews, this one conducted by Jeffrey M. Elliot and former U.S. Caribbean-American congressman Mervyn Dymally (1986),[13] he is asked: "What qualities make for a great leader? [And] Do you believe you have those qualities?" (37). In response, he offers a very nuanced and detailed analysis of different types of leadership and concludes that, ". . . you can't describe a leader with any one model" (38). Additionally, "many people," he concludes, "have leadership qualities" which circumstances produce and/or have to be brought out and cultivated" (40). Still Fidel Castro's model of leadership combined the charismatic and the patriarchal as liberator, benevolent father, successful military leader of the Cuban revolution and the attempted *Playa de Giron* (Bay of Pigs) attempted incursion and rhetorical challenger of United States imperialism.

Yet, the founding of the Cuban Federation of Women in 1960, is seen as the genesis of women's advancement. His speech at its first conference is still relevant to this discussion:

> Women in society have interests which are common to all members of society but they also have interests which are their own interests as women. Above all, when the creation of a different society is attempted, to organize a better world for all human beings, the women have great interests in that effort; among other things, the women constitute a sector which was discriminated against in the capitalist world in which we lived. In the world we are building it is necessary that every vestige of discrimination against women disappear. However, even if from the legal and from objective points of view all vestiges of discrimination were to disappear, there would still remain a number of circumstances of natural order and of custom which make it important for the women to be organized, to work, and to struggle. (October 2, 1962)[14]

The rise of women, in general, to leadership positions in Cuba, then, is perhaps the most hidden detail in the current global women's movement. Additionally, as we identify Black women as leaders one can also trace a slower but gradual movement of African-descended Cubans into more definite visible political locations within the last decade and into the current generation. Today, Inés Maria Chapman, is one of four Vice-Prime Ministers or Deputy Prime Ministers and Vice President of the Council of Ministers. Her charge, we learn, is also to ensure racial and gender representation in the society at large. Joel Quirpo Ruiz, Member of the Communist Party's Central Committee, serves as its Secretary. Within the parliamentary representation, Ena Elsa Velazquez leads the Ministry of Education and Nayra Arevich, Ministry of Communication; all the members of the Ministry of Foreign Affairs that I encountered were Black women including Patricia Pego Guerra and Ambassador Inés Fors Fernandez, Director Bilateral Affairs, United States Division.

Kenia Serrano who started her trajectory as a member of the Federation of University Students (FEU) as a youth representative of the Students association became a member of parliament and served in this capacity for years remains energized and very affirmative about the Cuban revolution's gains as it pertains to women and of its future possibilities. Now the Dean of the *Facultad Prepatoria*, at the University of Havana in charge of public education programs, one of her mandates include bringing more Black and urban youth into the educational process by creating community-based educational processes. This is the detailed work that will determine the next generation's ability to transcend all limitations.

Even more significant for my own academic context, a formal welcome meeting with the new *Rectora* (President) Miriam Nicardo Garcia, of the University of Havana provided a direct encounter with and understanding of the nature of Black women's leadership in Cuba. Also a member of the Council of State, she is described as having the ability to represent the University of Havana at the highest governmental level. A mathematician by professional affiliation, her rise was through becoming first a Dean of her school and then to the position of *Rectora*. Dr. Miriam Nicado Garcia, *Rectora de la Universidad de la Habana* and *Miembro del Consejo de Estado* (President of the University of Havana and Member of the Council of State), is a Black woman who represented well her leadership status. Consistently, she provided a very courteous, friendly, humble yet confidently proud sense of herself as a Black woman leader. Thus, in my assessment, she combines both aspects of positive transformative leadership at an academic and at a political and personal level. In my meeting with her when asked about women and leadership in Cuba, she not only proudly identified the range of women in leadership in Cuba, but detailed women's leadership in the university and also consistently underlined the presence of Black women in each of these contexts.

The logic of a "revolution inside a revolution is how some describe Cuban women's movement."[15] Thus, for scholars, researchers and activists in Cuba, the Cuban Federation of Women was central to this movement, guided by the initial impetus of its founding in the context of the Cuban Revolution and testified by Fidel Castro's speech to their first congress cited above. As a result, for all the women of the research unit of the Cuban Federation of Women with whom I talked,[16] it is less the idea of simply putting any women into leadership, but a process of women moving into leadership at local levels, exceling and being tapped for more advanced leadership positions based on proven records. Texts like *Mujeres Cubanas 1958–2008. Estadisticas y Realidades,* which I was given after a visit to one of their offices provide documentation of the steady participation of women in all sectors, including one statistic that shows that the majority of medical doctors in Cuba are now women. The Cuban Federation of Women, now a mature organization, functions as a lobbying group for women in general and provides the bases for policies and advantages for women to move forward. Women's participation is also structured, following their political system, with local leadership elected in each community which connect with the municipality and then to the national level. Leadership skills are cultivated formally and ideologically and women are promoted to higher levels based on the outcome of their preparation. In answer to the question: What was the percentage of Black women in leadership in Cuba, I was told that 21% of women in leadership are Afro descended women. And: Is it generational? Where are younger women? We learn that there are 35% of young women in leadership and the number is steadily increasing. Still the question of power remains as one consistently to be advanced. Thus the role of Teresa Amarelle Boye, Chair of the Federation of Cuban Women, is seen as significant as she is as well a Member of the Central Committee of the Communist Party of Cuba and of the Council of State of Cuba, identified as significant in advancing women's rights and the use of personal power to move policies which benefit women through to realization.

Yet in examining the issue of the representation of Black women in Cuba, the question of racial representation lingers at the popular level and the implications of global structural racism need always to be factored particularly as it pertains to the combination with gender discrimination which Black women experience in local and global contexts. This is significant given that in most socialist or communist contexts, the issue of class equality was seen as having the capacity to ameliorate racial inequalities. This has proven not to be the case anywhere because of the entrenched issues of racism that permeate most societies.

Still, because of those same historical presidential statuary representations bereft of women, indicated above, I was gratified to see, in the Vedado neighborhood in which I stayed, a park dedicated to Mariana Grajales (1808–1893), the mother of the Maceo brothers, the most well-known being Antonio Maceo Grajales (1845–1896), Cuba's legendary Blackgeneral who fought for both Cuban independence and the emancipation of enslaved Africans in Cuba currently represented too with a strong military statue in a prominent location in downtown Havana. The statuary representation of Mariana Grajales[17] presents her as strong Black woman, pointing the way forward as she holds a young man around his arms at waist length.

The study of race in Cuba, by Cuban scholars based in Cuba themselves, as distinct from Cuban expatriates living abroad, was advanced in the scholarship of Gisela Arandia Covarrubias, Afro Latin American, Afro Caribbean and Diaspora Women's Network (*Enlace Cuba de la Red de Mujeres Afrolatinoamericanas, Afrocaribenas y de la Diaspora*) whose work culminated in a doctoral thesis titled *"Estudio teórico crítico del racismo: un modelo de análisis epistemológico y político para el contexto cubano"* (Tesis de Doctorado, 2017).[18] While it addressed the question of race in Cuba sociologically, in her view, it requires all the various disciplines and fields to be brought to bear in studying racism. In a discussion of current manifestations of racism based on her work, she praised the 2010 Government Program for the Elimination of Racism and Racial Discrimination being instituted which she admits has created a more multi-racial society, but indicated a process of advances and delays. Thus, she says in reviewing her ongoing studies:

> During my research on Cuban raciality in Havana and Miami, starting in 1990, I verified the differences and analogies of two identity models opposed in their ideology, but culturally close in terms of this problem. In Cuba, there was a significant advance of people of African descent, particularly in the 1960s, with an inclusive impulse that diminished as the years of utopia passed. I am referring to the literacy campaign, volunteer teachers, revolutionary militias, young rebels, mass projects that mobilized society as a whole and through which people of African descent played a leading role and generated significant changes. These events contributed to the emergence of a new type of raciality, despite the fact that the proposal to which Fidel Castro (1926–2016) aspired for the elimination of racial discrimination made in a televised appearance on March 25, 1959, could not be completed.[19]

For Zuleica Romay Guerra head of Casa de las Americas, African American Division,[20] the social and historical context often determines the responses to racial disparity in Cuba, providing examples from her own family generationally and the larger Black community's response to race. Romay Guerra has a very insightful text "From Afro-Cubans To Black Cubans. Africanity And Skin Color In The Cuban Social Imaginary"[21] which ends with an assertion that both terms are usable: "I was satisfied with a definition that integrates us into the struggles that millions of women and men, descendants of Africans, have fought for almost half a millennium, always in disadvantageous conditions . . . let us be Afro-Cuban as long as it is necessary, if it brings strength and light to the effort to make Cuba a better country" (86).

The dearth of information on Cuba by those living and working outside of the Caribbean and Latin America or Africa, means the larger intellectual community or general public have little knowledge of these movements unless they actually visit or do current research in Cuba itself as was my experience, though literate in other aspects of the African diaspora. Ada Ferrer describes briefly some of the historical limitations as it relates to race: Fidel's initial assertion to eradicate racial discrimination and the "distress occasioned by his speech" which was so strong that Castro was forced to backtrack" (393). The result is a belated but steady movement of Black representation in political leadership. Generally today, there is a steady movement of Afro descendants into political leadership as in the case of Esteban Lazo Hernandez who was visible on news coverage as the head of the parliament while I was in Cuba in May 2022.[22] Contemporary Cuba is a recognizably demographically Afro-descendent and racially mixed Caribbean country which means one expects more physical representation of diversity in leadership. But racism and colorism its descendant is an issue which still plagues other countries across the world. Yet, there is tremendous pride for example at the presence of Esteban Lazo Hernandez the current President of the National Parliament (*Presidente de la Asamblea Nacional del Poder Popular*). From all accounts, Lazo as he was affectionately referred to, is a man who has worked for years in the context of the sustenance of the Cuban Revolution. Additionally, another Black man, Salvador Valdes Mesa is Vice President of Cuba as is Inés Maria Chapman, Vice President of the Council of Ministers with the responsibility for governmental activity and affairs who leads the National Program for the Advancement of Women with impact also on the National Program Against Racism and for the Racial Rights.[23] Dr. Julio Guerra Izquierdo Condecorado, a Black man was the chief of the medical mission of Cuba to Italy at the height of the COVID-19 epidemic which was honored for this contribution by the Italian government during the time of my stay in Havana.

Conversations with young Black women scholar-activists such as Aracelys Rodríguez Malagón, researcher in the Instituto Cubano de Filosofia, Analoy Lafargue Cau, a researcher with the Federación de Mujeres Cubanas, both working on analyses between the theory and the practice of the rights of Black women revealed a shared understanding of the need to better account for the work of activists against racism in Cuba and the need to do comparative work with other locations. Many young women feel that the Federation of Cuban Women still needs to understand and account for the different iterations of feminism in its various global formations and inter-pretations, and thereby achieve a much needed gender/racial transversaliza-tion. *Transversality*, a term Cuban scholars seemed to use in preference to *intersectionality*, becomes significant particularly as it emanates from new materialism discourses.[24]

Still as usual, there is always the caution that because there are women in power, there is no assumption that they will be feminists or will work on the issues that pertain to women; the same on issues of Blackness. If we use the United States African American experience as example, since it served for a long time as the vanguard of racial representation, we can learn from the extreme flaws in this approach. More in-depth analyses will be generated as one studies the actual practices of those in leadership positions over time as indicated at the outset. As in post-independence Africa or Caribbean, one cannot make an automatic assumption that one's ethnic or racial or gender identity will impact one's politics in support of that group's interests or offer a consistent ideological praxis.

In Cuba though, several internal battles have been fought and won by women. For example, legal battles have produced a Penal Code that states that there should be no violence against women and a Family Code that has been updated and is described as the best across the Americas. The Program for the Advancement of Women in Cuba with strategies against gender violence which was approved last September 2021 attains significance in these gains. The new Families Code, after revision for appropriate language and concepts in a nation-wide people's participatory process, was approved by the parliament members in June 2022 and will be voted in a people's referendum in August, 2022. The draft of the new Families Code has changed the structure of marriage as between a man and a woman to marriage between two people. Interestingly transgender rights have been identified in Western media but as advanced by the daughter of Raul Castro, Mariela Castro, a gay-rights advocate, member of Cuba's National Assembly and head of the country's institute of sex education. Unlike in the United States, particularly recent ominous Supreme Court decisions in June 2022, women have reproductive rights to control their bodies, abortion is not illegal, which was already an achievement of the Revolution which made abortions available at public facilities in hospitals and protected women's privacy in the control of their own bodies and provided child care and educational facilities of excellent quality.[25] Because Cuba has a very advanced medical system, women have several options to get care at local or national facilities.

Cultural representation is evident in another generation working fluently in social media with global connections on the valorization of Black culture as does Adriana Garcia from nearby artistic center Guanabacoa, the CEO of Beyond Roots, who has a base in *Havana Vieja* and is passionate about strategies to care for the Black body, inventing techniques to enhance and style Black women's hair naturally, maintaining clarity of mind, joy and a confidence in a sense of self. For this generation of young Black women, the real gains and challenges of the Cuban Revolution have to be spread so that young Cubans understand what they have to fight to keep.

Still a filmmaker like Gloria Rolando[26] despite her international reputation and wide range of successful films, often operates as do many independent filmmakers globally on budgets that have to be crafted to achieve the final product. Perhaps this is the strength of independent filmmaking everywhere. Yet work would be less tedious if there is more visible support of cultural workers who like Gloria the only Black woman in the Cuban Film Institute with a series of films, each exploring aspects of Black history in Cuba which have received international recognition, appointed to the American Film Academy in 2019, even as she herself lives in very modest circumstances within an urban working class community in which she functions often as one of the community's beacons. Her film "Dialogue with My Grandmother, 1912: Breaking the Silence, Chapter 1" traces her ancestral history with Africa as place of origin. Her current film project in process is on the Black nun soon to be canonized, Mother Maria Lange of the Oblate sisters (www .oblatesisters.com) founder of the Hermanas Oblatas de la Providencia who opened a high school for Black girls in Santiago de Cuba as she also had in Baltimore, Maryland, with the idea of providing educational pathways for the Black community.

For Nancy Morejón, Cuba's premier poet and a leading and well-represented representation of Black women's history and identity in her poetry such as the now classic "Mujer Negra" as in her life, there is a certain assurance and confidence in her own status in terms of simultaneous Cuban belonging and international recognition.[27] A steady rise of Black women to positions of leadership in many sectors (media, government, university administration) has happened in the last two decades.

Still all of these moves operate against the shadow of the US embargo following Cuba's post-revolutionary history even at the level of finding the exact shade of make up when one is denied access to the popular and more extensive range of shades that African American women have developed also over the last two decades. Brands like Fenty Beauty with a more extensive palette of shades for Black women, developed by Barbadian singer and national icon Rihanna are not yet available. Carmen Pacheco for example is creating her own cosmetic line as part of her project to provide make up using appropriate shades of foundation for Cuban women in her Carmen Pataki Company. I was happy to add to her cosmetic collection, an extra red Sacha (Trinidad and Tobago) lip color that I had brought with me precisely for such a recipient. I was overjoyed when I saw a beautiful and well-presented, perfectly coifed and made-up professional Black woman, Lissett Fillu Tellez [@filluT] anchoring the Cubavision's prime time news, with one of the sign language translators also as a Black woman, during one of my first nights in Havana. I quickly took her photo to share on social media with my friends. On the streets I observed how the continuing impact of the US blockade impacts the working poor even as they find creative ways around these limitations to achieve the economic necessities for daily living. Still people are often stylishly dressed wearing contemporary European fashion even as private second-hand (somewhat vintage) clothing sales are apparent. As usual, there is a natural love that people have for their native lands, and sometimes historical challenges often make like difficult wherever we are across the African diaspora, given the history of our arrival in the Americas and the various serious levels of oppression we have experienced and over which we still triumph.

"SOY PORQUE SOMOS"/I AM BECAUSE WE ARE

In the country of Colombia where Francia Márquez made a giant leap by running for president, and being elected vice president like other continental

American countries, there is an African-descended Black population the product of transatlantic enslavement from the 15th century onwards and subsequent European and North American colonialism and ongoing neo-liberal operations. While having one of the largest populations of Africans in the Americas, following Brazil, Afro-Colombians are nonetheless marginalized as non-existent, remain impoverished with a surprising visibility perhaps only during the regional or world cups for football (soccer) when one finally sees a large Black representation.

Perhaps most endearing is that as this aspect of the history of Black women in Latin America unfolds, we learn that Francia Márquez had started her activism in response to the attempt of a mining company to destroy her community. In a videotaped tri-locational interview with scholar-activist, Angela Y. Davis,[28] they highlighted her many positions on the displacement of indigenous people, mass incarceration of those same displaced people and the appropriation of land on which African and indigenous people had cultivated and lived for many years for the benefit of capitalist greed. All of these ills functioned collaboratively with a variety of governments over the years.

Of relevance to this book's theme is that Francia Márquez sees the leadership of Black women who make it to political power as not just personal accomplishments. Instead, she asserted then as she does now that once in power there is an imperative to represent more fully and that Black women who get to leadership have to be conscious of their leadership and its impact on communities beyond the individual. The message to those who would seek leadership power is deliberate: your acquisition of leadership is based on historic struggle of activist women in the United States, and various parts of the world, who struggled for social change in the lives of people who have been excluded and oppressed. Thus, one with an access to power should be an advocate, representing the need for peace and the end to the circulation of violence around the world. In her words, "To occupy the state is not the end; the end is to bring dignity to life, to care for life, to have more just spaces, to end the murder of the planet. Occupying the state is just a means for the struggles that we continue as a people, the struggles that are needed by humanity and for this planet."[29]

Testifying to the circularities of power which is this book's theme, I note that it is significant then that the Francia Márquez campaign motto translated the Ubuntu philosophical position, "I am, because we are," also used by Marielle Franco in Brazil, which Latin Americans now casually mouth "Soy porque somos."[30] Thereby, a particular African philosophical formation is translated and activated diasporically.[31] The echoes of Wangari Maathai, in self-presentation, language, personal African fashion aesthetic style are unmistakable: anti-imperial, anti-patriarchal, pro-environmental, and for an equitable assumption of Black women's rights to the world's resources are again actualized. Thus Francia's presence provides a tangible representation of what Besi Brillian Muhonja in her book *Radical Utu. Critical Ideas and Ideals of Wangari Muta Maathai*[32] defines as "Theorizing and Activating Utu Citizenships." Indeed, African women it is reported in Kenya have been energized by her victory with now three out of four presidential tickets for elections in August having women as presidential running mates which according to Mshai Mwangola, suddenly positions women for leadership as it did in Tanzania. Additionally, the major party which does not have a woman in its Presidential ticket is now promising parity, belatedly, indicating that 50% of the Cabinet will be reserved for women.[33]

The undying impact of these moves on the global community of Black women cannot be denied. Scholar-activist Angela Y. Davis herself in the discussion with Francia as in her prior assertions on the impact of activist strategies such as that of Marielle Franco in Brazil, reverses the paradigm of North to South influence by saying that some of these global movements should impact or influence Black women's movements in the United States. Thus, the significance of U.S.-based Black feminist scholars who worked as campaign watchers such as Jemima Pierre[34] in her capacity as the co-coordinator of Haiti/Americas Team for the Black Alliance for Peace reports[35] is expressed in her essay "Witnessing and Making History" in which she describes how their team went to observe: "after the results of the March 13, 2022 primary elections in Colombia clearly indicated that the two leading candidates of the leftist 'Pacto Historico' party were Gustavo Petro (a former guerilla activist turned mayor of Bogota) and Francia Márquez, his running mate." The preliminary 40% lead over all other candidates (10% short of the 50% necessary for victory) in the general election, necessitated a follow up run-off election between the leftist candidate Petro and a businessman who was still facing an earlier charge of corruption. In the final elections, following the first run-off Christen A. Smith[36] a scholar of Brazillian and Latin American gender studies accompanied the US group Afro Resistance as an observer of the elections, and was in place to witness Francia's victory.

It is easy to conclude then that Francia Márquez while she still faces the predictable combined racial and gendered discriminations, nonetheless, has also changed the expectations, language and culture of leadership in the African Diaspora, establishing a politics of care which we have also heard from Prime Minister of Barbados, Mia Mottley, as a basic principle. Hers is a praxis of diaspora literacy which VèVè Clark articulated.[37] Her confident position statements have challenged the assumption of white male patriarchy in leadership as the only model to move towards ending what she calls the debilitating effects of capitalist white male supremacy under which her people still suffer. Francia Márquez who had initially run for the presidency on her own and was indicated as the most popular candidate in party primaries, saw her campaign "not as an end but as a means" to achieve education, food, water, social justice, that aims to achieve a full liberation of Afro-Colombians. Leadership she asserts must come from the bottom up which she represents. The historic embodiment of Black woman's rights re-appears in the present.

My research and study of the African diaspora reveal that we are all still in recovery. For example, the new Dia Internacional da Mulher Negra Latino-americana, Caribenha e da Diáspora is a recognition of the need for understanding histories and activism relationally. Having Black woman access political power is only one step along that process of recovery. In such a larger historical context we must continue to study what, if anything, changes when Black women finally access political leadership.

NOTES

1. In the full contemporary mode of communication, Francia's website exists publicly for those wanting to understand the passions and commitments. Because of the recent context of her win, much of the information available exists on social media platforms. Her political website provides details of her political interests. See https://www.franciamarquezmina.com. Thank you Samuel Fiure, my generous host and then chair at University of Havana (FLEX-School of Foreign Languages) for organizing strategic interviews at community, university and other institutional levels and for reading this coda for accuracy quickly and above all supporting and encouraging this coda's and thereby Cuba's inclusion in this project. What a great outcome!

2. Thank you, Rosemari Mealy author of *Fidel and Malcolm,* Fidel and Malcolm X-Memories of A Meeting (Black Classic Press, 2014) and of "'Affirming the Right to be Revolutionary.' Assata: An Interview" in *Moving Beyond Boundaries.v.2. Black Women's Diasporas.* Ed. Carole Boyce Davies (NYU Press, 1995), 89–93.

3. Because of her recent electoral victory, a great deal of information on Francia Márquez Mina circulated on social media. This is her response to an interviewer indicated as at Noticentro 1, Bogotá, Colombia @CMILANOTICIA. Thank you to Jessica Alarcon for translation. This is the full translation of the exchange from Cornell graduate student Gina de la Rocha Goico:

Camila: [. . .] In the house that exists for the person who holds the position of vice president of the nation. My question is, if you are going to move to that house that is a block away, to the west, from the palace of Nariño, or if that does not entail what you call *"vivir sabroso"*?

Francia Marquez: Umm, I do not believe that *"vivir sabroso"* means to live in a house. Today, thank God I can say I have a decent house. So, if you believe that because I am an impoverished woman, and I now get presidential housing, is what will make *"vivir sabroso,"* you are mistaken. That [belief] is part of the classism in this country if you see it from that perspective.

I invite you to reflect on what does it mean the *"vivir sabroso"* for Black people. Within our entrails, in our cultural and ethnic identity, [*vivir sabroso*] means to live without fear, it means to live with dignity, to have guaranteed rights. So, when you put it as if I am going to *"vivir sabroso"* now because I will be living in the vice-presidential house, you are definitely mistaken.

Surely, *"vivir sabroso"* is me being able to live in my own house; it [*vivir sabroso*] would mean for me to have my security guaranteed in my own house, without having to count with armed people to protect me. That is not good living, that is not *"vivir sabroso."* Having to live everyday with 30 armed people is not *sabroso.*

Camila: [interrupting] Mrs Vice-President. Allow me to take advantage of these seconds left to ensure that what you understood is not what I was intending to ask you, of course, but as a way to ask you if you are indeed going to live in the vice-presidential house that is available for you or if you will be living in Cali? Or how are you going to be handling your housing since you have been a woman from the region?

Francia Marquez: That is a topic [. . .] That is a different question to what you posed to me in the beginning. With all due respect, I did not do this political career for a position in office. I wish I could be able to stay back in Yolombo, back there in my community. I wish I could stay in my territory, undisturbed, working the land [. . .]

4. Ada Ferrer, New York University professor won the Pulitzer Prize for *Cuba. An American History* (Scribner, 2021). Ferrer offers a concise overview of the movement of women into active participation in the society in her "New People" chapter, 389–391.

5. *No Longer Invisible: Afro-Latin Americans Today*. Ed. Minority Rights Group, 1995. In many ways this work was the first major recognition of the need for a field of Afro-Latin American Studies now a central aspect of African Diaspora Studies and Latin American Studies along with several studies of the Black presence in individual countries in Latin America and Brazil. See also, *Blackness in Latin America and the Caribbean.* V.1 & 2 Eds. Norma E Whitten, jr. and Arlene Torres (Bloomington: Indiana University Press, 1998) and entries on various Latin American countries in *The Encyclopedia of the African Diaspora* (Oxford and Santa Barbara: ABC-CLIO, 2008).

6. See his "Quilombo. Vida, Problemas Aspirações do Negro" (facsimile). Rio de Janeiro, nos. 1 & 10, dezembro de 1948 a julho de 1950. Editora 34 2003.

7. Natasha Gordon Chipembere, "Meet Epsy Alejandra Campbell Barr: Costa Rica's First Black Vice President," *Essence Magazine*, December 6, 2020. https://www.essence.com/news/politics/epsy-alejandra-campbell-barr-costa-rica-first-black-vice-president.

8. Ian I. Smart, "Eulalia Bernard: A Caribbean Woman Writer and the Dynamics of Liberation," *Letras Femeninas* 13:1/2 (Primavera-Otono, 1987): 79–85.

9. Personal communication with Myriam Moise, Associate Professor, University of the Antilles, who did a Caribbean connect research visit to Costa Rica in May 2022.

10. www.ipu.org and the Cuba government website: https://www.parlamentocubano.gob.cu/ [accessed June 24, 2022]. The Inter-Parliamentary Union reports that "The Americas are the first region to go above the 30-per-cent threshold, with 31.3 per cent of MPs who are female" and that the current move towards parity worldwide is

still 26.2% based on their Women in Parliament report for 2021 https://www.ipu.org/news/press-releases/2022-03/new-ipu-report-more-women-in-parliament-and-more-countries-with-gender-parity

11. See texts like *Mujeres Cubanas 1958–2008. Estadísticas y Realidades.* Federation de Mujeres Cubanas and Oficina Nacional de *Estadísticas* 2009.

12. See Anton Allahar, ed. *Caribbean Charisma: Reflections on Leadership, Legitimacy and Populist Politics* (Ian Randle, 2001).

13. *Nothing Can Stop the Course of History.* Interview by Jeffrey M. Elliott and Mervyn M. Dymally (New York and London: Pathfinder, 1986).

14. F. Castro, Address to 1st National Congress of Cuban Women, Havana, 1962. Also available in Fidel Castro Ruz, *Mujeres y Revolucion,* as "Discurso en el I Congreso Nacional de la Federacion de Mujeres Cubanas." Federacion de Mujeres Cubanas, La Habana, 2006: 87–92.

15. *Las Mujeres en Cuba Haciendo una revolución dentro de la revolución* is a collection edited by Mary-Alice Walters (Pathfinder Press, 2012).

16. Conversation hosted by Elpidia Moreno, Director del Centro de Estudios de la Federación de Mujeres Cubanas, Vedado, Havana, Cuba.

17. Bordering Calle 23 and 25, between Streets C and D in Vedado, and across from a major pre-university high school.

18. Gisela Arandia Covarrubias, "Estudio teórico crítico del racismo: un modelo de análisis epistemológico y político para el contexto Cubano" (Tesis de Doctorado). La Habana: Editorial Universitaria, 2017. e-ISBN 978-959-16-3466-5.

19. Gisela Arrandia Covarrubias, "Racism and Racial Discrimination in the Cuban Agenda," March 10, 2022. https://www.ipscuba.net/sociedad/racismo-y-discriminacion-racial-en-la-agenda-de-cuba [Accessed 6–21–2022]

20. Zuleica Romay Guerra director of Afro American Studies at Casa de las Americas, organizes a colloquium on Afro-America in its continental understanding, the most recent of which took place in June 2022. Afroamérica en coloquio, por primera vez en la Casa See https://www.afrocubaweb.com/zuleicaromay.htm

21. First published *Revista Brasileira de Estudos Africanos, (Brazilian Journal of African Studies)*| Porto Alegre | v. 3, n. 6, Jul./Dec. 2018 | p. 75–88. available on Afro Cuba Web as in https://core.ac.uk/download/pdf/196619762.pdf March 20, 2019 [Accessed 6/21/2022]

22. Lazo became president of the National Assembly (Parliament) in 2013, and ratified in the following legislature in 2018 https://www.parlamentocubano.gob.cu/juan-esteban-lazo-hernandez [accessed 6/24/2022].

23. "Cuba and Kenya Explore New Areas for Bilateral Cooperation." *Cuban News Agency,* which captions the article: Vice President of the Cuban Council of State and Ministers, Ines Maria Chapman, was also received by Kenya President Uhuru Kenyatta.

25. One of the texts I was given by the Federation of Cuban Women was a pamphlet by Vilma Espin Guillois, identified as Miembro del Comité Central del Partido Comunista de Cuba and Presidenta de la Federación de Mujeres Cabanas. "La Batalla por el Ejercicio Pleno de la Igualdad de la Mujer."

26. See a good listing of her films and her directorial statement on Afro Cuba Web https://afrocubaweb.com/rolbio.htm [accessed 6/24/2022].

27. See Miriam DeCosta Willis, "Orishas Circling Her House: Race as (Con) Text in Morejon's Poetic Discourse." *Moving Beyond Boundaries. v.2. Black Women's Diasporas.* Ed. Carole Boyce Davies (NYU Press, 1995), 97–111.

28. "'I Am Because We Are': A Conversation Between Francia Marquez Mina and Angela Davis" who described visiting her visit in 2010 in solidarity with her with whom she visited in La Toma in 2010 saw her representing Black women in Latin America as facilitated by Mamyrah Prosper for the People's Forum, September 7, 2021. https://www.youtube.com/watch?v=qOLZaA509dI [Accessed May 14, 2022]. Mamyrah Douge-Prosper, of Haitain origin, now a professor at University of California, Irvine, had visited Francia during her environmental activism struggles and had been taken to see the mining and degradation of communities. Thank you Mamyrah for reading this coda and for that great interview you moderated with Francia and Angela Davis.

29. Ibid.

30. https://blackagendareport.com/soy-porque-somos-i-am-because-we-are-black-women-led-and-life-based-project-new-colombia

31. https://www.spreaker.com/show/soy-porque-somos [Accessed 6–22–22]

32. Ohio University Press, 2020: 65–89.

33. Personal Communication from Mshai Mwangola of the African Leadership Centre in Nairobi, Kenya:

> The kind of scrutiny the potential VP candidates are getting in Kenya in general is definitely at a new level, in part at least because of the historic importance of the possibility of having a woman as Deputy President, even though we have previously had women running even for the Presidency before, including the one who is on the ticket that is the current front-runner Martha Karua. (Others preceding her in standing for the presidency itself had been the late Wangari Maathai and Charity Ngilu, but neither's candidacy was considered as realistically viable at the time, partly on the grounds of gender.) We are the last of the original EAC countries to have a woman in that position (and ours is just potentially so) but definitely, it's a whole new season for Black women, and will be interesting to see how those who have the opportunity to serve navigate the promise and pitfalls of political power.

34. Author of *The Predicament of Blackness. Postcolonial Ghana and the Politics of Race* (University of Chicago press), 2012.

35. https://blackagendareport.com/witnessing-and-making-history-observing-2022-presidential-elections-colombia [Accessed 6–21–2022].

36. Author of *Afro-Paradise. Blackness Violence and Performance in Brazil.* University of Illinois Press, 2016.

37. See Brent Hayes Edwards, *The Practice of Diaspora: Literature, Translation, and the Rise of Black Internationalism* (Harvard University Press, 2003); Veve Clark, "Diaspora Literacy," *Encyclopedia of the African Diaspora,* v.2: 382-3; Janis Mayes

professor emerita of Africana Studies at Syracuse University and founder of Paris Noir, defines the cultural practices of African diaspora translation work as "trans-atlantic translation."

Appendix

Selected Conversations with Black Women on Political Leadership

The following conversations are only a sampling based on a larger group of women with whom we have been in conversation. I say *we* because students in my classes on Black Women and Political Leadership have been engaged in ongoing conversations with a range of women in political leadership at the local and global levels. These are available at https://blogs.cornell.edu/ blackwomenlead.

What follows are mostly my own interviews/conversations generated from questionnaires which have guided this project, with responses submitted in writing rather than the more desired back and forth conversation. The only ones with whom I was able to do sit-down conversations were Aminata Dramane Traoré and Her Excellency Ellen Johnson Sirleaf both of which took place before the COVID-19 pandemic of 2020.

I deliberately wanted to include daughters of famous leaders and these are represented here by Samiah Nkrumah and Erica Williams Connell, daughters of post-independence leaders of Africa and the Caribbean, Ghana, and Trinidad and Tobago respectively.

Two phone conversations were done with Honorable Hazelle Rogers and Una Clarke. I conducted an extensive conversation with another former Minister of Culture of Mali, Ndaiye Ramatoulaye Diallo who was on government business in Dakar in June 2019 and she was the first to actually provide detailed written responses for me to all the questions ahead of time, which she embellished when we met. But, since then, the government that she was part of has been deposed and I have not been able to secure a good communication link with her to get her approval to include it in this group. In the process of doing this work though, her support and friendship provided encouragement and further ideas for advancing this project. I visited Dar es Salaam in January 2022 and tried to secure an interview with Honorable Samia Suluhu Hassan but did not do enough advance work to make this happen in time.

Many of the women leaders if in office at the time are so busy that it is difficult to get them to sit down for an extensive interview while they are in the business of governing. There are several others whom I contacted but have not yet been able to schedule interviews. I see this as an ongoing project which will eventually result in a much-needed database of interviews with Black women political leaders all over the world.

A CONVERSATION WITH ELLEN JOHNSON SIRLEAF, PRESIDENT OF LIBERIA, 2006–2018 (NOVEMBER 9, 2018)

I was invited to have a conversation with former president Ellen Johnson Sirleaf,[1] first elected woman head of state in Africa, at her sister's house in Uniondale, New York, in November 2018. The person I met was an elderly woman, casually dressed in beige slacks, not in her public/professional African photographed traditional attire. I realized then that what we see in photographs, especially presidential photographs, are images intended to build larger than life constructions. Still, here was a woman, humbly presented but still strong in her assertions of women's right to leadership. At the time of this interview, Ellen Johnson Sirleaf had already completed her two terms as president, from 2006 to 2018. We talked candidly, and I asked her many of the same questions raised in the introduction to this work and added others specific to her experience of being the first Black woman head of state in Africa. I was struck that the quiet, reflective woman I met had moved beyond all the pomp and circumstance of that role and had become to me like any of the senior women in my family, understated but with much power behind their words. So it was easy to talk with her casually about serious matters while family members were within earshot. Visible from where we sat in the dining room, a young woman was cooking what seemed to be a family meal in a large pot in the kitchen nearby. The former president's sister was the one who welcomed me to her home after I landed at JFK Airport on a quick return flight from a seminar I had led in Germany with Rhoda Reddock at the Justus-Liebig University in Giessen. On arrival in New York, I quickly rented a car and drove with excitement to Uniondale nearby.

My most important takeaway from our conversation was: "Yes, we want the power and if it helps the leadership." An interesting separation of leadership and power, framed within an affirmative sense that women are on a crest, "we have gained a platform and we should take advantage of it" while it lasts. Johnson Sirleaf saw her election to the presidency of Liberia as a "breakthrough" and hoped that it inspires other women. For her, many women are out there who can lead, with much "potential without full education" which bodes well for the future. For her, one limitation that hampers women's leadership is that many African women still lack access to formal education. "Education" is not "intelligence," in her words, but education does provide some of the knowledge and skills needed in leadership. Johnson Sirleaf also feels that women are more resolute once they have made a decision, and that women are more effective in getting things done and producing results.

Women, she believes, have sensitivity to humanity and are concerned about the consequences of not being thoughtful.

I was surprised that she did not share the "glass ceiling" or "concrete ceiling" view (that women have limits to acquiring leadership), finding it too negative a view which locks in conceptually a perpetual number of barriers to success. For Johnson Sirleaf, capacity and determination can overcome obstacles if one is willing to recognize these obstacles and overcome them. "Failing is success upside down," she argues, as Shirley Chisholm did. "It should strengthen you and that's precisely the time the strength will come." For this reason, she felt perceptively that even in her loss, Stacey Abrams held much promise for leadership: even knowing that she had contested an election fairly and it was taken away from her by several unfair practices, her initial loss in her quest for the governorship of the state of Georgia that it did not weaken her but gave her the fortitude to move forward and "established her prominence in leadership." "In the future any woman can feel she can run for governor of Georgia," Johnson Sirleaf said.

What changes when women get to power? "No, or fewer, wars, and violence is brought under control when women are in power. With women in power we can have happier societies."

On members of a subordinated group finally getting power, Johnson Sirleaf said:

> You have an obligation to lead, to set a goal if you have been deprived of leadership before as members of a subordinated group. Yes, there are times when one's values, cultural or otherwise, inform one's decision. And sexuality does often bring negative overtones when applied to leadership, but it is whether you are brave enough in the end to move past all of these social constructions. One should feel compelled and obligated to take charge and by doing this send a strong message that impacts everyone; but above all to motivate women to stand against the status quo.

Finally, she felt that as women we should encourage competence and experience and that a future leader should start deliberately grooming herself for leadership. She thought that we need, to aid this process, a leadership institute, where women learn from each other's mistakes, failures, and successes across Africa and the African Diaspora. Currently examples of Black women in leadership are isolated, occurring in disparate locations across the Caribbean, Latin America, North America, and Africa. She affirmed that history of leadership in Africa where there are women who were "paramount chiefs," and in many extended family systems women can often hold power. Still, we must continue to look for, and at, performance when women are in leadership.

HER EXCELLENCY PAULA WEEKES: FIRST WOMAN PRESIDENT OF TRINIDAD AND TOBAGO, 2018– PRESENT (JULY 23, 2020)

What is leadership in your thinking?

Leadership[2] is first the modelling of desired behavior by the leader in her public and private life. Second, it involves articulating clearly to those being guided the leader's expectations and desired outcomes. And third, assessing the strengths and weaknesses of the cohort in order to facilitate each person to best deliver. In so doing, a leader needs to be firm, though compassionate, observant, flexible and willing to admit her own shortcomings.

Are there issues you are able to address better as a woman?

There are certainly issues that as a woman I would address differently from a man, not that I am sure that is necessarily better. Women generally manage interpersonal relationships better, in my view, using the innate EQ that most of us possess.

Do you use a gender lens when solving problems?

I do not intentionally use a gender lens in problem solving, but I think it is almost inevitable that all of my experiences, including my gender, influence my problem-solving methods.

How do you balance your personal life and professional?

After 14 years at the public and private Bar, I was a Judge of the Supreme Court during the period 1996–2016. I learnt then to balance my personal and professional life by creating distinct lines which included keeping work at the workplace (in so far as possible), developing the ability to say no without apology or explanation, keeping personal and professional friends, largely separate, although that was by way of coincidence, establishing boundaries and pursuing a number of interests that had nothing to do with work.

And what is your advice to young girls and women today trying to figure out how they can balance their lives?

I am mindful in giving advice to young women and girls that being single and without children allowed me to operate in a manner that might not be easy for them, cultivating and maintaining extra-curricular interests that allow for physical and mental release is important. I also advise that young women, on joining a place of work, try to understand the full scope of what is required and work out how much of their time needs to be devoted to work, other activities and rest. This calculation will have to be revisited as responsibilities and circumstances change.

One often ignored factor is the need to find enjoyment in one's work as this helps to make the necessary sacrifices feel less onerous.

Is there a difference between women's leadership and men's use of political power? How would you describe your leadership style?

Open and collaborative, allowing those with competencies in particular areas to take ownership in their field. As President I work with a number of experienced professionals in different fields, e.g., protocol, communication, IT and unless there is good reason, I am guided by them. However, at the end of the day, I bear overall responsibility and so, if I am unable to agree with a view, I make it clear why I am unable to accept it.

In terms of regularity, punctuality and general conduct, I model what I expect of those working with me.

Do you see yourself carrying forward any traditional leadership methods in your various projects?

There are several tried and true traditional leadership methods that serve me well and which I employ with any necessary tweaking, as we execute Office of the President projects.

Do you think anything changes, or will change, when more women get to political power?

I have no doubt. Today, our President of the Senate and Speaker of the House are women, as are roughly 30% of our Parliamentarians. Women are also rising to the top of many national organisations which, while not "political" have effect on political decisions being made. The overall effect has been a subtle change in the method of communication, greater willingness to be collaborative and more sensitivity to the circumstances of women, children and other vulnerable groups in the society.

I believe that these changes will be magnified as more and more women access political power.

**Do you feel that women in positions of power are
scrutinized more heavily on issues such as competence
but also on issues like physical appearance,
clothing, family?**

I do not sense that women in positions of power are scrutinized more fully on competence, and suspect this is because at primary, secondary and tertiary levels, girls and women have been out-stripping their counterparts in significant numbers, including in the STEM fields, except engineering. At the University of the West Indies, female graduates outnumber males 2 to 1.

However, on matters which are often irrelevant to competence, there is unwarranted focus. Physical appearance and sexual orientation are two examples.

Even though my functions in the Judiciary caused both my name and photograph to appear regularly in the print and online media, I was relatively unknown when elected as President. With no information, but that I was unmarried and childless, there was rampant speculation on social media that I was lesbian. There was also curiosity about the make-up of my family. To this day, it baffles me why.

SAMIAH NKRUMAH, DAUGHTER OF GHANA'S FIRST PRIME MINISTER, HON. KWAME NKRUMAH; MEMBER OF PARLIAMENT, 2009–2013; 2020 INDEPENDENT PARLIAMENTARY CANDIDATE (DECEMBER 24, 2021)

**What is leadership in your thinking? Or; How do
you understand leadership based on your experience
as the daughter of one of the 20th century's most
important leaders?**

First of all, I will say, leadership is in my DNA. My father as a leader always exhibited admirable leadership characteristics. So, as I was growing up, I was having the enthusiasm to become a leader. Not to waste time, I will say my leadership came to the green light in 2008. This is when I started active politics in Ghana. In the year 2008, I contested for the parliamentary seat and for the first attempt, I won. So, on the 7th of January, 2009, I joined the parliament of Ghana as a member of parliament. In the year 2011, I was elected as the first woman chairperson of my father's founding party (CONVENTION PEOPLES PARTY). To brief it, I was the first woman chairperson of the party from 2011 to 2015. I was the Member of Parliament for the Jomoro constituency from 2009 t0 2013. In the December 2020 Election, I contested as an Independent parliamentary candidate in my constituency. I have received many awards but a recognition by OTUMFUO OSEI TUTU II and THE MILLENIUM EXCELLENCE FOUNDATION by giving me A LIFE TIME ACHIEVEMENT AWARD has boosted my positive energy to work as a woman leader. I will say this is how my leadership started. I am yearning more to become an African leader as well as a world leader in the years to come.

Are there issues you are able to address better as a woman? Do you use a gender lens when solving problems?

I will say yes. To the issues of gender equality, child rape, domestic violence etc. where women are treated badly, I am able to address cases like this when it comes to my table. As a woman, I know how it feels when a woman is treated in a way which is not encouraging. I have addressed many cases where women leaders were not given attention when it comes to decision making. As a woman leader, I understand the feelings of women and fight for their rights. I also teach them how they can work on their own to become acceptable in the society.

How do you balance your personal life and professional? And what is your advice to young girls today trying to figure out how they can balance their lives?

As a professional journalist and a politician, there are a lot of time-consuming activities but I do not let this negatively affect my personal life. I am a family woman. So, I adjust things so I satisfy the needs of my people as well as my family.

Also I have learnt that, as I work with a lot of people and meet a lot of people, I will come across a lot of stuff which I may not like but I have to adjust to them in order to become a successful leader.

My advice to young girls of today trying to balance their lives is, they should try as much as possible to suppress egotistical tendencies. I don't mean they should please people and harm their selves but rather have listening ears and be humble. They must also know that, one day, they will become what they are aspiring to become. Wherever they find their selves, they shouldn't allow time to be a barrier. They should schedule their time to satisfy everyone. They should put it behind their minds that, not everyone will like what they like so they adjust to everything in order to work progressively.

Is there a difference between women's leadership and men's use of political power?

This is a question I will say it is a controversial one. I will say there is a vast difference between women's leadership and men's leadership by the use of political power. Naturally, women have a caring heart and see their people as their own children and for that matter treat them as such. They therefore serve with kind and parental heart. But to men, I can say they most of the time abuse people with their political power. If I must rate, I will say, 80% of women serve with a caring heart but 90% of men do not serve like that.

How would you describe your leadership style?

In this civilized world, where democracy is paving the way, I go with the democratic leadership style. In my entire leadership, I listen to my people in order to satisfy them accordingly. I have promised myself not to be self-centered. I always come out with my clear visions and make it known to my people. With this, I have been able to achieve a lot. I have always strived to be a leader who helps her people to reach their goals and also bring people who are better than me on board in order to achieve a common goal.

Do you see yourself carrying forward any traditional leadership methods in your various projects?

I will say yes. Yes because, I see most of our traditional leadership in this our modern world as transparent and democratic. I therefore see myself carrying forward the democratic leadership method (traditional) which is helping boost my leadership roles.

Do you think anything changes or will change when women get to political power?

To me, leadership is one's ability to work and motivate others in achieving a common goal. Things really change when women get political power. Political power, in one way or the other, boosts the charisma of women. This in one way or the other, changes their way of thinking and doing things. It boosts their confidence and motivates them to work satisfactorily. They should try as much as possible to do better than the previous male presidents. When this is recorded, women would be fully recognized when it comes to presidency. And I think when they do better than the male presidents, it will be history they are making and by so doing, it will enhance other political women which gradually will make Africa's future a well living.

Do you feel that women in positions of power are scrutinized more heavily on issues such as competence but also on issues like physical appearance, clothing, family?

Starting with competence, I will say yes. Women are being scrutinized heavily. When a woman becomes a leader or comes in power, almost everyone looks up to her to deliver. Especially in Africa, where people have to come to believe that, men should be in power, all eyes are set on women when they are able to come to power. I won't concentrate much on physical appearance because I don't think people emphasize it much. They talk about it if any bad news comes from your camp.

Talking about clothing and family, there have been a lot of criticisms. Especially in areas where the people are looking up to the leader to work massively and it does not go that way, people will begin to talk when they see you in expensive dresses. Most cases in Africa, when they see you taking your children to schools outside the country, they will talk about it bitterly.

Personally, I haven't had much experience with these things except competency whereby your opposition uses it to campaign against you. It might be that, you may not be able to deliver all your promises and campaign messages. This is where your opposition will use it to campaign against you and tag you as incompetent. Scrutinizing my competence is where I have had some slight experience during 2012 election when I lost my parliamentary seat.

ERICA WILLIAMS CONNELL, DAUGHTER OF TRINIDAD AND TOBAGO'S FIRST PRIME MINISTER, DR. ERIC E. WILLIAMS (JULY 7, 2020)

What is leadership in your thinking? How do you understand leadership based on your experience as the daughter of one of the 20th century's most important leaders?

Well, leadership is the exact antithesis of what we are suffering in the US at this time!

> Fellow Party Members, allow me to end on a purely personal note. It has been my privilege to serve you, as Political Leader for six years and as Premier for five. I have sought always to keep faith with the Party and the People. I have placed all my knowledge, acquired at public expense, at your disposal. I have not spared myself in the performance of my duty to you, neither my time, nor

my energy, nor my health. You, in turn, have helped and inspired me more than many of you will ever understand . . . the most important contribution that you have made to me personally, one that I can never hope to repay, is that you have given life and meaning and vitality to a long period of training which would otherwise have been an academic exercise and mere intellectual decoration . . ." (Eric Williams, Address to PNM Special Convention, September 23, 1961)

THAT is leadership!

Are there issues you are able to address better as a woman? Do you use a gender lens when solving problems?

I would have to use a gender lens since I have no idea what it is like to be a man. I always said, half-jokingly, to my late father: "Behind every great man, there is an even greater woman!" And I meant it. Even though I am not a virulent feminist (I do believe that men are meant to do certain things, and women, others), in terms of leadership and its many parameters, women are far more suited to conflict resolution, patience, compassion, and inner strength. Men are not generally multi-taskers. The same certainly cannot be said of women. When men of old came home from work, their day's tasks were complete, and this has only minimally improved. By contrast, when women leave their day jobs, they begin anew as wife, mother, cook, house-keeper, launderer, nurse, teacher, psychologist, chauffeur, activities director, financial planner.

How do you balance your personal life and professional? And what is your advice to young girls today trying to figure out how they can balance their lives?

There IS no balance. I struggle daily to "keep all the balls in the air!" Every day I swear I'm going to get into bed earlier, eat better, relax more. It never happens. Despite my many responsibilities as an employee, grandmother providing childcare, etc., it is my extracurricular work helping to advance my late father's Library, Archives & Museum at the University of the West Indies in Trinidad and Tobago that is my passion. I am engrossed by this, enlivened and overly enthusiastic. Therefore, whatever extra hours I *don't* have that I put into this effort, never fail to revitalize me, to affirm my mission. My advice to the young, and especially to my granddaughter, is to always be involved in something bigger than yourself, something immensely fulfilling, something that nourishes the soul. All the while realizing that, on one's death-bed, no one bemoans the fact that they should have worked more diligently.

That final conversation is always about family and love. Therefore, do your best to put them first, and your passion after.

Is there a difference between women's leadership and men's use of political power?

The hand that rocks the cradle, rules the world! Nothing is more true. Women are fearless. I think we only have to look at the current state of affairs in the US today, and even around the world, to see that women can and do make the hard decisions, regardless of the consequences. Men, seemingly, tend to be sometimes tentative, bull-headed, with a penchant for self-interest and self-preservation that is stunning to witness. A mother will literally lift a car that is crushing her child, while men will ring their hands futilely. It is absolutely astonishing that the so-called glass ceiling has been well and truly breached, even in developing countries, but not yet in the US.

How would you describe your leadership style?

An iron hand in a velvet glove.

Do you see yourself carrying forward any traditional leadership methods in your various projects?

No. Were that the case, I hardly believe the Eric Williams Memorial Collection Research Library, Archives & Museum would have had such success. The word "no" is not in my vocabulary, in fact, it is like waving a red flag to a bull. In many instances, people can tell you one hundred ways from Sunday why such and such cannot be done. I offer a hundred ways from Sunday why it can . . . and should be!

Do you think anything changes or will change when women get to political power?

Yes. I believe there will be less war, more diplomacy, more effective negotiation and greater efficiency, for all of the reasons I mentioned in item 2. This does not mean that a female leader will allow herself to be taken advantage of, quite the contrary. She will bite the proverbial bullet when she has to.

Do you feel that women in positions of power are scrutinized more heavily on issues such as competence but also on issues like physical appearance, clothing, family? Have you had any experience with this and could you give examples of this?

Perhaps they are, but why shouldn't they be held to a rigorous standard? It's not as if they will fall short! In terms of physical appearance, I think the day has long passed when a kewpie doll was the epitome of female attractiveness.

Obviously, one cannot appear bedraggled but I, personally, have no doubt that even with such unwarranted scrutiny, women leaders will immediately dispel the notion that the outer packaging trumps—forgive the word—competence, vigor and productivity.

HAZELLE ROGERS, MAYOR OF LAUDERDALE LAKES, FLORIDA, FORMER DEMOCRATIC MEMBER OF FLORIDA HOUSE OF REPRESENTATIVES, 2008–2016 (JANUARY 13, 2021)

What is leadership in your thinking? What is your leadership story?

In 1969, seeing Shirley Chisholm run for office became a reference point for me so when I moved to Florida . . . having come to the United States as only a teenager, from the Caribbean I began to observe how people were treated differently. When I realized her (Chisholm's) roots: I said to myself: You can come to America and do this? It made me proud of her heritage . . . the same way I felt about Kamala putting herself out there to run as a democratic nominee for the presidency. She would not be in the position she is today had she not done that.

My Homeowners Association would be my first start. When there was a position I ran for it without knowing if it was paid, I knew I could do better than available leadership. And I was the youngest elected official and the only woman for 12 years on the Commission . . . I knew I was different, had to do things differently. Normally former businessmen who had come to Florida to retire went after these political positions. I ran for City Commission Lauderdale Lakes 1995 and lost by 2 votes. I was new to it, but the community was changing and growing. During the historic Al Gore race, the one with hanging chads in Broward County, I remember that those votes were not counted. (Under normal circumstances there should be a recount.) By1996 I had learned of things to do, followed guidelines, watched the votes, had people in the precinct outside and in to do better. Scars that you acquire along the way are not to be ashamed of. After serving on the City Commission, in 2008 I went to Tallahassee. There it was more partisan; a man's world; for example, no mirrors but places to hang your coat and cap. An open seat became available at the time and it was the District 94 for Eglison to the State House. State Representative for District 94/95 and I served in that capacity with Barack Obama and left with him 2008–2016.

When I went to Tallahassee I knew they were funding programs locally . . . so I wanted to fight for libraries, knowing my love for Broward County.

Roadways are always a challenging issue so I wanted my city to get attention. Monies for roads and bridges, educational programs, urban league and social programs and economic development, small business, minority business were issues I fought for. You had to speak that language for Black communities to get support: Black Colleges and Universities were always central. That was the focus to continue to fund those institutions as these educated most Black Americans (HBCUs) always the focus of these institutions. Someone in the next generation needs to push forward how we teach our history, not hide from it; not hiding from it, but rarely did they recognize the Caribbeans. I always credit The Association of Caribbean Elected Leaders which had members from all over the country and when my colleagues heard about it, they all had Caribbean roots; Frederica now talks about her Caribbean roots but at the time said we were dividing up the Black community. Many did not see our economic value, and certain health issues and language issues which needed to be represented. For example, the need to have the teachers in the room when you want to represent everyone. Growing Haitian community meant that materials have to be in the languages of the people. We are one but have different things we have to celebrate.

**Are there issues you are able to address better
as a woman? Do you use a gender lens when
solving problems?**
Women's Reproductive Rights is always in Tallahassee one of the biggest issues. That will never go away. They, the Christian fundamentalists, want to legislate whether you can have an abortion or not. As women we have to be bold and argue that we have to leave that up to the family. Generally, they work the background . . . They know how to negotiate and people end up voting with them. As a woman you have to make sure they are not putting you in a social bubble. I can do economics and science because most of them did not go to school for areas they wanted to serve in themselves. I made sure I used legislation to get my issues across. If you believe in something, they must see it is important; it cannot be kept in the chambers or in the Board Room . . . you have to get your issues out. So I always use the media to get my issues out, representing all the people . . . not just Black people or women, and they too are diverse with diverse issues. You have to know who you are and why you run for office and why you seek public office and because you end up involving your entire family. They carry them with you and all wounds are reopened. One has to speak to the issue and share the wounds and scars and everyone becomes real people. Nobody is perfect.

How do you balance your personal life and professional? And what is your advice to young girls and women today trying to figure out how they can balance their lives?

Challenging at first but God gave me an awesome husband. Any trip he is included and is there doing his thing . . . you have to find time and quality time. Nieces are around. When you are in the hospital and you see the volunteers they get exposed to the lifestyle; whatever I am doing they see. Now my niece is a State Rep. Anika Omphroy State Representative in Tallahassee and in the same district that I represented. Families pass on the connections . . . certain professions you see family . . . generations . . . part of that tradition and it comes with exposure. "I can do better" I know this.

Is there a difference between women's leadership and men's use of political power?

Men think they are entitled period. Women don't think we are entitled. We collaborate. We work hard. We believe in partnership. We are more inclusive. The only woman on my commission for 12 years and now back as Mayor now it is all women in the Commission. But I learned from the men what not to do. Women have grown up into knowing that they can also lead. We were always in the room thinking and working but now they realize they can go forward. We do everything. We are mothers and we wear style.

Do you see yourself carrying forward any traditional leadership methods in your various projects?

There is a mentorship component that came from Una Clarke, former Council member in Brooklyn and she reached out to me and stayed with me even today, her daughter Yvette Clarke is a colleague and friend. She knew her daughter would stay with me and Una would stay with me. She called me and when I got elected to Tallahassee came in from Brooklyn, as a mother and a mentor to be with me. She is that fireball, that Nanny of the Maroons. She would have known Shirley Chisholm. She ran for that seat Shirley Chisholm had and her daughter ran for it too.

Do you think anything changes, or will change, when more women get to political power?

That is a big change. We are now training more women. Men appoint men so lots of opportunities for women to follow if we open the door. I have a great deal of pride in Kamala. Biden selected Kamala because he wanted to win. I worked harder and smarter for Kamala, no stopping. Very proud of her boldness, her natural beauty, love her laughter. You have to be able. From the press, the idea that she presented was clear. The first picture we (Caribbeans) saw was with her grandmother. That was what she wanted us to see.

Do you feel that women in positions of power are scrutinized more heavily on issues such as competence but also on issues like physical appearance, clothing, family?

Family is important and understanding. They are proud of you and take that with you. I believe Black people know how to dress up . . . the clothes you wear in church and the year and the occasion to wear them. I went through every hairstyle. . . . gerry curl, big Afro, everything and have pictures with African outfits, tie die tops. You are who you are and should not be afraid to wear your African outfits, they are part of your culture, or in my case, my Jamaican colors. I have lived in America most of my life so I have learned a lot and know that we have been through the same class and color prejudices among ourselves that we also go though . . . brown skin gets more opportunities. I did not wear makeup until 1974 when I got married, I felt I was beautiful enough.

UNA S. T. CLARKE, FORMER COUNCILWOMAN FROM BROOKLYN, 1992–2001 (MOTHER OF CONGRESSWOMAN YVETTE CLARKE) (JANUARY 13, 2021)

What is leadership in your thinking?

There are many ways—pioneer in a special area, willing to take a position and on behalf of a community –the first person to take an issue forward.

What is your leadership story (your pathway to leadership)?

I knew Shirley and her husband before she ran for office. There is a definite influence because of our similar work in early childhood education. We also have a connection through Brooklyn College, Head Start and Day Care and when I ran for office being endorsed by her. In my time, Caribbean American people were emerging as a community and there was a movement to get Caribbean people to vote. Many would stay in the US and not know when or if they are ever going home but miss participation during those years. There was also a redistricting process 40th and 45th and a need for political representation. Very few of the men wanted to run so I decided to run. One had already served as a Panamanian in the Chamber of Commerce and after all the noise advocating on our community's behalf, no Caribbean wanted to run.

Are there issues you are able to address better as a woman? Do you use a gender lens when solving problems?

I think that women understand bread and butter issues and issues of budget-making sure that everything is covered. An innate gift for women have is to be able to do many things at the same time: raise a family and do civic or public life. I was always very active in the schools PTA, Block Associations.

How do you balance your personal life and professional? And what is your advice to young girls and women today trying to figure out how they can balance their lives?

Conrad was a great supporter not a competitor as a husband. He filled in the gaps always. People can grow to realize that you can complement and not compete. We should make sure it will not be an either/or. There are many things that propel women to enter public life . . . for example the Black Lives Matter mothers who lose a child often become active in politics.

Is there a difference between women's leadership and men's use of political power?

There is always a difference. People thought I worked for a councilman. They assume you work for a man if they meet you for example when traveling in elevators. Also, because I have a strong accent and maintain an accent they were not used to associating that [Caribbean] accent with leadership.

How would you describe your leadership style?

I don't see myself as different from community, I try to be a part, try to get consensus.

Do you see yourself carrying forward any traditional (US African American or other) leadership methods in your various projects?

Usually my theme was "a voice of the voiceless and a face of the faceless." Many things happen when I was in community that gave me a national profile, Abner Louima and two shootings on Church Avenue; Dorismon from the Haitian community . . . I had to take the issue on headlong and it became national news. Always had to be out front.

Do you think anything changes, or will change, when more women get to political power? Do you feel that women in positions of power are scrutinized more heavily on issues such as competence?

Depends on what office and how one carries herself. You should have a presence and command respect of people around you, so people know . . . during my time I once wore a short Afro, cut off all my hair. Being able to command respect from those people you represent is important. You have to let them know who you are and hold everything you want to do at heart.

The national Association of Caribbean Elected Officials and Leaders played a major role. Its focus was what can we do to enhance Caribbean women as nations and their residents. Appointed officials, clergy too participated as we went to Washington DC to Organization of American States to lobby, to the White House as well and to advocate for the advancement of trade with the Caribbean and countries who were being left behind. In the 90's, supporting and getting more leaders to come forward, we became a national organization. Health issues too at that time were also important. We had representatives from Hartford, Connecticut, Florida and so on, and included Republicans also so we were open to all interested in advancing Caribbean communities. . . . so that you felt the weight.

AMINATA DRAMANE TRAORÉ, FORMER MINISTER OF CULTURE AND TOURISM, MALI, 1997–2000, BAMAKO, MALI (JANUARY 30, 2018)

Tell me how you got to leadership? What is your leadership story?

I was the first girl in my family to go to school and the way I did it, in a colonial context, very far from here, going by myself and coming back. I also had to help my mother, like going to market and selling things while I was trying to do my work at school.

Then I got married in Cote d'Ivoire with my husband, we had a French university experience where I had my two daughters. I went to the University of Caen Calvados and then in Paris at the Sorbonne where I had a PhD in social psychology. And then I came back to Cote D'Ivoire and had been appointed as a researcher at The Institute Ethno Sociology of University of Abidjan and that was in 1975, International Women's Year. We were just two women in the Institute, I was appointed as Director of programs and Research in the

Ministry of Women's Affairs. This was where I spent part time in the university and doing things in the field, promoting women's role in different areas in Cote d'Ivoire. Then I started to get involved at the African continental level, in different meetings and I started to write and do consultations for the UN. This kind of leadership, intervening in debates was appreciated because we were not many to do that. In 1992, after the Ministry of Women's Affairs I was appointed by the UN to do a regional project, covering 12 countries, on the role of women in water and sanitation (PROWES). The objective was to raise people's consciousness on water and sanitation and so on. I was going from one place to another, here and Abidjan where I had my house and here I started to do this work, paving, working with young graduate women on women's issues. I started to write since we were facing problems linked to Structural Adjustment policies and I worked a lot on this — the impact on women; the social dimension of projects, if you don't treat these problems, what are the consequences for women?

And then in Cote d'Ivoire, there was the very first Ministry of Women's Affairs in Africa, created by Houphet Boigny in that period. It has been a very good experience to get involved in the field in different activities. The same thing at the . . . university, attending different meetings, during the last 3 decades of the 2000's. We have had all these meetings, the UN meetings on water the environment and so on.

In terms of leadership, I think that I did not face many problems with men "because you are women." I think that sometimes to be a Black woman in some areas, they listen, they are commanded to listen to an African woman dealing with macro and geo-political issues. Then when I came back here (Mali) I decided to do things like this. This is why once they called me to become the Minister of Culture and Tourism, I accepted.

I cannot say . . . (she interrupted to greet her grandchildren)

It is . . . Unfortunately it is even sometimes easy to work with men. The competition between women . . . very difficult. We were six women ministers in the government. I don't remember if we had close and good relationships between us as women. I know they try now to do that to create links between former ministers, but it is so superficial . . . I don't want to get to this thing that because you are women . . . if in terms of ideology you disagree.

What about the personal? This is still a big issue that women still have, how they balance their personal life. Do they compartmentalize?

It is quite easy in Africa because compared to Europe, and the US as well you always have family or somebody to assist you. My sister! my mother! Otherwise you can recruit somebody to help. I am quite lucky because I got divorced very early. (Side conversations with grandsons who had just returned from school and were talking with her.)

As far as the relationship with men, when I was Minister of Culture, honestly, I don't remember a problem.

Sirleaf, Ellen Johnson Sirleaf, describes in her book
that she was the recipient of violence in the house,
domestic violence . . . so she said she understands the
questions for women, but I don't know if that translates
into women being able to do policies that will affect
other women with the same problem.
My case I had to divorce because effectively I went through other problems. But my partner, in my case, it was a question of jealousy. Because otherwise he was nice; he would do whatever at home, he would clean the place. But when you go out, it is what did you do and so on then . . . It's not because you are a woman or a man but just because "I don't want you to do that." This is why in my work, my concern is more related to the consequence of policies and all these issues of democracy and I'm more alert towards this.

In Trinidad, for example, there was a question of trying
to get women ministers to take positions on issues like
child marriage, education of girls. Often those issues
don't get raised by the men because they don't realize
it as an issue. You say that you engaged with men on
issues of economics mostly . . .
Environment, water, sanitation, interior design, textiles how to give women economic opportunity, to have a part in all of this, how to improve the socio-economic conditions. All this port that you see. We designed the port. But people that you see, like politicians respect you because they see that you try to renew the reflection of our situation to see our specificity. I know that . . . I started to have problems as the Minister of Culture when I published my book on the World Bank. The problems I suffered were not in the relationship between men and women, less than the context of the way of African women contest the theories of the underdevelopment of Africa. That's why I say that the global market is not our market, it is their market. Because they need our raw materials. They need our work, like during slavery. But this line of thinking disturbed at that period because in the 1990's we were not many to raise this. So, this has been very hard so I had a bad relationship with those politicians. Today I think that honestly I don't see a difference between men and women politicians. Maybe if I decided to take part in elections, I would take more interest in those positions.

But do you see anything changing when women get political power? There are not that many examples in Africa.

I am a little bit disappointed because they tend to be appointed as women but when they are elected it becomes an issue of class; no more of gender. Because women politicians demonstrate the same behavior as men, fighting for power, going into corruption, whatever they can do to get where men are.

So your take it is a question more of ideology and political position. Any examples you use for women's leadership?

I have to develop my own strategy from my own experience, because each of us is quite unique, coming from a family where my mother is illiterate being part of a family of six brothers and sisters and then I am the only one educated. You study in difficult circumstances material-wise. Then going to France. When I write, or if I have to decide anything, it is from this experience.

I am not on very good terms with western feminists because of their concerns about your body as African Black women. I fight against female circumcision definitely and all those issues related to our body. But when they started to look with compassion and then to judge you and your culture as a victim, I say No! I have to tell you where I am wounded or hurt in this part my body, I decide to tell you what is my problem. This is my body so don't dictate to me what I have to say. It is very hard to French and Canadian women when you tell them what is your concern. They are like hysteric. No! Feminists like when you start to tell them, to what extent your men are bad, you culture is bad. So I say No! Malian women in my society and I have many problems and I think I know how to solve them. When I had problems with my husband, it was my brother who came to say to my husband don't touch her. For Malian feminism to me it is our struggle to fight according to our own sensibility and aspirations. But, historically white western women are in a dominant culture and they cannot tell me what to do. This issue is like all development issues. They come with projects, if you want money you have to write what they want. You have evaluation to assess what they want you to know or say. This the way they want us to operate.

NOTES

1. I thank Howard Dodson, former chief of the Schomburg, who provided the initial contact for a meeting in Washington, D.C., with former president Johnson Sirleaf a few months before, which was canceled precipitously because the former president had to attend a friend's funeral. Continued contact with Robert Sirleaf helped me to

secure an interview in Uniondale a few months later. This interview is not presented in full because it ended up being more of a conversation than an interview. I am presenting in quotation marks all direct statements, and the rest is a summary of our conversation.

2. President Weekes was careful to explain to me that her Presidency was only ceremonial. I wanted her voice included nevertheless.

Bibliography

Abbott, Diane. "I fought Racism and Misogyny to Become an MP. The fight is Getting Harder. *The Guardian,* February 14, 2017. https://www.theguardian.com/commentisfree/2017/feb/14/racism-misogyny-politics-online-abuse-minorities

Abrams, Stacey. *Lead from the Outside. How to Build Your Future and Make Real Change.* New York: Picador, 2019.

Abrams, Stacey. *Our Time Is Now: Power, Purpose, and the Fight for a Fair America.* New York: Henry Holt and Co., 2020.

Achebe, Nwando. *The Female King in Colonial Nigeria. Ahebi Ugbabe.* Bloomington: Indiana University Press, 2011.

Achebe, Nwando. *Female Monarch and Merchant Queens in Africa.* Athens: Ohio University Press, 2020.

Adamczyk, Alicia. "All These Countries Have Had a Female Head of State (Before the U.S.)" *Time.* July 9/11, 2016. http://time.com/money/4362191/female-heads-of-state/ [Accessed 2/11/2018]

Adams, A., ed. *Essays in Honour of Ama Ata Aidoo At 70: A Reader In African Cultural Studies.* Banbury: Ayebia, 2012.

Addai Kwarteng, Frederick. "Ghana, Barbados sign agreement to establish sister-port relationship between Tema, Bridgetown" November 15, 2019. https://www.abcnewsgh.com/ghana-barbados-sign-agreement-to-establish-sister-port-relationship-between-tema-bridgetown/ Accessed 7/25/2020

Adichie, C. N. *The Thing Around Your Neck.* New York: Anchor Books, 2010.

Adichie, C. N. "We Should all be Feminists." TEDx Euston, London, April 12, 2013.

Adichie, C. N. *Americanah.* New York: Anchor Books, 2014.

Adichie, C. N. *We Should All Be Feminists.* New York: Anchor Books, 2015.

Adichie, C. N. Chimamanda Ngozi Adichie: My Father's Kidnapping. *The New York Times.* Saturday May 30, 2015. http://www.nytimes.com/2015/05/31/opinion/sunday/chimamanda-ngozi-adichie-my-fathers-kidnapping.html (Accessed 22 06 2015).

Africa Woman 6 (September/October, 1976).African Union. "Protocol to the African Charter on Human and Peoples' Rights on the Rights of Women in Africa." 2005, https://au.int/en/treaties/protocol-african-charter-human-and-peoples-rights-rights-women-africa Accessed 10/30/2021

"African Voices" CNN International. Broadcast date 7.11.2009.

Agyeman-Duah, J.C.P. and Ivor Mahoune. *The Asante Monarchy in Exile: Sojourn of King Prempeh I and Nana Yaa Asantewaa in Seychelles.* Center for Intellectual Renewal, 2000.

Aidoo, Ama Ata. "The African Woman Today." *Dissent.* Summer, 1992: 319–325.

Aidoo, Ama Ata. "Ghana: To Be A Woman." *Sisterhood is Global. The International Women's Movement Anthology.* Edited by Robin. Morgan. CUNY: The Feminist Press, 1984: 258–263.

Aidoo, Ama Ata. *Our Sister Killjoy. Reflections from a Black-Eyed Squint.* London: Longmans, 1997 (1979).

Aidoo, Ama Ata. *Changes: A Love Story*. New York: Feminist Press, 1993.

Alexander, Ryan. "Beyond Michelle Obama's Arms. Media Representations of a Black First Lady." M.A. Thesis. Africana Studies, Cornell University, 2010.

Allahar, Anton L. "Charisma and Populism: Theoretical Reflections on Leadership and Legitimacy." *Caribbean Charisma. Reflections on leadership, Legitimacy and Populist Politics.* Edited by Anton Allahar. Jamaica: Ian Randle, 2001:1–32.

Allahar, Anton, ed. *Caribbean Charisma. Reflections on Legitimacy and Political Leadership in the Era of Independence.* Kingston, Jamaica: Ian Randle, 2001.

Amadiume, Ifi. *Male Daughters, Female Husbands: Gender and Sex in an African Society.* London: Zed Books, 1987.

Amadiume, Ifi. "Cheikh Anta Diop's Theory of Matriarchal Values as the Basis for African Cultural Unity." Introduction. The Cultural Unity of Black Africa: The Domains of Matriarchy and Patriarchy in Classical Antiquity. London: Karnak House, 1989.

Amadiume, Ifi. *Daughters of the Goddess, Daughters of Imperialism: African Women Struggle for Culture, Power and Democracy.* London: Zed Press, 2000.

Ampofo, Akosua Adomako. "Work as a Duty and as a Joy: Understanding the Role of Work in the Lives of Ghanaian Female Traders of Global Consumer Items," in *Women's Labor in the Global Economy. Speaking in Multiple Voices.* Edited by Sharon Harley. New Brunswick, NJ: Rutgers University Press: 182–220.

Andaiye. *The Point is To Change the World. Selected Writings of Andaiye.* Edited by. Alissa Trotz. London: Pluto Press, 2020.

Anderson, Marie. *Julia's Daughters. Women in Dade's History.* Miami Florida: Herstory of Florida, Inc., 1980.

Anker, Elizabeth. *Fictions of Dignity. Embodying Human Rights in World Literature.* Ithaca, NY: Cornell University Press, 2012.

Antrobus, Peggy. "Transformational Leadership: Advancing the Agenda for Gender Justice." *Gender & Development*, 8:3 (2000): 50–56.

Ashby, Solange. "Priestess, Queen, Goddess. The Divine Feminine in the Kingdom of Kush." Routledge companion to Black Women's Cultural Histories. Ed. Janell Hobson. London and New York: Routledge: 23–34.

Assie-Lumumba, N'Dri Therese. "Hillary Rodham Clinton and the 1995 Beijing International Conference on Women. Gender and the Nexus of Global and Domestic Power Dynamics." *The Global Hillary. Women's Political Leadership in*

Cultural Contexts. Edited by Dinesh Sharma. New York and London: Routledge, 2016: 78–93.

Bailey, Moya. *Misogynoir Transformed. Black Women's Digital Resistance.* New York: NYU Press, 2021.

Bairros, Luiza. "Lembrando Leila Gonzalez." *Afro-Asia* 23 (Salvador), 1999.

Baker, Ella. "We Need Group-Centered Leadership." *Let Nobody Turn Us Around. An African American Anthology.* Edited by Manning Marable and Leith Mullings. Rowman & Littlefield, 2009: 375–376.

Barreto, Raquel. "Lélia Gonzalez: A Brazilian Thinker." *Capire.* February 1, 2021 https://capiremov.org/en/analysis/lelia-gonzalez-a-brazilian-thinker

Barriteau, Eudine. "Enjoying Power, Challenging Gender." *Enjoying Power: Eugenia Charles and Political Leadership in the Commonwealth Caribbean.* Edited by Eudine Barriteau and Alan Cobley. Mona, Jamaica: UWI Press, 2006:3–25.

Barriteau, V. Eudine, ed. *Love and Power: Caribbean Discourses on Gender. Mona, Jamaica:* UWI Press, 2012.

Barriteau, Eudine and Alan Cobley, eds. *Enjoying Power: Eugenia Charles and Political Leadership in the Commonwealth Caribbean.* Mona, Jamaica: UWI Press, 2006.

Barrow-Giles, Cynthia. "Straight Roads or Bumpy Rides? Eugenia Charles's Path to Power." *Enjoying Power: Eugenia Charles And Political Leadership in the Commonwealth Caribbean.* Edited by Eudine Barriteau and Alan Cobley. Mona, Jamaica: UWI Press, 2006: 70– 107.

Barry, Boubacar. *The Kingdom of Waalo. Senegal before the Conquest.* New York: Diasporic Africa Press, 2012.

Batliwala, Srilatha et al. "Feminist Leadership for Social Transformation: Clearing the Conceptual Cloud." CREA: Creating Resources for Empowerment Action, 2010.

Beckles, Hilary Mc D. *Britain's Black Debt. Reparations for Caribbean Slavery and Native Genocide.* University of the West Indies Press, 2013.

Beckles, Hilary Mc D. *How Britain Underdeveloped the Caribbean. A Reparation Response to Europe's Legacy of Plunder and Poverty.* University of the West Indies Press, 2022.

Berry, Daina Rainey and Kali Nicole Gross. *A Black Woman's History of the United States. Boston: Beacon Press, 2020.*

Bridger, Emily. "From 'Mother of the Nation' to 'Lady Macbeth': Winnie Mandela and Perceptions of Female Violence in South Africa 1985–1991." *Gender and History,* (University of Exeter) *March* 19, 2018.

Black, Edda Fields. *Harriet Tubman, the Combahee River Raid, and Black Freedom during the Civil War.* Oxford University Press, forthcoming.

Blain, Keisha N. *Set the World on Fire. Black Nationalist Women and the Global Struggle for Freedom.* Philadelphia: University of Pennsylvania Press, 2018.

Blain, Keisha N. "Black Women Are Leading the Movement to End Police Violence." *Washington Post.* October 1, 2020. https://www.washingtonpost.com /outlook/2020/10/01/black-women-are-leading-movement-end-police-violence/ (Accessed 10/31/2021)

Blain, Keisha N. *"Until I am Free." Fannie Lou Hamer's Enduring Message to America.* Boston: Beacon Press, 2021.

Boahen, A. Adu. *Yaa Asantewaa and the Asante-British War of 1900–1.* Sub-Saharan Publishers and Traders 2003.

Boyce Davies, Carole. "Private Lives and Public Spaces: Autobiography and the African Woman Writer." *Crisscrossing Boundaries* by Ngate, Harrow and Zimra. Washington, DC: Three Continents Press, 1990: 109– 127. [Rpt.in *Neohelicon* (Hungary) 17:2 (1989): 183–210 and *CLA Journal,* 34:3 (March 1991): 267–289.]

Boyce Davies, Carole. "Representations of Urban Life in African Women's Literature." *Women's Lives and Public Policy. The International Experience.* Eds. Meredith Turshen and Briavel Holcomb. Connecticut: Greenwood Press, 1993: 171–181.

Boyce Davies, Carole. "Finding Some Space: South African Women Writers." *A Current Bibliography of African Affairs* 19: 1 (1986–1987) 31–45. [Rpt. in *Ufahamu: Journal of the African Activists Association* 14:2 (1986): 121–136.]

Boyce Davies, Carole. "Collaboration and the Ordering Imperative in Life Story Production." *De/Colonizing the Subject. The Politics of Gender in Women's Autobiography.* Minneapolis: University of Minnesota Press,: 1992: 3–19.

Boyce Davies, Carole. *Black Women Writing and Identity: Migrations of The Subject.* London: Routledge, 1994.

Boyce Davies, Carole. "Transformational Discourses, African Diaspora Culture and the Literary Imagination." *Macalester International* (Literature, the Creative Imagination and Globalization) 3 (Spring, 1996): 199–224.

Boyce Davies Carole. "Hearing Black Women's Voices: Transgressing Imposed Boundaries." *Moving Beyond Boundaries. International Dimensions of Black Women's Writing.* Edited by C Boyce Davies and Molara Ogundipe. New York: New York University Press, 1995:3–14.

Boyce Davies, Carole. "Afro Brazilian Women, Culture and Literature. An Introduction and Conversation with Miriam Alves." *MaComère. Journal of the Association of Caribbean Women Writers and Scholars* 1:1(1998): 57–74.

Boyce Davies, Carole. "Re-/Presenting Black Female Identity in Brazil: Filhas de Oxum in Bahia Carnival," *Representations of Blackness in the Performance of Identity* Ed. Jean Rahier. Connecticut: Greenwood Press, 1998): 49–67.

Boyce Davies, Carole and Monica Jardine. "Imperial Geographies and Caribbean Nationalism: At the Border Between A Dying Colonialism And US Hegemony." *Centennial Review* (3:3, Fall), 2003: 151–174.

Boyce Davies Carole. "Con-di-fi-cation. Black Women, Leadership and Political Power." *Feminist Africa* (6 March), 2006: 67–84.

Boyce Davies, Carole. "Enduring Legacies of Mrs. Garvey No. 1." *PROUDFLESH: A New Afrikan Journal of Culture, Politics & Consciousness:* Issue 6, 2007.

Boyce Davies, Carole. "Respecting African Cultures: Advancing Our Knowledge" in *Benin A Kingdom in Bronze.* Edited by Babacar Mbow and Osenwegie Ebohon. Exhibition Catalog. African American Research Library and Cultural Center, Fort Lauderdale Florida, 2005: 69–76.

Boyce Davies, Carole. *Left of Karl Marx. The Political Life of Black Communist Claudia Jones.* Durham: Duke University Press, 2008.

Boyce Davies, Carole. "Black Voting Rights, Kwame Toure, Barack Obama and the Im/Possibility of a Black President." *Pluriel Magazine* (June-July, 2008): 42–43.

Boyce Davies, Carole. "Beverley Manley—History on Her Terms." *Abeng News Magazine*, June 29, 2008.

Boyce Davies, Carole. "Sisters Outside: Tracing the Caribbean/Black Radical Intellectual Tradition." *Small Axe*. 28(March, 2009):193–202.

Boyce Davies, Carole. "'She Wants the Black Man Post': Sexuality in the Construction of Black Women's leadership." *Agenda* (South Africa) 90/25.4(2011):121–132.

Boyce-Davies, Carole. "Pan-Africanism, Transnational Black Feminism and the Limits of Culturalist Analyses in African Gender Discourses," *Feminist Africa* 19(2014): 78–93

Boyce Davies, Carole. "From Masquerade to Maskarade. Caribbean Cultural Resistance and the Re-humanizing Project." *Sylvia Wynter. On Being Human as Praxis.* Edited by Katherine Mc Kittrick. Durham: Duke University Press, 2015: 203–225.

Boyce Davies, Carole. "The Persistence of Institutional Sexism in Africana Studies" September 17, 2018. https://www.aaihs.org/the-persistence-of-institutional-sexism-in-africana-studies/

Boyce Davies, Carole. "Abuser-in-Chief Strikes Again." *Trinidad Express,* January 13, 2018. http://www.trinidadexpress.com/20180113/editorial/abuser-in-chief-strikes-again

Boyce Davies, Carole. "The Promise of Kamala Harris." *The Crisis* August 27, 2020. https://www.thecrisismagazine.com/single-post/2020/08/27/THE-PROMISE-OF-KAMALA-HARRIS

Boyce Davies, Carole & Elaine Fido. "African Women Writers: Towards A Literary History." *A History of African Literature in The Twentieth Century.* O. Edited by O. Owomoyela. Nebraska: University of Nebraska Press, 1993: 311–346.

Brathwaite, Edward. *The Arrivants. A New World Trilogy.* London: Oxford university Press 1973.

Brereton, Bridget and Barbara Bailey, eds. *Engendering History: Caribbean Women in Historical Perspective*. Palgrave MacMillan, 1995.

Bridger, E. "From 'Mother of the nation' to 'Lady Macbeth': Winnie Mandela and Perceptions of Female Violence in South Africa, 1985–91." *Gender and History.* ORE Open Research Exeter. 19 March, 2018. http://hdl.handle.net/10871/32162

Brown, DeNeen L. "The Black Women Who Paved the Way." *Washington Post.* January 12, 2021. https://www.washingtonpost.com/history/2021/01/12/black-women-who-paved-way/ Accessed 10/31/2021

Brown, Elaine. *A Taste of Power. A Black Woman's Story.* New York: Anchor Books, 1992.

Brown, Matthew. "Progressives Saw Kamala Harris as A Unique Champion. Lately, They're Disappointed." *USA Today,* November 5, 2021. https://www.yahoo.com/news/activists-disappointed-kamala-harris-isnt-090134600.html

Brown, Nadia. *Sisters in the Statehouse: Black Women and Legislative Decision Making.* Oxford: Oxford University Press, 2014.

Brown, Nadia. "It's More Than Hair . . . That's Why You Should Care": The Politics of Appearance For Black Women State Legislators, *Politics, Groups, and Identities*, 2:3 (2014): 295–312.

Brown, Nadia. "'If Not Now, When?': Black Women Seize Political Spotlight." *US News and World Report*, August 3, 2020 https://www.usnews.com/news/politics /articles/2020-08-03/if-not-now-when-black-women-seize-political-spotlight (Accessed 10/31/2021)

Browne-Marshall. *She Took Justice. The Black Woman, Law, and Power 1619–1969*. New York and London: Routledge, 2021.

Buddan, Robert. "Universal Adult Suffrage in Jamaica and the Caribbean Since 1944." *Social and Economic Studies* 53:4(2004): 135–162.

Bulawayo, Noviolet. *We Need New Names*. London: Chatto and Windus, 2013.

Bunce, Robin and Samara Linton. "How Diane Abbott Fought Racism—and Her Own party—to Become Britain's First Black Female MP." *The Guardian*. Tuesday September 29, 2020. https://www.theguardian.com/politics/2020/sep/29/how-diane -abbott-fought-racism-and-her-own-party-to-become-britains-first-black-female -mp Accessed 10/31/2021

Busby, Margaret. *Daughters of Africa. An International Anthology of Words and Writings by Women of African Descent from the Ancient Egyptian to the Present*. London: Ballantine, 1994; New Edition: Amistad, 2019.

Caldwell, Kia Lilly. (2001). "Racialized Boundaries: Women's Studies and the Question of 'Difference' in Brazil." *The Journal of Negro Education* (Black Women in the Academy: Challenges and Opportunities) 70:3(Summer, 2001): 219–230.

Cambridge, Alrick. "C.L.R. James' Socialist Future and Human Happiness" in *Decolonizing the Academy. African Diaspora Studies*. Trenton, NJ: Africa World Press, 2003: 61–91.

Cambridge, Alrick. "When Socialist Values Harmonize with Human Desire for Liberation: Assessing Claudia Jones' Politics," Afterword to *Claudia Jones. Beyond Containment*. Banbury UK: Ayebia, 2011: 207–220.

Carmichael, Stokely. *Ready for Revolution. The Life and Struggles of Stokely Carmichael (Kwame Ture)*. Edited by Michael Thelwell. Scribner, 2005.

Carneiro, Sueli. 2014. *Lélia Gonzalez: O feminismo negro no palco da história*. Brasília: Abravídeo. Center for American Progress, "The Women's Leadership Gap" https://www.americanprogress.org/issues/women/reports/2017/05/21/432758 /womens-leadership-gap/ [Accessed 2/28/18].

Castro Ruz, Fidel. Mujeres y Revolucion, 1959–2005. La Habana: Federación de Mujeres Cubanas, 2006.

Chacel, Julian, ed. *Brazil's Economic and Political Future*. Westview Press, 1988.

Cherry, Gwendolyn Sawyer, Ruby Thomas Rayford, Pauline Styles Willis. *Portraits In Color: The Lives Of Colorful Negro Women."* University of Wisconsin: Pageant Press, 1962.

Chipembere, Natasha Gordon. "Meet Epsy Alejandra Campbell Barr: Costa Rica's First Black Vice President," *Essence Magazine*, December 6, 2020. https://www .essence.com/news/politics/epsy-alejandra-campbell-barr-costa-rica-first-black -vice-president/ [accessed 6/29/2022]

Chisholm, Shirley. *Unbought and Unbossed* (1970). Expanded 40th anniversary edition. North Carolina: Take Root Media, 2010.

Chisholm, Shirley. *The Good Fight*. New York: Harper and Row, 1973.

Chisholm, Shirley. "Racism And Anti-Feminism." *The Black Scholar,* January-February 1970, Vol. 1, No. 3/4: 40–45.

Clark, VèVè. "Diaspora Literacy," *Encyclopedia of the African Diaspora,* Oxford and Santa Barbara: ABC CLIO: V.2. 2008: 382–383.

Clinton, Hillary Rodham. *Hard Choices.* New York: Simon and Schuster, 2014.

Clinton, Hillary Rodham. *What Happened?* New York: Simon and Schuster, 2017.

Coard, Phyllis. *Unchained: A Caribbean Woman's Journey Through Invasion, Incarceration and Liberation.* (self published), 2019.

Coates, Ta Nehisi. "Frederick Douglass: 'A Women's Rights Man.'" *The Atlantic,* September 30, 2011. https://www.theatlantic.com/personal/archive/2011/09/frederick-douglass-a-womens-rights-man/245977/

Cohen, Cathy J. "Punks, Bulldaggers and Welfare Queens. The Radical Potential of Queer Politics?" *GLQ* 3(4): 1997:437–465.

Cooper, Carolyn. "Supporting Sister P: Feminist Alliances in Class Prejudiced Jamaica." *JENDA: A Journal of Culture and African Women Studies.* Issue 9 (2006): 1–18.

Cooper, Carolyn. "Drawing Sister P's Tongue," *The Daily Gleaner*, December 25, 2011.

Cooper, Helene. *Madame President. The Extraordinary Life of Ellen Johnson Sirleaf.* New York: Simon and Schuster, 2017.

Cope, Suzanne. *Power Hungry. Women of the Black Panther Party and Freedom Summer and Their Fight to Feed a Movement.* Chicago: Lawrence Hill Books, 2022.

Covarrubias, Gisela Arandia. *Estudio teórico crítico del racismo: un modelo de análisis epistemológico y político para el contexto cubano.* Tesis de Doctorado, 2017.

Covarrubias, Gisela Arandia. "Racism and Racial Discrimination in the Cuban Agenda" March 10, 2022. https://www.ipscuba.net/sociedad/racismo-y-discriminacion-racial-en-la-agenda-de-cuba [accessed 6/21/2022]

Craig, Geoffrey. "Kindness and Control: The Political Leadership of Jacinda Ardern in the Aotearoa New Zealand COVID-19 Media Conferences." *Journalism and Media* 2, no. 2 (2021): 288–304. https://doi.org/10.3390/journalmedia2020017

Da Silva, Benedita. *Benedita da Silva: An Afro-Brazilian Woman's Story of Politics and Love.* Monroe, OR: Food First Book, 1997.

Dadzie, Stella. *A Kick in the Belly. Women, Slavery and Resistance.* London and New York: Verso, 2020.

Davie, Lucille. "Winnie's Pain and Torture in Prison." *The Heritage Portal.* Sunday, April 8, 2018. www.thehertiageportal.co.za/article/winnies-pain-and-torture-prison Accessed 6/15/2020.

Day, Lynda. *Gender and Power in Sierra Leone. Women Chiefs of the Last Two Centuries. New York: Palgrave Macmillan, 2012.*

de Araujo, Flavia Santos "Marielle, Presente!" *Meridians,* 17:1 (September, 2018): 207–211.

DeCosta Willis, Miriam. "Orishas Circling Her House: Race as (Con) Text in Morejon's Poetic Discourse." *Moving Beyond Boundaries.v.2. Black Women's Diasporas.* Ed. Carole Boyce Davies. NYU Press, 1995: 97–111.

DeJesus, Carolina Maria. (1967) *Child of the Dark. The Diary of Carolina Maria de Jesus [Quarto de Despejo]* Signet, 2003.

de Negreiros, Dalila Fernandes "Marielle Franco's Seeds: Black Women and the 2020 Brazilian Elections." *https://nacla.org/Black-women-Brazil-2020-elections*

Diallo, Halima. "Women Leaders in Senegal." Universite Paris, 13. MA Thesis, 2018.

Diop, Cheikh Anta. *The Cultural Unity of Black Africa: The Domains of Matriarchy and Patriarchy in Classical Antiquity.* London: Karnak House, 1989.

Discussing Women's Empowerment: Theory and Practice, SIDA (The Sweedish International Development Agency) Studies, 3. Stockholm: SIDA. 2001. https://www.sida.se/en/publications/discussing-womens-empowerment-theory-and-practice (Accessed 10/30/2021)

do Nacimento, Abdias. *Quilombo. Vida, Problemas Aspirações do Negro.* (facsimile). Rio de Janeiro, nos. 1 & 10, dezembro de 1948 a julho de 1950. Editora 34 2003.

Dunbar, Erica Armstrong. *She Came to Slay. The Life and Times of Harriet Tubman.* 37INK, Simon and Schuster, 2019.

Duncan, Natanya. *Crossing Waters and Fighting Tides: The Efficient Womanhood of the UNIA in the Atlantic World.* University of Illinois Press, 2021.

Dunn, Marvin. *Black Miami in the Twentieth Century.* Gainesville, Tallahassee: University Press of Florida, 1997.

Duster, Michelle and Hannah Giorgis. *Ida B. The Queen. The Extraordinary Life and Legacy of Ida B. Wells.* Atria, One Signal Publishers, 2021.

Dzidzienyo, Anani. "The Position of Blacks In Brazilian Society." Minority Rights Group. Reports, no. 7. January 1, 1971.

Edwards, Erica. *Charisma and the Fictions of Black leadership. Minneapolis:* Minnesota University Press, 2012.

Ekine, S. Interview with Uche Umez—Sokari Ekine, *November 5, 2012,* Nigerians Talk. Retrieved from http://nigerianstalk.org/2012/11/05/interview-with-uche-umez-sokari-ekine/ (Accessed 6. 23. 2015).

El Saadawi, Nawal. *Woman at Point Zero.* London: Zed Books, 1975.

Elliott, Jeffrey M. and Mervyn M. Dymally. *Nothing Can Stop the Course of History.* New York and London: Pathfinder, 1986.

Emecheta, Buchi. *The Joys of Motherhood.* New York: George Braziller, 1979.

Emecheta, Buchi. "Feminism with a Small 'f'!" *Criticism and Ideology: Second African Writers' Conference. Edited by Kirsten Holst Petersen.* Scandinavian Institute of African Studies, 1988:173–185.

Encyclopedia of the African Diaspora. Ed. Carole Boyce Davies et al. Oxford and Santa Barbara: ABC-CLIO, 2008.

Espín Vilma, Asela de los Santos, Yolanda Ferrer. *Las Mujeres en Cuba Haciendo una revolución dentro de la revolución.* New York: Pathfinder Press, 2012. Ed. Mary-Alice Waters

Evaristo, Bernardine. *Girl, Woman, Other.* New York: Black Cat, 2019.

Falcon, Sylvanna M. *Power Interrupted. Antiracist and Feminist Activism Insite the United Nations.* Seattle and London: University of Washington Press, 2016.

Fanon, Frantz. *The Wretched of the Earth.* Paris: Presence Africaine, 1963/New York: Grove Press, 2004. (Translated by Richard Philcox).

Farmani, Pari. "Aloisea Inyumba: Politician Who Played a Key Role in the Rebuilding of Rwanda." April 16, 2013. https://www.inclusivesecurity.org/2013/04/16/aloisea -inyumba-politician-who-played-a-key-role-in-the-rebuilding-of-rwanda/

Farmer, Ashley D. *Remaking Black Power. How Black Women Transformed an Era.* Chapel Hill: University of North Carolina Press, 2017.

Federación de Mujeres Cubanas. *Mujeres Cubanas 1958–2008. Estadísticas y Realidades.* Federation de Mujeres Cubanas and Oficina Nactional de *Estadísticas,* 2009.

Ferrer, Ada. *Cuba. An American History.* New York: Scribner, 2021.

Fields, Dorothy Jenkins. "Black in Time: Gwen Cherry's Enduring Legacy Creates Opportunities." *Miami Herald,* September 24, 2015. https://www.miamiherald .com/news/local/community/miami-dade/community-voices/article36478458.html (Accessed 1/3/2021).

Figueirdo, Angela. "Letter to Judith Butler." *Revista Internacional de Comunicación y Desarrollo,* 4 (2015): 133–144.

Fitzgerald, Ellen. *The Highest Glass Ceiling. Women's Quest for the American Presidency.* London and Cambridge: Harvard University Press, 2016.

Fitzgerald, Joseph R. *The Struggle is Eternal. Gloria Richardson and Black Liberation.* University of Kentucky Press, 2018.

Fitzpatrick, Scott. "The Pre-Columbian Caribbean: Colonization, Population Dispersal, and Island Adaptations." *PaleoAmerica* 1:4(2015): 305+.

"Five Ways Winnie Mandela Influenced the Lives of Women in South Africa." *African Impact,* April 6, 2018. https://www.africanimpact.com/winnie-mandela -blog/ Accessed 6/15/2020.

Folarin, Tope. "Miracle." *The Caine Prize For African Writing: A Memory This Size And Other Stories.* Oxford and Auckland Park: New Internationalist Publications Ltd, 2013: 10–21.

Folarin, Tope. *A Particular Kind of Black Man.* Simon and Schuster, 2020.

Foray, Joseph. "Liberia: Ellen Johnson Sirleaf to George Weah. Achievements, Challenges, the Way Forward. Lessons for Governance in Africa." *African Reality,* October 3, 2019.

Ford, Tamasin. "Ellen Johnson Sirleaf: The Legacy of Africa's First Elected Female President." *BBC News* 22 January, 2018.

Ford Smith, Honor. "Women and the Garvey Movement in Jamaica," in *Garvey: His Work and Impact,* eds. R. Lewis and P. Bryan. Kingston, ISER/UWI, 1988, 73–88.

Foucault, Michel. "The Subject and Power." *Critical Inquiry* 8:4(Summer, 1982): 777–795.

Fourie Reneva. "Deepening the Participation and Representation of Women in Politics in Africa." *The Thinker* (South Africa) 74(2017), 66–67.

"Francia Marquez es la candidata a la vicepresidencia junto a Gustavo Petro que aspira a la Presidemcia." *Deutsche Welle* March 23, 2022 [acessed 6/29/2022].

Franco, Marielle. "Entrevistamos Marielle Franco: mulher, negra, periférica e Vereadora do RJ—Mulheres na Política #1 Medium," May 16, 2017. https://medium.com/revista-subjetiva/entrevistamos-marielle-franco-mulher-negra-perif%C3%A9rica-e-vereadora-do-rj-mulheres-na-pol%C3%ADtica-7839b7fbfe06

Franco, Marielle. "After the Takeover." *New Left Review,* 110(March-April, 2018) (*Translated by Jamille Pinheiro Dias, Katrina Dodson and Deise Faria Nunes*) 'A Emergência da Vida para Superar o Anestesiamento Social frente à Retirada de Direitos: O Momento Pós-Golpe pelo Olhar de uma Feminista, Negra e Favelada,' in *Tem Saída? Ensaios críticos sobre o Brasil,* edited by Winnie Bueno, Joanna Burigo, Rosana Pinheiro-Machado and Esther Solano (Editora Zouk, 2017) https://newleftreview.org/issues/ii110/articles/marielle-franco-after-the-take-over

"From First Lady to Vice President of Liberia: Meet Jewel Howard Taylor." June 1, 2018 https://www.france24.com/en/20180105-first-lady-vice-president-liberia-jewel-howard-charles-taylor-sierra-leone

Garvey, Amy Ashwood. "The Black Woman" in Tony Martin. *Amy Ashwood Garvey. Pan-Africanist, Feminist and Mrs. Marcus Garvey No. 1, Or, A Tale of Two Amies.* Dover, MA: The Majority Press, 2007: 377–378.

Garvey, Amy Jacques (1925). "Women as Leaders Nationally and Racially." In Gregg, Veronica Marie. *Caribbean Women. An Anthology of Non-Fiction writing, 1890–1980.* Notre Dame: University of Notre Dame Press: 2005:108–110.

Gbowee, Leymah. *Mighty Be Our Powers. How Sisterhood, Prayer, and Sex Changed a Nation at War.* Beast Books, 2013.

Giddings, Paula. "Missing in Action: Ida B. Wells, the NAACP, and the Historical Record," *Meridians* 1:2 (Spring, 2001): 1–17.

Giddings, Paula. *Ida: A Sword Among Lions: Ida B. Wells and the Campaign Against Lynching.* University of Illinois Press, 2009.

Gillard, Julia and Ngozi Okonjo-Iweala, eds. *Women and Leadership. Real Lives. Real Lessons.* MIT Press, 2021.

Gilliam, Angela and O. Gilliam, "Negociando a subjetividade da mulata." *Estudos Feministas* 3(2): 479–489.

Glover, S. Tay and Flavia Meireles. "Towards a Transnational Black Feminist Theory of the Political Life of Marielle Franco," *Caribbean Review of Gender Studies,* 2020:14: 53–72.

Gomez, Michael A. *African Dominion: A New History of Empire in Early and Medieval West Africa.* Princeton University Press, 2019.

Gonzalez, Lélia. "For an Afro-Latin American Feminism." 1988. Republished as http://feministarchives.isiswomen.org/47-books/confronting-the-crisis-in-latin-america-women-organizing-for-change/828-for-an-afro-latin-american-feminism

Gonzalez, Lélia. "Racismo e sexismo na cultura brasileira." In Silva, L. A. (Ed.), Movimentos sociais urbanos, minorias e outros estudos. [Ciências Sociais Hoje, ANPOCS, 2], 223–244. "Racism and Sexism in Brazilian Culture." *Women's Studies Quarterly,* 49, Fall/Winter, 2021: 371–394.

Goodison, Lorna. "Bedspread" *Selected Poems.* Ann Arbor: University of Michigan Press, 1992.

Gouws A. "The Rise of the Femocrat." *Agenda,* 30, 1996: 31–43.

Gramsci, Antonio. *Selections from the Prison Notebooks*. New York: International Publishers, 1971.

Gregg, Veronica Marie. *Caribbean Women. An Anthology of Non-Fiction Writing, 1890–1980*. Notre Dame: University of Notre Dame Press, 2005: 108–110.

Guerra, Zuleica Romay. "From Afro-Cubans To Black Cubans. Africanity And Skin Color In The Cuban Social Imaginary." *Revista Brasileira de Estudos Africanos, (Brazilian Journal of African Studies)| Porto Alegre | v. 3, n. 6, Jul./Dec. 2018 | p. 75–88. available on Afro Cuba Web as in https://core.ac.uk/download/pdf /196619762.pdf March 20, 2019 [Accessed 6/21/2022].

Guild, Joshua. "To Make That Someday Come. Shirley Chisholm's Radical Politics of Possibility." *Want to Start a Revolution? Radical Women in the Black Freedom Struggle*. Edited by Dayo Gore, Jeanne Theoharis and Komozi Woodard. New York and London: New York University Press, 2009: 248–270.

Guyon, Stephanie. "Christiane Taubira, A Black Woman in Politics in French Guyana and in France." *Black French Women and the Struggle for Equality, 1848–2016*. Eds. Felix Germain and Silyane Larcher. University of Nebraska Press, 2018: 19–36.

Hall, Stuart. *The Hard Road to Renewal: Thatcherism and the Crisis of the Left*. London: Verso, 1988.

Hanchard, Michael George. "Identity, Meaning and the African-American." *Social Text* (1990): 31–42.

Hanchard, Michael George. *Orpheus and Power, The Movimento* Negro *of Rio de Janeiro and São Paulo, Brazil 1945–1988*. Princeton University Press, 1994.

Hanchard, Michael George. Ed. *Racial Politics in Contemporary Brazil*. Duke University Press, 1999.

Hanchard, Michael George. *The Spectre of Race. How Discrimination Haunts Western Democracy*. Princeton University Press, 2020.

Harper, Frances Ellen Watkins. "Women's Political Future." *Words of Fire. An Anthology of African-American Feminist Thought*. Ed. Beverly Guy-Sheftall. New York: The New Press, 1995: 39–42.

Hartman, Mary S. Ed. *Talking Leadership. Conversations with Powerful Women*. New Brunswick: Rutgers University Press, 1999.

Hassim, Shireen. "A Life of Refusal. Winnie Madikizela-Mandela and Violence in South Africa." *Storia delle Donne* 10(2014): 55–77.

Hassim, Shireen. "The Impossible Contract: The Political and Private Marriage of Nelson and Winnie Mandela." *Journal of Southern African Studies*, 45:6, 1151–1171.

Haywood, D'Weston. *Let Us Make Men: The Twentieth-Century Black Press and a Manly Vision for Racial Advancement*. University of North Carolina Press, 2018.

Head, Bessie. *A Question of Power*. London: Heinemann, 1973.

Heywood, Linda M. *Nzinga of Angola. Africa's Warrior Queen*. Cambridge: Harvard University Press, 2017.

Horwitz, Linda and Catherine R. Squires. "We Are What We Pretend to Be: The Cautionary Tale of Reading Winnie Mandela as a Rhetorical Widow." *Meridians* 11:1(2011): 66–90.

Hudson-Weems, Clenora. *Africana Womanism: Reclaiming Ourselves*. Bedford Publishers, 1995.

Hull, Gloria, Patricia Bell Scott, and Barbara Smith. 1982. *All the Women are White. All the Blacks Are Men. But Some of Us Are Brave*. New York: The Feminist Press, 1982.

Hutchinson Miller, Carmen. "Stereotyping Women's Political Leadership: Images of Eugenia Charles in the Caribbean Print Media." *Enjoying Power: Eugenia Charles and Political Leadership in the Commonwealth Caribbean*. Edited by Eudine Barriteau and Alan Cobley, eds. Mona, Jamaica: UWI Press, 2006:239–249.

Ibrahim, Shamira. "India Walton Isn't Slowing Down." *Essence Magazine,* January/February, 2022, 60.

James, Stanlie M. *Practical Audacity. Black Women and International Human Rights.* Madison: University of Wisconsin Press, 2001.

Jayawardena, Kumari. *Feminism and Nationalism in the Third World.* London and New Jersey: Zed Books, 1987.

John, Kesewa. 2021. "People Papers: The Pan-African Communities and Afro-Caribbean Radicals between Paulette Naardal and George Padmore 1918–1948." PhD diss., University of Chichester, 2021.

Johnson, Elizabeth Ofosuah. "Ndate Yalla Mboj, the Last Queen of Senegal Who Fought off the French, Arabs and Moors." *Face to Face Africa,* April 5, 2019.

Johnson Sirleaf, Ellen. *This Child Will Be Great. Memoir of a Remarkable Life by Africa's First Woman President.* Harper Perennial, 2009.

Jones, Claudia. "For New Approaches to Our Work Among Women," *Political Affairs,* 27(August, 1948): 738–743.

Jones, Claudia. (1949). "An End to the Neglect of the Problems of Black Women" *Claudia Jones. Beyond Containment.* Banbury, UK: Ayebia, 2012: 75–85.

Jones, Grace. *I'll Never Write My Memoirs.* New York: Gallery Books, 2016.

Jones, Hilary. "Originaire Women and Political Life in Senegal's Four Communes." *Black French Women and the Struggle for Equality, 1848–2016.* Eds. Felix Germain and Silyane Larcher. University of Nebraska Press, 2018: 3–18.

Joseph, Gloria. "Race, Class, Gender and Revolution." Unpublished paper. n.d.

Joseph-Gabriel. *Reimagining Liberation. How Black Women Transformed Citizenship in the French Empire.* Urbana: University of Illinois Press, 2020.

Kaplan, Flora Edouwaye S. Ed. *Queens, Queen Mothers, Priestesses and Power. Case Studies in African Gender.* New York: New York Academy of Sciences, 1997.

Kanogo, Tabitha. *Wangari Maathai* (Ohio Short Histories of Africa). Ohio State University Press, 2020.

Kellogg, Carolyn. "Beyonce's Song 'Flawless' Features Writer Chimamanda Ngozi Adichie." *L.A. Times*, December 13, 2013. http://www.latimes.com/books /jacketcopy/la-et-jc-beyonce-flawless-chimamanda-ngozi-adichie-20131213,0 ,3338347.story#ixzz2peTdpJeV (accessed 10/31/2021).

Krook, Mona Lena. "Electoral Gender Quotas: A Conceptual Analysis." *Comparative Political Studies, 47*(9), 1268–1293, 2014.

Krook, Mona Lena. "Reforming Representation: The Diffusion of Candidate Gender Quotas Worldwide." *Quotas for Women in Politics: Gender and Candidate Selection Reform Worldwide.* New York: Oxford University Press, 2009.

Kushkush, Isma'il. "In the Land of Kush." *Smithsonian Magazine,* September 2020. www.smithsonianmagazine.com

Lambert, Laurie L. *Comrade Sister: Caribbean Feminist Revisions of the Grenada Revolution.* University of Virginia Press, 2020.

Laó-Montes, Agustín. *Diasporic Counterpoints: Cartographies of the Political* in *Our Afroamérica.* Manuscript shared by author.

Lau Chin, Jean, Bernice Lott, Joy K. Rice and Janis Sanchez-Hucles, Eds. *Women and Leadership. Transforming Visions and Diverse Voices.* London: Blackwell, 2007.

Lavender, Natasha. "The Incredible Real-Life Story of Shirley Chisholm." Grunge, November, 2020. https://www.grunge.com/285238/the-incredible-real-life-story-of -shirley-chisholm. (Accessed 1/22/2021).

Lewis Desiree. "BalekeMbete: On Queens who would be Kings." 2009. *Amandla, Available from http://www.amandlapublishers.co.za/special-features/sa-national -womens-day/597-on-queens-who-would-be-kings.*

Lewis, Desiree. "Mother of the Nation." *Chimurenga Online,* December 22, 2003.

Lewis, Desiree. "Winnie Mandela: The Surveillance and Excess of 'Black Woman' as Signifier." *Southern African Feminist Revie* (Harare) Vol. 2, Iss. 1 (Jan 31, 1996): 7.

Lewis, Desiree and Gabeba Baderoon, eds. *Surfacing On Being Black and Feminist in South Africa.* Johannesburg: Wits University Press, 2021.

Lindsey, Lydia. "Black Lives Matter: Grace P. Campbell and Claudia Jones—An analysis of the Negro Question." Self-Determination, Black Belt Thesis. *Journal of Pan African Studies,* 12:9 (March, 2019): 110–143.

Liverpool H. *From the Horse's Mouth. Stories of the History and Development of the Calypso,* Port of Spain, Trinidad and Tobago: Juba Publications, 2003.

Lorde, Audre. "Age, Race, Class, and Sex: Women Redefining Difference." *Sister Outsider: Essays and Speeches.* Freedom, CA: Crossing, 1984: 114–123.

Lorde, Audre. "Grenada Revisited. An Interim Report." *Sister Outsider. Essays and Speeches.* Trumansburg: The Crossing Press, 1982:176–190.

Lorde, Audre. Interview with Pratibha Parmar and Jackie Kay. *Charting the Journey. Writing by Black and Third World Women.* London: Sheba Feminist Publishers, 1988: 129–181.

Loureiro, Gabriela. "To Be Black, Queer and Radical: Centring the Epistemology of Marielle Franco." *Open Cultural Studies* (University of West London), 2020: May, 4: 50–58.

Lugones, Maria. "Toward a Decolonial Feminism." *Hypatia* 25:4 (Fall, 2010): 742–759.

Maathai, Wangari Muta. *Unbowed. A Memoir.* New York: Anchor Books, 2007.

Maathai, Wangari. *The Challenge for Africa.* New York: Anchor Books, 2009.

Madikizela-Mandela, Winnie. *491 Days. Prisoner Number 1323/69.* Johannesburg: Picador Africa, 2013.

Magnolia, Tiffany. "A Method To Her Madness: Bessie Head's A *Question Of Power* as South African National Allegory," *Journal of Literary Studies,* 18:1–2 (2002): 154–167.

Madikezela Mandela, Winnie Nomzamo. "Being a Black Woman in the World." *V103 Expo for Today's Black Woman*, March, 2006. Chicago, Illinois. Part 1 *The Final Call*, March 28, 2006. http://www.finalcall.com/artman/publish/Perspectives_1/Being_A_Black_Woman_In_The_World_-_Part_1_2511.shtml

Madikezela Mandela, Winnie Nomzamo. "Being a Black Woman in the World." *V103 Expo for Today's Black Woman*, March, 2006. Chicago, Illinois. Part 2, *The Final Call*, April 18, 2006. http://www.finalcall.com/artman/publish/Perspectives_1/Being_A_Black_Woman_In_The_World_-_Pt_2_2569.shtml

Mama, Amina. "Khaki In The Family: Gender Discourses And Militarism In Nigeria," *African Studies Review*, 14(1), 1998:1–18.

Mama, Amina. "'We Will Not Be Pacified': From Freedom Fighters to Feminists." *European Journal of Women's Studies* (2020): 1–19.

Mama, Amina. "Nkrumah's Legacy, Feminism and the Next Generation." Inaugural lecture as the Fourth Kwame Nkrumah Chair in African Studies at the University of Ghana, Legon. February 15, 2022.

Mandela, Winnie. *Part of My Soul Went with Him*. New York and London: W.W. Norton, 1984.

Marshall, Paule. *Brown Girl Brownstones*. (1959). CUNY: The Feminist Press, 1994.

Marshall, Paule. *Reena And Other Stories*. CUNY: The Feminist Press, 1983.

Marshall, Paule. *The Chosen Place. The Timeless People*. New York: Vintage, 1984.

Marshall, Paule. *Triangular Road. A Memoir*. New York: Civitas Books, 2009.

Martin, Tony. *Amy Ashwood Garvey: Pan-Africanist, Feminist and Mrs. Marcus Garvey No. 1 or a Tale of Two Amies*. Wellesley, MA: The Majority Press, 2007.

Martins, Ana. "Running Away with Language: Inventing Wor(l)ds in the Work of Lelia Gonzalez in 1980s Brazil'" *Gender & History*, Vol.30 No.1 March 2018: 255–270.

McFadden Pat, "Cultural practice as gendered exclusion: Experiences from southern Africa." *Discussion of Women's Empowerment: Theory and Practice*, SIDA Studies, 3. Stockholm: SIDA, 2001: 58–71.

McFadden, Pat. "The Challenges and Prospects for African Women's Movement in the 21st century." *Women in Action*. Issue 1, 1997 http://www.hartford-hwp.com/archives/30/152.html Accessed 2/8/2021

McKittrick, Katherine, ed. *Sylvia Wynter: On Being Human as Praxis*. Duke University Press, 2015.

Mealy, Rosemari. *Fidel and Malcolm X-Memories of A Meeting*. Baltimore, MD: Black Classic Press, 2014.

Mealy, Rosemari. "'Affirming the Right to be Revolutionary.' Assata: An Interview," in *Moving Beyond Boundaries.v.2. Black Women's Diasporas*. Ed. Carole Boyce Davies. NYU Press, 1995: 89–93.

Meintjes, Sheila. "Winnie Madikizela Mandela. Tragic Figure? Populist Tribune? Township Tough?" *Southern Africa Report* (Toronto): August, 1998: 14–20.

Mensa, Nicole. "When Women Stand UP: The Stories of Yaa Asentwa and Leymah Gbowee." *Pan African Connections. Personal, Intellectual, Social*. Trenton, NJ: Africa World Press, 2020:

Mernissi, F. *Doing Daily Battle*. New Brunswick: Rutgers University Press, 1989.

Mfanga, Tina. "To the Red Carpet Feminists; Congratulations for Breaking a Glass Ceiling." *Sauti Ya Ujamaa.* July 22, 2021.Mfanga, Tina. "An Open Letter to My Ancestor, Nomzano." *Sauti Ya Ujamaa.* April 15, 2020.

Miller, Zoe. "When Women Got the Right to Vote in 25 places Around the World." *Insider.com* March, 1920.

Mills, Sara. *Michel Foucault.* London: Routledge, 2003.

Minha,Trinh T. *Woman, Native, Other. Writing Postcoloniality and Feminism.* Indiana University Press, 2009.

Minority Rights Group, eds. *No Longer Invisible: Afro-Latin Americans Today.* 1995.

Mohammed, Patricia. *Writing Gender into the Caribbean: Selected Essays 1988 to 2020.* Maracas, T & T: Hansib, 2021.

Moïse, Myriam. "Antillean Women and Black Internationalism." *The Black Scholar,* 51:2 (2021): 23–32.

Msimang, Sisonke. "Winnie Mandela and the Archive: Reflections on Feminist Biography." Desiree Lewis and Gabeba Baderoon, eds. *Surfacing. On Being Black and Feminist in South Africa.* Johannesburg: Wits University Press, 2021:15–27.

Msimang, Sisonke. *The Resurrection of Winnie Mandela.* Capetown & Johannesburg, South Africa: Jonathan Ball Publishers. Melbourne, Australia: The Text Publishing Company, 2018.

Mugo, Micere Githae. *Daughter of My People, Sing!* Kampala: East African Literature Bureau, 1976.

Mugo, Micere. "Dr. Micere Mugo, Kenya's Outspoken Intellectual and Academic Critic Talks to Nancy Owano." *Africa Woman* 6 September/October, 1976: 14–15.

Muhonja, Besi Brillian. *Radical Utu. Critical Ideas and Ideals of Wangari Muta Maathai.* Ohio University Press, 2020.

Munro, Brenna. "Nelson, Winnie, and the Politics of Gender." *The Cambridge Companion to Nelson Mandela.* Cambridge: Cambridge University Press, 2014: 92–112.

Murray, Pauli. *Song in a Weary Throat. Memoir of an American Pilgrimage.* Liverright, 2018.

Musila, Grace A. *Wangari Maathai's Registers of Freedom. Selected Writings of Wangari Maathai.* Cape Town, South Africa: Human Sciences Research Council Press, 2020.

"My Name Is Pauli Murray." Directed by Julie Cohen and Betsy West. Documentary. Amazon Prime, 2021.

Nadji, Hillal H. "A Garvey Comes Home to Africa," *Chicago Defender Magazine* (August 6,1949): 230.

Nama, Charles A. "Daughters of Moombi. Ngugi's Heroines and Traditional Gikuyu Aesthetics." *Ngambika. Studies of Women in African Literature.* Eds. Carole Boyce Davies & Anne Adams Graves. Trenton, NJ: Africa World Press, 1986: 139–149.

Ndebele, Njabulo. *The Cry of Winnie Mandela.* Banbury, UK: Ayebia, 2004.

Ngugi, Mukoma wa. *Nairobi Heat.* New York: Melville House Publishing, 2011.

Ngugi, Mukoma wa. *The Rise of the African Novel: Politics of Language, Identity and Ownership.* University of Michigan Press, 2018.

Ngugi, M.W. Beauty, mourning and melancholy. *Africa* 39, November, 9, 2014.

Retrieved from https://lareviewofbooks.org/review/beauty-mourning-melancholy
-africa39

Nnaemeka, Obioma. "Feminism, Rebellious Women, and Cultural Boundaries: Rereading Flora Nwapa and Her Compatriots." *Research in African Literatures* 26:2:1995: 80–113.

Nyambura, Zipporah and Donelly, Elizabeth. (Interview) "Liberia: Ellen Johnson Sirleaf's Presidential legacy." *DW* 27–12–2017. https://www.dw.com/en/liberia -ellen-johnson-sirleafs-presidential-legacy/a-41947808 Accessed, 7/10/2020

Nyanzi, Stella. *No Roses from My Mouth.* Uganda: Ubuntu Reading Group, 2020

Nzegwu, Nkiru. "Aloisea Inyumba: Mother of New Rwanda," *JENDA: A Journal of Culture and African Women Studies,* 10(2007): 10–46.

Nzegwu, Nkiru. Editorial: "Women and Political Leadership." JENDA 9(2006):1–5.

Nzegwu, Nkiru. "Indomitable Luisa Diogo: Prime Minister of Mozambique." *JENdA: A Journal of Culture and African Women Studies.* 10(2007): 2–9.

Obama, Barack. *The Audacity of Hope. Thoughts on Reclaiming the American Dream.* New York: Broadway Books, 2007.

Obama, Barack. *Dreams from My Father. A Story of Race and Inheritance.* New York: Crown, 2004.

Obama, Barack. *A Promised Land.* New York: Crown, 2020.

Obama M. "Remarks by the First Lady at Spelman College Commencement," Georgia, 2011. International Convention Center, Atlanta, Georgia. Available from http://www.whitehouse.gov

Obama, Michelle. *Becoming.* New York: Crown, 2018.

Obeng, Samuel, ed. *Selected Speeches. Kwame Nkrumah.* Ghana: Afram Publications, Ltd., 1979.

Ogundipe, M. "African Women, Culture and Another Development." *The Journal of African Marxists* 5, 1984: 77–92.

Okonjo-Iweala. *Fighting Corruption is Dangerous: The Story Behind the Headlines.* MIT Press, 2018.

Okpewho, I. and Nzegwu, N., Eds. *The New African Diaspora.* Bloomington: Indiana University Press, 2009.

Olazagasti, Ignacio. "The Material Culture of The Taino Indians," in Samuel Wilson, *Indigenous Peoples of the Caribbean.* University Press of Florida, 1997:

Olupona, J. K., and Rey, T. *Òrìsà Devotion As World Religion: The Globalization Of Yorùbá Religious Culture.* Madison, WI: The University of Wisconsin Press, 2008.

Onuzo, Chibundu. "Wole Soyinka: 'This Book is My Gift to Nigeria.'" *The Guardian* (London). Interview. September 25, 2021.

Osundare, Niyi. "The Unintended Feminist." *Sahara Reporters,* January 29, 2017.

Owens, Jill. "Powell's Interview Jennifer Nansubuga Makumbi, Author of 'A Girl is a Body of Water.'" September 11, 2020. https://www.powells.com/post/interviews /powells-interview-jennifer-nansubuga-makumbi-author-of-a-girl-is-a-body-of -water Accessed 2/7/2021.

Padmore, George. *Panafricanism or Communism? The Coming Struggle for Africa.* London: Dobson, 1961.

Palmer, Colin. *Eric Williams and the Making of the Modern Caribbean.* University of North Carolina Press, 2008.

Palmer, Lisa Amanda. "Diane Abbott, Misogynoir and the Politics of Black British Feminism's Anticolonial Imperatives: 'In Britain too, it's as if we don't exist.'" *The sociological Review* 68(3) 2020: 508–523.

Palmer Adisa, Opal. *Portia Dreams.* Jamaica: Herald Printers, 2021.

"Panafricanism and Feminism." Special issue of *Feminist Africa.* Issue 19 (2014).

Parker, Andrew, Mary Russo, Doris Sommer, Patricia Yaeger, eds. *Nationalisms and Sexualities.* New York and London: Routledge, 1992.

Patterson, Louise Thompson. "Toward a Brighter Dawn." *Woman Today, 1936.*

Persad-Bissessar K. *Through the Political Glass Ceiling. Race to the Prime Ministership. Selected Speeches.* Compiled with introduction by Kris Rampersad. Trinidad and Tobago, 2010. ISBN: 978–976-8228-00–0.

Persad-Bissessar K. Address by Prime Minister the Hon Kamla Persad-Bissessar in celebration of International Women's Day 2011 at the Diplomatic Centre, St Ann's http://www.news.gov.tt/index.php?news=7284 Accessed July 31 2011.

Perry, Jeffrey, ed. *Hubert Harrison. The Voice of Harlem Radicalism, 1883–1918.* New York: Columbia University Press, 2009.

Perry, Jeffrey B. ed. *Hubert Harrison. The Struggle for Equality, 1918–1927.* New York: Columbia University Press, 2021.

Perry, Keisha-Khan. "The Groundings with My Sisters: Toward a Black Diasporic Feminist Agenda in the Americas" *S&F On Line* 7:2(Spring, 2009). http://sfonline .barnard.edu/africana/perry_01.htm

Perry, Keisha-Khan. *Black Women against the Land Grab. The Fight for Racial Justice in Brazil.* Minneapolis: University of Minnesota Press, 2013.

Perry, Keisha-Khan Y. "The Resurgent Far Right and the Black Feminist Struggle for Social Democracy in Brazil." *American Anthropologist.* 122:1 (March, 2020): 157–162.

Perry, Keisha-Khan Y. and Eldiza Sotero. "Amefricanidade: The Black Diaspora Feminism of Lélia Gonzalez." *LASA Forum,* 50:3 (2019): 60–64.

Perry, Keisha-Khan Y. and Taís de Sant'Anna Machado. "Translation of 'The Black Woman: A Portrait.'" *Feminist Anthropology,* 2020 (online journal).

Philips, Tom and Caio Barretto Brito. "Brazil: Congresswoman and Friend Of Slain Politician Marielle Franco Flees Following Death Threats." *The Guardian* (London) November 13, 2020. https://www.theguardian.com/world/2020/nov/13 /congresswoman-taliria-petrone-flees-brazil-following-alleged-plot-kill-marielle -franco Accessed 11/30/2020

Phiri, Virginia. "Wangari Maathai. To Renew Our Earth." *African Visionaries.* Eds. Agnes Ofosua Vandyck, Molly Nyagura and Rosemary Brooks. Ghana: Sub-Saharan Publishers, 2019: 81–88.

Protocol To The African Charter On Human And Peoples' Rights On The Rights Of Women In Africa, 2003. https://www.un.org/en/africa/osaa/pdf/au/protocol_rights _women_africa_2003.pdf Accessed 7/29/2020.

Quijano, Annibal. "Coloniality of Power, Eurocentrism, and Latin America," *Nepantla: Views from South* 1:3(2000):533–580.

Ramey, Daina Ramey and Kali Nicole Gross. *A Black Women's History of the United States*. Boston: Beacon Press, 2020.

Rampersad S. "Women and Politics 101." *Trinidad Express*, December 25, 2009.

Rampersad S. "The Ascension of Kamla," *Trinidad Express*, February 5, 2010.

Ransby, Barbara. *Ella Baker and the Black Freedom Movement. A Radical Democratic Vision.* Chapel Hill and London: University of North Carolina Press, 2004.

Reddock R. "Douglarization and The Politics of Gender Relations in Trinidad and Tobago," in C. Barrow and R. Reddock (eds.), *Caribbean Sociology. Introductory Readings,* Jamaica: Ian Randle, 2001.

Reddock, Rhoda. "Catherine McKenzie." *Dictionary of Caribbean and Afro-Latin American Biography.* Edited by Henry Louis Gates Jr. and Franklin Knight. New York: Oxford University Press, 2016.

Reddock, Rhoda. "The First Mrs. Garvey and Others: Pan-Africanism and feminism in the early 20th Century British colonial Caribbean." *Feminist Africa,* 19(2014): 58–77.

Richardson, Gloria. "Civil Rights Pioneer Gloria Richardson, 91, on How Women Were Silenced at 1963 March on Washington." Interview with Amy Goodman on *Democracy Now.* August 27, 2013. Civil Rights Pioneer Gloria Richardson, 91, on How Women Were Silenced at 1963 March on Washington | Democracy Now!

Richardson, Riché. *Emancipation's Daughters. Reimagining Black Femininity and the National Body.* Durham: Duke University Press, 2021.

Rickards, Lisandra. "The Rise of Female Leaders in the Caribbean." August 24, 2017. https://www.virgin.com/virgin-unite/rise-female-leaders-Caribbean Accessed 7/16/2020

Rios, Flavia. (2019). "Améfrica Ladina: The Conceptual Legacy of Lélia Gonzalez (1935–1994)." LASA Forum, 50: 3: 75–79.

Robinson, Cedric. *The Terms of Order. Political Science and the Myth of Leadership.* Chapel Hill: University of North Carolina Press, 2016.

Robinson, Michelle La Vaughn. "Princeton-Educated Blacks and the Black Community." B.A. thesis. Princeton University, 1985.

Rodrigues, Felipe Fanuel Xavier. "The Politics of African Heritage in Black Brazilian Women's Literature." *Women's Studies Quarterly* 49(Fall/Winter, 2021): 297–315.

Russell-Brown, Katheryn and Eric Velasquez. *She Was the First. The Trailblazing Life of Shirley Chisholm.* New York: Lee & Low Books, 2020.

"Samia Nkrumah. Like Father, Like Daughter." *Glitz and Glamour* (Ghana), July, 2009. https://www.ghanaweb.com/GhanaHomePage/features/Samia-Nkrumah -Like-Father-Like-Daughter-184181

Sankara, Thomas. "The Emancipation of Women, And The Liberation Struggle of Africa: On The Liberation Of Women." March 8, 1987. Also available as *Women's Liberation and The African Freedom Struggle.* Pathfinder Press, 2007.

Santos de Araujo, Flavia. "Marielle, Presente!" *Meridians. Feminism, Race, Transnationalism.* 17:1 September, 2018: 207–211.

Saujani, Reshma, *Women Who Don't Wait in Line. Break the Mold. Lead the Way.* New York: New Harvest, 2013.

Schmid, Evelyne. "Liberia's Truth Commission Report: Economic, Social, and Cultural Rights in Transitional Justice." *PRAXIS - The Fletcher Journal of Human Security*, Vol. XXIV, May, 2009: 5–28. Available at SSRN: https://ssrn.com/abstract=1425543

Selasi, Taiye. "Bye-Bye Babar (Or: What is an Afropolitan)." *The Lip Magazine*. March 3, 2005.

Selasi, Taiye. *Ghana Must Go*. New York: Penguin, 2013.

Sen, G. and Grown, C. Development crisis and alternative visions: Third world women's perspectives development alternatives for women with a new era. *Canadian Woman Studies/Les Cahiers De La Femme*, l l(3), 1986: 16–18.

Sheller, Mimi. *Consuming the Caribbean: From Arawaks to Zombies*. London and New York: Routledge, 2003.

Sheller, Mimi. "Caribbean Futures in the Offshore Anthropocene: Debt, Disaster, and Duration." *Society and Space* 2018, Vol. 36(6): 971–986.

Sheller, Mimi. "Quasheba, Mother, Queen: Black Women's Public Leadership and Political Protest in Post-Emancipation Jamaica, 1834–65, *Slavery & Abolition*, 19:3, 90–117.

Sheller, Mimi. "Caribbean Futures in the Offshore Anthropocene: Debt Disaster and Duration." *Society and Space*, 36(6): 971–986.

Smart, Ian A. "Eulalia Bernard: A Caribbean Woman Writer and the Dynamics of Liberation," *Letras Femeninas* 13:1/2 (Primavera-Otono, 1987): 79–85.

Smith, Barbara. "The 'Creative Chaos' of Gloria Richardson (1922–2021)." *The Nation*. July 23, 2021. "The 'Creative Chaos' of Gloria Richardson (1922–2021)." | The Nation

Smith, Cristen. *Afro-Paradise. Blackness, Violence and Performance in Brazil*. Urbana: University of Illinois Press, 2016.

Spencer, Robin. *The Revolution Has Come: Black Power, Gender, and the Black Panther Party in Oakland*. Duke University Press, 2016.

Spillers, Hortense J. (1987). "Mama's Baby, Papa's Maybe. An American Grammar Book." *Diacritics* 17:2 (Summer): 65–81.

Steady, Filomina, ed. *The Black Woman Cross-culturally*. Connecticut: Greenwood, 1981.

Stillion Southard, Belinda A. "Crafting Cosmopolitan Nationalism: Ellen Johnson Sirleaf's Rhetorical Leadership." *Quarterly Journal of Speech* 103:4 (2017): 395–414.

Sumari, Nancy Mwandishi and Mchoraki Tito Fungo. Samia. Dar es Salaam, Tanzania: Bakita, 2021.

Sumari, Nancy. "Everyone Wants to Be Famous, but We Can Be Great." TWIGA 12. January-March, 2022: 21–25.

Swaby, Nydia. Amy Ashwood Garvey and the Future of Black Feminist Archives. Lawrence Wishart, Summer 2022.

Swift, Jaimee. "Afro-Brazilian Feminists and the Fight for Racial and Gender Inclusion." *AAIHS Black Perspectives*. February 2, 2017 https://www.aaihs.org/afro-brazilian-feminists-and-the-fight-for-racial-and-gender-inclusion/ (Accessed 1/11/2021).

Tadjo, Veronique. *Queen Poku.* Banbury: Ayebia, 2009.

"Talk Africa: African Women Leaders" CGNTV Africa. CCTVNews. September 17, 2016. https://www.youtube.com/watch?v=ySgvRrr10kA

Tamale S. *When Hens Begin to Crow: Gender and Parliamentary Politics in Uganda.* Kampala: Fountain Publishers, 1999.

Tamale, Sylvia. "Towards Feminist Pan-Africanism and Pan-Africanism." Nyerere Dialogue Lecture. Dar es Salaam, Tanzania: Nyerere Resource Centre, October, 2019.

Tamale, Sylvia. *Decolonization and Afro-Feminism.* Ottawa: Daraja Press, 2020.

Taylor, Keanga-Yamahtta. "Succeeding While Black." *Boston Review.* March 13, 2019. https://bostonreview.net/race/keeanga-yamahtta-taylor-succeeding-while -black

Taylor, Ula. *The Veiled Garvey: The Life and Times of Amy Jacques Garvey.* Chapel Hill: University of North Carolina Press, 2001.

"Tia Ciata" filme/Doc. 26/2017/RJB. Directed by Mariana Campos and Raquel Beatriz. https://www.youtube.com/watch?v=2-5-_6w8EBQ "The Global Gender Gap Report" http://www3.weforum.org/docs/GGGR16/WEF_Global_Gender _Gap_Report_2016.pdf.

The People's Forum. "I Am Because We are": A Conversation Between Francia Marquez Mina and Angela Davis" Facilitated by Mamyrah Prosper September 7, 2021. https://www.youtube.com/watch?v=qOLZaA509dI [Accessed May 14, 2022]

"The Rise of Female Leaders in the Caribbean." https://www.virgin.com/virgin-unite /rise-female-leaders-Caribbean

"The Status of Women's Leadership in West Africa." A Study Commissioned by West Africa Civil Society Institute (WACSI) Rome, August, 2008. Ref. OEDE/2008/4.

"The Words of Marielle Franco: Love and Dedication to Justice and Favela." Curated by Luisa Fenizola March 14, 2020. https://www.rioonwatch.org/?p=58297 #prettyPhoto

Theoharis, Jeanne. *The Rebellious Life of Mrs. Rosa Parks.* Boston: Beacon Books, 2013.

Thomas, Gregory and Sylvia Wynter. "Yours in the Intellectual Struggle." *The Caribbean Woman Writer as Scholar.* Ed. Keshia Abraham. Coconut Grove: Caribbean Studies Press, 2009: 31–69.

Tichy, Noel. *The Cycle of Leadership. How Great Leaders Teach Their Companies to Win.* Harper, 2002.

Tonnessen, Liv, and Samia al-Nagar. "Patriarchy, Politics and Women's Activism in Post-Revolution Sudan." CHR Michelsen Institute, University of Bergen, Sudan Brief, June 2020.

Traoré Aminata Dramane. *Le viol de l'imaginaire.* Libraire Arthene Fayard: Editions Actes Sud, 2010.

Tripp, A. M. Women in Movement: Transformations in African Political Landscapes. *International Feminist Journal of Politics* 5:2 (2003): 233–255.

Tripp, A. M. *Women And Power in Post-Conflict Africa.* Cambridge University Press, 2015.

Trotz, Alissa, ed. *The Point is to Change the World. Selected Writings of Andaiye.* London: Pluto Press, 2020.

Tyson, Cecily. *Just As I Am: A Memoir.* New York: Harper Collins Publishers, 2021.

United Nations, Department of Social and Economic Affairs. *The Worlds Women. Trends and Statistics.* 2015.

United Nations, Department of Social and Economic Affairs. *The World's Women. Trends and Statistics.* 2020

UNDP & UN Women. *Inclusive Electoral Processes: A Guide For Electoral Management Bodies On Promoting Gender Equality And Women's Participation.* https://www.undp.org/content/undp/en/home/librarypage/democratic-governance/electoral_systemsandprocesses/guide-for-electoral-manage

Vallely, Paul. "The Woman Who Has the Power to Change Africa." *JENDA: A Journal of Culture and African Women's Studies.* 9(2006):1–19.

Wainaina, B. "Kenyan writer Binyavanga Wainaina Declares: 'I am homosexual.'" *The Guardian*, Tuesday January 20, 2014. Retrieved from http://www.theguardian.com/world/2014/jan/21/kenyan-writer-binyavanga-wainaina-declares-homosexuality (Accessed 23 06 2015).

Wakefield, Shawna. "Transformative and Feminist Leadership for Women's Rights." Oxfam America Research Backgrounder series (2017): https://www.oxfamamerica.org/explore/research-publications/transformative-feministleadership-womens-rights.

Walker, Alice. *In Search of Our Mothers' Gardens. Womanist Prose.* Harcourt Brace Jovanovich, 1983.

Warner, Gregory. "It's The No. 1 Country for Women in Politics—But Not in Daily Life." *NPR,* July 29, 2016.

Washington, Margaret. *Sojourner Truth's America.* Urbana and Chicago: University of Illinois Press, 2009.

Waters, Roderick Dion. "Sister Sawyer. The Life and Times of Gwendolyn Sawyer Cherry." PhD diss. Florida State University, 1994. Proquest Dissertations and Theses Global.

We Charge Genocide: The Historic Petition to the United Nations for Relief from a Crime of the United States Government Against the Negro People. January 1, 1951 Civil Rights Congress and William L. Patterson et al. New York: Civil Rights Congress, 1951.

Wendt, Samuel and Pablo Dominguez Andersen, Eds. *Masculinities and the Nation in the Modern World: Between Hegemony and Marginalization.* Palgrave, 2015.

West, E. James. "A Black Woman Communist Candidate: Charlene Mitchell's 1968 Presidential Campaign." *AAIHS Perspectives,* September 24, 2019.

Whitten, jr. Norman E. and Arlene Torres. *Blackness in Latin America and the Caribbean.* V.1 & 2 Eds. Bloomington: Indiana University Press, 1998.

Williams, Dessima. "Bringing More Women into Leadership," *Boston Globe,* March 8, 2000.

Wills, Vanessa. "We Can't Let the Nomination of Harris Blunt Our Demands for Racial Justice." Truthout. August 12, 2020. https://truthout.org/articles/we-cant-let-the-nomination-of-harris-blunt-our-demands-for-racial-justice/ [Accessed 2/7/2022]

"Winnie" Documentary film by Pascale Lamche 2017 (Winner of the Sundance Film Festival, Director's Award). https://www.pbs.org/independentlens/videos/winnie/

Winslow, Barbara. *Shirley Chisholm. Catalyst for Change. 1926–2005.* Boulder, CO: Westview Press, 2014.

Wolverton, Mimi, Beverly L. Bower, and Adrienne E. Hyle. *Women at the Top. What Women University and College Presidents Say About Effective Leadership.* Sterling, VA: Stylus Publishing, 2009.

"Women on the March." Foreword. *The Journal of African Marxists 5* (February, 1984): 35–36.

"Women Political Leaders." *JENDA. A Journal of Culture and African Women Studies.* 9(2006) & 10 (2007).

Women and Political Leadership in the Caribbean. UN Women, 2018.

Wynter, Sylvia. "'No Humans Involved': An Open Letter to My Colleagues." *Voices of the African Diaspora* 8:2 (1992): 13–16.

Wynter, Sylvia. "Unsettling the Coloniality of Being/Power/Truth/Freedom: Towards the Human, After Man, Its Overrepresentation - an Argument," *New Centennial Review,* 3:3(Fall: 2003): 257–335.

Zeleza, Paul Tiyambe. "The Significance of Johnson-Sirleaf's Victory." *JENDA: A Journal of Culture and African Women's Studies.* 9(2006): 1–7.

Zeleza, P. (2009). Diaspora Dialogues: Engagements Between Africa and Its Diasporas. Edited by Isidore Okpewho and Nkiru Nzegwu. *The New African Diaspora.* Bloomington: Indiana University Press, 2009: 31–58.

Index

About the Author

Carole Boyce Davies is a pre-eminent scholar, writer, professor and community worker. Her past works include *Left of Karl Marx. The Political Life of Black Communist Claudia Jones* (2008); *Black Women, Writing and Identity: Migrations of the Subject* (1994); *Caribbean Spaces. Escape Routes from Twilight Zones* (2013). Her work spans the African diaspora, always reaching for the fullest representation possible. The editor of over thirteen critical editions on African, African Diaspora and Caribbean literature and culture such as the 3-volume *Encyclopedia of the African Diaspora* (Oxford: ABC-CLIO, 2008), *Claudia Jones Beyond Containment: Autobiographical Reflections, Poetry, Essays* (2011) and *Pan-African Connections* (2021), she has maintained visibility and practice of empowered teaching and mentoring of students along with intellectual production and community service. In this work, she reveals the breadth and depth of her engagement with Black women as political actors, creators and "movers of the world" and definitely as possible transformative leaders, offering always a politics that assumes and expects a more equitable distribution of material resources at every level of human existence.

www.ingramcontent.com/pod-product-compliance
Lightning Source LLC
Chambersburg PA
CBHW022300280326
41932CB00010B/930